African Leaders of the Twentieth Century

OHIO SHORT HISTORIES OF AFRICA

This series of Ohio Short Histories of Africa is meant for those who are looking for a brief but lively introduction to a wide range of topics in African history, politics, and biography, written by some of the leading experts in their fields.

Steve Biko
by Lindy Wilson

Spear of the Nation (Umkhonto weSizwe): South Africa's Liberation Army, 1960s–1990s
by Janet Cherry

Epidemics: The Story of South Africa's Five Most Lethal Human Diseases
by Howard Phillips

South Africa's Struggle for Human Rights
by Saul Dubow

San Rock Art
by J.D. Lewis-Williams

Ingrid Jonker: Poet under Apartheid
by Louise Viljoen

The ANC Youth League
by Clive Glaser

Govan Mbeki
by Colin Bundy

The Idea of the ANC
by Anthony Butler

Emperor Haile Selassie
by Bereket Habte Selassie

Thomas Sankara: An African Revolutionary
by Ernest Harsch

Patrice Lumumba
by Georges Nzongola-Ntalaja

Short-changed? South Africa since Apartheid
by Colin Bundy

The ANC Women's League: Sex, Gender and Politics
by Shireen Hassim

The Soweto Uprising
by Noor Nieftagodien

African Leaders of the Twentieth Century: Biko, Selassie, Lumumba, Sankara

African Leaders of the Twentieth Century

Biko, Selassie, Lumumba, Sankara

OHIO UNIVERSITY PRESS

ATHENS, OHIO

Ohio University Press, Athens, Ohio 45701
www.ohioswallow.com
All rights reserved

© Ohio University Press, 2015

To obtain permission to quote, reprint, or otherwise reproduce
or distribute material from Ohio University Press publications,
please contact our rights and permissions department at (740)
593-1154 or (740) 593-4536 (fax).

First published in North America in 2015 by Ohio University Press
Printed in the United States of America
Ohio University Press books are printed on acid-free paper ∞ ™

ISBN: 978-0-8214-2161-1

Contents

Steve Biko
by Lindy Wilson

Emperor Haile Selassie
by Bereket Habte Selassie

Patrice Lumumba
by Georges Nzongola-Ntalaja

Thomas Sankara: An African Revolutionary
by Ernest Harsch

STEVE BIKO inspired a generation of black South Africans to claim their true identity and refuse to be a part of their own oppression. Through his example, he demonstrated fearlessness and self-esteem, and he led a black student movement countrywide that challenged and thwarted the culture of fear perpetuated by the apartheid regime. He paid the highest price with his life. The brutal circumstances of his death shocked the world and helped isolate his oppressors.

This short biography of Biko shows how fundamental he was to the reawakening and transformation of South Africa in the second half of the twentieth century—and just how relevant he remains. Biko's understanding of black consciousness as a weapon of change could not be more relevant today to "restore people to their full humanity."

As an important historical study, this book's main sources were unique interviews done in 1989—before the end of apartheid—by the author with Biko's acquaintances, many of whom have since died.

Lindy Wilson is an independent South African documentary filmmaker and writer. Her films include *Crossroads, Last Supper in Hortsley Street,* and *Robben Island Our University.*

Steve Biko

Lindy Wilson

OHIO UNIVERSITY PRESS
ATHENS

Ohio University Press, Athens, Ohio 45701
www.ohioswallow.com
All rights reserved

© Lindy Wilson, 2011

First published in 2011 by Jacana Media (Pty) Ltd
10 Orange Street, Sunnyside
Auckland Park 2092
South Africa
(+29 11) 628-3200
www.jacana.co.za

To obtain permission to quote, reprint, or otherwise reproduce or distribute material from Ohio University Press publications, please contact our rights and permissions department at (740) 593-1154 or (740) 593-4536 (fax).

First published in North America in 2012 by Ohio University Press
Printed in the United States of America
Ohio University Press books are printed on acid-free paper ♾ ™

20 19 18 17 16 15 14 13 12   5 4 3 2 1

ISBN: 978-0-8214-2025-6
e-ISBN: 978-0-8214-4441-2

Library of Congress Cataloging-in-Publication Data

Wilson, Lindy.
 Steve Biko / Lindy Wilson.
   p. cm. — (Ohio short histories of Africa)
 "First published in 2011 by Jacana Media, Auckland Park, South Africa."
 Includes bibliographical references and index.
 ISBN 978-0-8214-2025-6 (pb : alk. paper) — ISBN 978-0-8214-4441-2 (electronic)
 1. Biko, Steve, 1946–1977. 2. Political activists—South Africa. 3. South Africa—History—1961–1994. 4. South Africa—Race relations. 5. South Africa—Politics and government—1994– I. Title. II. Series: Ohio short histories of Africa.
 DT779.8.B48W55 2012
 968.06092—dc23
 [B]
                                           2012020802

Cover design by Joey Hi-Fi

Photo credits: Steve Biko Foundation, p. 21; *Daily Dispatch,* pp. 9, 58, 66, 107, 121, 127, 134, 140 (with thanks as well to Wendy Woods); Bruce Haigh, p. 127; UWC Robben Island Mayibuye Centre, p. 51; UCT Library, p. 74; Historical Papers, Wits University Library, p. 37 (bottom left); Bailey's African History Archive, pp. 37 (top), 146; National Archives, p. 43; Benjamin Pogrund, p. 37 (bottom right); Peter Bruce, p. 154; John Reader/*Life Magazine* © Time, Inc.: p. 39.

Contents

Preface 7

1. Introduction 11
2. Early years, 1946–1965 18
3. Student action and style of leadership,
   1966–1972 30
4. To love and to work 54
5. Bantu – Son of Man, 1973–1977 76
6. Choices and dilemmas 112
7. Detention, banishment and international
   engagement 118
8. Arrest 129
9. A life still to be 'dug out'................. 143

Bibliography 155
Index 158

Preface

This brief biography of Bantu Stephen Biko is grounded in relevant published literature. Much written evidence has been lost, was deliberately destroyed or carefully not recorded, out of fear of reprisals in a fearful age. Thus Biko's story draws substantially from interviews. Some were done with Biko himself, particularly near the end of his life. Twenty-six were conducted in 1989 and 1990 before the end of apartheid. Interviews, of course, have weaknesses as historical sources. They are subjective and also rely on memory, often blurred and distorted by time and perspective. Further, describing another's life is sometimes a projection of one's own.

An earlier version of this biography was published in 1991 as a chapter in the book *Bounds of Possibility*. It was written at the invitation of Barney Pityana, Malusi Mpumlwana and Mamphela Ramphele, the co-editors of the book, who have kindly agreed to my revising it for publication in this form.

1

Introduction

September '77
In Port Elizabeth weather fine
It was business as usual
In Police Room 619
    – 'Biko', by Peter Gabriel

On 12 September 1977 'business as usual' for the South African Security Police claimed the life of Bantu Stephen Biko, the twenty-first person to die in a South African prison within a period of twelve months. Biko was 30 years old.

Ten days earlier Biko was reported to be physically sound when visited by a magistrate at the Walmer police cells in Port Elizabeth. He did, however, request 'water and soap to wash himself and a washcloth and a comb', and added: 'I want to be allowed to buy food. I live on bread only here. Is it compulsory that I have to be naked? I have been naked since I came here.'

On the morning of 6 September, Biko faced a

team of Security Police in Room 619 of the Sanlam Building under the leadership of Maj. Harold Snyman, appointed to interrogate 'the Black Power detainees'. According to evidence given to the Truth and Reconciliation Commission by Det.-Sgt. Gideon Nieuwoudt at his amnesty hearing in 1998, Biko sat down on a chair facing his interrogator, Capt. Daantjie Siebert, who immediately ordered him to stand. Later, when Biko sat down again, Siebert grabbed him by the chest and yanked him to his feet. Nieuwoudt asserts that 'Biko pushed the chair forward and lunged with his fist'. Five men then assaulted him simultaneously, 'Blows were aimed backwards and forwards', which also flung him against the walls of the narrow room. Nieuwoudt thrashed him with a reinforced hosepipe. 'In the momentum', he said, 'Mr Biko hit his head, fell, seemed confused and dazed ... Siebert then told me to chain him to the [horizontal] bars of the security gate with arms outstretched [at shoulder height] ... two sets of hand-cuffs and leg irons also attached – standing.' He was left in this crucifying position for six hours, only able to move his head. Three to four hours later, when Biko asked for water his words were incoherent as if 'under the influence of liquor', Nieuwoudt went on to testify.

That night Biko was left lying on a urine-wet mat, still shackled by leg-irons on his feet which were locked onto the walls. Although Lt.-Col. P.J. Goosen, Officer Commanding, Eastern Cape Security Police, spoke at the inquest into Biko's death about his suspicion at the time that Biko had 'suffered a stroke' and said he had called in a doctor, Nieuwoudt reported at the TRC hearing that the first doctor only appeared 24 hours after the injury and to no effect, leaving Biko shackled in leg-irons and handcuffs for another night. On 11 September, though specialist evidence indicated brain damage, medical approval was given for him to be driven (naked) in the back of a Landrover hundreds of kilometres to Pretoria, where he died from the head injuries he had earlier sustained.

The details of Biko's death horrified the world.

In spite of the inquest that followed, in which the doctors and police displayed a measure of callousness so shocking that their evidence would be transcribed, virtually word for word, into a theatrical performance for audiences world-wide to witness, the details of what actually happened still remain shrouded. None of the Security Police who applied for amnesty from the TRC in 1998 was granted it. The requirement was to tell the *whole* truth. This 'we may never know', commented chairperson George Bizos.

It is, however, Biko's life-giving force that concerns us here. His vitality drew people to him, not only for his sharp intelligence and generous counsel but for his exuberant energy and contagious laugh; not only for his clear thinking and his refreshing political insight but for his capacity to listen, his ability to place himself within a circle of people and not position himself upfront. Biko's gift of leadership was not that people should follow him in a slavish kind of way but that, suddenly, and to their great surprise, they discovered *themselves* and empowered themselves with their own resources.

Basically, Biko was appalled at what he saw all around him in South Africa at the time: 'the black man has become a shell, a shadow of man … bearing the yoke of oppression with sheepish timidity,' he said. He challenged blacks not to be a part of their own oppression, believing that 'the most potent weapon in the hands of the oppressor is the mind of the oppressed'. He defined Black Consciousness as 'an inward-looking process' to 'infuse people with pride and dignity'. 'We have set out on a quest for a true humanity,' he said clearly.

Young as he was, he realised that a new psychological climate had to be created if the liberation of his country was to come about. He expressed what he saw as the bitter truth. Of prime importance was 'to awaken the people as to who they are by getting them to state their identity. He thought that if you could do that, then there was no stopping them from revolution,' explained his colleague Malusi Mpumlwana.

This consciousness towards a realised identity, a refusal to mirror white apartheid's definition of black inferiority, gradually took root amongst the black youth and revived political energy in the 1970s. A new dignity and a refusal to be afraid helped fuel those in emerging trade unions; it gave determination to the many working in grassroots organisations; it empowered lawyers, doctors, priests, poets, mothers and fathers. Its youthful followers, scattered by the apartheid regime especially after 1976, later joined and vitalised new thinking in the ranks of the banned, imprisoned and exiled liberation movements of the African National Congress (ANC) and the Pan Africanist Congress (PAC).

Biko's life expressed in words only, diminishes him. His arrival in the doorway, his large physical frame relaxed into a chair, were essential elements of who he was. The welcome he gave, the sound of his laughter and his immediate questioning curiosity are glaringly missing here. He is not easily packaged. Biko was by no means a paragon of virtue. Though he could hold his drink, he often drank too much; he earned a reputation of being a 'womaniser'; and he could not always judge for himself his own emotional and psychological capacity. He was essentially human but also exceptional. Biko strongly criticised the institutional Church yet he believed in God and had insight into Christ's teachings. He was not a Marxist – indeed he was much criticised for this – identifying more with what his close friend Barney Pityana refers to as the 'Hegelian thesis–antithesis'. He believed in bargaining from a position of strength, as witnessed in the Saso-BPC Trial, where Biko stated in public: 'We certainly don't envisage failure ... We have analysed history ... the logical direction is that eventually any white society in this country is going to have to accommodate black thinking. We are mere agents in that history.'

Pityana would argue that Biko's historical analysis lacked the force of Marxist historical materialism. Biko regarded the common oppression of all blacks as being a stronger political motive for change, and more unifying, than that of class; he recognised that to forge a powerful identity among the majority would potentially shift political power. He was more at home in African socialism than in socio-political examples from Europe.

Although he set out to study medicine he never became a doctor. Although he never had time to complete his law studies, he donned the mantle of a lawyer of considerable skill when summoned to give evidence in defence of those in the organisations he helped establish. And although he never set out to become a martyr, this is what he became. Perhaps the thing he least set out to do was to convert white South Africans, yet the Black Consciousness Movement jolted white youth into a profound self-examination that changed the political direction of a whole generation; and he converted one of the leading liberal newspaper editors without apparent effort. Above all, although he advocated a philosophy called 'Black Consciousness', Steve Biko was not a racist.

This brief narrative of his life traces some of the origins of Biko's political thinking and the role he played in connecting Black Consciousness and self-identity. It reveals his innate curiosity and fascination with the human condition, with humanity, with what being human truly is, particularly in Africa.

2

Early years, 1946–1965

Bantu Stephen Biko was born on 18 December 1946 in Tarkastad, in the Eastern Cape, the third child of Mzingaye and Alice Nokuzola 'Mamcethe' Biko. His birth, in his grandmother's home, included the traditional smearing and burying of the umbilical cord into the floor of the room where he was born. Mzingaye chose to name him Bantu Stephen Biko. 'Bantu' literally means 'people'. Later Biko called himself 'son of man'. Although this was done often with tongue in cheek, Malusi Mpumlwana interprets Biko as understanding his name to mean that he was a person for other people or, more precisely, *umntu ngumtu ngabanye abantu*, 'a person is a person by means of other people'.

The name Stephen was prophetic of the manner of his death. It connects with that of his biblical namesake, Stephen, who was stoned to death. Stephen accused the Jews of being false to their vocation, of being stubborn, like their forebears, in refusing to acknowledge that truth. Mpumlwana adds: 'Jesus was actually the path of the Truth, which is very much in line with what the whole vocation of Israel was about. Even as he died he challenged them in the face of their anger.' Stephen Biko challenged people to recognise their humanity and acknowledge it. This included the authorities and those who persecuted him. But they could not see him as a human being nor recognise who he was. They, too, were bound to kill him.

Biko grew up in a Christian family. His parents met and married in Whittlesea when Mzingaye was sent to work with Mamcethe's father, both of them policemen. The Bikos were later transferred to Queenstown, then to Port Elizabeth, to Fort Cox and finally King William's Town, where they lived in a house in the black location of Ginsberg. In 1950, when Mzingaye was studying for a law degree by correspondence through the University of South Africa (Unisa), he fell ill. After being admitted to St Matthew's Hospital in Keiskammahoek, he died. Biko (who was called Bantu by his family) was 4 years old. The first-born, his sister Bukelwa, had been delegated by her father to look after him, while Khaya, an elder brother, was to look after his younger sister, Nobandile. Though the children kept asking where their father was, Mamcethe could not at first bring herself to tell them he had died. Because he was often away, she said he had gone to Cape Town for work and an aeroplane would bring him back. While playing with a group of other children they saw an aeroplane and shouted: 'Aeroplane, come back with our father!' But the other children said: 'No, your father died!'

As a widow with four young children, Mamcethe earned a meagre income for the next 23 years as a domestic worker. She remembers her first employer, the superintendent of Ginsberg, as a helpful and 'good man', who welcomed her children to play with his, included them at Christmas time and was generally generous. After he left, she had to take a job as a cook in the much tougher environment of Grey Hospital in King William's Town, the 'whites-only' town across the railway line from Ginsberg location.

Ginsberg was a closely knit community of about eight hundred families, every four families sharing communal taps and toilets. In spite of her slender means, Mamcethe's house, though simple, was by no means destitute, and with her quiet and singular dignity she always welcomed her friends and neighbours. 'Everybody knew the next person,' Biko's younger sister Nobandile remembers. 'It was common, then, if you didn't have food, you'd go to your neighbours and they'd give you samp, beans, mealie meal, sugar in dishes, and when you had [eaten] you'd just return the dishes.' Biko and Nobandile grew up side by side in the small township, where the languages of English,

Nobandile Biko.

Alice Nokuzola 'Mamcethe' Biko.

Khaya Biko.

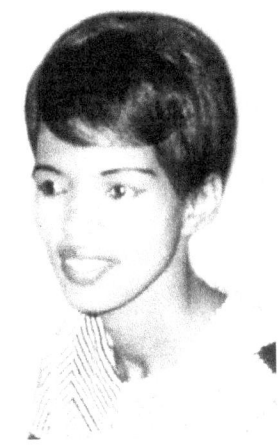
Bukelwa Biko.

Afrikaans and Xhosa intermingled. At the age of 6 or 7 he took Nobandile, aged 4, to the creche each day on his way to Charles Morgan Primary School and collected her on his way home.

From a young age Biko made people laugh, not only by tomfoolery and clowning but by the way he engaged in conversation. If he had been too busy playing soccer in the streets and had missed a meal, he would demand it with the next one. He avoided doing things that bored him: errands for aunts or feeding the chickens before school, when he would deliberately get up late. He loved experiments and, like most boys, used his younger sister as guinea pig, but Nobandile 'enjoyed every minute' of that shared childhood with him and, on reflection, remembers that 'We never regarded ourselves as poor though when I look back I realise that, in fact, we were poor'.

Soon, tall and slender, the youthful Biko went off to secondary school at Forbes Grant. His mother began to notice that when other children had parties he refused to have clothes bought for him and he would say: 'I know we don't have a father. We can't afford these new clothes.' Though she would tell him not to worry about such things, the truth is that he worried about his mother all his life. He was deeply committed to her well-being. It made a profound impression on him that she laboured for such long hours in such unrewarding jobs, for very little pay.

Mamcethe wanted her children to be educated. Biko was doing so well at school that the Ginsberg community gave him a bursary to go to Lovedale Institution in nearby Alice, where his brother, Khaya, was already in boarding school. The bursary was, in fact, from money collected to build two senior classrooms, which had not materialised. Biko was 16. Within the first three months of his arrival, Khaya was arrested, suspected of sympathies with the banned PAC. Biko was arrested too. 'They took us to the police camp, decided I was the younger of the two and sent me in first for a sort of heavy grilling, seven people around me. It didn't take long for them to discover that I didn't know a single thing about it. They were talking about "friends" of mine who had been arrested; I didn't know these people. They were talking about things I was *doing* with "friends"; I didn't know about this. This was how I got a glimpse into what was going to happen to my brother. I never saw him thereafter. He just disappeared. I saw him ten months later. It was a bitter experience. I was terribly young.' Khaya was convicted but acquitted on appeal. When Biko returned to Lovedale school, he was immediately expelled although he was entirely innocent. 'I began to develop an attitude which was much more directed at authority than at anything else. I hated authority like hell.'

In 1964, having missed a full year of studies, Biko went to boarding school at St Francis College in Mariannhill, outside Durban. He had just turned 18. It was run by Catholic nuns and monks, and he later described an atmosphere free of government intervention. 'I think it helped a lot in the formulation of ideas in a slow sense. We saw the principal and all the authorities [as] obviously not representative of the system but, all the same, they had an approach to us which was sort of provocative and challenging. That's where one began to see, in a sense, the totality of white power. These were liberals, presumably, who were enunciating a solution for us.' Biko was not loath to question anybody and did so: 'I personally had many wars with those guys, most of them non-political wars in a sense, but again this kind of authority problem.'

Biko began to question 'all sorts of [practices] within the Church, within the authority structure within the school'. He befriended a Catholic nun, who gave him a good deal of her time discussing such issues as the position of nuns within the Church, for example, and why it was necessary to have the institution anyway, which apart from other things imposed strictly disciplined relationships between nuns and monks. And, doubtless, he was curious about celibacy. He also sought answers to these questions by initiating a correspondence with Father Aelred Stubbs, of the Anglican Community of the Resurrection, who was principal of St Peter's College at the Federal Theological Seminary in Alice. Father Stubbs had, in his normal round of duty, come across the Biko family at the time of the two boys' arrest. It was the start of an important and long-term relationship between spiritual 'father' and 'son'.

As we shall see later when Biko befriended a challenging young Anglican priest, David Russell, he would continue to pursue with interest questions of faith and belief, his understanding of religion and his disappointment in the Church. Consciously, however, these questions were not central to his life. Already, at school in Mariannhill, he sought information of an increasingly political nature and he recalled how the pupils found intellectual debates valuable, particularly about Africa's independence from colonialism, which was then under way: 'We were great listeners to news services,' Biko recalled, 'and at that time [Hastings] Banda [of Malawi] and a whole host of other African leaders were coming up.' Several of them became 'heroes', particularly Algeria's Ahmed Ben Bella. Biko himself identified particularly with Oginga Odinga, one of Kenya's national leaders. Their ideas and stances were hotly debated while the whole question of military coups was carefully discussed. Biko remembered, however, that all of them agreed on the idea of a common society. 'I don't know to what extent Christian principles played a part here,' he mused, 'but I was always sold on the idea of a common society.' He added that nobody could enunciate the method or approach or design on his behalf but that, talking of himself as an 'oppressed person', he would do so for himself.

Biko was full of zest and youthful confidence whenever he came home. He would arrive at the door in high spirits, hardly pausing before describing his journey home and everyone he had met. 'He was like a father who comes home. We would hug and kiss and there would be laughter,' Nobandile recalls, and then the two of them might go off the next day and visit some of the older, more lonely people in the township, or they would sit on the verandah until late at night singing Gibson Kente songs. It was partly this zest for life, combined with incorrigible optimism and excitement at Africa's increasing independence, that drew him towards the future rather than the pessimism of the immediate present.

He had been only a boy of 13 when the protest against the carrying of passes took place with the subsequent massacre at Sharpeville in 1960 and both the major black political movements, the ANC and PAC, were banned and went underground. Spurred by the police action at Sharpeville, which killed 69 people in that non-violent protest, there was strong opinion in both organisations that the door had finally closed on passive resistance and that some form of insurgency was necessary for fundamental change in South Africa. Biko was 14 when Nelson Mandela proposed, in June 1961, the formation of the military wing of the ANC, Umkhonto weSizwe (MK). He was 15 when Mandela was arrested on his return from an illegal visit overseas and sentenced to five years' imprisonment, and he was 16 when most of the MK national high command were arrested at Liliesleaf Farm in Johannesburg (he himself also being arrested at Lovedale) and were sentenced to life imprisonment after the Rivonia Trial in 1964.

Running alongside the ANC's 'controlled sabotage' programme was the PAC's militant group, known as Poqo. It was with this organisation that his brother Khaya had been suspected of having connections. Biko talks of the only 'politicos' in his family being PAC and how 'at a very young age I listened to a whole host of their debates'. The PAC was not sympathetic towards Communist ideology nor did it readily accept white membership at that stage. In spite of his admiration for their courage and their 'terribly good organisation', Biko was not convinced by what he saw as an exclusive Africanism.

When Steve Biko matriculated from school in 1965, aged 19, all this history had only very recently come to pass. As far as the government was concerned, the black opposition was neatly rolled up into jails under lock and key or had fled into exile. To what extent all these events were known or in what way they affected the emergent ideas of the young Biko is difficult to judge. Whatever the case, Biko soon expressed his distaste at what he saw as 'this sort of appalling silence on the part of Africans and this tendency to play kids and hide behind the skirts of white liberals who were speaking for them'. Seemingly unscathed and certainly unafraid, Biko believed that blacks could be playing a far greater role. Possibly influenced by his Catholic school background, he believed, at that stage, in what was then known as the 'non-racial' approach – that already established institutions should be opened up to a far greater participation by blacks. Better recruitment and greater numbers of black students would mean that these institutions would shift from being predominantly white to becoming more representative.

Biko wanted to study law at university but there was a popular mentality in the Eastern Cape that equated law with political activism, and was therefore to be discouraged. Medicine was the safe alternative for a good profession, and Biko won a scholarship to study it. There was also a common pattern at the time that bright black students with good matric results should go to the medical school at the University of Natal

(Non-European Section, or UNNE), one of the few possibilities for good tertiary education. Thus many intelligent and remarkable young black students, for whom medicine was not necessarily their first choice, found themselves there in a core group with a measure of freedom which did not exist in any other long-established liberal university, where blacks were always a very small minority.

3

Student action and style of leadership, 1966–1972

In 1966 Biko went to UNNE at Wentworth in Durban to study medicine. He entered the university keen for debate and participation in student politics. In his first year he went as an observer to the July congress of the National Union of South African Students (Nusas), in spite of the many black student groups who disagreed with this decision and with his view of the non-racial approach. In the following year, 1967, he went as a delegate to the congress held at Rhodes University in Grahamstown. Biko immediately challenged Nusas to take an active stance against the segregated residential facilities which Rhodes University had imposed on the congress: those classified as 'Indians' and 'Coloureds' were to stay in the town whilst Africans were required to stay some distance away in a church hall in the 'location'; whites, on the other hand, could stay in the university residences. At the outset of the conference the executive of Nusas dealt with this by bringing in a resolution condemning the Rhodes University Council for not allowing blacks into the residences. Biko then moved a private motion proposing that the conference adjourn until they could find a 'non-racist venue'.

He later remembered that it was during the subsequent debate, which lasted throughout the night, that a lot of ideas became clear to him. 'I realised that for a long time I had been holding onto the whole dogma of non-racism almost like a religion, feeling that it was sacrilegious to question it … I began to feel there was a lot lacking in the proponents of the non-racist idea … They had this problem, you know, of superiority, and they tended to take us for granted and wanted us to accept things that were second-class.'

There was also the assumption that all affairs were automatically conducted in English. This gave an immediate disadvantage to those for whom English was not their mother tongue. It was an extraordinary experience for blacks to listen to their own lives being articulated by whites, who had had an infinitely superior education, yet had had no experience of the reality of being black. Biko recalls the effect: 'You are forced into a subservient role of having to say "yes" to what they are saying because you cannot express it so well. This in a sense [also] inculcates a sense of inadequacy. You tend to think it is not just a matter of language. You tend to tie it up also with intelligence. You tend to feel that that guy is better equipped than you mentally.' Biko identified and experienced, at first hand, the kind of mental process that led to an inferiority complex among blacks. He was certainly not going to succumb to this.

There stirred within him the germ of an idea, which was to flower into a student movement. It conscientised blacks into analysing their sociopolitical condition by recognising that they could be their own liberators by resisting their oppression with a different mental attitude. It was this mental attitude that became known as 'Black Consciousness'. Amongst other things it debunked long-standing myths whites had woven about Africa generally and South Africa in particular, myths present in school and university textbooks: the inherent inferiority of blacks, their skin-deep civilisation, the simplistic quality of their faith and beliefs, the inferiority of Africa's oral tradition as opposed to written history, the 'primitive' nature of its culture, and so forth. Blacks would be re-conscientised into discovering their true identity by refusing to live the lie. In the spirit of the 1960s world-wide, with the end to colonial rule in Africa, the emergence of Black Power in the United States, and the student revolts in Europe, the Black Consciousness Movement emerged to transform the minds of black South African students, thereby generating a lifestyle which eventually resisted oppression on a massive scale.

On leaving the Nusas meeting Biko went immediately to New Brighton, in Port Elizabeth, to talk to Barney Pityana, who remembers how 'We literally sat in my room for probably the whole night and he was talking through his annoyance and what I was saying to myself was: "Why did you go? You must have known before you went that it would be like that, that nothing is really different and if you did go, you were naive to have expected anything different."'

Pityana had also been dismissed from Lovedale school following a student strike in 1964. He was now one of the leading students in the Anglican Student Society, the English Dramatic Society and the Law Society at the University of Fort Hare. He was not a person easily convinced. He tested and questioned ideas with a legalistic mind: Why this? Why that? Why not the other? Not so much a devil's advocate, he was a person whose intelligence was to be thoroughly trusted and whose questions often brought out aspects not yet considered. In this instance Biko and Pityana were at one and began to work as a convincing team together. Pityana found Biko's idealism attractive. 'There was something about him that was really prepared to experiment with ideas, to really get going, could really take you away from the ordinary humdrum things and say there are other possibilities. He had the capacity to challenge and to make it a reality.'

In July 1968, Pityana and Biko attended a student meeting in Stutterheim of the University Christian Movement (UCM), a newly emerging radical ecumenical group of young people, using the Gospel to challenge the churches to take a more practical, robust approach to counter apartheid and participate to a far greater degree in social change. Under a provision of the Group Areas Act, blacks were allowed to be in any urban area only for 72 hours without a permit. The black participants met to discuss what to do about this. They presented a motion refusing to obey the rule. White delegates expressed displeasure at being left out, and a compromise motion was adopted whereby the whole conference was to march to the borders of the magisterial district. The black caucus also took a formal decision 'to work towards a conference in December to deal with the specific issue of a black student organisation as such'.

Pityana was not convinced about an on-going blacks-only caucus. In a country dominated by segregation, it might easily be seen as a group of students 'taken over by government-orientated thinking'. Shortly afterwards, he invited Biko to speak at Fort Hare at a UCM student discussion to put his point of view. When Biko told students that their responsibility was to the whole university, 'including the people that are working, underpaid, and treated like slaves', Pityana was convinced and saw the potential of the idea as 'a real link between student responsibility and the social concerns of the country'.

Pityana played a leading student role at Fort Hare and, at that time, was determined no Student Representative Council (SRC) should be formed that would be seen to collaborate with the pro-government appointees now ruling the university. In 1968 he was expelled during a strike. As regional director of the UCM, which was not allowed to operate on the Fort Hare campus, Pityana travelled to the Western Cape while Biko went to Natal and the Transvaal. 'We actually never sat down to agree about what we would say,' Pityana reflected, 'but it was, more or less, that it's about time that black people up and down the country began to speak together in one voice.' 'Black' meant all of the oppressed, which included anyone classified 'Coloured', 'Indian' or 'Asian' as well as those classified 'Bantu'. This new definition had a liberating effect on many people, freeing them from the categories defined by apartheid, though some were extremely dubious of something that sounded as though it smacked of racism. It took time to sow the seed. Biko and Pityana were in constant contact, travelling and writing each other long letters to keep in touch: 'He was a political writer and was very good at throwing out ideas,' Pityana emphasised. Biko displayed another quality too, 'an eye to discern people and human nature in a very penetrating way without having to get into great discussions about things'. Biko and Pityana spent most of the early months of 1969 doing the rounds of the university campuses across the country.

The result of all this energy, enthusiasm and growing conviction amongst the black student youth was the founding of the South African Students' Organisation (Saso) in July 1969 at one of the government's own tribalised universities, Turfloop (the University of the North). Biko was its first president. The first SASO communiqué has a breathless quality about it:

1. At a time when events are moving so fast in the country, it is not advisable to show any form of division amongst students' ranks – especially now that students appear to be a power to be reckoned with in this country.
2. Any move that tends to divide the student population into separate laagers on the basis of colour is in a way tacit submission to having been defeated and apparently seems in agreement with apartheid.
3. In a racially sensitive country like ours, provisions for racially exclusive bodies tend

Barney Pityana (centre), who was elected president of Saso to succeed Biko in July 1970.

Father Aelred Stubbs.

Neville Curtis.

to build up resentment and to widen the gap that exists between the races, and the student community should resist all attempts to fall into this temptation.
4. Any formation of a purely non-white body shall be subject to a lot of scrutiny and so the chances of the organisations lasting are very little.

Coincidentally, at this time, Nusas itself underwent some radical changes under the presidency of Neville Curtis, an independent-thinking 'outsider' who was not definable in the Nusas liberal tradition. Curtis and Biko met at conferences on several occasions. They both wanted to find a way of working on black and white campuses alike that was fresh and innovative and not just defensive; that would, said Curtis, 'enable us to mobilise students, that allowed us to *raise* issues, not just react to issues'. Though their tasks were different, the two had a breadth of vision that acknowledged the usefulness, at that point, of the continued existence of both organisations, co-operating but not coming under one umbrella.

Saso could have wrecked Nusas, but instead it passed a resolution recognising the latter as the national student body. By keeping this contact with Curtis, Biko picked up some of Nusas's most useful

Steve Biko addresses a meeting of SASO's second General Students Council held at the University of Natal, July 1971.

procedures, particularly the idea of training, which in Saso became known as formation schools. They concentrated on leadership training, which at the same time ensured that layers of leadership would persist. This was not only as a precaution in case people were 'knocked off' by the government but as a principle to avoid hierarchy. Both organisations were in a situation where neither might survive. Nusas and the UCM had the universities and the Church to draw on; Saso had neither. 'It was an extremely brave venture in organisational terms,' Neville Curtis recalls.

Biko built up different groups of people with whom he debated and discussed ideas and procedures. In February 1970 he wrote a letter to the presidents of all the SRCs of the English- and Afrikaans-speaking universities, to national student organisations and students overseas, giving the historical background, the structure, policy and aims of Saso.

In this letter the word 'non-white' was still used, but this was to be short-lived. 'Non-white' was a negation of being. It indicated a desire to become white eventually. It implied that 'whiteness' was the norm to which one attached all other people whose own culture and identity had been negated. It was soon removed from Saso's vocabulary. Mpumlwana elaborates: 'Over time, blacks had been made to see themselves as just a mass, one of a mass without any sense of responsibility about who you are, your destiny and your society. Just "non-whites", non-something. Everything that you are has been taken away from you. You're a non-person. In order to be a person you have got to claim your identity. You name yourself. And we named ourselves "black".'

In July 1970 Pityana became second president of Saso, and Biko editor of the *SASO Newsletter*. From

August Biko began his column 'I Write What I Like' and signed it 'Frank Talk'. Throughout the following two years it enabled the evolution of the philosophy of Black Consciousness to be recorded and expressed, ideas sounded out with colleagues and friends, tried and tested in the Saso style of consensus politics.

In January 1971 Pityana and Biko delivered two separate papers to an Abe Bailey conference in Cape Town, statements that were 'a major refinement of what we were doing'. Barney recalls how incredible it was that neither of them had read each other's paper in advance. As they had dealt with the far more ideological question of whether or not they should participate, it was quite clear to both of them, in the papers presented, 'that there was a lot there between us that was actually a result of conversations and writing and sharing and thinking through precisely how you present, in a hostile, in an ambiguous and uncertain climate, something positive and, in our view, certain. We felt certain about the capacity of black people to participate in their own struggle but that it needed to be said in a challenging and in a critical way.'

A particular style of leadership evolved which recognised the enormous advantage of widespread consultation. This meant not only consultation to win over a proposal but the creation of an atmosphere where individual opinions were considered and taken seriously. They were valued equally. It was time-consuming and costly in energy but it ensured true development and growth, both politically and in terms of human advance, so that people became more efficient and confident. This style was effective for Black Consciousness and developed at the height of some of the most oppressive years of apartheid. Its legacy and the whole leadership-training style remain relevant today in a country still grappling with crime and the effects of migrant labour, which destroyed family life; with one of the widest gaps between rich and poor in the world; where the burden of a previous inferior education system persists; where self-worth has been ravaged by the onslaught of HIV/Aids, coincidental with growing violence against women and children.

Black Consciousness drew intellectual and political inspiration and dialogue from the Civil Rights and Black Power movements in the United States, from Négritude and other forms of post-colonial thinking and writing in Africa. It concerned itself with the religious movements of Ethiopianism and African religious political prophecy, and some of its practices were confirmed and strengthened through the methods of Paulo Freire's rapidly spreading pedagogy. All this was fervently debated in a growing consciousness rooted in the South African situation. The impact was that, under the very gaze of a severely oppressive

Biko with fellow medical students Brigette Savage, Rogers Ragavan and Ben Ngubane.

regime, people began to live lives actively aware of forging their own identity. A fearlessness evolved. The aim of Black Consciousness was that this style of life should filter into the lives of all the oppressed, the vast majority of South Africans. It sought to use the greatest potential of each person, *any* person, within its ranks, never considering anyone incapable of contributing. Initiated in Saso, this was to become the hallmark of the Black Consciousness Movement as a whole. Because it was a lived experience, recognition of a new identity became an integral part of its proponents. In so far as was possible, leadership was rendered invisible. This was not only in preparation for the inevitable moment when the State would single people out to be banned, banished or arrested, but also an acknowledgement that multiple skills are the most productive.

Biko's personality had a large part to play in living and nurturing this style. His presence ensured that people would be heard and their opinion considered. He engendered trust and freed people to use their potential. To him it was clear that to obtain the common goal of a true humanity, the game of power politics would have no place – a spectre that haunts the ruling ANC today. He recognised and enabled participation in such a way that the sum of the whole was richer, more useful and politically more powerful when thoroughly worked through than that of individual leadership and domination. Time was needed for a group to identify the skills in one another and then to trust those skills so that delegation could take place with the urgency and speed that were often necessary. Pityana describes Biko as 'the person who brought ideas. He was the fundamentalist, if you like, the person who brought the basic ideas which were being bandied about and thrown around. He was actually quite stubborn in some ways because he was very keen to push his point and his ideas to the limit.' For this reason the very opposite of consensus politics might have been expected from a person like Biko. This was not so. He himself was also challenged by equally vocal and questioning people, which he encouraged. And although he talked a lot, he also listened. He did not dominate and he had the capacity to be delighted by counter-argument.

Biko's room in the old army barracks of the medical student residence, Alan Taylor, doubled up as the Saso office. Saso became a sub-culture of the university. It was there, Mpumlwana recalls, when he first came to UNNE, that you 'expected to find people in some conversation or another; very friendly people, warm and accommodating, non-hierarchical and always involved in debates, conversations, always something exciting with a new angle to develop'.

Everybody read books outside their university subjects. These provided the essence of the debates and the discussion that made the future have some kind of meaningful possibility. Many people were involved, people who later became psychologists, doctors, poets, writers, politicians and trade unionists. Among them were Charles Sibisi, who was considered the 'international' expert, while Mamphela Ramphele and Malusi Mpumlwana worked on practical community programmes; Mandla Langa had started writing poetry and was getting it published in journals by small publishing houses in Johannesburg; Strini and Sam Moodley, Asha Rambally and Saths Cooper were founding members of the Theatre Council of Natal (Tecon), a group that was concerned with creating 'relevant theatre' by producing plays and poetry readings to accompany student conferences.

To write and to perform became an intrinsic part of the many meetings, teach-ins and seminars held throughout the country, and the General Student Councils (GSCs). Mandla Langa recalls: 'You would find yourself with a certain captive audience, people who would criticise you or encourage you but who would be there to read your stuff and try and make sense out of it. Students were extremely instrumental in making sure that one continued writing.' This included writers like Mafika Gwala, Mongane Wally Serote, Njabulo Ndebele, Strini Moodley and Saths Cooper, who, working alongside musicians and performing theatre groups, all interpreted with anger, depth and humour 'the thrust of that time'. The very nature of being 'travelling players', Serote remembers, gave them a consciousness and a 'global understanding' of the problems in the country.

In political and theological matters Biko and Pityana led the field. Langa recalls how 'we started sharing libraries, sharing books and also going to all these bookshops which had all these expensive books which we needed and, you know, finding a way of appropriating them. We started widening our vistas and our minds by reading books which the regime never possibly thought we'd lay our hands on, anything from the [Heinemann] African Writers Series to, well, we read Marcuse, we read the existential philosophers such as Jean-Paul Sartre. There was Mphahlele and maybe some hidden copies by Alex La Guma, Lewis Nkosi, Can Themba, Nat Nakasa, Bloke Modisane. We read all that.'

One of the most significant writers whom Biko passed on to the others was Frantz Fanon. It seemed coincidental that Fanon's work was published in English for the first time in 1965. Born in Martinique, Fanon had studied medicine in France and practised psychiatry in the Antilles, where he wrote *Black Skin, White Masks,* a psychological and philosophical analysis of the state of being black, and then *The Wretched of the Earth,* a book which included theory on the colonising of the mind, experience of which he gained when working in Algeria during the French-Algerian colonial war. Another important writer was James Cone, the black American theologian. Malcolm X was the 'Black Consciousness' counterpart to the liberal integrationism of Martin Luther King. He published his autobiography in 1965 and the Saso group had twelve gramophone records of his speeches. 'Compared to Martin Luther King, we felt that Malcolm's preachings were much more gutsy, much more in tandem with what we were thinking and feeling. They were also very very influential in some of the plays which we wrote and performed.' Mandla Langa recalls that there was also a resonance with the kind of cultural awakening expressed by the Black Panthers, and 'consciously or unconsciously there was a lot of borrowing, which is why you find the poetry of that time became very derivative really'.

One of the main sources for information about relevant books came from the 'objectionable books' listed in the South African *Government Gazette* itself. Quite obviously these were the very books that became required reading. Pityana also recalls how a man in the United States consulate made much of the relevant American literature available while another source was a Lutheran bookshop which unobtrusively sold banned books.

Thorough discussion took place as a constant backdrop to student activity. In preparation for the 1971 GSC, regarding leadership training, Biko (now 25) began to make an extensive study of South African political movements, concentrating on the early so-called religious breakaways of the 1890s, the Ethiopian movement, the foundation of the ANC, the history of the Industrial and Commercial Workers' Union (ICU), and so forth. *Time Longer than Rope* was a favourite book. Pityana recalls much of this research as a 'subconscious act of transcending the visions of the past without denying the authenticity of that'. At the same time there was a clear recognition that 'we could no longer proceed on that same basis [to] capture the imagination of our people'.

And so a new energy and mood began to spread across the country. Without making him stand out too much, nobody would question that much of the setting in motion of that rolling spirit was initiated by Biko, or affirmed by Biko. Once moving, once in motion, he stepped back and others took over, and they, in turn, did the same. He was always of the belief that nobody should become cast in a mould, that diversity was educative, that people had different skills. No Saso president, for example, was in office for more than a year, a precedent set by Biko. This capacity to stand back, to put others forward, to initiate new ideas, get something going and make it practical, meant that although Biko was present, he managed not to be dominant. It was an infusion of ideas which he encouraged, resulting in a newly found energy that began to perpetuate itself country-wide.

He travelled extensively with different people. Not having a driving licence at this stage he always let others drive. 'It didn't matter where we were in South Africa, whether in rural areas, in townships, in town, in the suburbs, we always knew where to go, which shebeen to go to. We would arrive in a place, sometimes at three in the morning, when usually everything is shut. We would knock, the person would say "no", but as soon as they heard it was us they would open and we would get six boxes of beer, two quarts of whiskey and a *gumba* (dance party) started,' Serote recalls. 'We would all be tired and I would fall asleep and I would wake up and Steve would still be on his chair, talking and drinking. And the thing that struck you was his great joy at being among people. This seemed to inspire him, this seemed to give him the energy and even the willingness to challenge, you know. I think the *gumba* situation at that time was a very very important forum for us. Under a relaxed atmosphere we were able, then, to explore a whole lot of very complex issues, informally, of course always with Steve presiding.'

In Johannesburg, as elsewhere, socialising took on a new form with the arrival of Saso. Since the 1950s, there had been a considerable 'crossing of the colour bar', as it was called, which mostly took place in white liberal and Communist homes. Bokwe Mafuna, then working for the *Rand Daily Mail*, remembers the ambivalence he and others often felt in performing the role of 'interpreters' of the black townships and the black world at these parties. He remembers being introduced to Biko by Stanley Sabelo Ntwasa, the UCM's roving representative, at a 'garden party'. When Saso began to be active around that time, a new forum was established. Mafuna says that 'they were neither the quiet, intellectual discourse, sitting and drinking in the white suburbs nor were they getting drunk in

Mamphela Ramphele addresses the first Black People's Convention, December 1972.

the shebeen. They were social events which had a lot of political significance, where people met one another from all over the country, where you could speak out, pour out your souls to one another', a place where things raised in that informal atmosphere would be transformed into resolutions for later conferences.

Mafuna recalls how he had never been in such an environment before. He had been a worker since school-going age and a member of trade unions before he became a photographer and journalist. 'I had grown up in an environment of conflict all my life and here, for once, I was with people with whom I could be at ease, among whom I could start believing in myself

... I found myself organising trade unions throughout the country. We went to Port Elizabeth, Cape Town, Durban, Johannesburg, all over. We were organising youth. We were organising women. All these things I had never believed I could do and we were getting other people to do them with us.' He later joined Saso's Black Workers' Project and spent many intimate moments with Biko travelling all over the country, with the resultant hours of long discussions which ensue on long journeys across the vast landscape. 'Steve respected people and he made people respect each other. His whole attitude and his whole experience was a working-class attitude and experience. He had extraordinary gifts of knowing how to relate to people and be able to inspire confidence in people, and trust.'

Biko's style of leadership was similar when tensions arose in student or political meetings. With his various caucuses he usually worked through his ideas in advance. He stuck to them but also had the flexibility of recognising and accepting a majority voice. What is more, it is clear that he was concerned to look at the long-term, wider picture, and not get caught up in the emotional frustration of the moment. He had the capacity to allow things to happen without needing or trying to 'control' them, but would assume leadership when he saw possibilities of division or short-term misunderstanding. Father Stubbs speaks of Biko as having 'this deep-rooted profound intuition of togetherness. He wanted to be in the background. He couldn't be in the background in any ultimate sort of way. He wanted other people to take the lead. I think it was his intuition of what real leadership involves.'

4

To love and to work

'Freud was once asked what he thought a normal person should be able to do well,' Erik Erikson tells us. And Freud had replied: 'Lieben und arbeiten', to love and to work. Erikson goes on to say that 'it pays to ponder on this simple formula; it grows deeper as you think about it. For when Freud said "love", he meant the generosity of intimacy as well as genital love; when he said "love and work", he meant a general work productiveness which would not preoccupy the individual to the extent that he might lose his right or capacity to be a sexual and loving being.'

Work

Biko's work was to awaken the people: first, from their own psychological oppression through recognising their inferiority complex and restoring their self-worth, dignity, pride and identity; secondly, from the mental and physical oppression of living in a white racist society. Biko explained: 'I had a man working on one of our projects in the Eastern Cape on electricity … a white man with a black assistant. He had to be above the ceiling and the black man was under the ceiling and they were working together pushing up wires and pushing through the rods in which the wires are and so on, and all the time there was insult, insult, insult from the white man. "Push this, you fool." That sort of talk. And of course this touched me. I knew the white man very well, he spoke well to me, so we invited them to tea and I asked him: "Why do you speak like this to this man?" And he said to me in front of the guy: "This is the only language he understands, he is a lazy bugger." And the black man smiled. I asked him if it was true and he said: "I am used to him." This sickened me. I thought for a moment that I did not understand black society. After some two hours I came back to this black guy and said to him: "Did you really mean it?" The man changed. He became very bitter. He was telling me how he wanted to leave his job, but what could he do? He did not have any skills, he had no assurances of another job, his job was to him some form of security, he had no reserves. If he did not work today he could not live tomorrow, he had to work, he had to take it. And as he had to take it he dared not show any form of insolence to his boss.'

What mattered to Biko, Mpumlwana explained,

was what work *he* needed to do in order for this person to be himself all the time. He further understood that self-realisation and identity also depended on seizing the necessary tools to function in a technological world, tools deliberately denied blacks by the Bantu Education Act. As Dr Verwoerd, Minister of Native Affairs at the time, had explained in parliament, when speaking about the new laws of segregated education: 'There is no place for [the Bantu] in the European [white] community above the level of certain forms of labour … For that reason it is of no avail for him to receive a training which has as its aim absorption in the European community above the level of certain forms of labour … Up till now he has been subjected to a school system which drew him away from his own community and partially misled him by showing him the green pastures of the European but still did not allow him to graze there.'

Demanding those denied tools – at the same time recognising that the green pastures of white education were not so green after all – would lead to widespread disruption in the Bantu Education system, which was sustained by black students for a whole generation over the next two decades. In 1972, although reluctant to believe he could not manage both studying and political work, Biko chose the more difficult political road. This was formally affirmed by his dismissal from medical school in June 1972, having only officially passed three years out of six. What was more painful was that he would also have to disappoint his family's ambitions for him and those of virtually the whole Ginsberg community. The choice he made was one that thousands of black students would come to face: the choice of either becoming a political activist or taking the time to gain some sort of qualification towards a professional life, with inevitable compromises, under apartheid. Biko thus sacrificed his chance of becoming a professional doctor. For the time being, his work lay elsewhere.

Two months later, in August 1972, he joined Bennie A. Khoapa as a staff member of the Black Community Programmes (BCP), whose offices, at 86 Beatrice Street, Durban, were on the same premises as Saso. This programme was concerned to develop skills in the black community. 'Issues of empowerment, the development of the ability to decide, the ability to be critical', were some of these – as well as to create practical programmes to meet sheer need, Khoapa explained. Biko's brief was primarily to co-ordinate youth leadership training and thereby 'expand the thrust of conscientising to youth beyond the schools'. He worked closely with Harry Ranwedzi Nengwekhulu. Youth groups already existed, country-wide, and many of them were well defined. They consisted not only of

'At the heart of this kind of thinking is the realisation by blacks that the most potent weapon in the hands of the oppressor is the mind of the oppressed.' – Biko's address on 'White Racism and Black Consciousness', Cape Town, January 1971.

pupils in school but also those who had had to drop out of school early, for economic reasons, most of them now on the streets but also some young workers in industry.

In this regard Biko recognised the importance of the educational methodology of Paulo Freire. He had read his book *Pedagogy of the Oppressed,* and in July had sought out Anne Hope, who was running training courses on Freire's educational method in Johannesburg and Swaziland. Fifteen people enrolled, including Pityana, Mafuna, Cooper, Moodley, Johnny Issel, Mthuli Shezi, Jerry Modisane, Deborah Matshoba and others. They attended workshops over four months. Each month's session consisted of five days of intensive training, after which they returned to their local communities for three weeks of research and practice. Key to Freire's methodology is the recognition that teaching should be a political act, directly related to production, health, social conditions, to the regular system of instruction, and to the overall plan for a society still to be realised in the future. The act of teaching should not be separated from the act of learning. The trainees, therefore, needed to be able to submerge themselves in the context of the learners' life experience, primarily to be able to listen while encouraging learners to unveil and 'unpackage' their lives and problems. Listening did not mean only literally hearing but listening in order to create a curriculum or a meaningful training programme for people out of what they disclosed about themselves. This training influenced Biko considerably and dovetailed with his style of leadership.

In the meantime BCP had applied to the Ford Foundation for funds to produce a state-of-the-black-nation annual review, similar to the annual survey of the Institute of Race Relations but written, researched and produced by blacks. Ford favoured Race Relations. Undeterred, Biko set about organising the first issue of the *Black Review*. Khoapa says this was virtually paid for out of the petty cash of the Black Community Programmes and, as Biko explained, could be realised with 'the help of some boys who are being chucked out of school and are not going back to university, like Welile Nhlapo and Tomeka Mafole'. Biko assured Khoapa that 'All they need is some food and transport. I am sure they'll be glad to do the paper, the coordination and so on'. Biko was the editor. However, by the time it was printed in 1973 Biko had been banned. This banning order prevented him from preparing any material for publication, and so *Black Review* came out under Khoapa's name and was dedicated to Biko and Mafuna, who was also banned.

Early in that new year Biko enrolled for a law degree through the correspondence university, Unisa

– the degree his father had also aspired to. In this and in his decision to continue with his political work, he selected the career from which his relatives had sought to protect him and pursued his vision. Legal training would add professional skills to his natural intelligence and curiosity and add weight to his ability to take hold of facts and thrash them out. He already had the African gift of *ubuntu,* being a person for other people.

Generosity of intimacy

'He was best at helping you be who *you* are best,' Mpumlwana explains. Indeed, most people who knew Biko well felt an intimacy of their very own with him. He gave them his undivided attention, entrusted them to recognise their own potential, whether it was a friend, fellow student, lover, spiritual father, teacher or someone in authority. This intimacy did not often engender rivalry. It was part of his capacity to love generously, and he spent a great deal of his time giving each person his undivided attention.

Neville Curtis, Nusas president, recalls him in those student days as 'an incredibly attractive human being. He was good-looking and articulate. He was a sparkler, a vivid person, a wonderful person. He could hardly ever talk to you without putting his arm around you. And also this "no bullshit" thing.' At the same time 'he was far from a perfect personality, a perfect human being. He was apt to over-indulge, but he was living life to the full and doing it with vividness and style.'

This generosity of intimacy naturally grew in complexity when it involved women, a complexity he largely chose to ignore. In those early travelling days there was an element of exploitation towards women which certainly bordered on chauvinism. With his 'vividness and style', Biko gained the reputation of being a 'womaniser'. His view of himself was that he was always open. People could take it or leave it. There was a certain defiance in his attitude, reminiscent of his defiance against authority. Sexism, as being potentially similar in form to racism, did not enter his head. Even when it was pointed out to him by women in the groups he worked in, he tended to set it aside. Like those in the ANC and in other liberation movements in Africa, he possibly held the view that Black Consciousness would liberate everything at once. Dimza Pityana affirms that the women who were involved in the Black Consciousness Movement were involved as blacks, not as black *women*. However, 'there was an interesting disjuncture between the genuine comradeship one experienced within the movement and the sexism which reared its head at many levels,' Mamphela Ramphele recalls. 'For example, the responsibility for catering, cleaning-up and other entertainment functions tended to fall on women participants.' And 'becoming one of the boys' contained simultaneous approval and disapproval. 'Late nights, alcohol consumption and smoking became part of life' but 'the same men one socialised with took a dim view of women being seen doing the same things as them publicly, especially smoking.' At the same time, feminism, which had swept through Europe and the US, was seen as 'irrelevant to the needs of black women in South Africa' and dismissed 'as a "bra-burning" indulgence of bored, rich white Americans'. And thus 'interpersonal relationships remained largely unchanged, with the man as the dominant partner, and many women remaining trapped in unsatisfactory relationships that violated their dignity as people'.

Basically, Biko was insatiably curious. He loved people. He found exploring relationships consistently fascinating, and though his exploration bordered on exploitation and might lead to complications which he sometimes did not know how to handle, he was someone seldom without love and respect. Being the person he was, he was much sought after by women and did not hesitate to have relationships with many of them. Pityana, on looking back, feels that Biko had not yet come 'to judge for himself how much you could have a fulfilled relationship with a woman without all the sexual overtones'. At the same time, he observed, in the circles that emerged, it was also true that 'many of the women [themselves] did not accept that there could be an authentic relationship with a man without that relationship becoming sexually loaded'. Serote observed that 'When you looked at the women around Steve, whom you knew he had personal relationships with, somehow the relationship between them had made something bloom – put lots of energy into every one of them. Even in relations like that he would continuously discuss these very complex issues, so many of the women had no choice but to continuously be conscientised and politicised!'

Women are often drawn to men who manifest the winning combination of power and human understanding – Martin Luther King, John F. Kennedy and Nelson Mandela immediately spring to mind. Biko was still a young man and was not in that kind of political limelight. Nevertheless, he had a similar ease of manner and charisma that was magnetic. Pityana maintains that one of the reasons that so many people wanted to be associated with him was this very capacity to 'radiate joy and confidence, which gave people a sense of ease and of love'. He accepted people, all people, without prejudice. Even the Security Police he knew must be human and, initially, he appealed to that. If that potential humanity continued to hide itself he virtually demanded it by his action and behaviour. It was only when he finally gave up on somebody that he sometimes became very angry. He accepted people first and then challenged them and, in risking his own generosity of intimacy, this usually had a profound effect on them. There was certainly no apparent seeking of power. Father Stubbs had the sense that Biko was somewhat wary of this potential power within him and that his saving grace was his recognition of his own vulnerability. This enabled him to be open.

This kind of challenge, these relationships, not only enriched him personally but were the way he chose to become informed about his country. The parties and shebeening, apart from being an important antidote to his intense lifestyle, also provided the forum, the access to a variety of people he might otherwise never have met. Sometimes he did not assess correctly the emotional impact of his behaviour on others, and there were certainly times when he got himself into relationships he had not bargained for. Although he read and digested many materials and books immediate to his task, it was people who became the library of his life.

Love and marriage
Freud, by his own definition, would have found Steve Biko 'normal'. His love seemed bound to set people free and he certainly knew how to work. Work was seldom without a circle or group of others, without consultation

Steve Biko with his wife, Ntsiki, and his son Nkosinathi.

with colleagues and the trust of friends. Later he exhibited a fearlessness and a powerful reasonableness that demanded respect even from the Security Police. Biko never lost 'his capacity to be a sexual and loving being'. Indeed, as we have seen, this capacity led to some complexity in his relationships. Few of these, however, had significant bearing on the two basic relationships which were of paramount importance to him. These attachments were different and deeply personal. They ran parallel, each one fulfilling different dimensions and needs in his life, and he never found it possible to give up one for the other. One was with Ntsiki Mashalaba, who became his wife, and the other, Mamphela Ramphele, his colleague at medical school, who grew visibly in his presence and who became the doctor of the first BCP clinic, Zanempilo, near King William's Town, where she put into action much of the theory of Black Consciousness.

By 1969 Ramphele had known Biko casually for about a year, and had met him regularly in the Saso circle as she became part of it. She remembers a sense of deep attraction for him then, which she dutifully ignored as she was engaged to be married to 'homeboy' Dick Mmabane at the end of the year. In early 1970 she returned to medical school, married, and excitedly displaying wedding photographs and rings. It was only later that she discovered that Biko had written her a letter, which she never received, encouraging her to delay her marriage. Ramphele was 22. Biko met Nontsikelelo (Ntsiki) Mashalaba and they were married at the end of 1970. They were both 23.

Ntsiki was training as a midwife at King Edward VIII Hospital in Durban. On their marrying, Biko's mother gave her the name Nosizwe – meaning 'Mother of the Nation' – warning her that 'your husband's name is Bantu and you are Nosizwe and you must know you are going to have lots of people around you'. Later Steve and Barney Pityana found a four-roomed house in Durban and Nosidima (Dimza) Pityana, Barney's wife, joined them. The relationship between the two women was warm and easy as they became good friends. During those few years they played a more or less accepted traditional role, sharing their first two babies, Nkosinathi (Biko) and Loyiso (Pityana), who were virtually the same age. They also had the nursing profession in common, Ntsiki having finished her midwifery by the time she got married, Dimza still completing hers.

Nontsikelelo Biko, small and dark with large soft eyes, describes herself then as quiet. 'I was very quiet indeed,' she explained, particularly when she went to medical school and listened to the discussions, seldom participating but absorbing a great deal. She was a private person, owning herself but creating a sense of ease and welcome around her. 'You feel very safe with Ntsiki,' Dimza explains, 'and very comfortable. She was a non-threatening person.' 'Still waters,' says Malusi Mpumlwana.

Their house was always full of people, who would arrive with or without Biko, at any time of the day or night. The main room more often than not contained sleeping bodies in the mornings: people from Saso, students from different universities throughout the country, and others. 'The money was short, short! But because we were working together with Barney, at least we managed to have good meals,' Ntsiki recalls. 'Sometimes we cooked meat, meat which would have been enough for the whole month!' Biko expected everybody to be fed, as they had been in his mother's house, even when they were very poor. Although Biko led such a politically demanding life, Ntsiki chose not to get involved in that side in a superficial way, but to play a supportive role to this life. Biko, on his side, believed in his commitment to his family, loved Ntsiki, and, whenever he was there, nurtured his children. They loved being with him, this huge father, strong and full of humour. Later, in King William's Town, he sometimes took Samora (his younger son) to the office, forgetting to bring clean nappies to change him, to the infuriation of his co-worker and secretary Nohle Mohapi. 'He was often away from home but I accepted him as he was,' says Ntsiki, 'a husband deeply involved in his politics. I very much accepted him.' He used to say when he brought his friends over: 'This is my wife, she's the people's wife, but we mustn't share her!'

And yet he expected her to share him. This type of expectation, this particular attitude towards his wife, highlights the ambiguity that existed within Biko. While he questioned just about everything else, he accepted, without question, a traditional view of the role of a wife, and this included her total loyalty under all circumstances. His mother, to whom he was dedicated all his life, was herself a powerful model, a woman whose home and personality had enabled the community of Ginsberg to be welcomed, to be accepted in the true sense of community. And Ntsiki complied, as young wives willingly do, not knowing what great demands would be made on her in her marriage to Steve Biko, demands which, ironically, set her questioning and led her later to claim her own self-image with dignity and independence. Biko's expectations required what amounted to an inordinate degree of tolerance and forbearing. Deep down he wished and hoped to make a real go with his family and children, but he soon realised, Pityana explained, that, as with his medical studies, this would not be possible. As his political commitment grew, things which he had expected to stay in place were submerged in its wake.

Biko was often obliged to work late at night and would sometimes remain in medical residence, where the Saso office still flourished. Amongst many others, he found himself working regularly alongside Mamphela Ramphele. She remembers how, in 1971, she got more and more involved with his thinking in the writing of the 'Frank Talk' articles. A dynamic, exciting, symbiotic relationship grew up between them, their skills complementing one another in many ways. A new energy was born. Being alongside Biko, Ramphele admits that she learnt a great deal about how to relate to people. On the other hand, Ramphele's capacity to transform ideas into practical action made her presence strengthening and critically relevant to him. Apart from her obvious intelligence, she was disciplined and totally reliable. They were two powerfully attractive people and their attraction for one another rapidly grew in depth, both politically and personally.

Soon after Steve married Ntsiki, Ramphele separated from her husband. She was very upset but, once back at medical school and into the swing of things, she increasingly became her own person, her inhibitions disappeared and, as her colleague Jay Pillay says, she 'became very very energetic'. She removed her wig, and was more and more conscious of being proud of being black, sometimes expressing it with anger and verve.

Biko became bound into two relationships. In most cases, under these circumstances, choices and sacrifices eventually have to be made. But, until he died at the age of 30, Biko did not make them. All three people lived with another's shadow cast over them, sometimes more encompassing than at other times. Changing circumstances constantly affected their lives and equilibrium, but the complexity of this triangle remained. Both Ntsiki and Mamphela bore two of Steve's children. Ntsiki had two boys: Nkosinathi (1971) and Samora Mzontsundu (1975). Mamphela had a girl, Lerato (1974), who died at two months, and a boy, Hlumelo (1978), born after Biko's death.

It would be too bald to leave it at that. Biko was deeply sensitive and agonised over many things. This situation often moved into sharp focus, demanding some resolution, especially when his relationship with Mamphela became more open and public, moving beyond a student affection into a powerful force. It was difficult to contain it without exposing its dynamic, and a vow they made early on, when it had begun to grow, not to hurt Ntsiki, was not sustained. She was deeply hurt by this relationship.

It is difficult to know whether (and, if so, when) Biko felt a real need to face these circumstances. The fact that he never *acted* to change them indicates that for a long while either he did not know how to or they were more acceptable to him as they were, unchanged. Father Stubbs raised the matter with him in 1974 just as he was leaving the Zanempilo clinic after a visit. Whether it was a shock coming from his 'dear priest' or whether he felt it to be a slight on his judgment, Biko was hurt and reacted with uncharacteristic anger. 'I regard topics of this nature as being extremely private. I am in many instances aware of the complexity that can be introduced by a willingness to accommodate the feelings of friends in a matter that is essentially private between two – or in this case three – parties. I have never found it necessary to reflect on my friends' private activities except in so far as I thought they affected at any one stage their political standing and their performance. Similarly I could never wish to ask you about your love life, your sexual life, etc. because I regard that as strictly speaking your business.'

He went on to make a more general observation: 'There is a profound difference in the way Westerners basically believe in character analysis to that adopted by us here. In many discussions I used to have with David [Russell] I agreed with him in comparing our attitude on the whole to that of the European working-class approach to life. When you guys talk about a person you tear him apart, analyse the way he speaks, looks at someone, thinks; you find a motive for everything he does; you categorise him politically, socially, etc. In

Steve Biko and Mamphela Ramphele outside the East London Magistrate's Court during one of Biko's many appearances for breaking his banning order.

short you are not satisfied until you have really torn him apart and have really parcelled off each and every aspect of his general behaviour and labelled it.' He admits, in the same letter, however, that in the political sphere he had learnt to do these things himself. Did he feel, then, that it was all right, and maybe useful, to subject politics to what he describes as a Western analysis, but that his personal decisions were fiercely and culturally his own, in spite of affecting friends and colleagues around him? In Xhosa culture the cautioning of a young man by an older man would be acceptable; moreover, Steve had been brought up as a Christian. The puzzle was too great and too sensitive for rational answers. In someone who seldom failed to look at problems head on and act on them in order to solve them, Biko in this instance was defiant, not yet ready for the solution. He obviously decided to live with these circumstances the way they were, in some ways refusing to see the implications in his usual clear, rational and human way. And then, there was the daily reality and, thereby, the rationale, of never giving it sufficient time. It was only in prison, in 1976, during a forced 101 days of solitary confinement, that he indicated he had begun to ponder this side of his life more fully and seriously.

5

Bantu – Son of Man, 1973–1977

In October 1972, aged 25, Biko was interviewed by Gail Gerhart, the American academic and writer. In discussing the apartheid government Biko said that if they were intelligent, they could 'create a capitalist black society'; that South Africa was one country in Africa where blacks might compete favourably with whites in industry, commerce and other professions. If they created this, 'South Africa could succeed [in putting across] to the world a pretty convincing, integrated picture with still 70 per cent of the population being underdogs!' However, whites were terribly afraid of this and, instead, were creating 'the best economic system for revolution'. The way they were going about it made communication among blacks easier, made the 'communication of ideas' possible through a shared, common stimulus as no physical or intellectual distance existed. 'In this whole conscientising programme, this is what makes ideas easily flow amongst people; this common ghetto experience blacks are subjected to.'

Banning

Black Consciousness was a philosophy which grew directly out of a racist State. It seized the very word 'black', defined by the State as the innately inferior majority, and transformed 'being black' into a defiance against that State. In his famous phrase, Biko detached any aspirations to 'white' values and said bluntly: 'Black man, you're on your own'.

By 1972 Biko predicted that it was obvious the government would become more vigilant and would take more definite action against the movement. 'But,' he went on to say, 'it's too late in a sense. We don't need an organisation to push the kind of ideology we are pushing. It's there. It's already been planted. It's in the people. We've got a very broad front, which is completely unintimidated. This constant change in leadership in Saso is partly to accommodate a very quick gradation of people to a certain level.' Although BCP contained few workers, it is interesting to note that in the first three months of 1973 the dockworkers, whose significant strikes in Durban changed history, refused to elect a leadership that could be identified.

When the first BC bannings came in March 1973, the movement was determined to treat them as a kind of hiccup. The State order immediately scattered eight of its leaders to different parts of the country, to whatever was their designated magisterial district:

Pityana to Port Elizabeth, Mafuna to Johannesburg, Biko to King William's Town, and so forth. They removed some of the current Saso office-bearers – Jerry Modisane, then president, and Harry Nengwekhulu, permanent organiser; they took out two of the founding members of the Theatre Council of Natal – Strini Moodley (also editor of the *SASO Newsletter*) and Saths Cooper (public relations officer for the Black People's Convention) – and Drake Koka, a founding member of BPC and general secretary of the Black Allied Workers' Union.

The address given in the banning order to Biko was that of his mother's house in Ginsberg. There he returned, empty-handed as it were, to the community that had funded an important part of his education. His mother remembers saying to him: 'Bantu, things are now hard for you. You are at home. You are doing nothing. When I was educating you I thought that by now I would be able to rest. Now, I am not resting. I cannot rest. You are imprisoned forever.'

Biko responded to her in the paradigm she best understood and asked her what Christ's mission on earth had been, and she replied, 'To save the oppressed.' Then he said: 'I too have a mission.' She remembers looking at him standing in the doorway of her house and realising that 'there was something deep in this child and I had an understanding of what was going on'.

Quite soon Mamcethe overcame her disappointment and became an ally, developing an expertise in dealing with the Security Police. Her open home now became home to all the young people who came to work in King William's Town. Although she never said so, she lived in fear of Biko's life night and day, and often lay awake until the early hours of the morning until she would hear his car return, the door open and she would know he was safe.

Very soon after his arrival Biko located the Anglican priest, David Russell, who had broken the news of his banning to his mother. Russell lived in a small house in the grounds of the church of St Chad's in the heart of King William's Town's white residential area: 15a Leopold Street. The church had not been used for a year because of the collapse of the roof and the subsequent move of the congregation to the local townships of Zwelitsha and Ginsberg. When Russell approached the priest-in-charge, James Gawe, they agreed it should be used as an office for Saso and BCP. Very shortly all three organisations were functioning there, the BCP existing through the facilities of the other two with no official status of its own, and a new committed community began to form.

Russell had his own agenda, which was well under way when Biko arrived. Speaking fluent Xhosa, he had taken up the cause of people removed, by legislation, from farms and towns like Middelburg and Burgersdorp, to an area in his parish called Dimbaza. This was one of many ill-prepared resettlement places in the homelands where blacks were forced to go, where there was no form of subsistence, no proper housing on arrival, where old people died of shock and infants of malnutrition. The state pensions were R5 a month, and for widows with children about R3 a month plus rations. Russell had first fasted on the steps of St George's Cathedral in Cape Town to draw attention to this, and then himself lived on R5 per month, for six months, writing a letter each month to the Minister responsible describing what meagre rations he could afford to buy.

Biko was undoubtedly drawn to Russell as a kindred spirit – not only intellectually but also finding him helpful and trusting him as a friend and confidant. Russell knew about local conditions, including the Security Police. Biko trusted Russell's political antennae and would enjoy dropping in on him at different times of the day or night to relax, letting slip his own political persona to discuss all kinds of issues – one of which was Russell's own stance and the nature of his commitment. When Russell explained that, as a priest, he was called to poverty, chastity and obedience, which included leading a celibate life, Biko was curious enough to test himself against these in the light of *his* own commitment and wrote a rare six-page document, which he and Russell discussed at length.

'Does God exist? I have never had problems with this question. I am sufficiently convinced of the inadequacy of man and the rest of creation to believe that a greater force than mortals is responsible for creation, maintenance and continuation of life. I am also sufficiently religious to believe that man's internal insecurity can only be alleviated by an almost enigmatic and supernatural force to which we ascribe all power, all wisdom and love … God has laid for man certain basic laws that must govern interaction between man and man, man and nature at large. These laws I see as inscribed in the ultimate conscience of each living mortal.' He goes on to say that 'Obedience to God in the sense that I have accepted it is in fact at the heart of the conviction of most selfless revolutionaries. It is a call to men of conscience to offer themselves and sometimes their lives for the eradication of evil.'

Biko was a religious person in the broad sense of the word. Khoapa said Biko also knew that anybody who might try to influence the black population politically and de-emphasise religion would not succeed. In the document to Russell, Biko is at pains to be honest and grapple with the Christian faith, not only because he is talking to a Christian but also because he is exploring his own self in relation to the way he has absorbed some of that faith. Choosing the word 'revolutionary' distances him from the practice of the Church and seems to enable him the freedom to pursue obedience to conscience (what he calls 'ultimate conscience' as opposed to a person's own conscience) without the cloying aspects of an institution.

'To the revolutionary the Church is anti-progress and therefore anti God's wishes because long ago it decided not to obey God but to obey man; long ago the Church introduced segregated worship and segregated seminaries.' Further, the 'Churches have tended to complicate religion and theology' and 'to drive away the common man by immersing themselves in bureaucracy and institutionalisation'. Christ 'is so conservatively interpreted at times that I find him foreign to me. On the other hand if I accept him and ascribe to him the characteristics that flow logically from my contemplation about him and his work, then I must reject the Church almost completely.'

In Biko's definition, the Church as an institution was not so distant from other institutions like segregated schools and universities, which in turn were not distinct from the law and the State. In Biko's view all these were the antithesis of God's basic laws, and in working towards obedience to God as he saw it – the exploration towards his own 'ultimate conscience' – he fulfilled his definition of a selfless revolutionary by intuitively knowing before he died that he, too, would have to give his life for 'the eradication of evil'. 'I can reject all Churches and still be godly,' he wrote. 'I do not need to go to Church on Sunday in order to manifest "godliness".'

Early on, as we have seen, he had an intense dislike of mindless and destructive authority, and a healthy distaste for institutions that became ossified and limited and behaved accordingly. In the confined enclosure of apartheid he refused to be reactive to its system. Instead he ignored its desired psychological stranglehold and used its racism to forge a common cause with many others, a community dedicated to creative and practical action. He recognised that beneath the layered levels of anxiety and fear was a deep seam with which to work. He was convinced that the ground rules that made for human communication and interaction lay in coming to know this consciousness. This involved demanding in others an encounter with what was ultimately humane in them, a quality he sought and often brought forth. His life now turned him face-to-face with the law and the State in the form of both the Security Police and the courts. In this formidable encounter he was to put to the test his faith and the essence of who he was and what he understood, knowing that the revolutionary's task includes 'liberation not only of the oppressed but also of the oppressor'.

The culture of fearlessness

Banning was a drastic form of restriction. Essentially, banned people were put in charge of their own imprisonment. Movement was confined to a specific magisterial district – this was often the district where one was born – and could mean losing one's job if one worked elsewhere. It prevented one from entering any place of learning; from preparing anything for publication; from attending a gathering of any kind; from talking to the press. It prohibited a person from being with more than one other person at any time, even in his or her own home, and in some 'house-arrested' cases banned people had to report to the police once a week and were confined to their homes between the hours of 6 p.m. and 6 a.m., as if under a private curfew.

'Banning orders have a strong tendency to turn a person into a social leper', wrote David Russell, in the *Daily Dispatch* of 1 September 1973. 'The banned are legally innocent citizens incarcerated in an inhuman twilight existence. It is no exaggeration to say that banning is a form of violence; violence to justice, violence to family, violence to persons. [There is] no means of appeal or recourse to a just hearing. If he [Biko] has a meal with friends he can be dragged before the courts and smeared as a common criminal. He can be found guilty and sentenced to imprisonment for anything between one and ten years.'

As people were banned they were very closely watched by Security Police, who did everything to catch them out. Even if a person was meticulous, it was virtually impossible to live within the confines of the banning order. If one did, one began to despise oneself for being one's own jailer, which was exactly the psychological state of mind desired by the government, an unacceptable state for anyone involved in Black Consciousness. So life became a cat-and-mouse game.

The suppression came in waves. No sooner had the leadership of Saso, BPC and BCP, which was banned in March 1973, been replaced than those appointed were, in turn, banned in August; those who replaced the August people were banned in October, and so on. Harassment by the Security Police was relentless, and charges were constantly laid in a further attempt to secure impotence and a sense of despair.

How did the movement respond to the banning order? In King William's Town, to begin with, people were afraid of being seen with Biko. 'I mean, we had the police actually driving bumper to bumper behind us 24 hours a day, and that scared people,' Mpumlwana recalls. The basic principle was not to ban yourself but to let the police do all the work: to monitor the system, to have to trail around following people night and day, to be made to work hard to ensure that what they had implemented was their responsibility. 'So we didn't recognise the banning order in a sense. We put good locks on our doors. To all intents and purposes, if you're indoors the police have got no power.' There could be a party in one's house, but they would have to prove one was part of it. Mpumlwana laughed at the irony: 'You can't be held responsible for being in your house where the party is being held!' The banning order was studied, the loopholes found, and those banned began to interpret it for the police.

They also held to the principle of not being reckless, not giving the police the opportunity to have them in court. At the same time, Mpumlwana explained how 'we learnt not to trust lawyers' opinions on things. We found that they were very conservative legally, and so it was important, if you wanted to break the law, to make your own rules. If you happen to be wrong they will have to defend you, but don't ask them what is right!' This, in turn, led to a strategy of using the courts as a public forum. It was not new for South Africans, accused of political opposition, to use the dock for defence speeches, thus keeping alive historic political statements and realities which could be quoted down the years and put to use by the media and opposition world-wide, the most famous being the Rivonia Trial of 1963–4, at which Nelson Mandela made his memorable speech from the dock.

Black Consciousness, as such, was not banned, only individuals were. The courts could be used to their purpose as much as everything else, part of the defiance of every day. On the occasions when Biko, for example, was taken to court for infringement or violation of his banning order he displayed his new-found legal skills, having thought ahead before he broke the conditions as to what new legal point he could appeal to or what interpretation had not yet been tested. He was never jailed on that account. This helped strengthen the resistance of other banned people, who were isolated or particularly harassed by police vigilance, and of those in prison.

As banning persisted and detention without trial increased, the Black Consciousness style of leadership, passed on to many groups in formation schools and workshops, came into good effect. An indefinable community, country-wide, with no easily identifiable leadership was already in existence. And those banished by the State were never considered separate from the others. Rather, they were considered to have been 'relocated' and it was assumed they would become effective working in these areas. They were part of decision-making, part of a circuit, and were consulted. Just as in the early days Biko had visited the banned as a matter of course, this was extended to a wider community network created out of trust and regular interaction. Those people who could be, were constantly on the move. Pityana, who was banned in the tough Port Elizabeth district, remembers the extraordinary way in which each person, no matter where he or she was staying, would be considered. Nobody was allowed to feel abandoned, however remote and however harassed. Enormous risks were taken at times in order to ensure that this happened. Thenjiwe Mtintso, a Fort Hare student, who came to work in King William's Town, says that those around Biko often forgot he was restricted and admits that it was only later, when she herself was banned to Johannesburg, that she became aware of how Biko had 'given so much to us, politically and otherwise, done so much and lived under such pressure'. Biko was 26 when he was restricted.

It was necessary to become fearless, to conquer fear – the kind of quality that grows through exercise, explained Aelred Stubbs. 'They weren't polite, they were tough,' recalls David Russell, 'but they knew the kind of parameters of how tough you could be without overplaying your cards and so the [Security] Branch was scared of them. They didn't know how to handle them.' Russell recalls one incident when they raided Biko's home in Ginsberg at night. Biko asked them what they wanted. They usually said they had come to see if somebody was there or that they were looking for banned literature, or some such pretext. They wanted to go into rooms where people were asleep. Biko said, "Well, let me tell you now that you are not going into *that* room because that is where my mother sleeps and you're not going into *that* room," [indicating] where his brother-in-law was with his wife. But they *did* go in there. And he said: "You see what you are doing with yourselves; you are opening people's doors and looking at people sleeping in bed with their wives at night." Biko made them feel small. He was also angry and it was time they got out. He moved towards them, cigarette in one hand and put out the butt in the palm of his other hand. The police got a tremendous fright. He had, in fact, moved to flick it out of the window but they had thought he was going to attack them. He was big and physically strong. They were really thrown. They found it extremely difficult to handle his style, his intelligence, his statements; a man of that calibre. I think that set quite a tone of style for the grouping there.'

Biko challenged what was ultimately human in others. If those terms were not forthcoming he could be tough, as tough as anybody. Donald Woods reports one occasion when he was in an interrogation room, in detention, with 'seven security policemen standing along the walls all around him. [Warrant-Officer] Hattingh entered the room, walked straight up to where Steve was sitting, and slapped him hard across the face.

"'What happened then?' I [Woods] asked.

"'I hit him right against the wall,' Steve replied. 'Bust his false teeth.'

"'Then what?'

"'He went straight out of the room. I had the feeling he didn't know what to do, or how to react, so he just went out – presumably for further instructions from his superiors.'"

This unhesitant response to insult was a direct display of how Biko exhibited fearlessness and how he practised Black Consciousness as a way of life. He was not going to be bullied. He considered banning as just one more of the innumerable restrictions that apartheid placed on black lives and refused to change his lifestyle in spite of the attempts by the State to watch him night and day. Although he seldom showed the strain, it may well have been the reason for his occasional, sudden and violent outbursts of anger at something of no great significance, when he would even hit out physically and it became very difficult to calm him.

Biko, like all of the others, consistently broke every single banning condition. In spite of being prohibited from preparing material for publication, he had completed the editing of *Black Review* and, later, was part of a team which prepared material for a regular newspaper column that the Black Consciousness point of view secured in the local East London paper, the *Daily Dispatch*. Biko often met more than one person at a time but was careful not to be seen to be doing so. He found a quiet place, within his magisterial district, near a dam, where he would drive with friends or visitors who came to consult him, to avoid the offices, which were bugged. If it was necessary he went out of his magisterial district. On many occasions he drove to see his wife, Ntsiki, when she worked in Keiskammahoek during the week; in 1974 he and Mpumlwana went to Durban after the arrest of most of the Saso–BPC leadership in 1974 to sort out problems there.

Banning failed to destroy the spirit and development of Black Consciousness. The next four years saw the flowering of some of the most imaginative and practical projects it was to produce. King William's Town became an important place where many people touched base, including international visitors. The arteries of contact persisted more fiercely, which included many of those banned. On one occasion at least, I myself witnessed, at a late-night *gumba*, Biko putting his finger over his lips each time he opened the door to admit one person after another, none of whom, according to the law, was permitted to be there. *Gumbas* remained a forum and an essential palliative against isolation.

Growth of a community

Biko asked Mpumlwana, who was then 22, to help him settle down and find people with whom to work, and the office in King William's Town was set up. Mpumlwana had already been alongside Biko in Durban. Late at night, after politicking or completing work on an issue or a Saso pamphlet, they would end the long hours with wrestling. 'It was our game. I enjoyed felling him. I'd played rugby. I'd go for his legs, lift him off and throw him down.' This was no mean feat as Mpumlwana was no match for Biko physically, being small and slightly built. Mpumlwana, a committed Christian, was unafraid of confrontation or of challenging values. With his wide-set, sensitive eyes alert to human suffering and humour alike, he was willing to pursue uncomfortable truths and often mediated crises involving warring political factions. Like Biko, Pityana and Ramphele, his laugh was loud and infectious, cutting through tensions. Thinking he could spare a couple of weeks, Mpumlwana came willingly to King William's Town. The weeks turned into months and years; in fact he never left.

A new group gathered, which flowered for a while in the tough climate of the Eastern Cape. Its members became some of Biko's most trusted comrades. When one person was restricted in one way or another their joint effort protected that person, and he or she went on working. Initially Biko was regional director of the BCP; Mapetla Mohapi came in to work for Saso, and Nohle Haya (who married Mohapi) was Steve's administrative assistant. Thoko Mbanjwa worked with Malusi (they later married). She, Biko and others did the research for the *Black Review* and Thoko edited the 1974–5 edition. Mxolisi Mvovo, married to Biko's sister Nobandile, worked as marketing officer for the home industries that the BCP was running. Nobandile worked with Thenjiwe Mtintso for the Border Council of Churches. Her work was closely connected to the BCP work, running self-help projects, bursary schemes and support programmes while Mtintso was fieldworker for the Dependants' Conference, funding and working with ex-political prisoners in Dimbaza and elsewhere. Nomsa Williams did research for *Black Review*, and, later on, Peter Jones did the accounting of the BCP books.

The fact was that designation was irrelevant. Mtintso, for example, though she had had little writing experience, was assigned as journalist when Donald Woods gave Black Consciousness an opening on the newspaper he edited, the *Daily Dispatch*. Later, a regular column in the newspaper became Mapetla Mohapi's responsibility, in which the BC viewpoint was expressed. Its content was a group assignment, discussed and debated and even jointly written.

Mohapi later became administrator of the Zimele Trust Fund to aid ex-political prisoners, a totally different assignment. King William's Town soon had a research and publishing department running and a showroom to display clothes and leather-work made locally in home industry centres.

Several projects got under way throughout the country. A glance at the issues of *Black Review* of 1973–6 indicates the extent of what began to be researched and discussed, and underlines just how much there was to report. It attempted to be faithful to a wide range of aspects, thus making it today an invaluable source of information about youth, workers, education, theatre, writing, political organisations, political trials and so forth. *Black Review* had, as its companions, *Black Viewpoint* and *Black Perspectives*. Cottage industries, producing leather goods and cloth garments, were created in villages near King William's Town and, later, in Cape Town. The Zimele Trust Fund helped mainly ANC and PAC people, who were being released into the 'resettlement' areas where there was no employment; bursaries were also raised for their children. The Zanempilo Community Health Centre was officially opened in April 1975. Dr Mamphela Ramphele was its first medical doctor and came to live at the clinic. Training courses in leadership, which also conscientised blacks to their reality, continued throughout the country, particularly among the youth. Hierarchy was automatically discouraged. It was literally pointless and diminished the growth of what was possible. Apart from aiding the system, dominance by individuals would prevent the evolution of ideas. 'We must not create a leadership cult. We must centralize the people's attention onto the real message,' Biko said. Curiously the word 'democracy' was not part of the language; rather the word used was 'communal'. More and more people, who were themselves active elsewhere, dropped into 15a Leopold Street from all over the country.

Black Consciousness took root and grew in spite of the draconian restrictions of the 1970s, when each year claimed more banned, and more detentions were made, often under the ferocious Section 6 of the Terrorism Act. With no access to lawyers allowed, no certainty of being charged, detainees were often kept for months in prison in solitary confinement, taken away from their work for long periods of time. Almost everyone whose name is mentioned here suffered detention of one sort or another. Many left the country: Mafuna and Serote went to Botswana in 1974, around the time that the current Saso–BPC leadership was arrested for holding an illegal rally to celebrate the Frelimo victory in Mozambique. Others left later, many in the aftermath of the 1976 student uprising to join the armed wings of the ANC and PAC; some only returned from exile in 1990, after President De Klerk's declaration of 2 February, which put an end to apartheid.

Biko defined Black Consciousness as 'an attitude of mind and a way of life'. Its philosophy was to express 'group pride and the determination of the black to rise and attain the envisaged self'; its realisation was to recognise that 'the most potent weapon in the hands of the oppressor is the *mind* of the oppressed'; its methodology was to enable the evolution of ideas to flourish and thereby give a wider range of people the chance to voice opinions, even if some were inarticulate and hesitant at first. Those who lived and learnt through this method and understood it, became a nationwide community and took that rootedness within them into whatever area of the struggle they later found themselves. The influence of Black Consciousness stimulated and helped to change the nature of the major liberation movements with a surge of new thinking and energy. It is an integral part of that history, recognised at the time, though the nature of its contribution has not been sufficiently acknowledged.

In the context of the community which he helped to create, Biko was seen as one of the most selfless. He was consistently available to others in ways outlined earlier: his room at medical residence was everybody's room, his house in Natal was everybody's house, his mother's home in Ginsberg became the focal point until the Zanempilo Centre was created – a crucial asset in that time of banning and dislocation. Because of this, people were prevented from being isolated and went on functioning. Biko, too, could not have survived without the many others. His personality, however, broke the taboos of the time and had a freeing influence on those who worked with him. Instead of needing to consult him every day, they began to find it exhilarating to be independent, seeing him from time to time for sheer pleasure and for rejuvenation in defiance of the authoritarian State. Mpumlwana describes Biko as a visionary and an adventurer, being 'like the plough with virgin soil to till; but the field would not bear any fruit without all the other implements, including the seed and the rain'. Biko knew this. It would be an insult to separate him from the wholeness of the process. He also needed to be cared for, needed love. He sought it in other people as much as they sought it in him. In spite of the harsh realities he faced and dealt with, he had a softness and a gentle sensibility.

There were costs. Enormous dedication and extremely hard work were required. Ramphele remembers: 'I was on duty 24 hours a day, 7 days a week, 52 weeks of the year' at the clinic. This necessitated a submersion of individuality and sometimes the suppression of aspects of individual talent and growth.

'It became a duty to be tolerant and to listen; it was necessary to be able to accept criticism and act on it.' One of the drawbacks was that having experienced the support of the group and the circle, some found it difficult to adapt to other circumstances, especially when they went into exile.

For most, however, it was a nurturing ground for the potential within them that otherwise might not have been realised. Developing trust took its time but was rewarding and cost-effective in the end. Those who built it then have a particular bond, in spite of having taken different personal, political and professional roads.

On 19 October 1977, a month after Biko died, all the Black Consciousness organisations were banned and people further scattered through banishment and imprisonment. Out of anger over his death and in dedication to what he stood for, many of those who had worked with him refused to let things die. Ramphele, virtually single-handed, built a new clinic at Ithuseng, near Tzaneen, in the district to which she was banished; Mpumlwana continued his mediation work through the churches, preventing many a death in later years; Pityana went into exile and became a priest, later working for the Programme to Combat Racism in the international arena of the World Council of Churches; Thoko Mpumlwana stayed in King William's Town and expanded the Ginsberg Educational Trust to include the whole Border region – it became known as the Zingisa Educational Project. Nohle Mohapi joined Thoko and worked for Zingisa until 1990, when she began a new branch in Port Elizabeth, Khanyisa. Thenjiwe Mtintso, who suffered appalling treatment and torture in prison, went into exile and joined the armed struggle in MK. Later, she became the ANC's ambassador to Uganda. She remembers that 'When we built that community, around Steve, around King William's Town, it really made us. It really made the good parts of me. We were building together, we were fumbling along, starting so many things together, and that made us. And that created the political discipline that we think we have. If you simply look at that lot that came from King William's Town, then went to Lesotho – there were seven of us who went into exile in January 1979 – they were given responsibilities even when we had just joined the ANC. They were young people in their twenties – but quite mature, quite disciplined and very committed and serious. We worked like slaves. Work was not torture, it was part of your whole life.'

'King was my political home. The group began to be my political school. And Steve began to be my political mentor as a person. But [he] went further than that. He was my counsellor in my own private.life. He was a friend, he was a brother, he could actually be all these things, put together. I don't want to put him beyond being a human being. He had his faults, many of them, but one thing I liked about him was the care. Steve could read your mood, could take time to talk about your own life ... He had this attraction for all of us I think. He was not an enigma – he was ... I can't explain it, but I can only say that it was that attraction and that attachment and wanting to spend as much time as possible with Steve, whether in a political or social or informal context.'

Political strategy
The Black People's Convention (BPC) had been established in June 1972 to expand the work of Black Consciousness beyond the student and youth groups of Saso. At its first conference in December it debated two points of view: whether it was to be an umbrella, culturally orientated organisation acting as a parent body to all African organisations, or a direct political body through which blacks would realise their aspirations. Over the next two years it sought to find its feet despite continual harassment and banning of its leadership. In September 1974, in conjunction with Saso, rallies were planned in solidarity with the victory of Frelimo to mark the installation of Mozambique's new transitional government. The rallies in South Africa were banned the night before. It was decided,

however, that the rally due to take place at Curries Fountain in Durban would go ahead. Biko himself was not in agreement with this. According to the *Black Review*, about five thousand people had gathered there. The police arrived, broke up the rally and arrested people on the spot. They then rounded up many others from the numerous offices of Saso, BPC, the Black Allied Workers' Union, and so on – all the Black Consciousness groupings, in fact. Those arrested were held under Section 6 (1) of the Terrorism Act, which allowed for indefinite detention, incommunicado. Seven months after the arrests, 13 people were charged in April 1975 under the Terrorism Act. By the time Biko gave evidence in May 1976, there were nine accused.

As Mpumlwana drove the newly released Mohapi from Pretoria to Natal in early 1975, they debated the role that BPC might now play. An idea grew that it should explore its potential as a catalyst for uniting the liberation movements for several different reasons: the logic that Black Consciousness should now develop from its psychological unity to a political unity; the fact that, in spite of the personal bannings, Saso and BPC still had mobility and continued to operate nationally on the ground; the recognition that the ANC and the PAC were the established political movements and that BPC would not act as a third force but would endeavour to create a national consciousness involving all the existing historical political movements against the common enemy. It was a delicate matter and, compared to the two banned Congresses, BPC was a fledgling organisation. The proposal would need to get a mandate. Nevertheless they were convinced, as Pityana asserts, 'that Black Consciousness provided a common programme, one with which the entire liberation [movement] could identify', that they had to assert that the stature and leadership of the ANC and PAC were unassailable. 'So, again and again, we acknowledged both the authority of the liberation organisations and the authentic leadership in prison or in exile.' Pityana explains that 'it was really the only basis on which the ANC or PAC militants could associate with Black Consciousness'.

The idea was discussed with Biko and others from different parts of the country. Influenced by developments in Zimbabwe of unity between Zanu and Zapu, BPC set out to test its bona fides with the banned PAC and ANC and also with other, smaller political groupings like the Unity Movement. Contact was made with known ANC and PAC supporters in the country, notably the lawyer Griffiths Mxenge and Robert Sobukwe respectively. The two were sympathetic to the idea. They in turn agreed to contact their underground organisations internally and externally. Confidence grew and BPC people travelled extensively. Biko also travelled when necessary.

Saso and BPC had good standing with other political groupings still functioning in South Africa. A joint project was being planned to protest against the apartheid government's policy to make the Transkei 'independent' in October 1976. This involved the Unity Movement and other groupings in the Western Cape, where some community programmes were also founded in common, and good personal links were formed. BPC felt that if practical united action was possible along these lines it would later help to build trust for the idea of a greater political unity.

The next BPC congress was held in King William's Town in December 1975, the same month in which Biko's new restriction orders prevented him from working for the Black Community Programmes. At the congress policy documents were proposed and debated. The idea was that these were to be used as working documents in the negotiations with the ANC and the PAC. However, most people at the congress knew nothing about these planned talks. In the political climate of the time the security risk was too great for the normal open discussion on such matters. This undemocratic approach must be acknowledged, but there did not seem to be any alternative. It had taken nearly a year of 'delicate shuttle diplomacy to persuade both the ANC and the PAC representatives to agree in principle to a joint meeting to explore the question of mutual co-operation,' Mpumlwana explained. The meeting, due to take place immediately after Christmas, involved not only banned people but also the banned organisations.

An economic policy document was written to avoid possible withdrawal of either PAC or ANC. It took its starting-point as 'Black communalism', described in *Black Review* as 'a modified version of the traditional African economic lifestyle which is geared to meet the demands of a highly industrialised and modern economy'. It gave considerable power to the State and local communities but avoided defining itself in Marxist terms or employing the classical class analysis. This document, as well as one on the vision of a future State, met with considerable criticism. Mafika Pascal Gwala (editor of the earlier *Black Review* of 1973) saw it as a 'reversal of development and history' and remembers how he quarrelled with Biko about it. At a further workshop in Mafeking in May 1976, he and others like Diliza Mji, Faith Matlaopane, Norman Dubazana and Nkosazana Dlamini felt that proposing far-reaching policy documents was no business of the BPC but the prerogative of the ANC and should involve the 'fleshing out' of the Freedom Charter, Mpumlwana reports. Such policies could smack of the beginnings of a third force rather than an attempt to find common ground.

All this was happening at just about the very moment that Biko was subpoenaed to give evidence in the Saso–BPC Trial. In the confined space of the court in Pretoria, the heart of apartheid's power-base, Biko chose his words carefully. 'We are advocating black communalism which is, in many ways, similar to African socialism. We are expropriating an essentially tribal background to accommodate what is an expanded economic concept now. We have got to accommodate industry. We have got to accommodate the whole relationship between industry and politics. But there is a certain plasticity in this interpretation precisely because no one has yet made an ultimate definition of it.' He proceeded to talk of bargaining and the importance of dialogue between themselves, who held this African socialist view, and those 'who hold dear a free enterprise system, and out of these two clearly the synthesis will come'. Although he was talking in apartheid's law courts – this can hardly be defined as a clear economic policy – Biko was also speaking to a broader audience. He now determined that two things were critical to his agenda: to better understand the nature of economic forces and to further pursue the growing debate about the validity of class analysis.

The nine charged under the Terrorism Act were mostly people he knew, some close friends. His task was to define Black Consciousness so that they might not be given severe sentences – the mandatory sentence for anyone charged under the Act was a minimum of five years. The case tested all of Biko's skills and was an example of his obvious eligibility for becoming a lawyer. He displayed the capacity to walk through a minefield of cross-examination without compromising himself or incriminating the accused. In the dock Biko often appeared to control the argument, either as the astute politician or the story-teller, the humourist or the teacher. In the expression of his answers lies the compassion for his country and its people.

Having accepted the conditions of participating in the due process of the law of the land, his first test was to assess the situation. The evidence led by David Soggot, assistant counsel for the defence, gave him the chance to state clearly what Black Consciousness was as well as inspire people once again with dignity and pride, defining Saso and BPC to be concerned with 'the whole development of the human being, in other words the black man discarding his own psychological oppression', he explained. Under cross-examination by both the defence and the State, he emphasised why the historical logic of Black Consciousness was blatantly obvious and reasonable. His assessment of Judge Boshoff was to draw him into dialogue. He answered his questions as if in a genuine debate, drawing the judge into some insights where the judge indicated

Biko in conversation with Richard L. Baltimore III, a US diplomat and political officer.

interest beyond the scope of the case, about one-party states in Africa, the meaning of democracy and the merits of the gold standard.

Biko did not treat the prosecutor in the same manner. This was more the cat-and-mouse game he had practised for so long with the Security Police. Almost immediately he made it clear that shoddy definitions and bullying tactics held no sway with him. He displayed his ease of intellect by redefining questions or words, using the very techniques he would expect a good lawyer to use, with skill and apparent confidence. He used humour and ironic references to whites to express the ironic nature of their society. There was a discussion of the meaning of the apartheid system. The definition flowed from 'the police' into 'institutionalised racism', with a graphic example of Biko having to use the 'white' toilet in the very building they were in and the marked display of racism he encountered as he did so, even though there was no 'black' one. And when asked whether he described himself as a freedom fighter, he immediately knew where that came from and challenged:

Biko: 'I did use the expression once to Security Police who wanted to know what my profession was, and I said I was a freedom fighter.'

Prosecutor: 'I think that was with tongue in cheek, not so?'

Biko: 'Well, it was making conversation, and if you have got to live with the Security Police on your neck all the time you have got to devise a way of talking to them, you know, and this is one of the ways. Generally, they understand in only one language.'

Those four days must have helped to restore any morale that might have been low amongst those who were charged; it would have revitalised the fearful and restored solidarity, and assured them that they were amongst those pushing forward the struggle. Reading the evidence today makes us forget the tense and dangerous circumstances under which it was given, makes it tempting to assume that this *was* Biko's own true testament and the 1976 expression of Black Consciousness. Partly it is, but there were terrible pitfalls that were set up, which Biko avoided in a remarkable way. The atmosphere was one of deliberate intimidation. The prosecutor constantly led arguments in which he attempted to connect Black Consciousness, and those charged, with the politics of the banned movements and their leaders. Biko was called at the very time that the BPC was embarking on its unifying role aimed at making contact with those banned organisations, and his genius lay in the way in which he kept many balls in the air at once, not compromising, not intimidating and yet maintaining the attention of the judge.

Not everything he said was exactly the way it was. In the feature film about Biko, *Cry Freedom*, the script-writer used the court record to elicit evidence that Black Consciousness was non-violent. This was not entirely true in reality. The policy of BPC was to explore the non-violent route, but many BC people were disillusioned with this approach and were leaving the country to follow the political logic of the armed struggle and join it. The atmosphere of the court was highly charged. Mandla Langa, another witness, feared for Biko's openness and obvious display of a superior intellect, feared his manner would do him harm: 'It was like war, really; you could feel the enmity.'

Members of the international world began to

recognise Black Consciousness, as articulated by Biko, as a key political voice in the country, whereas for most white South Africans, Biko's reply to the prosecutor's question probably sums it up:

Prosecutor: 'So you agree with me that the whites basically are afraid of Black Consciousness?'

Biko: 'I would say that the majority of whites are not even aware of Black Consciousness.'

Within a month of Biko's giving evidence in Pretoria, on 16 June 1976, a transforming political event occurred, the Soweto Uprising. The school children of Soweto came out onto the streets en masse, protesting against the imposition of Afrikaans as a medium of instruction. Dissatisfaction and restlessness had been brewing for some time against many aspects of the inferior Bantu Education system but this new regulation was the last straw. It mobilised into action a national peaceful protest. The retaliation was police bullets, which claimed the lives of hundreds of young people throughout the country. Reminiscent of Sharpeville, this had major implications both at home and abroad. Thousands of students crossed the border illegally to take up arms. Some joined MK, others the military wing of the PAC. Their full stories are only beginning to be told. The Soweto Uprising and its aftermath changed the face of South African politics, including Black Consciousness. Biko told me personally that no specific organisation could claim the uprising. 'It took us all by surprise,' he said. How much of it was spurred by eight years of Black Consciousness and its contact with youth organisations is yet to be fully assessed.

6

Choices and dilemmas

In spite of not having been in agreement with the decision to defy the ban on the Curries Fountain meeting, it must have been a relief for Biko to have performed his task well at the Saso–BPC Trial. When those in the trial had begun to be arrested in 1974, Biko expressed in a letter to Father Stubbs that he felt 'a strange kind of guilt'; he felt a responsibility that 'so many friends of mine have been arrested for activities in something I was most instrumental in starting', a lot of them 'blokes I spoke into the movement'. He comforts himself somewhat by saying that nobody knows why some of them were included and also that no trend in the movement warrants the 'terror act' being invoked. He then reminds himself that 'one does not think this way in political life, of course'. Casualties are expected and should be bargained for. 'An oppressive system often is illogical in the application of suppression', he wrote to Stubbs in a letter.

In the same letter Biko admitted that for himself the going had been 'tough under the present restrictions'. Again, he qualified this with his usual optimism and confidence: 'I am nowhere near despair and frustration but can understand only too well why some of our guys are.' He saw the positives in his life: 'a supportive and defensive township', 'reasonably fulfilling work' and 'I live with a very supportive family, one which is fully committed to my commitment if not to the cause itself'.

Biko seldom revealed his fears openly. Both his sister Nobandile and his colleague Thenjiwe Mtintso say that if banning did get him down, it never showed. Emotionally he took on the mantle of the father to his extended family. Once he had a job he became joint supporter with his elder sister Bukelwa in looking after his mother, insisting that she stop working. After the sudden and tragic death of Bukelwa of a heart attack, in his mother's house in September 1975, he and Ntsiki carried the responsibility. He also displayed a responsibility to everyone with whom he worked, including those he had worked with, now banned or banished.

It was only to the very few that he revealed doubts and his own inner misgivings. Father Stubbs was one of these people and the evenings he spent with David Russell, he wrote, 'were very good palliatives to the mental decay that so easily sets in'. To Ntsiki he expressed the expectation that she would be widowed before he was 30. When his frustration occasionally burst into uncontrolled rage, to the shock of those around him, because it was rare and so uncharacteristic, Ramphele was one of the few people who could calm him down and get him to go away to some quiet place. He shared many of his innermost thoughts with her as well.

He talks of his supportive family being committed 'to *my* commitment if not to the cause itself'. Biko was surrounded by women who loved and nurtured him, and Mamcethe, Ntsiki and Nobandile, his younger sister, complemented his life with their dedicated care. Women's inclusion by men in the 'just causes' to which they are dedicated has often assumed that those women will always perform the functional tasks in the preparation of food and drink, provide a safe base, love and comfort. With this goes also the assumed superiority of the man's intellect and choice of work, which is given time and space to be expressed. In spite of her key role as doctor in charge of the clinic, Ramphele also did her fair share of this kind of nurturing support for all the visitors who came to see Biko there. (He sometimes ate two meals, one there and one at his mother's home, and he put on weight.) However, women in the BC movement were aware that it was exploitative. Mtintso remembers that 'there was no way you could think of Steve making a cup of tea or whatever for himself'. She herself once refused to do so for him and met the consequences.

Biko did, indeed, expect this 'traditional' support, but he and others also assumed an equality of purpose and capability from the women who worked with them. Biko was filled with admiration after Mtintso had withstood very rough treatment and torture in prison. Mtintso comments wryly: 'We would have our revolts. They do want women to be political, to be active, to be everything, but they still need a complement of women who are subservient', and this was why (other) women were always brought into the *gumbas* 'to add glamour to the party'.

Ramphele was more and more an example who defied these traditional codes. In relation to Biko, not only had Ramphele become the professional doctor with a secure income, but he had long sounded out his ideas with her, and expressed his excitement while she helped him to remain consistent in the application of his ideas. She had been a constant sounding-board in his political thinking and this made a huge difference in the restricted environment of King William's Town. He could also unburden himself to her when necessary. Ramphele took little notice of his flirtation with other women, being confident in herself and of the depth of their own recognition of each other. After 101 days in prison – much of it in solitary confinement – at the end of 1976, with considerable time to think about his life, Biko came clean with some of these flirtations; she couldn't believe it and laughed and laughed. He admitted that the two of them seemed bound in a common destiny and he admitted that it was partly *that* that he had been trying to escape. She remembers him saying something like: 'I know we are two strong personalities and there is no way you are going to submit to me nor am I going to submit to you, so we have to negotiate our relationship.'

Ntsiki Biko understood his nature well, too, and accepted it in a different way. 'It needed somebody with strong convictions, or strong – I don't know whether to call it love for somebody – to stay with him. I doubt very much, even if I had left him, I am sure he would have married several times. I know he wouldn't have lasted in marriage. And I know he was very fond of his kids.' However, by early 1977, Ntsiki took her own independent stance. She began to look for another post, and when a job came up in mid-year at All Saints Hospital in Engcobo in the Transkei, she told Biko she intended to move away and set about filing for a divorce. No matter how much she challenged Biko, he did not change. His approach to her as his wife remained what is perhaps best described as traditional, with that expectation of a role-model wife who was supposed to understand and accept whatever her husband chose to do. Ntsiki loved Steve but circumstances went beyond her endurance. Particularly as his wife and, maybe one should add, as the daughter-in-law of Mamcethe, for whom Ntsiki had deep respect, there was the added difficulty of making personal demands against the powerful circumstances into which she had fallen: her husband was banned and deeply committed politically; people came to consult with him night and day; there was the necessity for her to have a job to survive, not only financially but also personally; the job was outside her husband's magisterial district; there was the knowledge that Steve was bound in with Mamphela, politically deeply committed to the work she was doing and all that surrounded her, including the powerful status which being a doctor carried in the community, especially as a woman; the fact that the clinic had become his logical political base. Ntsiki was not aggressive, did not expect to perform the undignified task of fighting for her committed rights as a wife, her inalienable rights as a married woman. They had talked through the things that upset her, constantly, and she had conceded a great deal regarding his work, 'but the relationship part was becoming too much,' she said. 'It was beyond my acceptance,' she said. Ntsiki never stopped loving Steve.

7

Detentions, banishment and international engagement

There was a crackdown in the King William's Town area. One month after the Soweto Uprising, on 15 July 1976, Mapetla Mohapi was arrested and detained at Kei Road police station under the Terrorism Act. He died in detention three weeks later on 5 August. This was a tremendous shock. It was alleged that he hanged himself with a pair of jeans. It was clear that he hadn't. The post-mortem was conducted by Dr R.B.R. Hawke, a pathologist, in the presence of two doctors, Dr Ramphele and Dr Msawuli, who were themselves then detained on 13 and 29 August respectively under the Internal Security Act. Biko was detained on 27 August, and Mvovo, Mpumlwana, Mbanjwa and Mtintso in the same month. Mohapi's widow, Nohle, ran the office for four months until they were all released in December, when Mtintso was banned to Johannesburg and

Mvovo to Dimbaza. In March 1977 Mpumlwana, now married to Thoko Mbanjwa, was held under Section 6 of the Terrorism Act for another four months. At the beginning of April, Father Stubbs was stopped by police on his way from Port Elizabeth airport to a local church where he was to preach on Good Friday; he was body-searched and ordered to strip, an indignity Biko thoroughly disapproved of.

In the same month, Ramphele was banished to the northern Transvaal. She was removed, suddenly and swiftly, from the BCP offices in Leopold Street by the police, only having time to grab her handbag, and driven over 1200 kilometres north. Within days of her arrival, having been told where she was to work in a particular hospital, she realised that the number on the warrant for her arrest and banishment did not coincide with her Reference Book. Even her name was spelt wrongly. She rang her lawyer, Raymond Tucker, who agreed this made her banning order null and void. Her young brother, Thomas, had just arrived to see her. 'All she said was, "Good! I'm glad you've come. Now we're off," bundled him into the car and drove the 200-odd miles to Johannesburg.' At 4 a.m. Ramphele and Father Stubbs left St Peter's Priory in Johannesburg and drove to the Zanempilo Centre, arriving twelve hours later. Great reunions, but only for ten days, before the system, slightly embarrassed, got its act together and banished her again for seven years. In those few, defiant days Hlumelo Biko was conceived, to be born after his father's death, miles away in Lenyenye, where Ramphele, having refused to work in the place assigned to her, began to establish the remarkable clinic of Ithuseng. After the long detentions of 1976 the State continued to break up and destroy the carefully established network all over the country by consistently removing people. Staff in the office and at the clinic went down to a minimum, the column in the *Dispatch* ceased. The signs were ominous and the State was menacing, but there was nothing to do except carry on.

Peter Jones, who was an activist in the Western Cape region of BPC in 1975–6, was asked by Biko to come and help manage the office in King William's Town. He had been part of a team, including Mpumlwana, Mvovo and Thandisizwe Mazibuko, who travelled widely to enlist support for the campaign to protest against the government's move to make the Transkei an 'independent' country. By now it was conceded by a growing political consensus that the Black Consciousness Movement was 'the least contentious' of the political organisations to attempt some kind of unity of focus for all the liberation movements in spite of the fact that the planned meeting between the banned organisations had had to be postponed

Biko (right) accompanied by Donald Woods (left), editor of the Daily Dispatch, *who gave the Black Consciousness Movement a column in his newspaper to put across its viewpoint.*

in December 1975. 'The relationship with anyone outside [the country] was based on the nature of the relationship we had with people inside the country,' says Jones. By 1977 these 'people were very close to us. There was no credibility problem. And because of Steve's quiet position he [was] the best placed to personally promote it.' In January 1977 Biko was appointed honorary president of BPC in order to provide him with the leadership identity necessary. Jones explains that he was 'more visible than a lot of other leadership within our organisation, not media visibility but a crucial kind of visibility'. It was decided that Biko should secure an invitation from abroad. In April, when Father Stubbs had delivered Ramphele back to the clinic, Biko asked him to procure some such invitation in the UK or Europe, which he did. Biko made the same request of Lein van den Bergh, a Dutch lawyer who, representing a Dutch funding agency, visited King William's Town around that time.

Representatives and diplomats of foreign countries, constantly on the look-out for personalities representing different opinion, began to consult Biko as someone who held the key to what was going on in the black world. This was partly the result of his performance in the Saso–BPC Trial but also because of the arrest of virtually all the leadership of the Black Consciousness Movement, including himself.

In December 1976 Senator Dick Clark, chairman of the US Senate Sub-committee for Africa, who was attending a conference in Lesotho, applied to the government to see Biko while he was still in detention. Biko was released just before they were due to meet. Mpumlwana reports that immediately Biko knew this, he 'sent word to us in prison that he was out, was seeing Dick Clark and asked, "What should I say to him?" That evening we battered our way at a statement, which we smuggled out early to influence his presentation.' Even under these circumstances there was consultation. Biko presented Clark with a memorandum entitled 'American Policy Towards Azania'. After a polite preamble the memorandum pointed out that although words had been abundant by US politicians in condemning apartheid, 'very little by way of constructive action has been taken to apply concerted pressure on [the] minority white South African regime'. Clark made a press statement after meeting Biko, saying that 'I talk to Vorster [the South African prime minister] when I want to find out what the Government are thinking. I have talked to Mr Biko to find out what blacks are thinking'.

Soon after this Biko was invited to the US, under the auspices of the USA-SA Leadership Exchange Programme, but he refused, explaining that he would only accept such an invitation when 'America had given proof of a radically changed policy towards South Africa'. In most of the liberation movements, the US was considered 'imperialist', a country whose foreign policy towards other countries preferred 'economic stability' under an oppressive regime, rather than supporting a people's struggle for democratic human rights which might invoke radical political views in order to attain them. Biko expressed to Donald Woods how Western countries merely 'slapped the wrist' of the South African government but 'maintained their diplomatic and economic links that helped to bolster the regime'.

As repression closed in on the Black Consciousness Movement, contact with the outside world became more and more important. It was, metaphorically, the only 'court of appeal' in the increasingly dangerous atmosphere in South Africa, where the judiciary was virtually castrated by the legislature. Biko immediately recognised the usefulness of diplomacy amidst the growing danger that surrounded him and his colleagues. More and more people were dying in detention. The strategy was to inform the outside world as precisely as possible about the nature of that detention and the necessity to act against the South African government.

In a recorded interview with an American businessman, probably made around January 1977, Biko speaks about what detainees were up against. It was after Mtintso had been beaten up and tortured, and Biko was very angry. 'When I went into jail, my friend [Mohapi] had just died. He was the 24th person to die in jail since 1973. When I came out, they were talking about number 27. And this is happening increasingly now, because of the frustration the police are having. They want quick information. Now, there's an extent to which a person can absorb beating without revealing information. But sometimes it so happens that, in fact, the person being assaulted doesn't [have the information]. And they simply go on and on with a towel around your neck saying "Speak" – and you say nothing – "Speak" – you say nothing – and the bloody brutes are not trained well enough to realise when enough is enough. So by the time they release the towel you have been dead for a couple of minutes.'

In January 1977 he met with Bruce Haigh, second secretary in the Australian Embassy. As they drove out to a quiet and secluded place of Biko's choice (to avoid the bugged BCP office), Biko expressed interest in the current political and economic situation in Australia, stating that he looked to that country and others, like Scandinavia, Britain and the US, for some answer as to how the process of democracy would deal with the demands of an evolving technocratic society.

Biko led the discussion throughout, covering a wide range of topics, giving Haigh important information

– for example, what he felt were the reasons for his own detention. Haigh reports: 'They [the police] were trying to find out how many students had fled to Botswana and Swaziland and what they were doing there. They knew very little and he had been unable to help them.' Biko then gave Haigh the real information: that several thousand students had fled since the Soweto and country-wide uprising, and that 'lines of communication had been established between them and the students still in South Africa', and that Biko believed demonstrations would now be smaller in order to avoid loss of life; his expectation was 'that in future small groups of two or three people would probably start using explosive devices against selected buildings and government installations'.

Further, it was his opinion that 'the students felt that as activists they had a legitimate claim to lead the protest movement', that 'the ANC and PAC were building up their organisations within South Africa once again, but this was only after the students had created the preconditions for their return and re-organisation'. The youth who went into exile helped inject new energy and life into the liberation movements, informing and influencing them directly in assessing the thrust of the current political climate. Some went in the hopes of further education but most went to take up arms.

Biko treated Haigh as an intelligent ally, giving him

In 1976–7, foreign diplomats, academics and journalists sought out Biko. Bruce Haigh, Second Secretary in the Australian Embassy, realised he was in danger and asked his government to 'Please protect Biko'.

careful political information throughout the visit. Haigh himself was strongly aware of the danger surrounding Biko. In his very last entry in his report he wrote an appeal to his government: 'Please protect Biko.'

In these last recorded interviews with Biko – notably by foreigners – the strategy was to get information out fast. It was important to understand each interviewer and Biko assessed what would be the best information for each one of them so that it could be carried as far as possible to the right quarters. In these interviews we are again struck by Biko's astute understanding of the people he is meeting and of the situation at hand, in spite of the banning to isolate him. In August 1977, speaking to the American Committee on Africa, he explained that BPC's 'line' was to explore the non-violent road within the country, but that there was also the view 'that the present Nationalist government can only be unseated by people operating a military wing'. His own opinion was that 'in the end there is going to be a totality of effect of a number of change-agencies operating in South Africa'. He would also like to see fewer groups: 'I would like to see groups like ANC, PAC and the Black Consciousness Movement deciding to form one liberation group and it is only, I think, when black people are so dedicated and so united in their cause that we can effect the greatest result.'

8

Arrest

When he spoke those words, Biko had long since set out on that course. Only a few days later, he left for Cape Town on 17 August, once again breaking his banning order. Through Peter Jones he had a long-standing plan to meet with various people there. There was also a need to settle some possible dissension within the BC ranks. Biko hoped as well to meet Neville Alexander, who, having once been a member of the Unity Movement in the 1960s, now represented an important political grouping in the Western Cape. Alexander had served ten years in prison on Robben Island with the major ANC and PAC leadership and had been banned and house-arrested on his release in 1975. He was an articulate exponent of the class analysis and had considerable influence in this regard. Although Biko wished to see Alexander for other reasons, he had expressed interest in his political views and might have hoped for a stimulating debate as well.

But the times were very risky, and before he left King William's Town, Alexander had said he would not be able to see him. 'I had not been mandated to see him and could not get such a mandate in time,' he later said. This message was not communicated to Biko, who only discovered it on arrival.

This attitude was difficult for Biko to accept, and he waited for three hours outside Alexander's house while Fikile Bam, a comrade who had also served ten years on Robben Island with Alexander, was brought in to discuss whether he might change his mind. This was a high-risk operation for all three men: Alexander was banned and house-arrested and under constant surveillance; Bam had been banished to the Transkei homeland and had to get special permission to enter the Republic of South Africa; and Biko could have been recognised at any moment.

Jones intimates the growing unease they felt. 'A few other things happened in the course of that night. We just felt that we were not in control of the situation. There were too many shadows around us.' In the very early morning they decided to 'disappear'. Driving back to the Eastern Cape, Jones recalls that Biko obviously had things on his mind. 'For the first time we were actually talking personal things. We were going through his life, his marriage and stuff, and I was going through my girl-friend at the time

– I wasn't married – and my aspirations, and so on. What hit me was I couldn't recall any other time when we spoke with so much clarity.' Nearing the end of the long journey, round about 10.20 p.m., Jones was driving into Grahamstown. Biko had a tape-recorder on his lap and they were listening to a tape. Both were lighthearted and relaxed. As they came round the bend they ran into a roadblock of uniformed policemen and 'a number of plainclothes men I realised were Security Police'.

When requested to open the boot, Jones had difficulties because it was not a car he knew. While waiting for this to be executed, one of the plainclothes officers asked Jones where he was going. 'East London,' he replied. Then the man looked at Jones and said: 'Jy gaan seker vir ou Biko sien' (You're no doubt going to visit that chap Biko). Peter showed no reaction and said: 'Who's Biko?'

Impatient with the intransigent boot, the same plainclothes officer, Lt. Oosthuizen, 'suggested I should follow them to the charge office where the car could be searched,' Jones remembers. At the charge office, having identified Peter Jones by his wallet, the police then asked Biko what his name was. '"I am Bantu Stephen Biko," he replied. For several moments there was absolute silence with police just looking at both of us. "Biko?" Oosthuizen asked. "No, Bantu

Stephen Biko," said Steve, giving the correct Xhosa pronunciation to the *b*'s.'

Next morning they were 'viciously handcuffed' and removed to Port Elizabeth to the sixth floor of the Security Police headquarters at the Sanlam Building, handcuffed by one hand to the bars, then photographed, taken back outside, 'separated by two squads of police who surrounded each of us ... I was in front and Steve a few paces behind me.

'My entourage stopped at a Kombi [van] and I was told to enter and lie face down on the floor between the seats. I turned to look at Steve who just passed and called his name out loud. He stopped to look at me and called my name and we stared, smiling a greeting, which was interrupted when I was slapped violently into the Kombi. That was the last time I was to see my close comrade ever – alive or dead.'

Peter Jones was held for 533 days without trial. He was finally released in February 1979. For the first 25 days during which time Biko was also held, he tells us what happened to him in the hands of the Port Elizabeth police, the same team which interrogated Biko. 'The first session lasted for more than twenty hours. I left my cell at about 22.00 hours [on 24 August] and was brought back at about 18.00 hours the following night. ... We drove at high speed to Sanlam Building ... Immediately I entered the room I was held by several police while one of my hands was freed and my clothes taken off. I was made to sit naked on a chair with my left hand chained with the handcuff to the chair. Snyman and Siebert occupied chairs at desks respectively to the left and right of me.

'On the desk in front of Siebert was a length of green hosepipe. I was able to look right into the hole of the pipe and noticed that the hole was filled – with what, I cannot say, but it was something metallic.' General questions followed. 'Then suddenly they focused on the trip Biko and I had been on … I repeated my original story that I had gone down to Cape Town to attend to a newly established project there (a clothing factory) and that Steve's presence was incidental and unplanned with no other intention than giving him an "outing" … Siebert suddenly jumped up and hit me with the hosepipe across my face and chest and arms, and then returned to his seat … Siebert told me they knew we had been in Port Elizabeth, that we had dropped pamphlets and that we had seen or met some people with whom we distributed these pamphlets. After some time of following this trend I told the police that in fact we had been in Cape Town to have discussions with our BPC men there.' Jones was given pen and paper to write two statements: his political history and the story of the trip. This did not satisfy Siebert, who ordered two policemen to put him *op die stene*

Marthinus Prins, inquest magistrate.

Dr Ivor Lang, the first doctor to examine Biko.

B. de V. Pickard, counsel for the doctors.

Capt. D.P. Siebert, one of Biko's and Jones's interrogators.

(on the bricks). Soon after this Siebert re-entered, accompanied now by Snyman, Nieuwoudt, Marx and Beneke.

After some resistance Jones was forced onto two small pieces of brick. 'Two chairs (heavy steel ones) were placed one on top of the other (the one upside down), and both Beneke and Nieuwoudt had to lift these until I could hold them high above my head. Siebert told me that should the chairs lower or fall I would "get it". I told him it was impossible to hold. I was already experiencing cramps in my legs.' Questions followed on Jones's involvement in BPC and BCP. Jones lowered the chairs to his shoulders. They were taken away and he was again chained to the chair and, again, the subject of the pamphlets and Port Elizabeth came up. When he repeatedly said he knew nothing, he was again placed on the bricks.

'Snyman started calling me names and calling me a liar. He got up from his chair and kicked me on the left leg. I stumbled and the chairs came tumbling down, one hitting him on the head and the other landing on Siebert's desk … I was taken from the bricks, on which I had by now spent several hours. Siebert got up and asked me when I was going to stop lying, and started to deliver heavy blows with both hands (open) to my face. I grabbed both his hands and pulled him down towards me. I told him that the treatment was unnecessary as I was answering their questions. Siebert, who is smaller than me, told me to let go of him, and did I want to fight? Two fist blows followed, delivered by Nieuwoudt and Beneke ... these two grabbed my arms.

'Siebert removed his watch and rolled up his sleeves. For a very long time he slapped my face with both hands (open) continuously and without pause. I remained silent, felt my senses dimming gradually to the stage where I could with a detachedness just feel the blows going through my head while I looked straight into Siebert's eyes.

'Just behind Siebert was a mirror hanging on the wall and I could see my face ... amazed that my face could assume such dimensions. Another "lip" was forming, blood from my mouth and nose, mixed with spittle, dribbled down my face onto my chest ... Marx and Snyman now stood to the left and right of Siebert, facing me, and Nieuwoudt started delivering fast and heavy blows to my head with the hosepipe, which was excruciating in the kind of shocks it sent through my body.

'Then Beneke started hitting me with his fist in my stomach and I started to stumble. Marx got a boot to my right leg as a warning to stand still. Beneke left and from a drawer of a filing cabinet took another hosepipe, black this time. Marx shouted: "Give him both – black power and green power!" Beneke took up his position again, on my left, and from then on he and Nieuwoudt hit me mainly on the head with hosepipes while Siebert carried on smacking my face. Snyman and Marx delivered kicks to my shins whenever I moved out of the way.

'Every time I tried to defend my head with my hands the pipes would move to the back, the kidney area, or attack the hands. I found it impossible to cope with all the immense pain and I turned and faced the wall and, closing my eyes, began hoping for oblivion, which never came, as blows rained down on my head and back.'

This interrogation of Jones took place on 24–25 August. According to the evidence at the inquest and amnesty hearing, Biko's interrogation began on 6 September in the same small, isolated room. For the eighteen days prior to this he was apparently held naked, in solitary confinement, in the Walmer police cells. There, 'he was deprived even of the negligible rights he had as a section 6 detainee. He was not taken out for a minimum period of exercise … not allowed to purchase food … not allowed proper washing facilities.' We do not know whether Biko was interrogated like Jones before 6 September, but on that day he was told to put on a shirt and trousers and taken to the Sanlam Building. In Room 619 Biko was interrogated by precisely the same team under the leadership of Maj. Harold Snyman: Warrant-Officer Ruben Marx, Det.-Sgt. Nieuwoudt, Capt. Siebert and Warrant-Officer Beneke.

Peter Jones lived to tell his story. Bantu Stephen Biko did not.

At the inquest into Biko's death – Jones was still in prison – Lt.-Col. Goosen, head of the Eastern Cape Security Police, said: 'Major Snyman reported to me that Mr Biko had become very aggressive and had thrown a chair at him and had attacked Warrant-Officer Beneke with his fists. A measure of force had to be used to subdue him so that he could be handcuffed again. I immediately visited Mr Biko. He was sitting on the sleeping mat with his hands handcuffed and the leg-irons fixed to an iron grille. I noticed a swelling on his upper lip. There was a wild expression in his eyes. I talked to him but he ignored me.'

We still do not know the whole truth of what happened to cause the fatal injury in Biko's case. In spite of the opportunity to tell the truth to the TRC in 1998, none of the five men who simultaneously assaulted him has owned up to the actual blow or blows to the head, or to causing his head to hit the wall, which left major brain injuries and changed Biko from a perfectly healthy human being into a physical and mental wreck in a very short space of time. At the inquest into his death in detention, Advocate Sydney

Kentridge put the Security Police 'on trial' in so far as was humanly possible in a State that ensured police protection by law. Callousness, lies and brutality were in evidence day after day.

The doctors who supposedly examined Biko displayed a pathetic weakness in the face of the Security Police – a chronic lack of care or compassion. They disgraced their profession. At a point when Biko's brain was damaged, when he was deranged to the extent of no longer being in control of his bodily functions, Col. Goosen cynically described his condition as that of 'shamming'. 'Neither I nor any of my colleagues, nor the doctors saw any external injuries'. Goosen then put in the order for Biko to be transported, naked, in the back of a Landrover for the distance of hundreds of kilometres from Port Elizabeth to Pretoria. This was conceded to by Dr Benjamin Tucker, Chief District Surgeon, Port Elizabeth, who at the inquest averred: 'I didn't know that in this particular situation one could over-ride the decisions made by a responsible police officer.'

In the judgment, Magistrate Marthinus Prins pronounced that 'on the available evidence the death cannot be attributed to any act or omission amounting to a criminal offence on the part of any person'.

Whether Biko defended himself with the chair on which he sat without permission – if this was not

Sydney Kentridge, Ernie Wentzel and George Bizos at the inquest.

itself a fabrication – or whether what happened to Jones happened in more or less the same way to Biko is not of major significance in the face of the violence of his death. South Africa's security laws enabled policemen to be unaccountable. Protection of the most irresponsible policemen ensured that no court could condemn them. Beatings and other torture resulting in deaths were safely, symbiotically, locked into a protective conspiracy between police witnesses and the State. What happened in Room 619 happened countless times. The security laws allowed detainees to be held in terror without any protection. Doctors, magistrates and others were willing to compromise the integrity of their professions in the shadow of these laws, thus making the law a mockery but ensuring that it was played out as if it was not. Perjury was a matter of course.

A supreme arrogance persisted into and throughout the 1980s. At the time of Biko's death, the Minister of Police, Jimmy Kruger, was at a National Party congress in the Transvaal. In his first announcement reporting it, he said that Biko had died 'following a hunger strike', adding that 'Biko's death leaves me cold'. A quip from the audience by one Christoffel Venter responded that Mr Kruger was so democratic that he allowed detainees 'the democratic right to starve themselves to death'.

Twelve years later Father Aelred Stubbs cast his mind back on Biko and the preservation of the innermost person in that extreme situation. 'I am trying to work from my knowledge of Steve and my knowledge of his deepest values and instincts,' he said. 'I am sure that there was a kind of inner fortress of integrity that he would not suffer to be violated.' He knew that Biko was prudent with a sense of self-preservation and, although only a stupid person would have no fear, Biko had conquered fear in an intelligent way. 'He had a much greater fear of betraying himself than a fear of physical violence even to the point of death. He had conquered fear by his inner conviction of his outer undefeatability if he was prepared to give everything. That kind of quality grows with exercise.

A deep instinct; very very deep, absolutely rooted in the roots of his culture. Steve grasped the essential goodness of what was there and worked from that, allowed that to work within him, always broadening it as his own horizons did.'

9

A life still to be 'dug out'

Barney Pityana was still in prison on 12 September, the day Biko died, and was not told of his death. That night he had a dream. He dreamt that he had 'this enormous discussion with Steve where he was saying, more or less, "I am leaving. You must look after my children", and I saying, "You know it's not *my* business to look after your children – you must do something responsible."' Biko went on, insisting in a friendly sort of way, until Pityana reluctantly agreed that, all right, if he *had* to go somewhere, he, Barney, would look after his children. The next day Pityana was allowed to have a shower, something not allowed before, and 'this white boy was reading the paper and I managed to see in his paper a statement by Kruger. I would otherwise never have known and then suddenly this sort of funny discussion I was having in the middle of the night came back. I was in a very very lonely state in that cell. I was absolutely distraught, angry – much more, [I was] almost suicidal.'

'It was the fire – the fire went out.' Ramphele looked out of the window as she spoke. 'When Thenjiwe phoned me on 13 September I was in hospital. When I heard, everything went dead. I literally wondered if I could walk across that room, if I could survive physically. Everything was dead.' Mamphela Ramphele was banished, isolated in Lenyenye, far in the north, in hospital, trying to save the life of her unborn child – Biko's child.

Biko's funeral took place on 25 September at the King William's Town stadium. Oxen drew the coffin until it was lifted and held shoulder-high by his comrades, an impulsive gesture which was to become the hallmark of the many funerals of comrades to come. The only visible presence of the State was one lone soldier seen on a tower high above the crowd. Otherwise the police were not present. But, as Mafika Gwala explains, they were present elsewhere: 'Most Natalians missed [Steve's funeral], the result of police action in turning the cars and buses carrying mourners back on the Transkeian borders ... [but] I did not miss the symbolism that such burial carried ... Those who have attended the funerals of all those who have died in detention must have gone to these funerals with an inner understanding that a scratch on a black man is a scratch on every black man. And that death in detention at one centre is death in detention all over the country ... When we heard that Steve was dead many of us must have said, deep down in our minds, if the time must come, let it begin now.'

Biko knew that it *had* already begun. The youth of Soweto, of Natal, of the Eastern Cape, of Langa, Nyanga and Guguletu in the Western Cape – the youth of the whole country – had understood that. As Biko explained, 'The dramatic thing about the bravery of these youths is that they have now discovered, or accepted, what everybody knows: that the bond between life and death is absolute. You are either alive and proud or you are dead, and when you're dead you can't care anyway. And your method of death can itself be a politicising thing; so you die in the riots. For a hell of a lot of them, in fact, there's really nothing to lose – almost literally; given the kind of situations that they come from. So if you can overcome personal fear for death, which is a highly irrational thing, you know, then you're on your way.'

Biko's mother understood this too. 'In truth he was not my child. He was the son of the people. I have come to understand that I must comfort myself and accept that truth: that this child was not my child. Moreover, there are many children of other people who have gone before Steve. When a battle is fought, not all the soldiers come back home. It is God's will in which this

At Biko's funeral: wife Ntsiki, son Samora and mother Mamcethe.

whole thing happened. After such a long time *bube ubomi bakhe busombiwa* [his life is still being dug out]. Accepting that, I have a humble view of myself as a person from whom he comes.'

Biko foresaw his death in the nature of what he was doing, and he was prepared to die. Thus, along with many others, he became a martyr in the struggle for freedom in South Africa. He fulfilled his own concept of obedience to God, which was, as he explained, 'at the heart of the conviction of most selfless revolutionaries, a call to men of conscience to offer themselves, and sometimes their lives, for the eradication of evil'.

Biko was only 30 when he died. In the slow and tortuous manner of his death he endured a kind of crucifixion, chained and unable to move, his feet in irons hooked into the wall; with people always watching. After suffering a blow to his head so severe that it gradually undermined his mind and consciousness, his capacity to function as a human being, he was, after five days, declared fit enough to be driven, naked, in the back of a Landrover 1133 kilometres overnight. Yet, on arrival in Pretoria, he was still not dead. He died alone shortly thereafter.

In his own words, his 'method of death' was, indeed, 'a politicising thing'. It woke up the world to the true nature of apartheid and accelerated commitment to fight for change in all forms inside and outside South Africa. Dying young, Biko left a life of such promise in the air, so to speak. Of those who knew him at the time, Mpumlwana said: 'We all each individually experienced it. You can't replace the catalyst that he was. None of the other people we related to were *that* to you – and yet he didn't get to you. He was best at not making you grovel with gratitude. We couldn't have another Steve.' Donald Woods, in his exuberant style, said that he was simply 'the greatest man I ever met'. Lein van den Bergh, a Dutch lawyer, who was a member of the Resistance in the Second World War and experienced imprisonment at Dachau, met him only once and saw in him the qualities of a man whom he would expect to become 'the leader of the government'. Some of his political critics then were less impressed. In the *African Communist*, for example, Biko was accused of 'being a "liberal", an idealist, insufficiently anti-capitalist, a pacifist, and lacking any understanding of the mass struggle', but in a recent radio interview Kedibone Molema said, 'Biko took people out of an ethnic identity and allowed us to have another. That was a galvanising thing,'

Biko had a clear insight into the psychological aspect of the oppression of his time which had resulted in momentary political impotence. As politics was racialised by apartheid, the movement was called *Black* Consciousness. His message was simple and clear: *Do not be a part of your oppression.* It was a crucial intervention, a fresh, youthful and distinctive voice that mobilised people when all the major political opposition was banned, their leaders in exile or in jail. It provided a new, vital, unifying element giving to the ANC, as Wally Serote said, 'oxygen and new life, which the movement desperately needed'.

Black Consciousness worked with consensus decision-making. It instilled independent thinking, self-reliance, fearlessness and dignity. It had a wider concept, black power, which connected both with the emergence of Africa's independence from colonial rule and with that other significant struggle for black liberation in the US. In South Africa, Biko and his contemporaries broke the stunned silence of their time.

The refusal of a new generation of young blacks to be subservient or humiliated, even in the face of death, changed the nature of the struggle. Biko himself lived and died by this truth. Just before his death he was on the verge of meeting the leadership of the ANC and the PAC in exile to discuss the possibility of a unifying force. Biko's leadership and the role of Black Consciousness have yet to be truly estimated and cannot be tucked away into a small paragraph of history. A key catalyst of transformation, Biko's generation inspired a culture of fearlessness. This was made more resolute when the government responded by killing hundreds of young people in the Soweto Uprising and its aftermath. Fearlessness was sustained throughout the 1980s, when apartheid's policies manifested a mounting violence with secret assassination squads and army troops with teargas and bullets daily in the townships. Protests on the ground escalated whilst a growing number of MK guerrillas – including many from the BC movement – infiltrated South Africa country-wide. The situation was becoming ungovernable and evolving into an undeclared civil war. Funerals of black cadres were vast and became political platforms for further resistance. The flags of the banned organisations re-emerged in the carrying of the coffins. It was, indeed, 'the awakening of the people' whose sheer numbers made the politicians move. Black South Africans never felt inferior again.

Black Consciousness held the value of not wanting to be rich at the expense of the poor. 'If we have a mere change of those in government positions, what is likely to happen is that black people will continue to be poor and you will get a few blacks filtering through the so-called bourgeoisie and our society will be run almost as of yesterday,' Biko said. How, then, would he view the current, growing gap between rich and poor in South Africa's new democracy? What would he do about it? What would he think of the cult of materialism and greed? Or the jousting for status, money and position amongst South Africa's new elite – anathema to his style of leadership – with its failure of delivery to the majority, still imprisoned by the legacy of apartheid, whose youth continue to be undereducated and unemployed? In 1972 Biko ironically suggested that if the apartheid government was smart and wanted to be re-accepted into the world, it should create a black minority elite, a wealthy middle class, and retain the vast majority in poverty to provide a pool for cheap labour from which to draw. Is this close to the scenario emerging today in South Africa after the intense struggle and supreme sacrifices made for freedom and equality? Where would Biko stand today? Would he be inside the tent or outside? What is certain is that, first, he would interrogate the facts as to what exactly is going on in all spheres of South African life. If true to form, he would ensure this information was followed with country-wide debate around the issues; this would be led by consensus leadership and result in informed action.

One feature of South African society that would undoubtedly claim his attention and dismay him is the prevalence of violence and abuse of women and children, South Africa's rape statistics being one of the highest in the world – a stark negation of 'group pride and the determination to rise and attain the envisaged self'. 'Do not be a part of your own oppression'. His words sustain well into the 21st century. They determine analysis of the individual self and the call for action. In the 1970s Biko's words often spoke directly to 'the black *man*'. In 2011 the substitution of 'black *women*' might aptly apply to these words of his: 'The essence is the realisation by *women* of the need to rally together with *her sisters* around the cause of their oppression and to operate as a group to rid themselves of the shackles that bind them to perpetual servitude. It is based on a self-examination which has ultimately led them to believe that by seeking to run away from themselves, they are insulting the intelligence of whoever created them *women*. The philosophy of Black Consciousness expresses group pride and the determination … to rise and attain the envisaged self.'

Biko's spirit is far from dead. Nor is it confined to the movement he inspired but extends to the wider truths he held and expressed through the liberating experience of recognising that Black Consciousness could be the transforming agent of his time. It will always be true that 'the most potent weapon in the hands of the oppressor is the mind of the oppressed'. Biko's life is still 'to be dug out' as a transforming agent wherever oppression is rife. His life-force was an antidote to pessimism. Biko was essentially *living*. He would thoroughly object to becoming a myth locked away in the room of a museum or in the rigid, inappropriate statue of himself in East London. With his intellect, huge presence and raucous laughter and the 'no bullshit thing', he liberated the spirit of those he met. He used every opportunity available, weighing up a situation precisely and swiftly, seeing its limits as much as its potential, understanding how to make it work for the common purpose, knowing nothing was perfect and that you had to work very hard to transform anything. He worked with the potential of individuals, often locked away within them, knowing that without the recognition and subsequent growth of that potential a nation could not function fully. He worked with whoever came his way. He was not elitist in spite of having commenced initially as a student leader from a university. There was no time to waste and he knew he had to sacrifice his formal education. Later, he sensed that he would have to sacrifice his life. The strength of his particular style of leadership stemmed from his capacity for astute political insight coupled with his faith and recognition that anyone could grow, learn, and participate and lead once challenged with meaningful ideas, and from this could emerge a meaningful life.

Biko's perception and energy freed people to take their destiny into their own hands. How they will continue to draw on his insight and legacy is up to new generations. But his memory would best be served by the growth of a broader consciousness that remains wary of mindless authority, that recognises that ideas are strengthened through consensus decision-making, which has the capacity to be persuaded by a majority vote, even if it sometimes seems inappropriate, and, simultaneously, has the ability to then work with that decision, ensuring its soundness.

Bibliography

Apartheid Museum, *Biko: The Quest for a True Humanity – Exhibition*

Arnold, Millard, *Steve Biko: No Fears Expressed* (Skotaville, 1987)

Bernstein, Hilda, *No. 46: Steve Biko* (IDAF, 1978)

Biko, Steve, *I Write What I Like* (Heinemann, 1988)

Bizos, George, *No One to Blame* (David Philip, 1998)

Black Review, 1972–1976

Erikson, E.H., *Identity* (Faber & Faber, 1968)

Gerhart, G.M., *Black Power in South Africa* (University of California Press, 1978)

Freire, Paulo, *The Pedagogy of the Oppressed* (Penguin, 1972)

Lodge, T., *Black Politics in South Africa since 1945* (Ravan, 1983)

Marx, A.W., *Lessons of the Struggle* (Oxford University Press, 1992)

Mngxitama, A. et al., *Biko Lives* (Macmillan, 1998)

Moore, Basil, *Black Theology* (C. Hurst, 1973)
Mutloatse, Mothobi, *Reconstruction* (Skotaville, 1981)
New Republic, January 1978
Pityana, Barney et al., *Bounds of Possibility* (Zed Books and David Philip, 1991)
Ramphele, Mamphela, *A Life* (David Philip, 1995)
Van Wyk, C., *Steve Biko*, Freedom Fighters Series (Maskew Miller Longman, 2003)
Wilson, Monica and Leonard Thompson, *The Oxford History of South Africa*, 2 vols. (Oxford, 1969, 1971)
Woods, Donald, *Biko* (Henry Holt, 1987)

Notes taken by Pamela Reynolds at the Biko Amnesty Hearing, 30 March 1998

Interview with Steve Biko by Gail Gerhart (1972)

Interviews with Lindy Wilson:
Neville Alexander (Hogsback, 1991)
Nokuzola 'Mamcethe' Biko (Ginsberg, 1989)
Nobandile Biko (Mdantsane, 1990)
Nontsikelelo (Ntsiki) Biko (1990)
Neville Curtis (Harare, 1990)
Mafika Gwala (London, 1989)
Anne Hope (Cape Town, 1991)
Bennie A. Khoapa (Roma, Lesotho, 1990)
Mandla Langa (London, 1989)

Bokwe Mafuna (Paris, 1989)
Malusi Mpumlwana (Grahamstown, 1990)
Thenjiwe Mtintso (Harare, 1990)
Nyameko Barney Pityana (Geneva, 1989)
Dimza Pityana (Geneva, 1989)
Mamphela Ramphele (Cape Town, 1989)
David Russell (Grahamstown, 1990)
Mongane Wally Serote (Harare, 1990)
Aelred Stubbs (Sunderland, 1989)
Francis Wilson (Cape Town, 1991)

Videos and DVDs:
Biko Inquest (102 mins), 1984: dramatisation of the transcripts of the Biko Inquest by John Blair and Norman Fenton (with Albert Finney as Sydney Kentridge)
Biko: Breaking the Silence (52 mins), 1987
Biko: The Spirit Lives (67 mins), 1988
Steve Biko: Journey of the Spirit (52 mins), 1997
Steve Bantu Biko: Beacon of Hope (53 mins), 1999

Index

African National Congress (ANC) 15, 26, 48, 94, 96, 101–4, 110, 127
African socialism 16
Alexander, Neville 129
Bam, Fikile 130
bannings (March 1973) 77–8, 84–91; (August 1976) 118–24; (October 1977) 98
Beneke, Warrant-Officer 135–8
Biko, Alice Nokuzola 'Mamcethe' (mother) 18–3, 79, 114, 145
Biko, Bantu Stephen (Steve): birth and early years 18–29; schooling 22–7; as university student 30–56; medical studies 16, 28–9, 57, 70; law studies 16, 28, 105–8; president of Saso 36; joins BCP in Durban 57; banning to Ginsberg (1973) 77–9, 84–91, 113; further restriction (1975) 103; gives evidence at Saso-BPC Trial 105–10; imprisonment (1976) 75, 115–16; honorary president of BPC 122; arrest (August 1977) and death (12 September 1977) 11–13, 129–42; funeral 144–5; inquest 13; gift of leadership 14, 41–2, 44, 49, 52–3, 87–7; generosity of intimacy 15, 61–5, 114–15; love and marriage 65–75; socialising 49–51, 91–2; writing 40–1; reading 45–8; on religion 16, 24–6, 75, 80–3
Biko, Bukelwa (sister) 19, 113
Biko, Hlumelo 72, 120
Biko, Khaya (brother) 19, 23, 27
Biko, Mzingaye (father) 18–19
Biko, Nkosinathi 72
Biko, Nobandile (sister) 19, 20–1, 93, 113, 114
Biko, Nontsikelelo (Ntsiki) (wife) 67, 68–72, 113, 114, 116–17
Biko, Samora 72
Bizos, George 13
Black communalism 104
Black Community Programmes (BCP) 57, 60, 77, 79, 85
Black Consciousness 14, 17, 41–3, 62, 77, 87, 91, 95, 96, 101, 106, 148–54
Black Panthers 48
Black People's Convention (BPC) 85, 100–3, 105–10, 128
Black Power 32, 42
Black Review 60, 91, 93, 94, 101, 104
Black Workers' Project 52, 101

Boshoff, Judge 107
Cape Town 41, 52, 80, 94, 129, 133
Charles Morgan Primary School 22
Christianity 24, 26, 75, 81–3
Church, the 16, 24–5, 39, 82–3
Civil Rights movement 42
Clark, Dick 123
communism 27
Cone, James 47
conscientisation 32, 57, 95
Cooper, Saths 45, 46, 59, 78
Cry Freedom 109
Curtis, Neville 39, 61
Daily Dispatch 91, 93, 120
Dimbaza 80, 93, 119
Dlamini, Nkosazana 104
Durban 39, 52, 57, 68, 77, 91, 92, 101
Erikson, Eric 54
Fanon, Frantz 47
fearlessness 84, 88, 90, 141, 149
Forbes Grant Secondary School 22
Freedom Charter 104
Freire, Paulo 42, 59
Frelimo 95, 100
Freud, Sigmund 54, 65
Gabriel, Peter 11
General Student Council (GSC) 46, 48
Gerhart, Gail 76
Ginsberg 19, 20, 57, 70, 79, 88, 97
Goosen, P.J. 13, 138
Grey Hospital 20
Gwala, Mafika 46, 104, 144
Haigh, Bruce 125–6
Hope, Anne 59
Internal Security Act 118
Issel, Johnny 59
'I Write What I Like' 40, 71
Ithuseng Clinic 98
Johannesburg 50, 52, 59, 78, 88, 118, 119

Jones, Peter 93, 120–2, 129–38
Kentridge, Sydney 138–9
Khoapa, Bennie 57, 60, 83
King William's Town 19, 20, 67, 78, 85, 103, 118
King, Martin Luther 47, 64
Koka, Drake 78
Kruger, Jimmy 141, 143
Langa, Mandla 45, 46, 47, 109
liberalism 24, 28, 39
Lovedale Institution 23, 33
Mafuna, Bokwe 50, 51, 59, 78, 95
Malcolm X 47
Mandela, Nelson 27
Marcuse, Herbert 46
Marx, Ruben 135–8
Marxism 16
Matshoba, Deborah 59
Mbanjwa, Thoko 93, 99, 118, 119
Mji, Diliza 104
Modisane, Jerry 59, 78
Mohapi, Mapetla 93, 101, 118, 125
Mohapi, Nohle 69, 93, 99
Moodley, Strini 45, 46, 59, 78
Mphahlele, Eskia 46
Mpumlwana, Malusi 15, 40, 85, 86, 92, 97, 98, 101, 118, 120, 123
Mtintso, Thenjiwe 88, 93, 99, 114, 115, 118, 125
Mvovo, Mxolisi 93, 118, 120
Mxenge, Griffiths 102
National Union of South African Students (Nusas) 30–1, 39
Ndebele, Njabulo 46
Négritude 42
Nengwekhulu, Harry R. 57, 78
Nieuwoudt, Gideon 12, 13, 135
non-racism 31
non-violence 109
non-white 40
Ntwasa, Stanley 50
oppression 14, 54–5

Pan Africanist Congress (PAC) 15, 23, 26, 94, 96, 101–4, 110, 127
Pityana, Barney 16, 33, 34, 35, 40, 41, 46, 48, 59, 63, 68, 78, 88, 98, 143–4
Pityana, Nosidima (Dimza) 62, 68
Poqo 27
Port Elizabeth 11, 19, 33, 52, 78, 88, 99, 119, 132, 135, 139
Prins, Marthinus 139
Rambally, Asha 45
Ramphele, Mamphela 45, 62–3, 67, 71–2, 94–5, 97–8, 114, 115–17, 118, 119–20, 144
Rand Daily Mail 50
Rhodes University 30–1
Rivonia Trial 27, 86–7
Russell, David 25, 79–81, 84, 88, 113
Sartre, Jean-Paul 46
SASO *Newsletter* 40
Saso-BPC Trial 16, 105–10, 122
Security Police 11, 64, 79, 83, 85, 107–8, 132–41
Serote, Mongane Wally 46, 50, 64, 95
Sharpeville 26, 110
Shezi, Mthuli 59
Sibisi, Charles 45
Siebert, Daantjie 12, 133–7
Snyman, Harold 12, 133–7
Sobukwe, Robert 102
Soggot, David 106
South African State 43, 77, 97, 120
South African Students' Organisation (Saso) 36–8, 39, 40, 43, 50, 71, 85, 100, 105–10
Soweto Uprising 110, 118, 149
St Francis College 24, 25
St Matthew's Hospital 19
Stubbs, Aelred 24–5, 52, 65, 73, 88, 112, 113, 119, 122, 141
Terrorism Act 95, 101, 106, 118, 119
Theatre Council of Natal 45
trade unions 15, 52–3
Transkei 103, 120, 130
Truth and Reconciliation Commission (TRC) 12, 13
Tucker, Benjamin 139
Tucker, Raymond 119
Umkhonto weSizwe (MK) 27, 99, 110
Unity Movement 103, 129
University Christian Movement (UCM) 34, 35, 39, 50
University of Fort Hare 33, 34, 35
University of Natal Medical School (UNNE) 28–9, 30, 45
University of South Africa (Unisa) 19, 60
University of the North (Turfloop) 36
Van den Bergh, Lein 122, 148
Verwoerd, H.F. 56
Vorster, B.J. 123
Woods, Donald 89, 93, 124, 148
Zanempilo Community Health Centre 67, 73, 94, 119
Zimele Trust Fund 94

OHIO SHORT HISTORIES OF AFRICA

EMPEROR HAILE SELASSIE

BEREKET HABTE SELASSIE

EMPEROR HAILE SELASSIE was an iconic figure of the twentieth century, a progressive monarch who ruled Ethiopia from 1916 to 1974. This book, written by a former state official who served in a number of important positions in Selassie's government, tells both the story of the emperor's life and the story of modern Ethiopia.

After a struggle for the throne in 1916, the young Selassie emerged first as regent and then as supreme leader of Ethiopia. Over the course of his nearly six-decade rule, the emperor abolished slavery, introduced constitutional reform, and expanded educational opportunity. The Italian invasion of Ethiopia in the 1930s led to a five-year exile in England, from which he returned in time to lead his country through World War II. Selassie was also instrumental in the founding of the Organization of African Unity in 1963, but he fell short of the ultimate goal of a promised democracy in Ethiopia. The corruption that grew under his absolute rule as well as his seeming indifference to the famine that gripped Ethiopia in the 1970s led finally to his overthrow by the armed forces that he had created.

Haile Selassie was an enlightened monarch in many ways, but also one who became blinded by his own absolute power. This short biography is a sensitive portrayal of Selassie as both emperor and man, by one who knew him well.

Bereket Habte Selassie is William E. Leuchtenburg Professor of African Studies and Law, University of North Carolina at Chapel Hill and former attorney general of Ethiopia as well as associate justice of the Supreme Court of Ethiopia.

Emperor Haile Selassie

Bereket Habte Selassie

OHIO UNIVERSITY PRESS

ATHENS

Ohio University Press, Athens, Ohio 45701
ohioswallow.com
© 2014 by Ohio University Press
All rights reserved

To obtain permission to quote, reprint, or otherwise reproduce or distribute material from Ohio University Press publications, please contact our rights and permissions department at (740) 593-1154 or (740) 593-4536 (fax).

Printed in the United States of America
Ohio University Press books are printed on acid-free paper ⊚ ™

24 23 22 21 20 19 18 17 16 15 14   5 4 3 2 1

Library of Congress Cataloging-in-Publication Data
Bereket H. Selassie, author.
 Emperor Haile Selassie / Bereket Habte Selassie.
   pages cm. — (Ohio short histories of Africa)
 ISBN 978-0-8214-2127-7 (pb : alk. paper) — ISBN 978-0-8214-4508-2 (pdf)
1. Haile Selassie I, Emperor of Ethiopia, 1892–1975. 2. Ethiopia—Kings and rulers—Biography. 3. Ethiopia—Politics and government—1889–1974. I. Title. II. Series: Ohio short histories of Africa.
 DT387.7.B47 2014
 963.055092—dc23

2014029648

Cover design by Joey Hi-Fi

Contents

	List of Illustrations	7
	Preface	9
1.	Leadership in the Context of Ethiopian History and Mythology	15
2.	Tafari: Orphaned Prince Steeled by Adversity	23
3.	Harar, Ras Makonnen, and Menelik's Court	27
4.	The Feud with Iassu—the Plot Thickens	32
5.	The 1916 Coup d'État and the Rise of a Man of Destiny	39
6.	From King to Emperor: Proclamation of the Central Elements of Change	51
7.	The Italian Invasion and the Emperor's Exile	59
8.	World War II and the Return of the Emperor to Ethiopia	65
9.	Postliberation Developments	70

10. Diplomacy: The American Connection and Nonalignment	82
11. Turning of the Tide: A Shaken Emperor on the Horns of a Dilemma	90
12. Last Days: Revolution and the End of the Monarchy	102
Conclusion	122
Notes	131
Selected Bibliography	137
Index	143

Illustrations

Following page 124

Tafari with his father Ras Makonnen, ca. 1905

The newly crowned King Tafari, 1928

The emperor in his exile years, appearing before the League of Nations, 1936

Emperor Haile Selassie, mid- to late 1950s

A delegation of the Dergue meeting with the emperor, 1974

Preface

I must start by making a declaration that, beginning in the mid-1950s until the early 1970s, I served in the government of Emperor Haile Selassie. I served in different capacities, including holding the post of attorney general; thus I had ample opportunities to observe the emperor at work. Some portion of this book is, therefore, informed (and I hope enriched) by insights gained as a result of that experience. Nonetheless, for the most part I employed the usual research methodology of examining material about the emperor's life and work, principally biographical works, including the emperor's own two-volume autobiography.

It is tempting to write at length about the life and work of this historical figure of great fascination. Alas, the requisite size of this volume dictates concision; one has to be selective even in the works consulted, as the bibliography shows. The few pictures are chosen to represent different phases of the emperor's life. Then there is the English spelling of his name. Some use Haile Sellassie;

others Hayle Selase; others Hayla-Sellase. Here, as in all my writings about him, I follow the one used in the English translation of his autobiography—Haile Selassie. There are several different approaches to the spelling of Ethiopian names. The spellings I have adopted are, for the most part, sanctioned by use and should not occasion undue controversy. Titles like Ras and Dejasmach are written separately from the names; thus, Ras Imru should not be RasImru, and Dejasmach Balcha should not be DejasmachBalcha.

I must also note that I grew up hearing about Haile Selassie long before he changed his name, when he was still called by his given name, Tafari (he took the name Haile Selassie when he was crowned emperor in 1930). During my childhood in my Eritrean homeland, which was an Italian colony until 1941, my father and some of his close friends used to whisper his name and even quietly sing songs of praise, such as "Etiopia tenageri: bniguski bteferi" (Speak, O Ethiopia: speak in the name of your king, Tafari). As I mention in my memoirs, "Tafari was his given name . . . it was with the name Tafari that he had become well known as a popular and progressive ruler. His fame had spread across the Ethiopian border, to the then Italian colony of Eritrea and beyond, as the cult of Rastafarianism (Rastas) demonstrates."[1] Thus, I will say more on this and other aspects of his extraordinary life and work.

Of the biographical data that I consulted, none are more important than the memoir (in Amharic) of Ras

Imru Haile Selassie, *Kayehut, Kemastawsew*. Ras Imru was the emperor's cousin and close confidant, and was at his side, in good as well as bad times, from childhood through the stormy years of his feud with Lij Iassu until he assumed supreme power as emperor in 1930, and thereafter. Imru was with him during the last, fateful moment in September 1974 when a unit of the military junta, the Dergue, burst into the imperial palace and its leader informed the emperor that they had come to take him to a place of detention. The stunned emperor was speechless, whereupon Ras Imru intervened and was heard quietly counseling him to accept the inevitable gracefully. Then they led the once all-powerful monarch to an awaiting Volkswagen Beetle and drove him away as the jeering crowd shouted, "Leba! Leba! Leba!" (Robber! Robber! Robber!).

Thus ended a glorious reign, in ignominy. As historians have said about the passing of a Caesar, *Sic transit gloria mundi!*

Before deposing the emperor, the Dergue had asked Ras Imru to persuade his royal cousin, who had become their virtual prisoner, to provide them with information about his foreign bank accounts. The emperor was not willing to oblige the usurpers; through Ras Imru, he told them that if they could find any foreign bank account in his name, they were welcome to it! As this book will show, the Lion of Judah was nothing if not willful and tenacious, and he remained thus to the bitter end.[2]

Here a word is in order on the illustrious Ras Imru. I knew and greatly admired Ras Imru, not least because he interceded on my behalf at a time of my "troubles" with the emperor. He was universally loved and admired by the Ethiopian public for his uprightness and progressive politics as well as for his heroic role during the Italo-Ethiopian war of 1936. After Ethiopia's defeat, he was taken to Italy as a prisoner of war and spent five years in an Italian prison on the island of Panza.

His memoir is a priceless gem, containing as it does valuable information and insight on events and issues touching on the emperor's life and work. The editor of the memoirs says in the foreword that aspects of Ras Imru's descriptions in his memoir "have infused the raw material of history with a corporeal substance, making it breathe and smell human."[3] It is an apt and poignant remark. Ras Imru's memoir paints an intimate portrait of Haile Selassie as if he were his alter ego. It is an authentic testimonial of a life that was at once glorious and tragic.

The aim of this book is to give an account of the rise and fall of one of the twentieth century's truly remarkable leaders. Long before the rise in Africa of such men as Nkrumah and Nyerere—indeed, when most of them were still students—Haile Selassie had become world renowned. As the head of Africa's only (truly) independent nation, the emperor exerted considerable influence on Africans on the continent as well as those in the Diaspora. And when Italy invaded Ethiopia, Africans shared the sense of loss, as Nkrumah, Mandela, and others have written. When the emperor appeared at the League of Nations in Geneva to plead his people's case, he had become a world figure of no mean importance, as we shall see.

As part of the Ohio Short Histories of Africa series, this book is designed to provide a concise but well-rounded account of the emperor's life and work—his birth into the royal lineage, his struggle to attain the imperial throne, his championing of his country's modernization, and the challenges he faced through it all. His triumph and his tragedy.

1

Leadership in the Context of Ethiopian History and Mythology

The Question of Legitimacy

> By virtue of His Imperial Blood, as well as by the anointing He has received, the person of the Emperor is sacred, His dignity is inviolable and His power indisputable.

The words above are from Article 4 of the Revised Constitution of Ethiopia (1955). The same constitution also codifies the oral tradition according to which legitimate claim to the Ethiopian throne depended on the claimant's ability to trace his genealogy to the Solomonic dynasty, which was purportedly established by the union of King Solomon of Israel and the Queen of Sheba of Ethiopia through their son, King Menelik I, who was born during the queen's visit to behold Solomon's fabled wisdom.

For most Ethiopians, when they proudly spoke of their country's three-thousand-year history, that union loomed large, as, by some accounts, it did in the young mind of

Tafari Makonnen, the future Emperor Haile Selassie. This point is underscored by some of the emperor's biographers, who contend that belief in his dynastic genealogy gave him confidence that he was the legitimate heir to the throne of the ailing Emperor Menelik II, at a time when the question of who would succeed Menelik was an issue of momentous significance, as we shall see. Nonetheless, in his quest for the imperial throne, Tafari did not lie low, depending only on such claims of legitimacy; on the contrary, as we shall see, Tafari single-mindedly applied his indomitable will, political skills, and enormous energy to manipulate people and events toward the attainment of his goal.

As to the real basis of the story and whether the claim can be historically proved, that is immaterial. If the story is indeed based on myth, its durability shows the role of myth in history and society. The mythology of the Solomonic dynasty, believed by its originators to be based on history, acted as a powerful substitute for historical fact.

Belief was all.

This raises the question, why was it necessary for Ethiopian kings to rest their claim as legitimate heirs to the throne on such a story? Why would an African people insist on basing the legitimacy of their royalty on a story which happened long ago in a faraway land?[1]

Add to this the official title of the Ethiopian emperor—"the Conquering Lion of Judah"—and the puzzle becomes a mystery. In fact, that title provides the key to understanding why Ethiopians resorted to the Solomonic dynasty as a source of the legitimacy of their kings. Two biblical references are relevant here. The first is Matthew 1:1–17, which tells the story of the genealogy of Jesus Christ, "the son of David, the son of Abraham." The second is Revelations, which describes Jesus Christ as the conquering Lion of Judah: "And I saw in the right hand of Him who sat on the throne a book written inside and on the back, sealed up with seven seals" (5:1). "And I began to weep greatly," says John, the writer of Revelations, "because no one was found worthy to open the book, or to look into it. And one of the elders said to me, 'Stop weeping; behold the Lion that is from the tribe of Judah, the Root of David, has overcome so as to open the book and its seven seals" (5:4–5).

The relation between church and state has been a constant theme since the coming of Christianity to Ethiopia in the fourth century AD. Together, they conspired to elevate the notion of legitimacy based on the Solomonic dynasty as a defining principle of royal succession. According to some writers, the Ethiopians, or rather their ingenious scribes, penned the *Kebra Nagast*, the first written work to tell the story of the union between Solomon and Sheba, which also links the Ethiopian monarchy to Jesus Christ. Hence the critical relevance of the reference to Matthew's Gospel and Revelations. Some have further claimed that the Jews, by crucifying Jesus Christ, had relinquished their privileged position as God's chosen people and been replaced by the Ethiopians. Would this make such claimants "uppity wannabes," to use a much-abused colloquial phrase? Is such a claim far-fetched? No more far-fetched than the idea of the Solomonic dynasty. But I digress, and I will not push the argument one way or the other.

We shall see the relevance of the Solomonic dynasty in the contest over who would be the rightful heir to the great Emperor Menelik II—would it be Tafari or others? But for now we will leave it there and proceed with the narrative of Haile Selassie's life and work.

A Man of Destiny

Emperor Haile Selassie is one of the twentieth century's illustrious leaders, who won almost universal accolades for bringing Ethiopia kicking and screaming (according to some) from tradition-bound backwardness to the light of modern times.[2] Several biographies have been written about him, in addition to his two-volume autobiography, and a growing number of memoirs, including some by former members of his government, have started appearing, attesting to the fascination he still inspires. Many of these memoirs are critical of his failings while lamenting the tragic manner of his demise, if not the end of his regime. One Ethiopian writer, a former functionary of his government, has faulted him for neglecting the nation's interest in favor of his own selfish ends.[3]

In this volume, I attempt to focus on the core elements of his contributions as well as his failings. He was an enlightened monarch, but his earlier promise was unfulfilled and his historical legacy and stature have been diminished by his inordinate concentration and exercise of absolute power. Those who value the modernizing aspect of his work, however, may well argue that without that power he could not have accomplished his aim of modernizing Ethiopia. This is obviously a controversial issue, and I hope to address it below.

The Context

As we assess Haile Selassie's role in modernizing Ethiopia, it is worth bearing in mind that he was a product of his country's history and culture. Needless to say, there is no value without context; and the core values that he imbibed from childhood, which affected much of his work, were rooted in the specific historical and cultural context of Ethiopia, with Christianity a dominant factor in that context. Some of those received values the emperor rejected and sought to change or abolish, such as the hated practice of slavery. He was also actively engaged in promoting modern ideas and institutions, which he would use as instruments in centralizing state power. As both the product of a traditional polity and the beneficiary of a modicum of modern education, he often found himself in the middle of heated controversies occasioned by a clash of values, which more often than not involved conflicting interests. Indeed, his modernizing blueprint, particularly as embodied in much of the 1931 constitution, was aimed at, and partially succeeded in, diminishing the powers of the potentates in favor of a centralized modern national state apparatus.

A prime example of such a clash was the feud between Menelik's grandson Lij Iassu (b. 1894) and Haile Selassie, then known by his given name, Tafari. The feud had degenerated into an open military confrontation in 1916, which ended in Lij Iassu's defeat and the triumph of Tafari and his "modernizing party." That triumph, which will be described in more detail in chapter 4, was a crucial blow for progress and enlightenment. It meant the introduction of more modern education and the start of the building of infrastructures befitting a modern state.

Both before and after ascending to the imperial throne, Tafari faced incredible challenges. How he met those challenges, sometimes with success, other times suffering temporary setbacks, is a story that reflects his remarkable political skills and his dogged determination to impose his will on a backward nation.

The Ethiopian State

What is the core essence of the Ethiopian polity that Haile Selassie inherited? To answer this question, it is necessary to make reference to three related historical facts.

The first concerns the Christian origin of the state, which began in the fourth century AD with the conversion of the Axumite kingdom to Christianity.

The second is the expansion and consolidation of the Christian state, incorporating a wide variety of linguistic, cultural, and ethnic groups. The expansion continued for centuries until it reached its apogee by the end of the nineteenth century with Emperor Menelik's conquests, which expanded the state to include much of present-day Ethiopia, adding more territory and different ethnic groups and making the country an empire-state.

The third concerns the emergence of Islam in the seventh century AD. As it spread in and around the Horn of Africa subregion, including around Ethiopia, the challenge it posed to the Ethiopian state led to religious (Christian) nationalism becoming, in reaction, the defining characteristic of the Ethiopian state. The first serious threat to the survival of the Ethiopian Christian state was the Ahmed Gragne campaign in the sixteenth century. Although the state survived politically, Ethiopia's complexity in social and cultural terms originates in the Ahmed Gragne campaign and its aftermath. As the religion of a significant proportion of the Ethiopian people, Islam is an important part of the complexity—indeed, the richness—of the Ethiopian sociocultural reality. Moreover, the influx of the Oromo, who would become the single most numerous ethnic group in the country, into much of central and northern Ethiopia after the Gragne campaign added to the country's demographic and ethnolinguistic complexity.

A fact of great political significance in contemporary Ethiopia is that until recently the core of the state remained a monopoly of one ethnic group. At the center was the king, professing the Orthodox Christian faith and provided by the church with ideological backing in return for economic support, principally in the form of land grants and related privileges. The church-state coexistence, with the armed forces and bureaucratic apparatus providing, respectively, security and administrative structure, is the historic Ethiopian version of what is known in Egypt these days as the "deep state."

The crisis during the pre-1916 coup d'état, particularly as it concerned the Islamic sympathies and predilections of Lij Iassu, was a twentieth-century version of the Islamic challenge to the deep state, and the deep state's response resulted in Lij Iassu's overthrow, as we shall see in chapter 4.

2

Tafari

Orphaned Prince Steeled by Adversity

Tafari was born in the village of Ejersa Goro, five kilometers east of the city of Harar, to Leul (Prince) Ras Makonnen, a devoted cousin and trusted servant of Emperor Menelik, and Woizero Yeshimebet. Ras Makonnen took mother and child to his palace in Harar, where he was governor-general. Woizero Yeshimebet died delivering her second child a year and a half after Tafari was born.

When Tafari was four years old, Ras Makonnen decided to relocate him and his cousin Imru (later Ras), who was of the same age and also an orphan, to the small town of Kombolsha, not far from Harar. They lived in a gated compound under the watchful eyes of women guardians, who no doubt provided the missing maternal element to both children. Soldiers guarded their residence, and the boys were allowed to venture outside the compound only with the permission and in the company of their guardians. At age five, they were introduced to traditional Ethiopian studies, reading and writing Amharic and Geez, as well as studying the Psalms and *Melk'a*

Mariam and *Melk'a Yesus* (Life of Mary and Life of Jesus). Their Amharic and Geez teacher was Memh'r (teacher) Woldekidan, who on one memorable occasion took them to meet and receive the blessing of Abune Yohannes, a Coptic (Egyptian) bishop.

Ras Makonnen traveled frequently as Menelik's emissary to Europe. On the rare moments of his return, he would send for the boys to visit him in his government house in Harar, where they enjoyed his warm fatherly company for a few days. It is easy to imagine how much Tafari missed his father, to whom he was very much attached. At age eight, the boys were relocated to Harar to live in a more pleasant environment in a much larger house with more amenities. There they continued the traditional Ethiopian education that they had begun in Kombolsha, to which were added other subjects in a normal school curriculum, including learning French. Their teacher, who also acted as their guardian, was Dr. Vitalia, whom Ras Makonnen had brought from France for the purpose. Another teacher was an Ethiopian Catholic cleric named Aba (Father) Samuel, who belonged to the Catholic Mission of Aba Indrias. Between the two of them, the teachers organized morning and afternoon classes, alternating between French and other academic subjects, including reading and writing Amharic. In his memoirs, Ras Imru remembers with fondness the happy times they passed at the school, where they were also given riding lessons once a week. Ras Makonnen's decision to import teachers to instruct Tafari and other children of the nobility in Harar was a reflection of the larger program of modernization introduced by Menelik, which Makonnen earnestly emulated.

Some accounts of Tafari's childhood education contend that from the age of seven, when he first started to read and write Amharic, he seems to have become aware that he would one day succeed Menelik as a ruler of Ethiopia. He demanded from his Amharic tutor all the available books on Ethiopian history, and listened avidly to tales of the Solomonic dynasty, of which he understood himself to be an offshoot. By the time he was eleven, he had learned enough French to converse with Aba Samuel. His father proudly told Menelik about it, and Menelik, curious, requested that Tafari be brought to his court.

The introduction of modern education to Ethiopia under Menelik was accompanied by other modernization projects, including in particular the expansion of infrastructure. In this respect the Franco-Ethiopian Railway, running from Djibouti to Addis Ababa, was the most important, not only because it facilitated the expansion of trade and investment, but because it exposed Ethiopians to the rest of the world and opened it up to modern values and institutions, including banking and an early appreciation of the value of money. An illustration of this is the fact that Ras Makonnen opened a bank account abroad, as Tafari would do later when he became regent and crown prince.

Conditioned by Adversity

Ras Makonnen died suddenly in 1905. The loss of the popular governor of Harar hit his admirers and supporters hard, and none was more affected than the young prince, deprived of his one surviving parent, who had acted as both mother and father to him. A touching photograph of Ras Makonnen and young Tafari, taken a couple of years before Makonnen's death, shows deep filial attachment. In his memoirs, Ras Imru gives dramatic descriptions of the public reaction to Makonnen's death, including the colorful ceremonies of his funeral and the wailing and demonstrations of loyalty exhibited by his servants and all the grandees of Harar.

In all the public display of support for and commiseration with the young Tafari, who had just turned thirteen, he maintained the stoic self-control and discipline that would mark his behavior throughout his life and illustrious career. His quiet and calm behavior throughout the public mourning, which lasted over a week, impressed all observers. It was as if he had been prepared for yet another misfortune and had steeled himself for it. Ras Makonnen's frequent travels must have added poignancy to the motherless prince's loneliness, but at the same time they must have helped prepare him for the tough years ahead, which would involve him in the deadly feuds between the contending forces in Menelik's palace and elsewhere in the empire.

3

Harar, Ras Makonnen, and Menelik's Court

Harar: Model Province of the Empire

In the last decades of Menelik's imperial expansion campaign, Harar was the crown jewel of the empire. In terms of the advent of modern ideas and institutions, it had become the leading city in Ethiopia. Following in the footsteps of his imperial predecessor, Emperor Yohannes, Menelik snatched Harar from the Harar city-state, ruled by Emir Abdullahi. After the decisive battle of Chelenko in 1887, when Menelik's victorious forces occupied the city and all the surrounding area of what is today Harar region,[1] Menelik appointed his cousin, Ras Makonnen, as Harar's governor. Tafari's birth in Harar was thus a consequence of that appointment.

The Harar region, with its diverse topography and great geographical contrasts, is a microcosm of Ethiopia. Lying on the eastern part of the country, Harar is bordered by Djibouti to the east and Somalia to the east and southeast. To its west it is bordered by the Shoa and Arsi regions, and to its south and southwest lies Bale. Its most distinctive features are a highland zone with temperate climate, as well as an arid zone stretching to the east.

Ras Makonnen was, by most accounts, a popular governor, who administered Harar with a firm hand but with justice and fairness, especially in regard to the way his minions, the empire's agents, treated the "conquered" peasantry. Makonnen also played a significant role in rallying thousands of the best regiments from Harar, forces that played a key role in Menelik's victory over the Italians at the historic battle of Adua in 1896. He was also a top advisor and close confidant of Menelik, who sent him as his envoy to special occasions such as coronations as well as to negotiate treaties on his behalf. In today's parlance, he would be minister of foreign affairs. In 1902, Makonnen made his second trip to Europe as Menelik's envoy to attend the coronation of King Edward VII of England. Such exposure to Europe reinforced his desire for modernization. As already noted, Menelik, on being told how well Tafari spoke French, had had the boy brought to Addis Ababa. At Menelik's court, Tafari conversed with a French-speaking diplomat. Menelik was duly impressed not only by the boy's fluency in French, which the diplomat confirmed, but by his confident conduct. Menelik, evidently seeing brightness and promise in the young boy, ordered that he attend the court to learn about royal governance, and also that he enroll in the newly opened Menelik School.

Makonnen was so close to Menelik that many considered him a possible successor to the imperial throne after Menelik's death. It is also likely that Makonnen himself entertained that idea. That may be why he appointed Tafari as Dejasmach (military commander) when he was thirteen years old, in the expectation, shared by Makonnen's party of modernizers and all Harar grandees, that Menelik would make Makonnen his successor and that Tafari would then be in a position to succeed his father.

Alas, that was not to be. Makonnen's sudden death proved a deadly blow to such expectations, opening the question of succession to more dramatic controversies, court intrigues, and infighting, which would eventually be resolved by military confrontation and war. Any idea that Tafari's brightness and Menelik's favorable regard toward him and his father might automatically entitle Tafari to succeed to Menelik's throne seemed to be relegated to oblivion. At least so it seemed at first.

Menelik's Court before and after His Death

Just as there were people who wanted Makonnen to succeed Menelik, there were also those at Menelik's court who were pleased at Makonnen's death. Of the latter, the two most important were Menelik's wife, Empress Taitu, and King Michael of Wollo, father of Lij Iassu. Taitu had her own ambition of succeeding her ailing husband, and King Michael wanted his son, who was Menelik's grandson through his mother, to become emperor. Both Taitu and Michael knew that if Makonnen attained the throne, Tafari would eventually succeed him, dealing a deadly blow to their aspirations.

Then Menelik suffered his first stroke. Upon his recovery, he summoned Tafari from Harar and on November 1, 1905, appointed him governor of Selale, an important district in the central province of Shoa. Tafari, aged thirteen, administered Selale by proxy and remained at the court, where over the next few years he learned the art of government. He was also, by acutely observing instructive cases of court intrigue, studying and making mental note of schemers, connivers, and plotters, learning the art of survival.

To the surprise of many, Menelik decided to appoint Lij Iassu his successor under the guardianship of a trusted warlord, Ras Bitwoded Tesemma. The records do not indicate how Menelik's unexpected decision affected Tafari. But one can speculate as to how disappointed he must have been, particularly when Iassu's behavior and poor performance in governing became an open secret and were widely resented. Menelik then suffered a second stroke, after which his wife and some of her court allies ruled in his name for a short while. This development did not sit well with most of those in Menelik's court and the provincial potentates (Rases) with their own militia as well as other men of influence, whom we can call power brokers.

When Ras Bitwoded Tesemma died in 1911, Iassu, still a teenager, was free to assert his power. Encouraged by

Empress Taitu, he indulged in acts of debauchery and brutality, while completely neglecting his governing duties. Effective central government disappeared. Then, following a third stroke, Menelik died in 1913. Taitu engaged in power manipulation, dismissing people appointed by Menelik and replacing them with her own kinsmen from the north. Tafari was by then a very mature and generally well-regarded man of twenty-one, but Iassu's supporters and Iassu himself did not look on him with favor. Tafari had to walk a fine line between appearing loyal to Menelik's chosen successor and at the same time monitoring the situation like an eagle surveying a field filled with innocent sheep abandoned by their shepherd.

The ambitious Empress Taitu sealed her fate by overstepping her bounds, causing a decisive reaction against her by the ministers appointed by Menelik. The ministers, who represented the general sentiment of the Shoan ruling group, ousted Taitu and banished her to live a life of penance near a church around Entoto Mountain.

4

The Feud with Iassu— the Plot Thickens

Before her ouster from power, one of Empress Taitu's significant acts was to appoint Dejasmach Tafari as governor of Harar, to the general applause of the modernizing forces in Ethiopia. The Shoan ministers who overthrew Taitu canceled all her appointments, save that of Tafari; in fact, they reviewed his case and publicly confirmed it sending him to his father's domain with added prestige and power to continue the modernizing programs that had been started by his father. Ras Imru, who was a key figure in Tafari's camp and part of Harar's governing establishment, recorded the details of some of the modernizing programs, including administrative reforms, education, and open encouragement of new approaches to economic and fiscal policies.

All these measures increased Tafari's popularity, which proved to be a double-edged sword. On the one hand, it confirmed him as the authentic leader of the few young, educated elite and their supporters in the government and emboldened him in his quest for the empire's supreme power, confirming his rightful place in the succession to the Solomonic dynasty. On the other hand, it stoked fear and resentment in Iassu and his supporters. Before his appointment as governor of Harar, Tafari always played by the traditional rule book of protocol, taking care to pay the homage due to Iassu as his political superior, despite his own secret ambitions. It was a delicate situation, involving a game of duplicity, ambiguity, and subterfuge, and Tafari had become a master player by that time, thanks to his own personal experience, particularly at Menelik's court. An example of Tafari's political skills is his response when Iassu, wishing to put him under his control, suggested to Tafari that he marry one of his relatives. Tafari deftly used the language of ambiguity—not refusing, but not exactly accepting the suggestion.

Meanwhile, Iassu's rule (or rather misrule) went from bad to worse. He almost destroyed the central government carefully erected by Menelik, and the imperial court, which under Menelik functioned smoothly, was turned to a hornet's nest in which confusion and uncertainty prevailed. In that chaos, only Harar was stable, as Tafari put into practice revolutionary forms of governance, including improvement in the treatment of peasants, land tenure, and taxation.

Some well-known nobles, led by one Ras Abate, actually planned a coup to overthrow Iassu. But those opposed to the coup were able to thwart it. Empress Taitu was at the center of it, and a member of her camp tried to enlist

Tafari's support. In language that exemplified Tafari's skill, he answered by saying he was too young to get involved in so momentous a scheme: "It is simply over my head." In his memoirs, Ras Imru, who had inklings of Tafari's ambitions, expresses admiration of such uncanny ability.

It was at this time that Taitu appointed Tafari to be governor of Harar, while also suggesting a suitable marriage with one of her relatives. Though the decline in her power was already known, and a plot to oust her was already a foregone conclusion, Tafari paid her a respectful farewell visit before he headed to Harar. In the language of gambling, he hedged all his bets. At the same time, he did not miss an opportunity to demonstrate by example how his mode of rule differed from the disastrous rule of Iassu. One of the serious complaints leveled at Iassu was that he consistently favored the Muslims of the empire, showing complete disregard for the old system of government and especially for the Christian Orthodox Church's teachings. In an interesting contrast, whereas his father, King Michael, was born a Muslim and was converted to Christianity by Emperor Yohannes, Iassu seemed to wish to become a Muslim. Those who defend Iassu's Islamic tendencies claim that he was a visionary who wanted to unite Ethiopia by building a firm bridge between the two religions. If that is a fair assessment of Iassu's vision, it was not accompanied by the requisite need to take into account the stubborn reality of Ethiopia at the time, or the key role of the Christian Orthodox Church in Ethiopian history and politics.

Additionally, Iassu's partiality to the Muslims of Ethiopia was complicated by his partiality to the wrong powers in the World War I conflict, the Germans and Turks, which went against the interests of the European powers that surrounded Ethiopia, the British and the French. In the slowly developing drama pitting the modernizing or "progressive" forces rallying behind Tafari and those of Iassu, the position of the European powers was crucial. Tafari, ever the clever manipulator of forces and events, used his British and French contacts as well as Ethiopians sympathetic to his cause to discredit Iassu's politics of support for the wrong side.

He also expressed his dismay and bitter disappointment at Lij Iassu's continued abuse of the sacred duties of his imperial office, entrusted to him by no less a historic personage than his maternal grandfather, Menelik. A historic denouement was approaching. Lij Iassu was spending more time away from the capital, hunting, wenching, and fraternizing with Muslim leaders in the Danakil plains and elsewhere. In some historical accounts, there is even a hint of his being engaged in slave trading at least once in the southern district of Ghimira, as well as in atrocious behavior such as rape and massacre.[1] Tafari's response is interesting in its subtlety and suggestiveness. He said, "Lij Iassu sought in everything the company and counsel of worthless men who only wanted their immediate profit, while the great nobles and ministers became hostile and removed their hearts from him."[2]

As Tafari's popularity increased, with his supporters openly praising his leadership qualities, the relationship between him and Iassu worsened. This led Tafari's supporters to imagine the worst, including the danger of his being kidnapped by the powerful Ras Mikael, Iassu's father, governor of the Wollo region, where the famous Meqdela fortress with its inaccessible royal prison called Wohni Amba is found. Readers of Samuel Johnson's 1715 novel, *Ras Selas,* will recall that the locus for the novel was the same Wohni Amba, in which princes who were considered potential threats to the reigning monarch were incarcerated. Ras Mikael was so determined to have his son rule Ethiopia that it was feared he would not hesitate to remove his son's potential rivals. During Menelik's last days, his powerful consort, Empress Taitu, had consigned a disgraced Ras Abate to Mikael for imprisonment at Meqdela.[3]

As unrest mounted, Iassu's open defiance of the political reality of Ethiopia and association with Islam provided the conservative Orthodox Christian nobility with a pretext for orchestrating his removal from power. As the reasons for his removal are well established, and the result was the eventual rise of Tafari to become Ethiopia's leader, a few words of reflection on Iassu's vision would be worthwhile.

Iassu's Vision

There is a yet unanswered oral tradition that challenges the official version of modern Ethiopian history as regards the place of Lij Iassu. The gist of the challenge is that all official history is the "victor's version," written to please the powers that be and to suit their scripted version. Implicit in this oral tradition is a demand for a fairer and more accurate rendering of Iassu's place, which would require a reinterpretation of the reasons for and circumstances of the charge of his apostasy and his alleged Islamic favoritism. As to Iassu's fitness to rule the complex empire-state built so carefully by Menelik, the record supports a judgment that is not favorable to him. Certainly, again on the record, in terms of mental fitness—of sobriety and balance—there is no comparison to Tafari.

However, in the context of a constitutionally guaranteed equality, one wonders whether such a victor's version of history would pass muster today, particularly in view of an aroused Ethiopian Muslim community that contends that the constitutional guarantee of equality extends to all citizens in every respect. Such a challenge inevitably raises issues of the right balance between human rights (including religious rights) on the one hand, and stability of the state on the other. The fear on the part of those who cling to what we may call the officially sanctioned version of history is a genuine fear that their dearly held values would be under threat of being, at the very least, devalued. These are predominantly adherents to the Orthodox Christian faith, to whom the close ties that bind church and state form part of the historical DNA of the Ethiopian state. They feel discomfort from the kind of challenge the Iassu story and his supposed unifying vision implies.

Was Iassu's vision a mirage, or does it contain within it the possibility of reimagining a history in which Christian and Muslim citizens would be made to feel equally secure by a constitutionally guaranteed principle of equality, leaving the actual mutual acceptance and accommodation to be worked out in the crucible of social and political interactions? This is a serious question that all thoughtful citizens of Ethiopia (and of Eritrea) should reflect upon. To that end, the history of the Iassu-Tafari feud provides useful lessons.

5

The 1916 Coup d'État and the Rise of a Man of Destiny

> The same arts that did gain
> A power, must it maintain.
> —Andrew Marvell

Between Two Worlds

The world of Tafari and of his cohort of modernizing supporters was an imagined world of progress pitted against a backward-looking traditional society. The first time the Ethiopian state confronted modern (European) ideas and institutions in a serious way was during the tumultuous reign of Emperor Teodros in the mid-nineteenth century. Teodros was shocked to find that his country was at a disadvantage compared to European countries, notably Britain, with which he corresponded and by which he was later defeated. Teodros strongly believed that Ethiopia needed to emulate Europe and catch up in its material and technical achievements; but he fell short of achieving his goal.

Menelik, who spent his youth at Teodros's court, first as prisoner, then as a favored adopted son, learned a thing or two from him. Much of his policy of what we can call modernization was inspired by Teodros's vision of a united Ethiopia with modern administration and a national army and civil service. Through a combination of good fortune and an expanded and more richly endowed country than Teodros had ruled over, Menelik was able to fulfill some of Teodros's aims. And whereas Teodros dealt harshly with any opposition, including an ultraconservative clergy, Menelik followed a policy of accommodation and compromise. It was because of his wise policies as well as his popularity that Menelik was able to hold a backward church leashed and fearful of crossing him by standing in the way of the progress achieved under his reign, such as it was. But with Menelik incapacitated by a debilitating stroke, the forces of tradition seemed to have a new lease on life, with the backing of powerful feudal lords who were masters of their own domains. Menelik's expanded empire provided many of these lords with profitable land and subject peoples whom they could exploit. In this, the church worked hand in hand with the state as an integral part of the "civilizing mission" in a new imperial enterprise engineered and driven by Menelik and his minions. In that sense, therefore, Menelik is truly the creator of a new and expanded Ethiopia.[1]

It was in this context that the daring idea of modernization imagined by Tafari and his modernizing group of followers was advanced. In the proverbial opposition between an irresistible force and an immovable object, the forces of change led by Tafari were opposed by the forces of reaction, including Menelik's widow, Empress Taitu, and the provincial and feudal lords. The opposed forces represented not only conflicting ideas about modernity and progress but, perhaps more importantly, conflicting interests. It was a power struggle between a reactionary feudal class and an incipient investing bourgeoisie that was small in number but dynamic and forward-looking, with knowledge as its initial capital.

Tafari, standing at the center of that dynamic class, attracted all the young men with a modern education and those among the products of traditional education who had nevertheless seen the advantages of modernization. Two of the best known among the latter were Takele Woldehawariat and Woldegiorgis Woldeyohannes, who would later play key roles in Haile Selassie's government.

Tafari the Antifeudal Modernizer

It seems a contradiction in terms to characterize as antifeudal a prince like Tafari. The truth is that he was a prince born to a progressively inclined father, Ras Makonnen, who was Menelik's principal point of contact with the world of European ideas and institutions like banking and trade. When Makonnen traveled to Europe, one of the things he did was to open a bank account in Europe. Makonnen appreciated the power of money and the monetized economy, as did Tafari, and they both used the geographical position of Harar and the French-Ethiopian Railway company as the principal entry point for advancing trade and commercial development in Ethiopia. But while Tafari was a prince-entrepreneur who appreciated the power of money and of modern ideas and institutions, he was also keenly aware of the power of the landed gentry and handled them with care until he was in a position to control them through the agency of a centralized modern state. Tafari's conviction of the power of modern ideas and institutions would be further reinforced by his visit to European countries after he was secure as crown prince and chief executive officer following the coup d'état versus Iassu.[2]

During the period of uncertainty, with Tafari's star shining more and more brightly, a fearful Iassu agreed to Tafari's appointment as governor of Harar, presumably hoping to keep him away from the center, where the drama was being played out. Iassu also made Tafari swear an oath of loyalty. With his growing influence, Tafari faced the danger of being kidnapped by King Michael, Iassu's doting father, and imprisoned in Wohni Amba (the dreadful royal prison where former kings had kept potential rivals). The relationship between Iassu and Tafari had deteriorated. In 1915, Iassu traveled to Harar where his close connections with Muslim leaders became evident.

It was also during this period that Tafari nearly drowned in Haremaya (Alemaya) Lake. His former teacher, Aba Samuel, lost his own life in saving him. The suspicion that Iassu had bribed an agent to cause the accident, if true, only shows how desperate he had become about Tafari's growing power and influence. In May 1916, Iassu summoned Tafari to Addis Ababa. This gave Tafari an opportunity to consult with the Shoan power brokers, including the Council of Ministers. In his memoirs, Ras Imru describes how, while Tafari was in Addis Ababa, Iassu, in a last desperate act, traveled to Harar to mobilize his Muslim followers in the province and to distribute arms, preparing them for a final confrontation with Tafari's forces.[3] By September of that year, the forces were aligning, and there was tension in Addis Ababa, as some of Tafari's educated supporters felt their lives to be threatened. Two of these, Paulos Menameno and Aba Petros of the Catholic mission in Dire Dawa, happened to visit Harar, where they warned Ras Imru to take cautionary measures.[4]

According to Ras Imru's account, in addition to mobilizing and arming Muslim forces, Iassu also gave a banquet to prominent members of the Christian gentry, including veteran statesman Dejasmach Balcha, and gave a speech accusing Tafari of conspiring against him. In a dramatic exchange of words, Iassu was told in no uncertain terms that it was he who was conspiring against the state by consorting with Islam forces. Iassu denied the charge and, putting his hand on the Bible, swore an oath of loyalty to the Christian faith before a disbelieving audience.

Soon thereafter, Iassu removed Dejasmach Tafari from his governorship of Harar, and at the same time ordered an invasion of his Harar residence. This act provided Tafari a reason to release himself from the oath of loyalty, thus allowing himself to take a leading role in the 1916 coup.

The Coup d'État

Aware of Tafari's influence, the Shoan power brokers, headed by Fitawrari Habtegiorgis, had extracted a promise from him not to seek the throne. On February 11, 1917, they decided to depose Iassu and appoint Menelik's daughter, Zewditu, empress, with Tafari as chief executive and heir to the throne and Habtegiorgis as minister of war. This gave rise to what historians of the period have called a triumvirate, though Zewditu was a "sleeping partner," overwhelmed by Tafari's dynamic power.

Iassu was deposed but not finished; he escaped capture and headed to the Danakil plains, where he felt safe among people he considered loyal Muslim devotees. He was eventually captured, and died in prison in 1936. The Iassu-Tafari saga was finally settled in October 1916 at the battle of Sagalaye, in which the forces of Iassu's father, King Michael, were defeated by Tafari's forces. In sum, there were three factors that caused Iassu's fall. First was his dismissal of Tafari from his Harar governorship, which provoked a hostile reaction from Tafari's loyalists. Secondly, his alliance with the Germans and Turks in the 1914–18 war aroused the anger of the British and the French, pushing them to Tafari's side. Thirdly, his dalliance with Muslim leaders and appearance of abandoning the Christian faith alienated the powerful Christian establishment. The patriarch publicly proclaimed an act of excommunication, releasing all concerned from the oath of loyalty they had sworn in accordance with Emperor Menelik's demands upon designating his grandson, Iassu, to succeed him.

Conflicts arose within the triumvirate, which inevitably led to plots and counterplots. In one such conspiracy, the Council of Ministers, presumably under Habtegiorgis's urging, proposed to rein in Tafari's power, which Tafari vigorously resisted. In the power struggle, Tafari's loyalists everywhere showed superior organization and determination. In a showdown at the Jan-Meda plains, Tafari's forces were able to literally shout down the opponents and secure the support of a majority of the power brokers, thus defeating the conspiracy.

To confirm his freshly gained executive power, Tafari was able to banish all members of the Council of Ministers, except Habtegiorgis, to their respective provinces. Tafari learned a great lesson from all this plotting and counterplotting. It was probably at that time that a popular verse was composed:

> Harar'n babatu shoa'n begulbetu
> Wollo'n begabcha
> Ingdih Man Alla, Teqil ante b'cha!

(He got Harar through his father. He got Shoa by dint of force, and Wollo through marriage. Now who else is there except you—O Teqil!)⁵

A Man of Destiny

Throughout the time of bitter conflict that ended in his favor, what distinguished Tafari Makonnen (soon to be renamed Haile Selassie) was his clear vision for his country, a vision defined by his acute sense of the need for his country to adopt modern ideas and methods in order to join the family of civilized nations. While Menelik entertained similar sentiments, Tafari had to fight for them tooth and nail, nearly losing his life in the attempt. His toughness and determination as well as his unique political skills equipped him for the enormous task, involving some serious conflict with an old established system. But as the title of chapter 2, "Orphaned Prince Steeled by Adversity," suggests, a deep desire to attain the supreme power of the state must have been conditioned by deeper psychological factors having to do with losing a nurturing mother and having a frequently absent father who also died when he was still young. One can doubtless cite other examples of historical figures whose single-minded quest for certain things in life (such as power) was conditioned by similar experiences.

One example will suffice to distinguish Tafari from another great Ethiopian historical figure, Habtegiorgis, with whom he was involved in a tug-of-war during much of the triumvirate period. Tafari's quiet mode of operation, which masked an iron will and guile, enabled him to persuade his foes to relent, particularly in his dogged struggle to end slavery. The issue of slavery came to the fore when, in 1923, Tafari vigorously advocated that Ethiopia should apply for admission to the League of Nations. There was opposition within the league to Ethiopia, as a state that permitted slavery, being allowed to join, as well as tremendous opposition from conservatives within Ethiopia, most of whom owned slaves. Tafari was able to persuade some of the most influential men, such as Habtegiorgis, that membership in the League of Nations would be good for Ethiopia's security, and convince the most important provincial governors to back a proclamation to abolish slavery. Considering the conditions of the time, this was no mean achievement, for slavery was part of the socioeconomic fabric of society. To put it succinctly, the abolition of slavery meant the liberation of a mass of humanity that was chained to the feudal lords and their hangers-on. It would mean the end of the privileges of feudal lords and their eventual impoverishment. Their resistance would make Tafari's task enormous, if not impossible. That slavery was not ended (indeed could not be ended) then is a function of the hard reality the emperor was up against. It had to wait until another day. But the war against slavery (and slaveholders) had been declared.

Tafari's next bold stroke occurred in 1924, when he proposed to go on an extended tour of Europe, and to take along a number of the figures who were posing a threat to him at the time, including the provincial governors Ras Hailu of Gojam and Ras Seyoum of Tigray. Including them was a risky and delicate task, as he explains in his autobiography.[6] Before Tafari, no Ethiopian head of state had ever ventured out of the country. Prior to the European visit in 1924, he had traveled to the then British possession of Aden.

Before reaching Europe, Tafari visited Cairo and Jerusalem, then proceeded to Marseilles, Rome, Paris, and London. During his four and a half months of travel, he visited educational institutions as well as government and commercial enterprises and industrial plants, while Ras Hailu and Ras Seyoum and other members of his entourage went on a sightseeing and shopping spree. Tafari set out to turn his diplomatic tour de force into a propaganda weapon that would change the minds of the conservative opponents of progress. For example, once the Rases and their kind got used to such products of industrial civilization as cars, they would be more inclined to accept the idea of progress in general. Cars needed roads, and building roads would mean the building of further infrastructure. It would be the beginning of a long process of development.

Tafari knew, of course, that at the heart of all development lay education. Therefore, immediately after his European tour he opened a school, the Tafari Makonnen

School, with his own money and sent for teachers to be brought there. At the opening ceremony of the school, Tafari harangued the conservative assembly of Rases and others who had been dragooned to attend. "The time has passed for mere lip-service to our country," he said. "The crying need of our people is education, without which we cannot maintain our independence. The proof of real patriotism is to recognize this fact and—in the case of those who possess the means—to found schools and to forward the cause of education in every way. I have built this school as a beginning and as an example, which I appeal to the wealthy among the people to follow."[7]

Commenting on Tafari's speech and initiative, British traveler Charles F. Rey presciently wrote, "If it succeeds and extends [it] may affect profoundly the future of the country. It is of course for this reason that it was opposed by the reactionary elements." When the school opened in 1926, it had places for 180 children, bringing the total of places available at the time in the whole of Ethiopia to 291.[8]

In view of these simple facts, it is not difficult to imagine the scale of the effort and resources it would take to advance the education of Ethiopians to fulfill the developmental needs of the country. Any leader in his place, whether a king or president, would have had his work cut out for him; it was not an enviable position to be in. Yet Tafari then, and later as Haile Selassie, was not awed by the enormity of the challenge. Indeed, he seems to have thrived on meeting it.

The resistance to change that was the cause of so much conflict in the governing triumvirate slowly gave way to reluctant acceptance. When Habtegiorgis died in 1926, Tafari was left to deal with the aging and gradually weakening Empress Zewditu. Not long after Habtegiorgis's death, the empress, presumably at the behest of some ambitious chiefs in her court, tried to overthrow Tafari in what became known as the Aba Wukaw incident. Aba Wukaw was out to arrest Tafari in his palace in the name of the empress on the grounds that Tafari was undermining her authority and usurping her power. Aba Wukaw failed and was brought in chains before Tafari, where the assembled noblemen (whose actions were less than noble) recommended that he be hanged for his crime. Tafari spared his life but sent him to prison. The occasion provided Tafari's supporters a golden opportunity to force the empress to name Tafari king, a title that in a traditional society such as this one would significantly enhance his authority. Never one to miss an occasion warranting publicity, Tafari ordered that his coronation be attended by envoys of foreign powers, especially those with colonies around Ethiopia. Accordingly, preparations were planned for a grand ceremony. But a ceremony on an even grander scale was to take place soon, to which governments of almost all of Europe would be invited to send their envoys. That occasion was the coronation of Tafari as emperor upon the death of Empress Zewditu.

6

From King to Emperor

Proclamation of the Central Elements of Change

In early April 1930, two years after she was forced to crown Tafari king, Zewditu died. Hers is a sad tale of an unfortunate princess who was a prisoner of circumstance, caught in the middle of a power play among ruthless people, her position making her the object of their ambitious schemes. These people included Menelik's widow, the redoubtable Empress Taitu, who wedded Zewditu to her nephew, Ras Gugsa, a northern warlord. All her life the unfortunate woman had been a target for ambitious men who sought to marry her by hook or crook. One such was Ras Abate, who made an unsuccessful attempt to invade the palace and kidnap her. Had he succeeded, their marriage would have been a fait accompli, according to the traditional Ethiopian practice of *tilfia* (elopement). He failed miserably.

Gugsa was still married to Zewditu when the Shoan men of power elevated her to her father's throne, replacing Iassu. For reasons of state, these men prevented Gugsa from becoming consort. Tafari in particular feared Gugsa's influence as a threat to his own plans. This was one of the many examples in which the mild-mannered Tafari showed his iron will and ruthlessness. He simply forbade the empress to see her husband, announcing to her that henceforth she was divorced from him. She had no choice but to resign herself to her fate as a pawn in the merciless intrigue of palace politics. Zewditu apparently loved Ras Gugsa and did not forgive Tafari for denying her the love and comfort of her husband. Love, in this case, did not conquer all, contrary to the old adage *amor omnia vincit!*

The frustrated Gugsa rebelled, raising a northern army and posing a serious threat to Tafari's position and even the unity of the country. The full fury of the Shoan armed forces was brought upon him, including the use of air power for the first time in Ethiopia as a weapon of war. He was defeated and killed, and it was the news of her husband's death that dealt the coup de grâce to the ailing empress.

Immediately upon Zewditu's death, Tafari issued a proclamation informing the Ethiopian public of her death and his succession to the throne as emperor under the name of Haile Selassie. The substantial part of the proclamation reads as follows:

> PROCLAMATION . . . In accordance with the Proclamation which our Creator abiding in His people, and electing us, did cause to be made, we have lived without breach of our Covenant as mother and son.

> Now, in that by law and commandment of God, none that is human may avoid return to earth, Her Majesty the Empress, after a few days of sickness, has departed this life. The passing of Her Majesty the Empress is grievous for myself and for the whole of the Empire. Since it is the long-standing custom that when a King, the Shepherd of his people, shall die, a King replaces him, I being upon the seat of David to which I was betrothed, will, by God's charity, watch over you.
>
> Trader, trade! Farmer plough! I shall govern you by the law and ordinance that has come to me, handed down from fathers.[1]

The sentiment that the death of the empress was grievous for him shows hypocrisy in the service of "reasons of state," for in view of the decade-long struggle that preceded her death, no one could have been happier than he at her passing.

So, under the name of Haile Selassie, King Tafari, at the age of thirty-seven, became emperor of Ethiopia.[2] He decided to make his coronation a memorable occasion, one that would add value to his diplomacy and domestic politics. He wanted to send a clear signal to the international community, especially European powers, as well as impress upon Ethiopians the principal objectives of his vision, stressing the dire need for education and for the introduction of centralized administration as the backbone of unity and peaceful development.

Central Elements of the Required Change

Haile Selassie did not waste time in reordering his priorities and reorganizing his principal supporters. He made it abundantly clear to all concerned, especially his band of followers, that the first agenda was clipping the wings of the provincial potentates, the Rases, and bringing them under the control of a centralized state effectively controlled by him and a select cadre of modern-minded people. Next, he repeatedly mentioned education as a necessary instrument of modernization as well as a culture-enhancing force, and thus of great value in and of itself. This he had always emphasized by taking initiative and spending his own money to establish educational institutions. The rest of his program, such as economic development, including building infrastructure, would follow suit inevitably. Additionally, and no less important, social issues, including the need to create a regime of equality as a fundamental basis of peace and social solidarity, would have to be guaranteed under a new constitutional dispensation. Emperor Haile Selassie showed once again his considerable political skills in planning and organizing his coronation. First of all he secured the services of the few educated Ethiopians in the planning. Principal among these was Fitawrari Teklehawariat, a protégé of Ras Makonnen, who had studied military science in Russia, sent there by Ras Makonnen with Menelik's blessing. He had also spent time in France studying agricultural science.

The emperor summoned all the Rases to Addis Ababa to attend the coronation, and subsequently kept them as hostages for a whole year until he was ready to spring on them the most important instrument of his modernizing scheme.[3] In 1931, one year after his coronation, he announced that a modern constitution had been drafted that would be the basis of his government, including the government in the provinces. Modeled on a number of foreign constitutions, including that of Japan, it was drafted by a committee in which Teklehawariat played a key role. He was also given the privilege of reading and explaining its basic features to an assembly of all the most important personalities of the empire, including the Rases and their associates in the capital. Teklehawariat was eloquent and bold in explaining the basic features of the constitution.

In his speech delivered at the signing of the constitution, the emperor affirmed that it would mark a transformation of Ethiopia into a limited monarchy, "whereby the whole people may be made to share our labors in accomplishing the heavy task of government at which former Emperors labored alone." To those ends, the constitution introduced two deliberative chambers—a senate, appointed by the emperor, and a chamber of deputies, chosen by dignitaries and chiefs to advise the emperor. The members would come from the various provinces, chosen under the authority of the emperor "until such time as the people have reached a degree of education and experience enabling them to make the choice themselves.... Decisions taken in parliament and approved by the Emperor will be executed for the whole of Ethiopia and by Ministers."[4]

This, for the time, was indeed revolutionary.

Many commentators in Europe sneered at all this, calling it "window dressing," while a few well-wishers thought it a brave first step from feudalism toward democracy. Time would tell which of these views was well founded. But in its objectives, it was a blow for change, striking at the root of the powers and privileges of all potentates on three issues: security, taxation, and local administration.

With respect to security, henceforth there would be a salaried national army under the control of the central government. The Rases would no longer have the right to keep a private provincial army that could threaten or undermine the central government. Needless to say, this was a blow to the power of the Rases. With respect to taxation, all taxable income would be regulated by law issued by the central government; all regional potentates, from the Rases down to their local agents at the village level, were thus denied the financial basis of their feudal power. With regard to local administration, the plan was to send central government–appointed personnel to the regions and their local administrative units. For the first phase of the scheme, however, the governors would be chosen from loyal members of the old guard. The full implementation of the administrative reform would begin after the restoration in 1941, as we shall see in a later chapter.

By 1932, the emperor had established the principle of central government as a central guiding concept and forced the Rases to accept it. What remained was to apply it in fact, not just in theory. That would come in time. What counted now was that he had assumed supreme power, having vanquished all his adversaries. Among the diehard feudal lords, the Tigrean lords and Ras Hailu of Gojam, who had been kept in Addis Ababa since the coronation as "honored guests" of the emperor, had no choice but to accept the idea of central rule as defined in the constitution. The emperor had seen to it that the Rases were involved in discussions on the draft constitution. In one of his speeches, he said he wanted to promulgate a constitution "to bequeath to our heirs a rule that is based on law to bring our people into partnership in the work of government."[5]

It was probably at this time that the place of his birth, Ejersa Goro, was renamed Bet-Lehem. I have found no written evidence of who was responsible for deciding to name it after the place where Jesus Christ was born; perhaps some ecclesiastic true believers, assisted by imperial bureaucrats, were carried away by their fanatical enthusiasm. But it was obviously another aspect of the attempt to connect him to Christ. There is no record of whether the emperor encouraged the renaming of Ejersa Goro; nor is there evidence that he discouraged it. Nor did he take any steps to discourage the Rastafarians in Jamaica from adopting him as their God. Indeed, he made land grants to some of their members in southern Ethiopia, at a place called Shashemenne.

7

The Italian Invasion and the Emperor's Exile

The memory of Ethiopia's crushing victory over the Italian forces at Adua in 1896 haunted the successive leaders of Italy. Among these, none was more adamant in seeking to avenge the humiliating defeat than the Fascist leader Benito Mussolini. He had signed a Treaty of Friendship with Ethiopia in 1928, but would use it only as a wedge to invade Ethiopia later. While Emperor Haile Selassie put his trust in the treaty, just as he did in the Covenant of the League of Nations, European powers dismissed such trust as naïveté, aware of Italy's interest in making Ethiopia at best a client state beholden to Italy, and at worst a future colony. As it turned out, the European powers were right: Mussolini was secretly planning a military attack on Ethiopia, using the defeat at Adua as a pretext to arouse Italian public opinion in support of his project. In secret correspondence between Mussolini and General De Bono, his close military advisor, the general wrote,

> The political conditions in Abyssinia [Ethiopia] are deplorable; it should not be a very difficult task to effect

> the disintegration of the Empire if we work at it well on political lines, and it could be regarded as certain after a military victory on our part.... [I]t is incumbent on us to prepare ourselves, so that we could withstand the shock of the whole Abyssinian force in our present position and then pass to the counter-attack, and go right in with the intention of making a complete job of it, once and for all.[1]

The diplomatic history of the Italo-Ethiopian war of 1936 is a sordid story of duplicity and betrayal in which Emperor Haile Selassie made the mistake (as some have argued) of placing undue trust in international treaties and the notion of collective security guaranteed under such treaties. Whether Italy's motive in invading Ethiopia was to avenge the "shame of Adua" or to further her territorial expansion, the League of Nations' betrayal of Ethiopia is one of the twentieth century's tragic episodes. But it also elevated Haile Selassie into an important figure in international affairs, as the embodiment of victimhood and the rights of small nations. His Geneva speech to the League of Nations was a stern rebuke to the world powers for their betrayal of international law and morality in failing to live up to their treaty obligations to sanction an aggressor and come to the defense of the nation it invaded. As presented in the media, his appearance in Geneva, draped in a royal Ethiopian cape, his gentle manner and attractive persona, and above all his historic speech rebuking the world powers, telling them that God and history would be their judge, impressed itself on the psyche of a troubled world at a time when Hitler in Germany was posing a clear challenge to Britain and France. Most thoughtful people in Europe saw Haile Selassie as a symbol of a troubled world in which the dark cloud of war was looming on the horizon.

Having failed to move the League of Nations, Haile Selassie settled in Bath, England, where he began a five-year exile that would last until the start of the Second World War. Throughout that sad episode, a few devoted supporters in England never stopped espousing Ethiopia's cause as represented by the emperor. Among them, the indefatigable and indomitable Sylvia Pankhurst figured prominently, ceaselessly writing and lobbying members of the British Parliament.[2]

By some accounts, the emperor faced financial difficulties and may have undergone depression during the earlier part of his exile. For someone who had been busy all his life ruling over people, making decisions that affected the lives and deaths of thousands, it must have been hard to be without work, at the head of a family that faced, if not penury, certainly great discomfort. In his autobiography, he says that when he left his country he had a fervent hope that the League of Nations would help him recover his lost kingdom. How bitter he must have been to realize that the provisions of the League's charter were no more than empty words. Due to his misplaced trust in the League and in "collective security," he says, he was not able to take much with him when he left his country. And what he had, he shared with some needy exiles among his close kinsmen. Despite the generosity of some individuals in England, therefore, he was left mostly to his own devices. It was during this depressing period that he chose not to address the Council of the League, dispatching, in his place, the loyal and ever-optimistic Dr. Lorenzo Taezaz. All to no avail.

During these hard times, he was also faced with a cruel choice. The Italian government offered to let him return if he would accept a reduced status and acknowledge their sovereignty. Many among the Ethiopian nobility, including Rases, had been bribed to denounce him and recognize the Italian occupation. Only Ras Imru, true to his character, rejected the blandishments of Mussolini and his minions with the contempt they deserved and refused to denounce his royal cousin and sovereign. He spent five miserable years in an Italian island prison, mocked by his jailors but honored and hailed by his compatriots. Upon Haile Selassie's return to his throne, one of his first actions was to inquire into Imru's whereabouts. His British allies traced Imru and brought him back to his country, where a tearful reunion took place between the two cousins and comrades when Imru arrived at the Addis Ababa airport. This was the only occasion when the protocol-conscious Haile Selassie went to the airport to greet a fellow Ethiopian, exhibiting a rarely expressed emotional side of him.

During the five bitter years of exile, the emperor stayed in contact with the *arbegnas*, the guerrilla fighters in Ethiopia, who saw to it that the occupation would not be a bed of roses for the Italians. The heroic acts of the guerrillas kept alive, for the emperor and all the other exiles, the hope of eventual liberation. Led by Abebe Aregai (who would be promoted to Ras following liberation) in the central region of Shoa and by prominent people like Takele Woldehawariat and Amoraw Wubneh in the Gondar region in the northwest, the guerrillas continually harassed the occupying regime. While some Ethiopians defected to the enemy and acted as collaborators, others, under the guise of working with the Italians, gathered needed information for the guerrillas

It is worth noting that several units of Eritreans who had been part of the invading Italian forces defected to join their Ethiopian brothers to fight the common enemy. Two notable figures are Abraha Deboch and Mogues Asgedom. One day in February 1937, these young Eritreans, who were in the employ of the Italian government in Addis Ababa, made an attempt on the life of Marshal Graziani, the Fascist governor of Ethiopia, throwing a bomb at him while he was addressing a public meeting. He was badly wounded but survived. In a recent book, *The Plot to Kill Graziani*, Ian Campbell has unearthed some intriguing details about Deboch and Asgedom.[3] They were betrayed by Ethiopian residents of the Wolkait region of Gondar and handed over to the Italian rulers, who executed them; their remains were later unearthed and reburied at the cemetery of the Church of Qidiste Selassie (Holy Trinity Church), an honor reserved for patriots and heroes of the war. Incidentally, Lorenzo Taezaz was also buried in the same cemetery, as was Sylvia Pankhurst, in recognition of her service to Ethiopia during the hard times.

8

World War II and the Return of the Emperor to Ethiopia

It was as if his words had been fulfilled—the words of the tragic figure who, standing on the podium of the League of Nations in 1936, warned the members that God and history would judge them. When war broke out in 1939, with Mussolini's Italy siding with Hitler's Germany, Haile Selassie instantly became a prophet among thoughtful people, particularly in Britain. For people in the African Diaspora, particularly in the United States and the Caribbean region, his name became a talisman for Africa's liberation. And it did not take long for the leaders of the British government to call on him, telling him to get ready—it was time to go back home! This, from those who wouldn't touch "the little man" with a ten-foot pole during his bitter days of exile.

Italy occupied Ethiopia for five years. At the very beginning of the occupation, the Italian government announced the creation of an Italian Eastern Africa (*Africa Orientale Italiana*), joining Eritrea, Ethiopia and Somalia. With the declaration of war, the entire territory would become part of the African theater of war when the Allied troops attacked all Italian possessions, including Libya in North Africa. It was as a part of that war effort that the British government under Winston Churchill called on Haile Selassie to proceed to Sudan, from which he would go back to his occupied country to dislodge the Italians. He had been well aware of the state of his country, having sent Lorenzo Taezaz to test the mood of his people. Lorenzo, a brilliant Eritrean-born doctor of law, was the principal draftsman of the emperor's famous Geneva speech, and also read his second address to the League when the emperor could not attend due to illness. As the emperor's special emissary, he had trekked through Gojam and Gondar in 1938 and 1939, openly telling people to rise up for liberation.

Haile Selassie traveled to Khartoum via Egypt accompanied by a British journalist, his son, Makonnen, and his two principal aides, Lorenzo and Woldegiorgis Woldeyohannes. Following months of delay caused by the reluctance of the British military high command to assist the emperor in his desire to enter Ethiopia at the head of his patriotic forces, the emperor crossed the border from Sudan on January 20, 1941. His forces were commanded by Major Orde Wingate, a British officer with a messianic sense of his cause who saw the emperor as a David facing the Italian Goliath. So, after five years of painful exile, Emperor Haile Selassie landed on the soil of his country and raised the red, green, and gold standard with the Lion of Judah inset to flutter in the light breeze. In his speech, delivered in Amharic, the emperor thanked the British public, saying, "Before I go I would like to say that I shall never forget the sympathetic feelings which the British public have shown me in my hours of painful tribulation. I understand, and I am grateful to them."[1]

The journey was hard, testing even a hardy soldier like Wingate, but the Ethiopian patriotic forces fought their way to Debra Marcos, the capital of Gojam, on April 4, 1941. Two days later, the emperor accepted the surrender of Ras Hailu, Gojam's governor, who had collaborated with the invaders. Haile Selassie forgave Ras Hailu, but kept him under close surveillance for the rest of his life.

The duplicity and ulterior motives of the British government at the time are evident in an exchange at this point between Wingate and the high command. Wingate, a true believer in Ethiopia's total liberation and the restoration of its sovereign to his throne, was known for his defiance of orders when they conflicted with his sense of right. When he received a radio message from Khartoum informing him that the South African armed forces under General Cunningham were about to enter Addis Ababa and he was to halt all operations and keep the emperor at Debra Marcos, Wingate's response was to request that a plane be sent immediately so that the emperor could be flown to his capital and receive the homage and welcome of his people. The high command refused the request and sternly ordered Wingate to keep the emperor where he was. The reason they gave was that there were over twenty-five thousand Italians in Addis Ababa—white people, for heaven's sake! "If the Emperor arrives, the natives will panic. They will go wild and start looting and raping, and the Italians will all be killed. *So keep the little man out*" (my italics).[2]

The high command's order was repeated by General Cunningham, who told Wingate to halt by "everything short of force" any attempt of the emperor to approach Addis Ababa. Neither Wingate nor the emperor was in any mood to be dissuaded from entering Addis Ababa, and so the emperor entered his capital on May 5, 1941. He stopped at the Dabra-Libanos Church and also at the Entoto Church of Saint Mary to offer prayers of thanks, after which his procession formed for a triumphal entry to his capital. They entered with Wingate seated on a white horse and Haile Selassie in the back seat of an Alfa Romeo taken from Ras Hailu in Debra Marcos. Surely one cannot imagine a more poignant sense of the irony of history and poetic justice.

The emperor waxed eloquent in his speech.

> On this day, which men of earth and angels of heaven could neither have foreseen nor known, I owe thanks unutterable by the mouth of man to the loving God who has enabled me to be present among you. Today is the beginning of a new era in the history of Ethiopia. ... Since this is so, do not reward evil for evil. Do not

commit any act of cruelty like those which the enemy committed against us up to this present time. Do not allow the enemy any occasion to foul the good name of Ethiopia. We shall take his weapons and make him return by the way he came.[3]

A journalist who was present reported that the emperor told him, referring to his speech, "Vraiment, j'ai été très émotionné" (I was really overcome with emotion). The same journalist, who wrote a book on the whole experience, reported that the emperor's speech was received with joy, and that the public left quietly and peacefully "to celebrate but not to loot." He added, "It was just five years to the day since Marshal Badoglio and the Italian Army had marched into Addis Ababa."[4]

9

Postliberation Developments

In his speech, Emperor Haile Selassie spoke of a new era in Ethiopian history. *Addis Zaman* (New era), the leading Amharic daily newspaper, was named in commemoration of the country's newfound freedom and to give institutional expression to the symbolism of liberation articulated by the emperor.

However, the emperor was not able immediately to exercise the sovereignty implicit in his country's newfound freedom. His British war allies, or rather a segment of their government officials, including the military high command in Africa, raised legalistic arguments against full sovereignty. The emperor fought them tooth and nail and, with the help of such figures as Anthony Eden and Churchill, was able to overcome. With the signing of the Anglo-Ethiopian Agreement on January 31, 1942, Ethiopia regained full sovereignty; the two nations signed a renegotiated agreement on December 19, 1944. Opposition remained to Ethiopia joining the United Nations until the peace treaty with Italy was signed. But Emperor Haile Selassie fought hard, and in 1945 Ethiopia became one of the UN's charter members. Ethiopia also signed the Peace Treaty along with the United States, Britain, France, and the other Allied nations.

The Italians had left behind an impressive infrastructure and fledgling industrial and commercial enterprises, and the emperor lost no time in exploiting these legacies to his benefit and to that of his loyal followers. At the same time, he set about organizing his government, forming a cabinet of twelve ministers, of which the political ministries were those of the Interior, Defense, Justice, and Foreign Affairs. The emperor himself held the portfolio for the Ministry of Education, which he held for many years, based on his conviction that education is the key to all other aspects of development.

Back to the Imperative of Centralized Administration

As already mentioned, Emperor Haile Selassie and his followers placed a premium on centralized administration as the backbone of Ethiopia's peaceful development. For that reason, the centerpiece of the new government became the Ministry of the Interior, and for its minister the emperor chose a man whose competence and loyalty to him were beyond question: Woldegiorgis Woldeyohannes, who, since the mid-1920s, had been prominent among his followers and whose value was based on what one writer has called a "nobility of merit," as opposed to the nobility of privilege enjoyed by feudal lords and their hangers-on.[1] When the emperor (still named Tafari at the time) first noticed Woldegiorgis's bright competence and his command of French, he asked him, as it was his wont, "M'n innarghilih?" (What can we do for you"). He eventually appointed him his private secretary and interpreter, and the emperor's appreciation of his qualities is demonstrated by the fact that Woldegiorgis was among the select chosen few to go into exile with him, where he remained the emperor's loyal aide throughout the years of exile in England.

The work Woldegiorgis accomplished as minister of the interior, particularly the administrative structure of the new regional government administration, envisaged in a law proclaimed in 1943, shows an active and creative mind at work laying down the basic framework of a new centralized administration to replace the outmoded and oppressive feudal structure. In that structure, the center was the Ministry of the Interior, from which a new educated and modern-minded cadre, mostly young, was dispatched to mind the store, so to speak, as directors. The directors were supervised by an older provincial governor whose authority was mostly ceremonial, though handled with care by the modern faction appointed to do the work. The directors reported directly to the minister, who reported to the emperor on essential matters concerning controversial issues. Otherwise the minister was given complete authority on how to run his ministry and oversee the work of the provincial personnel.

Woldegiorgis was also minister of the pen, that is to say, principal secretary to the emperor and custodian of the imperial seal. At one time he also acted as minister of justice. For fourteen years, until his fall in 1955, his power was thus second only to that of the emperor. All people who worked with Woldegiorgis attest to his competence, analytical skills, hard work, and loyalty and generosity to all his subordinates.

Woldegiorgis's commitment to the cause of modern, progressive administration was evident as early as the 1930s, just before the Italian invasion. A journalist who visited Ethiopia at the time quoted him as saying that "we of the younger generation, are the friends of progress and humanism, while they [the Rases] are its enemies! And we do not want to work in vain."[2]

An organizational genius, Woldegiorgis also made sure that young educated people were placed in key positions in all the important ministries, including the position of secretary-general of the ministry. The function of a secretary-general included receiving and filing incoming correspondence and stamping and dispatching outgoing correspondence, which made him the overall supervisor of the ministry's archives; as instruments in the control of the flow of information, the secretaries-general marked the ubiquitous presence of Woldegiorgis, as this author personally witnessed. The position of secretary-general finally came into disuse with the arrival of the computer age.

Other Parts of the Central Elements of Change

Next to central administration, or rather as a complementary part of it, Emperor Haile Selassie's modernizing project included creating a national army and police force, as well as rationalizing the taxation system—which necessarily included taking away taxing powers from the Rases and their hangers-on in the provinces. Not only was this necessary to relieve the citizens of onerous tax burdens exacted by an avaricious local gentry, but it established a system that would ensure a steady income to the central government, regulated by law and overseen by the Ministry of Finance.

The Revised Constitution of 1955

Fourteen years after liberation, on the jubilee anniversary of his coronation as emperor, Haile Selassie proclaimed a revised constitution. Apart from greater length, the 1955 constitution rests on a seemingly more modern foundation, both in form and substance, than the 1931 constitution. It has been described as a blueprint for the modernization of the Ethiopian state, particularly in respect of its promise to give the people equal rights under the law, which answers the question about the place of the rule of law in the country. Additionally, as if to answer the question of the people's sharing of sovereignty—an essential feature of the notion of modernity—the constitution also promised the vote to the public. Thus, whereas in the

1931 constitution the members of both chambers were not elected by the people, under the revised constitution, the members of the Chamber of Deputies (the Lower House) were to be elected by the people in a universal suffrage to be defined in an election law.

But the constitution's implementation was delayed, diminishing the promises of democracy and the rule of law, and the result in the end was a denial of the promise of democracy. The band of young educated Ethiopians who were the nucleus of his modernizing policies apparently did not imagine that their leader and idol, the progressive, antifeudal Tafari, would break that promise. Indeed, the fact that one-third of the articles of the constitution dealt with the monarchy and the emperor's traditional powers and privileges, intimating that the position of the emperor was central, undermined the possibility of the installation of a regime of democracy and rule of law in the foreseeable future. It must also be remembered that since the person of the emperor was declared to be sacred, his dignity inviolable, and his power indisputable, one could not imagine any minister defying the emperor, including the pliable prime minister, who served him to his last days, protesting that he had no power.[3]

The emperor retained control over the army and foreign affairs, the power to introduce legislation, and supreme executive power, which he grudgingly shared with his prime minister and ministers under his close and strict supervision. Given that centralization was imperative if the power of the feudal lords was to be destroyed, the emperor's extensive power as both head of state and chief executive was a matter of necessity. In that sense, he was a crucial part of the modernizing project. However, his declared ambition of gradually introducing democracy and a regime based on the rule of law was denied by the constitution's codifying the power and dignity of the emperor, sanctioned by his anointing as well as by tradition. All in all, in the judgment of all close observers and based on the emperor's words and acts, Haile Selassie remained an absolute monarch with absolute power. Whether he was corrupted by such power is a matter of judgment that I will reserve for final assessment at the end of this book.

The Codes of Law

As I have noted elsewhere, Emperor Haile Selassie liked to compare himself to the Roman emperor Justinian, who codified Roman law. He considered his revised constitution and the codes of law he promulgated in the late 1950s and early 1960s his prime achievements, and did not take kindly to criticism of them.[4] The most significant codes of law were a Civil Code, drafted by a noted French professor of law, René David; a Penal Code, drafted by a noted Swiss professor of law, Jean Gravin; a Commercial Code; a Maritime Code; and Codes of Civil and Criminal Procedure.

Based on modern systems of law and drafted by some of the best legal minds in the world, but imposed on a traditional society and a semifeudal polity with a modernizing but absolute monarch at the helm, these laws, especially the Civil Code, were the subject of much controversy, as can be imagined. Having been one of those entrusted with the application of some of their provision, I can attest to the immense tension involved in their application and the administration of justice in general, which presented quite a challenge, at times approaching a nightmare. An example of such challenge concerns the age of marriage under the Civil Code compared with the law in traditional systems.

In the original draft of the Civil Code, René David had proposed that the minimum age of marriage be eighteen. When the draft was submitted to the Senate, the older members of that chamber raised a horrific row. Eighteen? Why, the girl will be an old maid! Some of the more enlightened members suggested reducing the age to sixteen. Not acceptable; too old, cried the more traditionally minded. The Senate thus arrived at a deadlock.

What to do?

The draftsman of the Code took the matter to the final arbiter, namely His Imperial Majesty the emperor. Employing the well-known Gallic logic and eloquence, Professor David implored the emperor in the name of progress and historical responsibility to resolve this impasse. Future generations of Ethiopian women will bless you, Sire! Moved, the emperor suggested fifteen as the minimum age. Thus ended the controversy, and the old guard swallowed their pride. To them even fifteen was too old, but they had no option but to accept the imperial judgment. From the perspective of social progress, the law had the effect of protecting young girls from being forced into childhood marriages, which interfered with their education. This was only one of many examples of the tension between the new laws and the old system and old attitudes which died hard.

The Emperor and the Administration of Justice

One of the precepts of the rule of law is the administration of justice by independent judges who decide cases without fear or favor. Again, I draw from the experience I was privileged to have in the matter of the emperor's role as final judge, which by tradition he was entitled to be. His *Chilot*, or final emperor's court, was held daily to hear appeals from any lower court. Citizens had a constitutional right to petition the emperor, and so no one could stop them from applying to the *Chilot*. All serious commentators on this practice agree that it had more political than judicial value. It was also a way for the emperor to stay in touch with his ordinary subjects, and thousands flocked to the palace to petition him. Only a change in the constitution could provide a solution to that judicial anomaly.

The Emperor and Economic Development

Ethiopia's economy was and is primarily based on agriculture, which is the mainstay of the lives of the people. Much of farming is dependent on rain, and the failure of rain, followed by drought, has led to periodic famines, including the one that ended the emperor's rule in 1974. This raises the question of what can be done. Is industrialization the answer, the way out of the cycle of famine caused by drought? Well, it is part of the answer, but industrialization is a long process, one that depends on surpluses provided from agriculture. So we have a vicious circle.

Emperor Haile Selassie had been in the forefront, acting as example and source of inspiration in investment in private enterprise, beginning from his days in Harar as prince-entrepreneur. Such encouragement was not limited to his considerable private enterprise efforts, organized under charitable trusts; it also involved the public sector, which he oversaw as leader of the government, promoting investment in commercial and light industrial enterprises. Indeed, this was one of the charges that the revolutionaries made against him in 1974, accusing him of abuse of power, corruption, and neglect of the population. The fact that the headway made in economic development under his watch was lost under the Dergue is a kind of poetic justice rendered to him posthumously.

The Emperor and Education

As noted earlier, from the very beginning, the emperor saw education as a key factor in Ethiopia's development, and even its independence. He gave a considerable part of his wealth for building schools and other educational institutions, urged other wealthy people to follow his example, and encouraged students in various ways, including visiting them in their schools and asking them questions, as this writer can testify from personal experience. Until almost the end of his reign, he received in audience graduate students returning from studies abroad, quizzing them about what they studied and how they proposed to apply their knowledge for the general welfare of the people. When I returned from law studies in England, he asked me that question; I told him my wish was to practice law as a private attorney. He was not amused, and after an exchange that some who were present during the audience considered impolitic on my part, he told me with a dangerous glint in his penetrating eyes that it was payback time: I must serve in the Ministry of Justice, and that was that.

During his 1954 world tour, the emperor instructed the Ethiopian ambassador in London to arrange for a banquet in the emperor's honor. Every Ethiopian studying in Britain, including myself, was invited to the special occasion. After the banquet was over, His Majesty met every student and quizzed each on his or her area of study. After that, he spoke to the gathering in a fatherly fashion, abandoning the imperial plural and using the singular pronoun, which was rare. He called us his children that he had conceived and delivered in education ("Ba'tmhrt yeweldekuachuh lijochie"). Some of us were moved to tears.

Four years prior to that, he had inaugurated the first university college in the country—the Haile Selassie I

College, later promoted to a university and, after the emperor's fall, renamed Addis Ababa University. In quick succession, colleges of agriculture and health were opened, followed over the years by different institutions of higher education that catered to the industrial and managerial needs of the country and accompanied by the development of industrial and commercial enterprises, all of which would contribute to political and social change, including the 1974 revolution.

10

Diplomacy

The American Connection and Nonalignment

After having become a world-renowned leader with his appearance at the League of Nations in 1936, and following his return to his country and restoration to his throne after the Italian occupation, Emperor Haile Selassie made the acquisition of Eritrea (or, as some would prefer to say, its recovery) his number one diplomatic agenda. That agenda was expressed both in terms of the legitimate historical ties between Ethiopia and Eritrea and in economic and strategic terms. The economic rationale was that a landlocked Ethiopia was disadvantaged, despite the connection to the sea through the Addis Ababa–Djibouti railway, because its central and northern regions were too far from the line. Without its own outlet to the sea, the country remained a hostage to foreign powers. And in terms of the strategic imperative, recent history showed that the Eritrean region had been used repeatedly as a launching pad by foreign invaders, the latest example being Mussolini's 1935 invasion.

The pertinent questions involved in the dispute between Eritrea and Ethiopia have been rehearsed in numerous back-and-forth arguments between the two sides, played out in their bitterest form in recent times during the so-called border war of 1998–2000. At this point, it is sufficient to say that just as Emperor Haile Selassie's imperial appetite overreached itself in 1962 when he abolished the UN-arranged Ethiopia-Eritrea federation, Eritrea's current president, Isaias Afwerki, also overreached in provoking the recent war. It is ironic that in annexing Eritrea the emperor flouted the very international law and morality to which he had appealed when his own country was invaded. The Eritrean war of independence (or of secession, according to some) began following the annexation, and would haunt Emperor Haile Selassie to his last days, as it has haunted his successors. As to why Haile Selassie made the "recovery" of Eritrea his number one diplomatic agenda, one theory is that in addition to the above mentioned reasons, he was dedicated to what may be called one-upmanship—doing something that would place him in the history books above Menelik, who "sold" Eritrea to the Italians.[1] Whether this is true or not, the emperor's obsession with Eritrea did finally help cause his downfall.

The American Connection

The emperor first met U.S. president Franklin Roosevelt in 1945 when the latter was passing through Cairo en route back home from the Yalta meeting with Stalin and Churchill. The emperor had settled his differences with his British allies and was on friendly terms with them, but on the urging of his minister of the pen, Woldegiorgis, who distrusted the British, he flew to a meeting with Roosevelt on a warship off Suez, where he recited the problems Ethiopia was facing as well as his earnest desire that Eritrea be joined with Ethiopia. Roosevelt invited him to visit after the war and in the meantime promised to send an economic mission, which he did. This was followed by a loan and the replacement of British advisors by Americans. It was the beginning of the American connection that would dominate Ethiopia diplomacy for three decades. Roosevelt died soon thereafter, and it was during the Eisenhower presidency that Haile Selassie visited the United States, in 1954.

Perhaps the most important achievement of the emperor through American help was the decision by the United Nations to pass Resolution 390 A(V) of 1950, which joined Eritrea with Ethiopia in a lopsided federation "under the sovereignty of the Ethiopian Crown." It was that federation, brought about through the use of an international instrument, that Emperor Haile Selassie abolished in 1962, thus provoking a long and bloody war of liberation. The UN General Assembly was under an obligation to protest and insist on the reversal of the emperor's act of annexation, but failed to do so, just as the League of Nations had failed to come to Ethiopia's help when Italy committed an act of aggression in 1935. It is interesting to speculate whether Haile Selassie learned a lesson from his tragic experience of relying on international law—that it is force that matters, not law or morality. The Eritreans in turn learned the same lesson, for having unsuccessfully relied on diplomacy, they were forced to take up arms to secure their right to self-determination, which they finally achieved after thirty years of heavy sacrifice.

Haile Selassie and Nonalignment

The nonalignment movement grew out of the response of some countries, including some newly liberated Third World nations, to the post–World War rivalry between the Soviet Union and the Western countries, led by the United States. The period known as the Cold War began in 1945 and lasted until the fall of the Soviet Union in 1989. It saw the liberation of much of Africa from European colonial rule, and soon Africa became an ideological battleground for the opposing forces. The guiding principles of the nonalignment movement were first discussed and framed at an international conference held in Bandung, Indonesia, attended by leaders such as India's Pandit Nehru, Yugoslavia's Josip Broz Tito, Egypt's Gamal Abdel Nasser, China's Chou En Lai, and Ethiopia's Haile Selassie.

Haile Selassie and Africa

Haile Selassie was an elder statesman who had become an internationally renowned figure long before any the other African leaders who shared the platform with him in May 1963 at the creation of the Organization of African Unity (OAU). Most of the men who became leaders of their respective countries in the late 1950s and early 1960s were students when the emperor made his famous appeal to the League of Nations in Geneva in 1936. One was Nelson Mandela, who was a boy of seventeen when Mussolini conquered Ethiopia. In his memoirs, *Long Walk to Freedom*, he writes, "Ethiopia has always held a special place in my own imagination." In 1962, on the eve of the OAU summit, almost thirty years later, he was finally able to meet Haile Selassie, which, he says, was "like shaking hands with history."

Haile Selassie's failure to stop the march of fascism had made him a martyr among the peoples of the world, and in particular among Africans both in the continent and throughout the Diaspora. It also helped reinforce the emerging spirit of Pan-Africanism. Indeed, Haile Selassie's position as a martyr gave him elevated status as a leader in African affairs, particularly in the early days of decolonization, before people like Nkrumah and Nyerere began asserting themselves as leaders in the African liberation agenda. Although African liberation and unity was a universally held value in Africa, different people had different ways of achieving it. Some, feeling that the countries could not all unite across the vast continent against their colonial oppressors, preferred to fight colonialism country by country. While leaders such as Nkrumah saw unification as a goal unto itself, Haile Selassie, a late bloomer in African affairs, had to be coaxed and challenged to take up the cause of Pan-Africanism. But when he did, persuaded by his advisors, it was in earnest and with characteristic single-mindedness. When Nkrumah convened the conference of African Heads of State and Government in the spring of 1958, the emperor sent his youngest son, Prince Sahle Selassie.

Haile Selassie's engagement with Africa prompted him to establish a scholarship fund for students to study at the University College of Addis Ababa. Two hundred scholarships were awarded, and students came from West, East, and Central Africa; I taught some of them in my classes at the college. A number of these students ended up occupying important ministerial and other positions in their own countries, such as Robert Ouko of Kenya, who was foreign minister of his country until he was brutally murdered, allegedly by agents of President Daniel Arap Moi.

The emperor's government also invited leaders of African liberation movements, encouraging them and providing assistance. Young African political and labor union leaders began frequenting the Ethiopian capital, and the Ethiopian media began putting a positive spin on African liberation movements. Among the emerging leaders with whom I struck up a friendship at the time were the late Tom Mboya of Kenya and Felix Moumie of Cameroon. They all met with the emperor with the help of those of us who had formed the ad hoc African Liberation Assistance

Committee, which the emperor's government approved. Tom Mboya ended up becoming the second most important political figure in Kenya until he was assassinated by jealous rivals. Felix Moumie was poisoned by an agent of the French Secret Service. These and other African leaders like Nyerere and Kaunda enriched the political experience of Ethiopians through speeches at public as well as at private meetings that some of my friends like Richard and Rita Pankhurst and I arranged.

The culmination of the emperor's engagement with African affairs was the establishment of the OAU in May 1963. That signal event in modern African history occurred following two years of intense negotiations among African leaders, hitherto polarized along ideological and personal axes of division. The main groups were known, respectively, as the Monrovia and Casablanca group of nations; the first was generally understood to be pro-Western, while the second, including Egypt and Ghana, was said to be socialist in orientation and critical of the West. One of the achievements of the creation of the OAU was to put to rest the division by creating a body that sought to speak with one voice on behalf of the continent.

Emperor Haile Selassie, who acted as host to the conference, played a crucial role in the negotiations to unite the divided groups. The world did not expect the conference to succeed in establishing a united African body; indeed, it was assumed that African leaders were too divided culturally and politically to agree. The writer attended the conference as a member of the drafting committee of the OAU Charter and could, therefore, gauge the temper of the meeting.[2] The foreign press in particular warned of impending disaster among feuding African leaders, especially since Nkrumah had proposed the creation of a United States of Africa, which was not favorably received by most of the other delegates. The critics would be disappointed. When Nkrumah threatened to walk out of the conference, Haile Selassie worked his African magic. He called on Guinea's President Sékou Touré and, holding Touré's hand like a father and looking him in the eye, said, "Mon fils, je vous prie. Allez amenez votre frère Nkrumah" (My son, I implore you to go and bring your brother Nkrumah). Touré did not hesitate in responding, "Oui Père. Je vais essayer" (Yes, Father. I will try), and brought Nkrumah back to the conference hall to a rousing standing ovation.

Africans felt proud of the achievement of the May 1963 conference, and Emperor Haile Selassie took much of the deserved credit.

11

Turning of the Tide

A Shaken Emperor on the Horns of a Dilemma

The 1960 Attempted Coup and Its Impact

It was a sunny morning in mid-December 1960. The emperor was in Brazil for a weeklong official visit. That day, the people of Ethiopia woke up to martial music on the radio at the hour when normal music should have been heard. We waited... and waited... and waited. Neighbors came to report that they saw groups of troops in battle gear being taken in jeeps toward the city center. Meanwhile, the martial music continued.

Suddenly, a radio announcer told a puzzled population to await an important announcement. I and my family and a group of friends who came to my house then heard the tired voice of the emperor's son and heir to the Solomonic throne, Crown Prince Asfa-Wosen.

Everyone in the room was shocked as the crown prince denounced the regime presided over by his royal father, a regime that he had been patiently waiting to inherit. The speech, which later turned out to have been written by Germame Neway, the Columbia University–educated intellectual and brain behind the coup attempt, was an indictment of the "oppressive feudal system," and promised to inaugurate a better system under which the crown prince would be a salaried constitutional monarch. Germame was the younger brother of General Mengistu Neway, head of the emperor's bodyguard. In addition to the Neways, the plotters included Workneh Gebeyhu, head of the emperor's intelligence service. They had arrested almost all the cabinet ministers and other dignitaries close to the imperial throne, and kept them in the palace. Germame had also summoned people whom he considered sympathetic to the revolution or fellow travelers. I later found out that my name was on the list of those who would be appointed as cabinet members following the overthrow of the emperor.[1]

The December revolt, as it became known, was the first direct challenge Haile Selassie had faced in his thirty years of rule. The fact that the revolt came from his trusted bodyguard added a painful element. More painful and a shock to the emperor was the involvement of his trusted Workneh, whom he loved like a son. The crown prince's speech, which was greeted by almost everyone with confusion and suspicion, did not seem to surprise his father, who forgave him instantly when the prince lay prostrate at his father's feet asking for forgiveness. The emperor knew that his son was being used as a puppet and had neither the courage nor the moral fiber to be martyred rather than betray his father. So he forgave him with a wry smile on his lips.

The diehard supporters of the imperial system, who had a strong vested interest in it, as well as the absentee landowners and the emperor's kinsmen, were outraged by the crown prince's action. On the other hand, my generation of Ethiopians, as well as a few disgruntled older people, welcomed the coup as a wakeup call. Some were naturally anxious about what would happen to their civil rights under a new government, considering the bad record of military regimes in human rights and the rule of law. But the general view was that nothing could be worse than what we had and that a military regime of the Nasser variety, guided by progressive individuals like Germame, would clear the way for a better republic. For those who held that view, the disappointment to come would be a bitter education. Certainly, on one point the outcome of the failed coup proved a step forward toward progress: it loosened the bonds that held the feudal system together.

The coup failed because the bulk of the armed forces and the air force remained loyal to the emperor and defeated his rebellious bodyguards. When they knew they had lost, the Neway brothers decided to take the top members of the imperial regime with them, and there was a horrendous massacre of ministers and other dignitaries in the emperor's palace in Sidist Kilo. They did not even spare Italian war hero Ras Abebe Aregai. It was later reported that when Abebe Aregai challenged Germame's right to treat him the way he did, denying him water to drink, for instance, Germame brought him water and then reminded Ras Abebe of the guerrilla fighters who had made him a hero and whom he had forgotten. The exact words related to me by a survivor were "Did you think of the peasants who sold their oxen and followed you and who made you Ras?"

The principal coup makers were either killed or captured a few days after the rebellion had failed. Germame was killed resisting arrest some fifty miles south of Addis Ababa. Workneh committed suicide, and General Mengistu was wounded and captured. His trial became the object of great curiosity and a bellwether of what would happen to the other rebel officers. Most of them, as it turned out, were banished and put under detention in distant places for several years.

The Loosening of the Bonds

Despite its failure, the coup had an impact on government and society, as well as implications for future changes. Its impact on government was felt first in the shape and behavior of the executive. The massacre of most of the cabinet members left the government truncated; the whole government system was shaken, and the bureaucracy was left dithering for some time. The emperor decided to donate his palace, the scene of a bloody massacre, to the university. Perhaps a more profound effect of the coup was that it released the suppressed energy of the public and emboldened progressive voices. One manifestation of this was student activities, which were the most threatening to the imperial regime. Students began organizing poetry festivals in which the content of the poems was revolutionary, lamenting the condition of the oppressed peasants. In these poems and in other forms of popular expression, Germame and his associates acquired the status of martyrs.

The military and the labor unions, too, were aroused. With the assistance of university students and teachers, labor unions began organizing clandestinely and demanding better wages and conditions of work, threatening strikes. True to his ability to adapt to new situations, the emperor decided to appear as an advocate of full union rights, and ordered his prime minister to prepare what became the Labor Relations Proclamation of 1963, which, while giving labor unions hitherto unknown rights, created mechanisms of control for the government. Still, the law represented progress; previously, companies could hire and fire with no legal redress, leading to periodic confrontations and violence, but the law now provided for mutual accommodation between unions on the one hand and employers and the government on the other.

The December 1960 coup created a whole host of challenges, of which the most important was the issue of security. For the first year after the coup, the emperor and his principal advisors were principally concerned with survival. After all, it was his most trusted aides who had revolted against him. He was particularly stung by Workneh's involvement. For a long time he was in denial, often remarking that Workneh must have been compelled to go along with Germame's scheme under duress. He had been especially fond of Workneh, part of whose duties, in fact, had been to spy on the top military brass, including General Mengistu of the bodyguards. The emperor's survival strategy included distrust of even his closest kinsmen, on the basis of the Machiavellian dictum "If I take care of my close friends, I can take care of my enemies." (The emperor was an avid reader of Machiavelli; Workneh told this writer that the emperor lent him an Amharic translation of *The Prince*.)

A matter of great significance after the coup situation was the disposal of hundreds of officers and enlisted men and some civilians who had taken part in it. This raised security issues as well as legal questions related to land reform, administration of justice, and constitutional reform. A military general was appointed on a temporary basis to deal with the security issues. The decimation of the cabinet and the dissolution of the imperial bodyguard had left a vacuum in the government system, which was filled by ambitious and willful men like Ras Asrate Kassa, son of the emperor's loyal kinsman Ras Kassa. Asrate was openly disdainful as well as resentful of the "commoners" whom the emperor had raised to positions of prominence, such as the prime minister and other ministers. In the twilight period during the year following the coup, in which the emperor temporarily lost his bearings and became vulnerable, Asrate had himself appointed head of a commission dealing with the disposal of all cases related to the rebellion, and in particular focusing on the rebellious officers.

Impact of the December Coup on the Imperial System

Apart from the decimation of the government's top personnel, what impact did the coup have on the system? All progressively inclined people had great expectations, believing that the emperor, shaken by what had happened, would allow political and social changes. The wily emperor raised their hopes by throwing a few crumbs, so to speak. He ordered the creation of several commissions tasked with bringing about changes, such as a Commission on Land Reform, a Commission on Judicial Reform, and a Commission on Social Reform. The commissions started their work promisingly for three to four months, then gradually ceased their operations with no explanation provided. The Commission on Land Reform created the expectation for many people, including the writer, who was a member of the Commission on Judicial Reform, that the peasants might finally be given land rights. But it all came to naught; despite his proclaimed intentions, His Majesty was not willing or able to alienate the class that was the backbone of the imperial system. For many of us, it was a moment of truth that showed the emperor's true colors, dashing our hopes for real social change.

As for political change, things continued for some five years before the emperor introduced cosmetic changes in the cabinet system. The prime minister was given the power to nominate his ministers for appointment by the emperor; previously, the emperor chose the ministers, and the prime ministers had no role in the process. Writing a commentary, in a British legal journal, this writer voiced his disappointment, and paid for it by being banished to a distant province for three years.

Most people settled down to live with the status quo, except for the university student activists, joined by high school students, who continued demands for change. "Meriet l'arashu" (land to the tiller) was their mantra. Their protests kept gathering strength until they were joined by the military, which had its own complaints, including insufficient salaries that did not meet the challenges of runaway inflation and the fact that their love for their commander-in-chief seem to be unrequited. Everything seemed to point to revolution, and everyone expressed fear of an impending disaster: everyone, that is, except the eighty-two-year-old emperor.

On the Horns of a Dilemma

For anyone who had followed the ups and downs of Emperor Haile Selassie's career and seen the dogged but supple manner in which he responded to different challenges to his position and even to his life, his response to the attempted coup of December 1960 was disappointing.

He had set the clock for real changes that might have left a brilliant legacy to mark his famed life and career. The Rases had been tamed, whatever residue of power was left to them by the 1931 constitution having been finished off by five years of Italian occupation. And after the restoration, he passed legislation that introduced administrative structures and organizations that opened the way for real changes. He proclaimed the 1955 Revised Constitution, which provided the framework for the changes that he had spoken about throughout his career. Then, when the moment of truth arrived—the hour of real decision—he retreated to a comfort zone, siding with the traditional forces that he had fought for decades.

Why did he retreat? To answer this, we must ask why, not just how, he achieved and maintained his power, including the reason why he stood in opposition to the conservative forces in the first place. As to how, it is instructive to cite the seventeenth-century English poet Andrew Marvell. In his "Horatian Ode upon Cromwell's Return from Ireland" (quoted above as an epigraph to chapter 4), he wrote, "The same arts that did gain / A power, must it maintain." The political skills of Tafari / Haile Selassie exemplify and confirm Marvell's poetic insight.

Between Progress and Absolute Power

From the time he sought and ascended to the Ethiopian throne, Haile Selassie (then called Tafari) appeared to the world as a progressive prince dedicated to bringing his country into the modern world. All observers agree on his success in taming the traditional nobility by imposing upon them modern ideas and institutions, and in creating a centralized administration that curtailed their power, if not eliminated it. Throughout most of his reign he was generally considered a progressive statesman; and the status of martyr he gained in consequence of the Italian invasion added a peculiar mystique to his power. That mystique and his progressive reputation sheltered him from the critical appraisal that all statesmen receive, but the 1960 attempted coup and his response opened him up for serious criticism even from people considered friendly to him and his government.

Within Ethiopia, radical student movements demanding "land to the tiller" raised questions about the emperor's power and his attitude toward the continued power of the traditional forces who abused the impoverished peasants. If he is a progressive leader, they asked, why does he allow such abuse, and when would he cause changes to be made so that peasants had rights in land tenure? By the time of the 1960 attempted coup, such questions had become part of the daily discourse among the literati, and after the coup failed, the students' repeated demands for change on the land question became the emperor's nightmare. Those demands reverberated throughout the empire, and the labor unions and the armed forces began to voice sympathy and gradual support for them. It is an irony of history that these, the very products of his modernization programs, became his most persistent critics, and would eventually combine to end his rule, as we shall see in the next chapter. It was a sign of the emperor's loss of control and of a weakening of his critical faculties that he did not give these demands the attention they deserved. Close observers of the imperial palace scene suggested that by the late 1960s the emperor had lost his phenomenal memory, with some even saying that he was affected by some form of dementia.

Another issue in daily conversation was the inordinate amount of time and energy the emperor was spending in travel, mostly to other African countries. His success in helping establish the Organization of African Unity (OAU) and his mediation in the Algeria-Morocco territorial dispute had established him as an elder statesman and whetted his appetite to engage in African affairs more frequently. In their petitions to the emperor, some Ethiopians started referring to him as Africa's Father. But critics complained that, like a wayward husband, he was neglecting his first duty to his spouse, Ethiopia, in favor of his mistress, Africa. People close to the palace claimed that he was annoyed by the constant attacks leveled at him by student radicals and other critics, considering them ungrateful ruffians who did not know what they were talking about. And the palace sycophants continually massaged his ego, while his ministers would not confront him with the reality. Those who did ended up being dismissed or "frozen." He had also become unresponsive to reasonable proposals that he had accepted gracefully in the past. In other words, he had become more autocratic. As Bahru Zewde, a distinguished Ethiopian historian, has put it, "the progressive and reactionary features of [Haile Selassie]'s reign are not mutually exclusive but tend to overlap. Power, which remained the abiding concern of the emperor, was their locus of interaction. In the long run, his obsession with power lent reactionary character to what at the outset could have been regarded as progressive measures." Bahru adds that the political centralization, once considered to be an instrument of progress in the Ethiopian setting, "negated the legitimate wishes of regions and nationalities for internal autonomy."[2]

12

Last Days

Revolution and the End of the Monarchy

The Gathering Storm

For over a decade before the revolution in early spring 1974, the country was beset by student agitation and labor union demands for fair labor practices and improvements in working conditions. There were also regional rebellions, with the war in Eritrea posing the most serious threat to imperial rule. Then, more ominously, there began to be grumblings in the armed forces, quiet at first, but growing louder. In these protests, the name of the emperor was invoked at first with respect, in the expectation that he would settle the grievances. The emperor was still seen as the dispenser of justice and equity, and his minions as selfish rascals who were betraying his trust. But the emperor's failure to respond finally led to more radical demands.

Student Movement

The first to question the emperor's legitimacy and boldly and unambiguously declare the imperial system to be the source of all the country's problems were the university students. By the mid-1960s, student organizations within Ethiopia as well as in America and Europe were espousing Marxist ideology, demanding social and political change. Within the student movement, divisions emerged based on disagreements on objectives and tactics. Some favored an evolutionary model, with social democracy as the objective and peaceful democratic change as the method. Others, who ultimately commanded the majority voice, insisted on radical reconstruction through Marxist strategy and tactics. Lenin's famous tract *What Is to Be Done?* was first in the list of works examined by student study groups and adopted as the means of achieving the aims of the revolution. Marxism-Leninism, the gospel of twentieth-century leftist revolutionaries, became the standard, which necessarily meant the rejection of "bourgeois" democratic aims and methods.

Inevitably, a split occurred in the movement, later complicated by the split between Soviet Union and China. The emperor's intelligence service, by that time expertly advised by American and Israeli professionals, saw in it an opportunity to weaken the student movement and thus postpone, if not prevent, the eventual revolution. The split arose from a disagreement between the faction whose leaders lived in the United States and the faction whose leaders lived in Europe. Attempting to find a real difference between the pronouncements of the two groups, each grounded in leftist scripture, is like reading the different pronouncements of Roman Catholic and Eastern Orthodox Christians at the time of the historic schism. To neutral observers, it was a case of a difference without a distinction. As with the split of Russian revolutionaries into Bolshevik and Menshevik factions, the difference was over tactics, including the issue of membership. A hidden struggle for power developed; it was as if Russian history were repeating itself in Ethiopia.

The two factions became known as the Ethiopian People's Revolutionary Party (EPRP), whose leaders were based in America, and the All-Ethiopia Socialist Movement (Meison, an acronym for the group's name in Amharic), whose leaders were based in Europe. The EPRP commanded the majority of supporters within the country, and the relative strength of the two factions would determine their respective behavior when the revolution exploded in 1974, as we shall see. Each faction published pamphlets in attempts to recruit followers, particularly within the country. The EPRP's popular pamphlet, called *Democracia*, was published in Amharic; its editors were outstanding writers, including poets, in the Amharic language. Meison published a pamphlet called *Sefiew Hisb* (Broad masses), which was not as widely distributed. Both factions endeavored to recruit followers within and outside government circles, which gave the imperial intelligence service a means to monitor and exploit the differences between them.

In the final phase of the revolutionary adventure, the larger and more popular EPRP would decide to adopt the Maoist strategy of conducting a rural guerrilla insurgency, working with the peasants and gradually encircling the state and capturing power. In the final phase of that strategy, the EPRP itself would split into two factions, one keeping to the Maoist strategy and the other wishing to conduct urban guerrilla warfare and overthrow the military government that had taken over from the emperor. Meison, in turn, decided to collaborate with the military government, which further complicated the role of the student movement and ultimately resulted in mutually inflicted damage, to the delight of the government.

The Emperor's Interest

The final fate of both factions is part of the tragic story of the misadventure of the student movement, which had started with much fanfare and great expectations for a transition to a democratic postimperial system. Throughout the events, the emperor continued to practice his well-honed skills of divide and rule, even as his reactions were being slowed, his knowledge of the facts was incomplete, and his analytical powers were diminished by advancing age. In July 1969, the present writer was summoned by the emperor to his palace in Dire Dawa, during his annual retreat, to be harangued about the fallacy of the student demands for socialism. His government, he said, had put in place national institutions like the Imperial Highway Authority, the National Airlines, and the Imperial Board of Telecommunications. Was that not socialism? What else did the students want? To my response that I did not know, he vehemently asserted that I did indeed know but was being cagy. (What he actually said, in Amharic, was "Debaqqi, shemmaqi," which is quite a bit more strident than "cagy.") I stood silent; there was nothing I could say, given the tone of his remarks. When he pressed me for an answer, I replied that the institutions he mentioned did indeed contain aspects of socialism. It was an answer given under duress, but I knew there was an element of truth in it, for a classic definition of socialism is public ownership of the means of production, distribution, and exchange. What I did not, could not, say was that the critical question was who the beneficiary of these institutions was! Before he dismissed me, the emperor seemed to relent, and asked me about my work as mayor of Harar.

That His Imperial Majesty would summon someone whom he had banished to a province far from the center was a sign of how desperate he was feeling. I couldn't help being sorry for this man, who at the ripe old age of seventy-seven felt cornered by the aggressive demands for change voiced by students and labor unions, beset by social forces that were the products of his own modernizing programs. In some of their demands, the students used language that could hardly be described as polite or respectful to the man whom much of the world respected and the majority of his subjects seemed to adore. The constitution stated that his dignity was inviolable, but clearly the student radicals did not care about that. What a comedown!

From his perspective, bitterness and a feeling of betrayal were understandable; but not from the perspective of those who saw his autocracy as an obstacle to progress. That difference in perspective was created not only by ideological disagreements, but also by a generational change with regard to how one ought to address an emperor who also happened to be an elder and therefore deserving respect in accordance with traditional values.

To what extent their Marxist-Leninist ideology, with class struggle as the critical imperative, influenced the students' lack of respect is anybody's guess.

Labor Unions

Just as the students were a product of the emperor's education programs, of which he was rightfully proud, the labor unions were the products of his programs for building the industrial, manufacturing, and commercial enterprises that largely came into being during his reign, if not completely at his behest. He may not have consciously wished for the emergence of the social forces that eventually would lead to demands for change; but his modernizing programs gave rise to them, and he thus had some legitimate right to claim that he was ultimately responsible for their creation.

Was he also responsible for responding to the workers' claims for fair and equitable treatment from their employers? There's the rub; the emperor's private interests, suitably camouflaged by his charitable organization, the Haile Selassie Charitable Trust, as well as the interests of members of the royal family and their hangers-on, inevitably clashed with the interests of the workers, despite the claims made by his agents that the workers were being treated neutrally and equitably even where their interests were opposed to his. Again, the writer was a witness to the invisible hands that brought pressure to bear in favor of the interests of the emperor and of those associated with the imperial system. In 1968, I was an umpire in a labor dispute between the Ethiopian factory workers of the Japanese-managed cotton factory in Dire Dawa and the company's management. The governor of the region warned me that I should decline the appointment as umpire. I did not decline, and as a result was subjected to all kinds of subtle and not-so-subtle pressures to deliver a verdict that favored the company. I resisted those pressures and handed down a verdict that satisfied the legitimate claim of the factory workers, which the Japanese management found to be fair and acceptable. I gambled in relying on the rhetorical commitment of His Majesty to the rule of law and due process—and I won. Far from being punished, I was told indirectly (by the governor—my "jailer"—who had been against my involvement in the arbitration) that in that arbitration dispute justice was rendered and the major shareholder, the emperor's charitable organization, was satisfied with the award.

The emperor's attitude toward the emergence of organized labor was pragmatic; as was his habit, he accepted the inevitable unless it posed a real threat to his power. After many years of hesitation, he was finally persuaded that it was time to legally recognize the labor unions. By doing so, and creating a mechanism of mediation to settle disputes, it might be possible for government and employers to control the unions more effectively. And so it was; the creation of a nationwide labor organization, the Center of Ethiopian Labor Unions (CELU), resulted in a period of peaceful coexistence of management and labor for a number of years, until the leadup to the revolution in 1974, when the CELU joined the chorus of demands for political change.

Regional Rebellions

Rebellions occurred in regions across the country, mostly caused by maladministration or mistreatment by local authorities of influential elites, or inspired by irredentist sentiments, as in the Harar and Bale regions. But, as mentioned above, by far the most serious rebellion was in Eritrea, later joined by that in the neighboring Tigray region. What made it more serious was that what the Eritreans demanded was complete independence from Ethiopia, as well as the military strength of the fighters there, the support they received from the people, and the region's geographical location along the Red Sea. The powerful Eritrean People's Liberation Front (EPLF) would join with the Tigray People's Liberation Front (TPLF), the next most strongly armed political organization in the area, which would become the major organization to form a coalition government after the fall of the military government in 1991.

Eritrea was an Italian colony until its liberation by the Allied forces in 1941. As noted in a previous chapter, the Eritreans were the victims of a U.S.-instigated scheme that had the effect of denying their legitimate claim to independence when they were joined with Ethiopia under a UN-arranged federal structure in which Emperor Haile Selassie's government had the upper hand. Even the modicum of autonomy given under the UN-sponsored scheme was taken away when the emperor unilaterally abolished the federation, declaring Eritrea a mere province. The result was a war that lasted thirty years.

The emperor's action prompted an Eritrean sage and respected elder by the name of Asmach Mirach to make a memorable comment: "How foolish the Shoans [Ethiopians] are! They have swallowed a piece of hard rock that will destroy them." In the war's last phase, on the eve of a decisive battle, a commander of the Eritrean regiment was ordered by the high command to attack the formidable Ethiopian regiment known as Nadow. The following morning, he told his soldiers that the day of battle would be the funeral of Nadow. Such was the sense of pride and determination of Eritreans with respect to their rights—such their clarity and passion.

Emperor Haile Selassie and his government were dead certain that Ethiopia would win the war. His army, next to that of Egypt, was the strongest in Africa, and almost every observer concluded that the guerrilla army of the small nation of Eritrea was doomed to failure. In battle after battle, the emperor's forces sent waves of attacks, killing people and animals and even poisoning wells. A quarter of the population fled to neighboring countries as refugees. But instead of submitting, the Eritrean fighters and the people behind them only grew stronger, drawing the invading forces further and further into a harsh landscape. By the eve of the Ethiopian revolution, an exhausted and dispirited Ethiopian army was caught in a murderous battle in Sahel, the base area of the guerrillas, where it suffered huge losses of dead and wounded.

That was the spring of 1973, the year when the Horn of Africa, including Eritrea and Ethiopia, was hit by a two-year drought that devastated the land and left the population desperately in need of food. The emperor's government was not able or willing to supply the necessary food, and an estimated one million Ethiopians in the northern regions of Wollo and Tigray died in the famine. The fickle international press was suddenly galvanized by the sight of emaciated bodies, and reported the plight of the people to a general public outcry the world over. Notably, a British TV and radio journalist named Jonathan Dimbleby made a film that caused an uproar in Europe and America. Confronted with the question why the government did nothing to prevent the deaths of so many Ethiopians, the minister of information denied that there was famine.

The Revolt of the Armed Forces

At the same time, word of the disaster in Sahel had reached not only the Ministry of Defense but all units of the armed forces, and it set in motion a serious rebellion in the military. "Sympathy strikes" occurred instantly, in which soldiers voiced complaints about their own conditions of service, which were deplorable. In the Negalle Borena region, the noncommissioned officers (NCOs) and enlisted men took the unprecedented step of detaining their superior officers and asking the government to send an inspecting team. The government sent the chief of staff of the armed forces, and the rebellious soldiers detained him as well. The news of the Negalle soldiers' action spread, and set off a chain reaction; the forces in Eritrea also detained their commanding officers, and others followed suit. The high command and the government felt helpless to do anything.

The next stage was critical in the unfolding of the revolution of 1974. All the units of the armed forces began to communicate with one another, breaking a pattern of discipline and the chain of command. They then agreed to choose representatives to send to the capital to guide the progress of the revolution.

The original demands of the rebelling military were couched in the trade union mode of demands for the improvement of working conditions—higher salaries, affordable housing, family allowances, medical services, and so on. But members of civil society, including students and teachers, began to call on the military to push their demands beyond their own narrow interests. The crescendo of protests continued to build. The students became more daring, and were rewarded by open public support, including that of labor unions and small traders. Coincidentally, inflation had struck at every sector of urban society, following a worldwide rise in oil prices. All were now geared for change. And as a result of the war in Eritrea and the famine in Wollo and Tigray, Ethiopia had become the center of world attention.

By late 1973, Addis Ababa's nervous system was showing signs of breakdown and paranoia. People hoarded essential supplies. Absenteeism from school and work, disobedience of authority, bold exchanges of obscenities, the flight of capital, and the purchase of goods at astronomical prices became the order of the day. Other large cities soon followed suit.

The Quickening March of Events

As 1973 gave way to 1974, the pace of the revolution was accelerating. A brief chronology of events in early 1974 will give a picture of the irreversible slide of the imperial regime toward its demise.

Thursday, February 21

Tension was mounting. Government employees failed to report to work due to a lack of transportation. There were reports of random shootings. Two students were killed by soldiers guarding buses and installations, and soldiers toting machine guns on open army trucks patrolled the streets. The government announced on radio and television the suspension of the World Bank–initiated Education Sector Review, which had aroused public opposition, led by the teachers unions, who argued that it would put nine- and ten-year-old children (of the poor) to work after only four years of education.

Friday, February 22

More soldiers were visible everywhere. The prime minister's car was stoned, along with those of other dignitaries. Shops were closed. Buses were back in service, escorted by armed guards. Fear crippled the city—the fear of the unknown.

Saturday, February 23

The emperor appeared on TV and radio, announcing the suspension of the new education policy and a reduction in oil prices.

Sunday, February 24

The streets were deserted. The government had arrested one thousand taxi drivers who had demonstrated protesting high gas prices. The soldiers, now everywhere, were coordinating, not opposing, the stone-throwing students. More cars were smashed. On the evening news it was announced that the salary of soldiers would be raised to $100 a month (then equivalent to US$20), comparable with salaries of other civil service employees, effective in March.

Monday, February 25

There was a mass promotion of officers, and some of the officers were taken to the palace to thank the emperor.

Tuesday, February 26

Early in the morning, it was reported that the ground forces in Asmara, the Eritrean capital, had mutinied. The soldiers, having seen that the emperor had no clothes, demanded a monthly salary of $150. Some also demanded political changes and dismissal of ministers and generals. The Asmara soldiers arrested all officers above the rank of captain.

Wednesday, February 27

The air force and navy officers joined in the mutiny, and a delegation was dispatched from Addis Ababa to negotiate terms and conditions of release of the officers. Only one member of the delegation returned; the rest were detained. On television it was announced that the government of Prime Minister Aklilu had asked to resign and that the emperor was considering the request.

Thursday, February 28

Troops were sent to guard important installations, including the Ministry of Information, the banks, and the airport. At two p.m., the emperor read a short speech announcing the appointment of a new prime minister. This was followed by an announcement of more salary increases.

As the above blow-by-blow recitation of developments shows, things were falling apart; the center no longer held. Soldiers were now everywhere, stopping cars and checking identity papers.

An OAU meeting of African foreign ministers was postponed because the government could not guarantee their safety.

Endalkachew Makonnen, the new prime minister, an Oxford-educated aristocrat, made an unsuccessful attempt to bring the situation under control. Students gathered at the Arat Kilo campus in Addis Ababa shouted demands for his removal. The students had been brought by soldiers, who urged them to keep up their demands.

On March 1, more students demonstrated, and shots were fired, with some students killed. Confusion followed. The armed forces were divided between a minority who supported the new prime minister and a majority who wanted him out.

The new prime minister appointed a new cabinet whose composition reflected an attempt to bridge the gap between the old and the new, between the emerging middle class and the retreating nobility. In this he seemed to continue the policy of the emperor, with the difference that young technocrats predominated in the cabinet. Many believed that had the emperor done this a year before, the country might have welcomed it as a great leap forward. As it was, the unleashed forces would not be satisfied with what they considered cosmetic changes. Above all, the military was now out to grasp power in its own name.

On March 1, the emperor addressed the nation, promising constitutional reform. But his promises were drowned out in the clamor for radical change. The same day, the labor unions staged a countrywide general strike. Even clergymen struck for pay raises.

Emergence of the Dergue

As the situation went from bad to worse, people started talking about a shadowy coordinating committee of the military that was directing events and controlling or influencing the forces of change. The members of this committee, later known as the Dergue (Amharic for "committee"), numbered 120 and came from the rank and file, the NCOs, and the junior officers, up to the rank of captain, of the entire military: the army, the police, and even the militia, traditionally looked down upon by the military establishment. With no organized political parties to challenge them, it was as if the revolution landed in their lap.

As membership expanded beyond the original leaders who had initiated the revolt, rivalry and competition for leadership caused the core body to reaffirm its power and elect as chairman an individual the leaders saw as lacking a strong social base and therefore malleable. It proved to be a tragic mistake. It was thus that in June 1974, an obscure man with the rank of captain, who had a reputation for drunken brawling, emerged as the leader of the Dergue. His name was Mengistu Hailemariam. Mengistu and his enthusiastic supporters made certain that all power was tightly controlled by his inner circle. Even the popular General Aman Andom, who had acted as the gray eminence advising the Dergue on strategy and tactics, was to be kept out. Not only had he outlived his usefulness, but he stood in the way of Mengistu, who turned out to be what no one had anticipated: an ambitious man determined to ascend to the summit of power.

Mengistu, no doubt aware of Aman's popularity, consented to his being named acting head of state and minister of defense following the fall of Endalkachew's new government. Endalkachew and his predecessor's cabinet ministers were arrested, together with many prominent civilians and high-ranking military officers. Nor did the Dergue allow Aman to stay in his position long. On September 12, 1974, six months after the revolution broke out, the Dergue announced the overthrow of the emperor's regime and its replacement by a constitutional monarchy. As a sop to fans of constitutional democracy, in what one historian has called a cruel joke, the emperor's ailing son, Crown Prince Asfa-Wosen, was named monarch.[1]

The End

So what some commentators called the "creeping coup" came to an end. Emperor Haile Selassie was pushed off the stage of history, which he had dominated for over half a century. All hopes of establishing a civilian democratic system after the end of his rule were dashed when the Dergue established a military government. They called it a provisional military administration, but few were under any illusions that the military would give up power. As twenty years of African history have shown, once they have tasted power, the military rarely give it up. And those civilian political forces that might have answered hopes of civilian-based democracy were engaged in mutual recriminations that later degenerated into a murderous factional war, encouraged by the Dergue. But that is another story.

In the preface, I described the scene when the emperor was overthrown by the Dergue. On that sunny September day in 1974, the military of Ethiopia, who had sworn oaths of loyalty to their emperor and commander-in-chief, consigned a man of history to the dustbin and became men of history themselves. News that the emperor had been deposed had been broadcast on the radio early that morning. The city was mad with joyous celebration.

People left their work and shops and streamed to the emperor's Jubilee Palace, as if driven by an inner force to become part of history. Those among the motley crowd who had a sense of balance and decency were astounded by the extreme reaction of the public. But theirs was the small voice of conscience in the midst of a mob. The military had prepared the stage over months of hostile propaganda demystifying the emperor, including showing film of him feeding cows at a time when people were dying of famine in parts of the country. Their clever work stripped him of his clothes, to vary the metaphor, and left the emperor stark naked!

As they took him in a Volkswagen Beetle to his place of detention, the crowd shouted words of abuse. A rumor would circulate that the emperor told his captors in the car that his beloved people thought the palace was being robbed, and that was why they were shouting, "Robber! Robber! Robber!" If the rumor is true, it means he had taken leave of reality and retreated into an inner world. He remained in detention for some months before he was taken to the old palace, Menelik's Ghibbi, where he died one year after his overthrow.

The manner of his death is shrouded in mystery. There is a story that he was quietly murdered by Mengistu and secretly buried underneath the office from which Mengistu would rule Ethiopia for seventeen years, before being overthrown by the combined forces of the EPLF and EPRDF. When former servants of the emperor informed the new government about his secret burial, they had the decency to disinter his remains and allow him to be buried properly beside the tomb of his beloved Empress Menen.

However Emperor Haile Selassie died, it was a lonely death, with few to mourn him. Most of his relatives were either dead, exiled, or in detention, and his ministers and the palace hangers-on were detained or dispersed. It was reported that at the time of the reburial of his remains, there was only one blood relative openly mourning for him: his granddaughter (the illegitimate daughter of his late son Makonnen). It is also noteworthy that representatives of the Rastafarians were present on the occasion.

Conclusion

The pathos of the emperor's lonely death must have shocked and saddened all who admired him, Ethiopians and non-Ethiopians. To those who followed his career closely, however, it is a tragic reminder of the fact that he was a lonely man in much of what he did all his life. It was an integral part of the mystique of his majesty. (It was not without reason that his title was "His Imperial Majesty.") He always made his decisions alone, never divulging his views or plans even to his closest confidants. All decisions made by the young Tafari while struggling to ascend to the throne, or by the older Haile Selassie, served one goal—gaining and maintaining power. The means he deployed to gain power, including intellectual and monetary resources, were amazing. The way he disposed of threats by some of the traditional nobility, such as Dejasmach Balcha, was masterly. And he exhibited incredible calm throughout the struggle to ascend to the throne and to guard it against adversaries. These qualities were, to a large extent, forged during his orphaned childhood, "steeled by adversity," as the title of a chapter of this book puts it.

Was Haile Selassie a progressive modernizer who shaped Ethiopia's destiny? The answer to this question is undoubtedly in the positive. Did his pursuit of power reflect a commitment to a higher purpose, such as modernization and centralization of the Ethiopian state? This too must be answered in the positive, despite some opposed views that contend that his use of power was purely for selfish ends that went against the interests of the nation. One commentator divides the record of the emperor's policies and politics into a progressive phase and a reactionary phase, concluding that his progressive phase ended in 1955 with the promulgation of the Revised Constitution. According to this view, the acquisition and maintenance of power was "a matter of obsessive concern" to the emperor. In other words, he did not stand for progress for its own sake, "but rather that progress was a concomitant of his quest for power."[1]

On this view, even the centralization of the state, which meant destroying or diminishing the power of the reactionary forces opposed to progress, was not altogether altruistic but was pursued in the service of monopolizing power, and had a negative side, denying people the exercise of regional power. The better view seems to be that such a judgment needs to take into account the historical circumstances. The emperor's unwarranted abolition of the federation of Ethiopia and Eritrea, for example, was an unfortunate example of a decision taken in pursuit of personal (imperial) power that ended tragically. The argument that the emperor's policy, beginning with the 1943 decree, which consummated Haile Selassie's early modernizing and centralizing aims, was in accordance with the needs of an underdeveloped state is justified, in my view.

The consensus is that the denial of democracy is the central issue on which the emperor finally stumbled. Democracy was one of the exciting promises of his earlier work, and in refusing to grant more power to the central institutions of the state, including the cabinet and the parliament, he certainly chose personal power over national interest. This was indeed his principal failure as a leader, and contributed to his tragic end. Perhaps a more critical cause of his fall was his inability or unwillingness to change the condition of the Ethiopian masses, who lived in abject poverty contrasted with the few who monopolized land and other resources. The rapid decline of his authority in the last days of his reign, the disrespect shown by the mob, and his ignominious end should be a lesson to actual and would-be autocrats. For what was once considered an impregnable imperial edifice crumbled like the walls of ancient Jericho at the sound of Joshua's trumpets.

Tafari with his father, Ras Makonnen, who raised the motherless child, ca. 1905

The newly crowned King Tafari, 1928

The emperor in his exile years, appearing before the League of Nations to plead his country's case, 1936

Emperor Haile Selassie, mid- to late 1950s

A delegation of the Dergue informs the emperor that he will be removed from the palace, 1974 (courtesy of Tsehai Publishers)

Notes

Preface

1. Bereket Habte Selassie, *The Crown and the Pen.*
2. The author, who was a close friend and confidant of General Aman Andom, was privy to information about the general's attempts, via Ras Imru, to convince the emperor to relinquish his funds in Swiss bank accounts.
3. Ras Imru's memoirs were edited by Fekade Azeze.

Chapter 1: Leadership in the Context of Ethiopian History and Mythology

1. In an unpublished paper, Donald Levine suggests geographical distance as a source of legitimacy. A copy of the paper is in the author's possession.
2. Imru, *Kayehut, Kemastawsew.*
3. The reference is to Ato Gaitachew Bekele.

Chapter 3: Harar, Ras Makonnen, and Menelik's Court

1. The victory of Menelik's army over that of Emir Abdullahi and the exchange of notes between the two on the eve of the battle of Chelenko are the subjects of legends. One legend is that the emir advised Menelik to convert to Islam if he wanted to receive the victorious emir's mercy

after the battle. For Menelik's response, see Monfreid, *Ménélik tel qu'il fut*.

Chapter 4: The Feud with Iassu—the Plot Thickens

1. Thesiger, *Life of My Choice*.
2. See Selassie, *My Life and Ethiopia's Progress*, 1:44.
3. Prouty, *Empress Taytu and Menilek II*, 337.

Chapter 5: The 1916 Coup d'État and the Rise of a Man of Destiny

1. Menelik is considered the creator of modern Ethiopia, a much expanded version of the core part of ancient Ethiopia. Many Ethiopians believe that what Menelik accomplished was not conquest but a recovery of what had been lost.
2. See Imru, *Kayehut, Kemastawsew*, 61–66.
3. Ibid., 27.
4. Ibid.
5. *Teqil* was Tafari's *yeferess sem* (nom de guerre).
6. See Selassie, *My Life and Ethiopia's Progress*, 1:83. In his visit to Aden, he was able to fly in an airplane and was also given an exhibition of bombing from the air, something that he used to good advantage a few years later in a conflict with a local feudal lord. He also used bombing against a rebellion in northern Ethiopia, for which he was criticized.
7. Mosley, *Haile Selassie*, 123, citing Rey, *In the Country of the Blue Nile*.
8. Ibid., 122.

Chapter 6: From King to Emperor

1. Haile Selassie is his baptismal name, which is recited by priests during the funeral service. All Christians of the Orthodox denomination are given baptismal names.

2. Cited in Mosley, *Haile Selassie.* 163.

3. By tradition, "invited guests" are required to obtain the permission of the host before departing. It would amount to the crime of lèse-majesté to break this custom.

4. Cited in Mosley, *Haile Selassie,* 172.

5. Ibid.

Chapter 7: The Italian Invasion and the Emperor's Exile

1. De Bono, *Anno XIII*, cited in Mosley, *Haile Selassie*, 176.

2. For a detailed description of the Italo-Ethiopian War of 1936, see Steer, *Caesar in Abyssinia*, cited in Mosley, *Haile Selassie,* 188–99.

3. I am indebted to my friend Mezgbu G. Amlak for bringing Campbell's book to my attention.

Chapter 8: World War II and the Return of the Emperor to Ethiopia

1. Cited in Mosley, *Haile Selassie,* 246.

2. Ibid., 250.

3. Ibid., 251. The Amharic version of the speech is more poetic.

4. Mosley, *Haile Selassie,* 251–52.

Chapter 9: Postliberation Developments

1. Getachew, *Beyond the Throne.*

2. Farago, *Abyssinia on the Eve,* 70–71, quoted in Makonnen Tegegn, "Walda-Giyorgis Walda-Yohannes," 135.

3. That the emperor did not take kindly to criticism of his laws is borne out by my own experiences with him. In 1966 he banished me to Harar for three years as a result of a critique I wrote in a British law journal on his "reform" of the cabinet system.

4. See my memoirs, *The Crown and the Pen*, especially chap. 10.

Chapter 10: Diplomacy: The American Connection and Nonalignment

1. Eritrea became an Italian colony in January 1889, when the Italian government consolidated its conquest of the area, giving it the name Eritrea. The conquest began with the acquisition of the port of Asab by an Italian company, which later relinquished it to the government, and gradually expanded from the Red Sea area to the highlands, ending in the declaration establishing the colony. Throughout, there had been military engagements in which the forces of Emperor Yohannes thwarted earlier Italian attempts at conquest. But Yohannes was killed fighting the Sudanese Dervishes in 1889, and Menelik succeeded him. The claim that Menelik "sold" Eritrea is related to Menelik's dealings with the Italians, obtaining from them arms and ammunition and expanding the empire southward while Yohannes was engaged in defending the country against foreign incursions. People ask: Why didn't Menelik press his advantage to push the Italians out following his victory over them at Adwa in 1896? From this question follows the conclusion that he "sold" Eritrea to the Italians. This is one of the endlessly debated questions among Ethiopians.

2. As a witness to the process of creation of the OAU, I can attest to the critical role Haile Selassie played in its success.

Chapter 11: Turning of the Tide: A Shaken Emperor on the Horns of a Dilemma

1. Kalekristos Abai, a former member of the emperor's bodyguard, wrote his memoirs (in Amharic) on the 1960 attempted coup, in which he gives a list of names that the coup

makers had planned to make up a cabinet of ministers. The author's name figures in the list (at p. 142).

2. Bahru Zewde, "Hayla-Sellase," 107.

Chapter 12: Last Days: Revolution and the End of the Monarchy

1. Bahru Zewde, "Hayla-Sellase," 109.

Conclusion

1. Bahru Zewde, "Hayla-Sellase," 101.

Selected Bibliography

Abbink, Jon. "The Organization and Observation of Elections in Federal Ethiopia: Retrospect and Prospect." In *Election Observation and Democratization in Africa*, edited by Jon Abbink and Gerti Hesseling, 150–79. Basingstoke: Macmillan, 1999. Accessed June 12, 2013. Africa-Wide Information, EBSCOhost.

———. "Religion in Public Spaces: Emerging Muslim-Christian Polemics in Ethiopia." *African Affairs* 110, no. 439 (2011): 253–74.

Abraham, Emmanuel. *Reminiscences of My Life*. Rev. and updated, 1st American ed. Trenton, NJ: Red Sea Press, 2011.

Almagor, Uri. "The Year of the Emperor and the Elephant among the Dassanetch of Ethiopia." *Northeast African Studies* 7, no. 1 (2000): 1–22.

Araia, Ghelawdewos. *Ethiopia: The Political Economy of Transition*. Accessed June 12, 2013. Lanham, MD: University Press of America, 1995. Africa-Wide Information, EBSCOhost.

Asfaw, Kumsa. "Ethiopia, Revolution and the National Question: The Case of the Oromos." *Journal of African Studies* 15, nos. 1–2 (1988): 16–22.

Bahru Zewde. "Hayla-Sellase: From Progressive to Reactionary." *Northeast African Studies* 2, no. 2 (1995): 99–114.

Bedasse, Monique. "Rasta Evolution: The Theology of the Twelve Tribes of Israel." *Journal of Black Studies* 40, no. 5 (2010): 960–73.

Bekele, Getachew. *The Emperor's Clothes: A Personal Viewpoint on Politics and Administration in the Imperial Ethiopian Government, 1941–1974.* East Lansing: Michigan State University Press, 1993.

Bekele, Getnet. "Food Matters: The Place of Development in Building the Postwar Ethiopian State, 1941–1974." *International Journal of African Historical Studies* 42, no. 1 (2009): 29–54.

Bereket Habte Selassie. *The Crown and the Pen: The Memoirs of a Lawyer Turned Rebel.* Trenton, NJ: Red Sea Press, 2007.

Berhanu, Abebe. "The Haile Selassie I Prize Trust." *Northeast African Studies* 2, no. 3 (1995): 53–66.

Beseat, Kiflé Sélassié. "Convaincre, controler ou contraindre? Systèmes et mécanismes de contrôles du pouvoir en Afrique." *Présence africaine: Revue culturelle du monde noir*, nos. 127–128 (1983): 79–113. Accessed June 12, 2013. Africa-Wide Information, EBSCOhost.

Campbell, Ian. *The Plot to Kill Graziani.* Addis Ababa: Addis Ababa University Press, 2010.

Clapham, Christopher. *Haile Selassie's Government.* London: Longmans, 1969.

———. "How Many Ethiopians?" *Africa* 63, no. 1 (1993): 118–28.

Coleman, Sterling Joseph, Jr. "Gradual Abolition or Immediate Abolition of Slavery? The Political, Social, and Economic Quandary of Emperor Haile Selassie I." *Slavery and Abolition* 29, no. 1 (2008): 65–82. Accessed June 12, 2013. Historical Abstracts, EBSCOhost.

Copley, Gregory R. *Ethiopia Reaches Her Hand unto God: Imperial Ethiopia's Unique Symbols, Structures, and*

Role in the Modern World. Alexandria, VA.: Defense and Foreign Affairs, International Strategic Studies Association, 1998.

Courtlander, Harold. "The Emperor Wore Clothes: Visiting Haile Selassie in 1943." *American Scholar* 58, no. 2 (1989): 271. Accessed June 12, 2013. Historical Abstracts, EBSCOhost.

De Bono, Emilio. *Anno XIII: The Conquest of an Empire.* London: Cresset Press, 1937.

D'Souza, P. P. "The Ethiopian Parliament: Origin and Evolution." *Africa Quarterly* 20, nos. 3–4 (1981): 19–29. Accessed June 12, 2013. Historical Abstracts, EBSCOhost.

Erlich, Haggai. "Haile Selassie and the Arabs, 1935–1936." *Northeast African Studies* 1, no. 1 (1994): 47–61.

Farago, Ladislas. *Abyssinia on the Eve.* New York: Putnam, 1935.

Gebeyehu, Temesgen. "The Genesis and Evolution of the Ethiopian Revolution and the *Derg*: A Note on Publications by Participants in Events." *History in Africa* 37 (2010): 321–27. Accessed June 12, 2013: Historical Abstracts, EBSCOhost.

Gebissa, Ezekiel. "The Italian Invasion, the Ethiopian Empire, and Oromo Nationalism: The Significance of the Western Oromo Confederation of 1936." *Northeast African Studies* 9, no. 3 (2002): 75–96.

Gebrekidan, Fikru Negash. *Bond without Blood: A History of Ethiopian and New World Black Relations, 1896–1991.* Trenton, NJ: Africa World Press, 2005.

Getachew, Indrias. *Beyond the Throne: The Enduring Legacy of Emperor Haile Selassie I.* Addis Ababa: Shama Books, 2001.

Girma, Amare. "Education and Society in Pre-revolutionary Ethiopia." *Northeast African Studies* 6, nos. 1–2 (1984): 61–79.

Haile Selassie. *My Life and Ethiopia's Progress: The Autobiography of Emperor Haile Selassie I*. 2 vols. Oxford: Oxford University Press, 1976.

Imru Haile Selassie. *Kayehut, Kemastawsew*. Addis Ababa: Addis Ababa University Press, 2010.

Jacobs, Virginia Lee. *Roots of Ras Tafari*. San Diego: Avant Books, 1985.

Juniac, Contran. *Le dernier roi des rois*. Paris: Plon, 1979.

Kapuscinski, Ryszard. *The Emperor*. New ed. London: Penguin, 2006.

Keller, Edmond J. "Ethiopia: Revolution, Class, and National Question." *African Affairs* 80, no. 321 (1981): 519–49.

Larebo, Haile Mariam. "The Ethiopian Orthodox Church and Politics in the Twentieth Century: Part II." *Northeast African Studies* 10, no. 1 (1988): 1–23.

Legum, Colin. *Ethiopia: The Fall of Haile Selassie's Empire*. New York: Africana, 1975.

Levine, Donald. *Greater Ethiopia: A Multiethnic Society*. Chicago: University of Chicago Press, 2000.

Lockot, Hans Wilhelm. *The Mission: The Life, Reign, and Character of Haile Selassie I*. London: Hurst, 1989.

Lyons, Terrence. "The United States and Ethiopia: the Politics of a Patron-Client Relationship." *Northeast African Studies* 8, nos. 2–3 (1986): 53–75.

Makonnen Tegegn. "Walda-Giyorgis Walda-Yohannes and the Haile Sellassie Government." *Northeast African Studies* 4, no. 2 (1997): 91–138.

Mandela, Nelson. *Long Walk to Freedom: The Autobiography of Nelson Mandela*. Boston: Little, Brown, 1994.

Marcus, Harold G. *Haile Selassie I: The Formative Years, 1982–1936*. Berkeley: University of California Press, 1987.

Mcvety, Amanda Kay. "Pursuing Progress: Point Four in Ethiopa." *Diplomatic History* 32, no. 3 (2008): 371–403.

Milkia, Paulos. *Haile Selassie, Western Education, and Political Revolution in Ethiopia.* Youngstown, NY: Cambria Press, 2006.

Mockler, Anthony. *Haile Selassie's War.* New York: Olive Branch Press, 2002.

Monfreid, Henri de. *Le masque d'or, ou Le dernier négus.* Paris: B. Grasset, 1936.

———. *Ménélik tel qu'il fut.* Paris: B. Grasset, 1954.

Mosley, Leonard. *Haile Selassie: The Conquering Lion.* London: Weidenfeld and Nicolson, 1964.

Pankhurst, Richard. "Emperor Haile Sellassie's Arrival in Britain: An Alternative Autobiographical Draft by Percy Arnold." *Northeast African Studies* 9, no. 2 (2002): 1–46.

Prouty, Chris. *Empress Taytu and Menilek II: Ethiopia 1883–1910.* Trenton, NJ: Red Sea Press, 1986.

Rey, C. F. *In the Country of the Blue Nile.* London: Duckworth, 1927.

Sandford, Christine Lush. *Ethiopia under Hailé Selassié.* London: J. M. Dent, 1946.

Schwab, Peter. *Haile Selassie I: Ethiopia's Lion of Judah.* Chicago: Nelson-Hall, 1979.

Shehim, Kassim. "Ethiopia, Revolution, and the Question of Nationalities: The Case of Afar." *Journal of Modern African Studies* 23, no. 2 (1985): 331–48.

Steer, George L. *Caesar in Abyssinia.* London: Hodder and Stoughton, 1936.

Thesiger, Wilfred. *The Life of My Choice.* London: Collins, 1987.

Vestal, Theodore M. *The Lion of Judah in the New World: Emperor Haile Selassie of Ethiopia and the Shaping of Americans' Attitude toward Africa.* Santa Barbara, CA: Praeger, 2011.

Index

Aba Indrias, 24
Aba Petros, 43
Aba Samuel, 24, 43
Abate, Ras, 33, 36, 51
Aba Wukaw, 50
Abebe Aregai, guerrilla fighter against Italian occupation, 63, 92
Abraha Deboch, Eritrean who attempted to assassinate Graziani in 1937, 63
Abuna Yohannes, 24
Addis Zaman (New era) (daily newspaper), 70
administration of justice, 78
Ahmed Gragne, 21
Aman Andom, 118
armed forces revolt, 112–13
army, salaried national, 56
Asfa-Wosen, 90
Asmach Mirach, 110
Asrate Kasa, 95

Bahru Zewde, 101
Balch, Dejasmach, 10, 43
Battle of Adua, 28, 59
Bet-Lehem, 57
British-French contacts, 48-49

Campbell, Ian, 63
Catholic Mission, 24

CELU (Confederation of Ethiopian Labor Unions), 109
Chilot, final emperor's court, 78
Chou En Lai, 85
Christian faith, 17
Christian state, religious nationalism, 17–18
Churchill, Winston, 66, 70, 83
Code of Civil Procedure, 76
Code of Criminal Procedure, 76
Codes of Law, 76–77
Cold War, 85
coup attempt by the emperor's bodyguard, 39, 44
coup of 1974, 112–19
Covenant of the League of Nations, 59–61, 86
"creeping coup," 119. *See also* coup of 1974
Cunningham, General, 67–68

David, René, drafter of Ethiopia's Civil Code, 76, 77
De Bono, General, and Mussolini, 59–60
democracy, lack of, 75–76
Dergue, armed forces coordinating committee that toppled Haile Selassie, 117–19

Dimbleby, Jonathan, British journalist who exposed the Ethiopia famine, 111
diplomacy, 82

East-West Rivalry (Cold War), 85
economic development under Selassie, 78–79
Eden, Anthony, and his support of Ethiopia's case, 70
education: under Tafari, 48–49; under Selassie, 79–81
Edward VII, King: Ras Makonnen as Menelik's envoy at coronation, 28
Ejersa Goro, emperor's birthplace, 23, 57
Emir Abdullahi, last emir of Harar, 27
Endalkachew Makonnen and his short-lived premiership, 116–17
Eritrean People's Liberation Front (EPLF), 109–11
Eritrea's rebellion, 109–11
Ethiopian People's Revolutionary Party (EPRP), 109–11

Geez, ancient Ethiopian language of liturgy, 23
Germame Neway, and 1960 coup attempt, 91–95
Gospel of Matthew: genealogy of Jesus and Ethiopian royal mythology, 17–18
Gravin, Jean, drafter of Ethiopian Penal Code, 76
Graziani, Rodolfo, Italian fascist governor of Ethiopia, 63
Gugsa, Ras, husband of Empress Zewditu, 51–52; rebellion against Tafari, 52

Habtegiorgis, Fitawrari, gray eminence under Menelik and his successors, 44, 45–47, 50
Haile Selassie Charitable Trust, 108
Hailu, Ras, governor of Gojam, 48, 57, 67, 68
Harar province, 23, 26, 27–29, 32–34, 42–44, 45–46
Haremaya (Alemaya) Lake, and near-drowning of Tafari, 42–43
Hitler, Adolf, 61, 65

Iassu, Lij. *See* Lij Iassu
Imru, Ras, cousin and ardent supporter of Haile Selassie, 10–12, 23–24, 32, 34, 43, 62
Italian East Africa, 65–66

Jan-Meda power showdown, 45
justice, administration of, 78
Justinian, 61

Kalekristos Abai, 134n1 (chap. 11)
Kaunda, Kenneth, 88
Kebra Nagast (Glory of Kings), source of mythology on the Solomonic Dynasty, 17
King Menelik. *See* Menelik II
King Michael, Lij Iassu's father, 29–30, 34, 36, 42, 44
Kombolsha, where Tafari (later Haile Selassie) lived as a child with Imru, 23–24

Labor Relations Proclamation, 94
labor unions, 107–9
League of Nations, 59–61, 84, 86
legitimacy, criteria for royal succession, 15–17

Levin, Donald, Ethiopianist/sociologist, 131n1 (chap. 1)
Lij Iassu, 20, 51; feuding with Tafari for succession, 20, 29–31, 33, 35–36, 42–44; Islamic inclination of, 20, 22, 29, 30, 33–35, 42, 43–45; vision of Christian-Muslim Congruence, 36–38
Lion of Judah, a title of Ethiopian kings, 11, 16–17
Lorenzo Taezaz, principal draftsman of Haile Selassie's Geneva speech, 62, 66

Makonnen, Ras, Haile Selassie's father, 23–29, 41–42, 54
Mandela, Nelson, 13, 86
Maritime Code of Ethiopia, 76
marriage, minimum age of, 77–78
Mboya, Tom, Kenyan labor leader and statesman, 87–88
Meison (All-Ethiopia Socialist Movement), 104–5
Melk'a Mariam (Life of Mary, 23–24
Melk'a Yesus (Life of Jesus), 24
Memh'r Woldekiodan, Tafari's early teacher, 24
Menelik II, creator of an expanded Ethiopian empire, 16, 18, 21, 25, 30–31, 33, 36, 40; Menelik's conquest, 27–28
Mengistu Haile Mariam, head of the military that overthrew Haile Selassie, 118 et seq.
Mengistu Neway, leader of 1960 coup attempt, 91–93
Michael. *See* King Michael
Mogues Asgedom, Eritrean who attempted to assassinate Graziani, 63

Moi, Daniel Arap, former president of Kenya, 87
Moumie, Felix, Cameroun leader killed by French Secret Service, 87–88
Mussolini, Benito, 59, 62, 65, 82, 86

Nehru, Pandit, 85
Neyerere, Julius, 12, 86
nonalignment movement, 85–89

Organization of African Unity (OAU), 85–89
Orthodox Christianity, 34
Ouko, Robert, former Kenyan foreign minister, 87

Pan-Africanism, 87–89
Pankhurst, Richard, 88
Pankhurst, Rita, 88
Panza, Italian island where Ras Imru spent five years as a POW, 12
Paulos Menameno, 43
Psalms (Mezmure-Dawit), subject of elementary Ethiopian education, 23

Rastafarianism (Rasta), 10, 58
rebellions, regional, 102; in Horn of Africa, 109–11
reform commissions, established after 1960 failed coup, 96
Revelations, Book of, 16–17
revised constitution of 1955, 74
revolution of 1974. *See* coup of 1974
Rey, C. F., British writer and early visitor of Ethiopia, 49
Roosevelt, Franklin Delano, 83–84
rule of law and its challenges, 76–78

Sahle Selassie, Haile Selassie's youngest son, 87
salaried national army, 56
Segaley, decisive battle in which Haile Selassie prevailed against Lij Iassu, 44
Sékou Touré, president of Guinea, 89
Seyoum, Ras, Tigrayan nobleman, 48
Shoa, central region of Ethiopia, 32
Solomon, King, progenitor of the "Solomonic dynasty," 15–18
Stalin, Joseph, 83
student movement, 99

Tafari Makonnen (Haile Selassie's name until 1930), 16, 20, 23, 26, 30, 32–35, 41–50, 51–53, 75; belief in dynastic genealogy, 16; crowned emperor as Haile Selassie in 1930, 52–53; early education, 23–25; European tour, 48; as orphaned prince, 23–26; cro
Taitu, Empress, Menelik's consort, 29–31, 33–34, 36, 41, 51
Takele Woldehawariat, Haile Selassie's staunch supporter, and later opponent, 41, 63
Teklehawariat, Fitawrrari, Russian-educated statesman and draftsman of the 1931 constitution, 54, 55

Teodros, Emperor, nineteenth-century modernizing figure, 39-40
Tito, Josip Broz, 85

United Nations Resolution 390A(V) of 1950, joining Eritrea with Ethiopia, 84
University College of Addis Ababa, 80–81

Vitalia, Doctor, teacher and guardian of Tafari Makonnen, 24

Wingate, Major Orde: helping Haile Selassie return to his country after exile in England, 66–68
Wohni Amba, royal prison, 42
Woldegiorgis Woldeyohannes, the emperor's close advisor and most influential minister, 41, 53, 57 58, 59, 67
World War I, 27

Yalta, 67
Yeshimebet, Woizero, Tafari's mother, 15
Yohannes, Emperor, Menelik's predecessor, 26

Zewditu, Empress, Menelik's daughter and Haile Selassie's predecessor, 44, 50–52

OHIO SHORT HISTORIES OF AFRICA
PATRICE LUMUMBA
GEORGES NZONGOLA-NTALAJA

PATRICE LUMUMBA was a leader of the independence struggle in what is today the Democratic Republic of the Congo, as well as the country's first democratically elected prime minister. After rising through the colonial civil service and the African political elite, he became a major figure in the decolonization movement of the 1950s. Lumumba's short tenure as prime minister (1960–61) was marked by an uncompromising defense of Congolese national interests against pressure from international mining companies and the Western governments that orchestrated his eventual demise.

Cold war geopolitical maneuvering and coordinated efforts by Lumumba's domestic adversaries culminated in his assassination at the age of thirty-five, with the support or at least the tacit complicity of the U.S. and Belgian governments, the CIA, and the UN Secretariat. Even decades after Lumumba's death, his personal integrity and unyielding dedication to the ideals of self-determination, self-reliance, and pan-African solidarity assure him a prominent place among the heroes of the twentieth-century African independence movement and the worldwide African diaspora.

Georges Nzongola-Ntalaja is a professor of African, African American, and diaspora studies at the University of North Carolina at Chapel Hill and professor emeritus of African studies at Howard University. He is a past president of the African Studies Association and the author of *The Congo from Leopold to Kabila: A People's History*.

Patrice Lumumba

Georges Nzongola-Ntalaja

OHIO UNIVERSITY PRESS

ATHENS

Ohio University Press, Athens, Ohio 45701
ohioswallow.com
© 2014 by Ohio University Press
All rights reserved

To obtain permission to quote, reprint, or otherwise reproduce or
distribute material from Ohio University Press publications, please
contact our rights and permissions department at (740) 593-1154 or
(740) 593-4536 (fax).

Printed in the United States of America
Ohio University Press books are printed on acid-free paper ∞ ™

24 23 22 21 20 19 18 17 16 15 14   5 4 3 2 1

Library of Congress Cataloging-in-Publication Data
Nzongola-Ntalaja, Georges, 1944– author.
  Patrice Lumumba / Georges Nzongola-Ntalaja.
    pages cm. — (Ohio short histories of Africa)
  Includes bibliographical references and index.
  ISBN 978-0-8214-2125-3 (pb : alk. paper) — ISBN 978-0-8214-4506-8 (pdf)
  1. Lumumba, Patrice, 1925–1961. 2. Prime ministers—Congo (Democratic Republic)—Biography. 3. Congo (Democratic Republic)—Politics and government—1908–1960. 4. Congo (Democratic Republic)—Politics and government—1960–1997. I. Title. II. Series: Ohio short histories of Africa.
  DT658.2.L85N96 2014
  967.5103092—dc23

2014029924

Cover design by Joey Hi-Fi

Contents

Preface and Acknowledgments 7
Abbreviations and Acronyms 15
Name Equivalency 17
Map of the Congo 18
Introduction 19

1. Early Years, Youth, and Formal Education, 1925–44 29
2. Civil Service Career and Political Apprenticeship in Kisangani, 1944–56 37
3. Years of Transition, 1956–58 53
4. The Struggle for Independence, 1958–60 66
5. The Short Political Life of Congo's First Prime Minister, 1960–61 85
6. Lumumba and the Counterrevolution in Central and Southern Africa 101
7. Lumumba's Assassination 117
8. The Political Legacy of Patrice Lumumba 134

Chronology	141
Notes	149
Bibliography	155
Index	159

Preface and Acknowledgments

Having grown up as a teenager in the second half of the 1950s, I belong to a generation of young people who were politicized by the struggles of Africans living in colonial territories for decolonization, or freedom from colonial rule. In the Belgian Congo, the country known today as the Democratic Republic of the Congo (DRC), Patrice Lumumba was the most eloquent and the best known of the leaders of the national independence movement. As high school students with some knowledge of world history and current affairs, we were greatly impressed by his vision of a united and strong country that, given its enormous wealth in natural resources, was likely to play a major role in Africa's unity and development.

Although I never met Lumumba, I was greatly inspired by his wonderful speeches on the radio and his statements in the newspapers. I became so involved in active advocacy for independence that in April 1960, two months before Congo's independence on June 30, I was expelled for anticolonial activities from the Methodist-Presbyterian secondary school in which I was enrolled. Unfortunately, the joy we felt on that momentous day was quickly dissipated by the crisis our country fell into for reasons that were beyond our comprehension. That a person who was democratically elected prime minister and enjoyed majority support in Parliament would be driven out of power and then imprisoned, tortured, and assassinated in less than seven months after independence was too traumatic for most of us to cope with.

Thus, to the trauma suffered by the country due to the heinous crimes of Belgian King Leopold II in an effort to maximize his colonial investment with enormous profits from the brutal exploitation of Congolese resources between 1885 and 1908, was now added the trauma of Lumumba's assassination and the tragic political crisis surrounding it. This crisis took place in the context of the cold war as part of the counterrevolution against national liberation in Central and Southern Africa by a coalition of mining companies, white settlers, and right-wing political groups in the West. A very idealistic young man without much political experience, Lumumba was isolated among unprincipled politicians eager mostly to amass power and wealth, and an international community dominated by those who feared his independence and thus found it convenient to frame his militant nationalism as sympathy for communism.

This book is designed to tell the story of Lumumba's life. Who was he? What made him such an illustrious leader not only in the Congo but also all over Africa, the African diasporas of North America and the Caribbean, and the Third World? Given his centrality to the history of the independence struggle in the Congo and his stature as a pan-African leader, Lumumba deserves a volume in the Ohio Short Histories of Africa. His short, tragic, but inspiring life will certainly enrich this series of informative and concise introductions to important topics in African history. I am very grateful, indeed, to Gillian Berchowitz of Ohio University Press for asking me to contribute this volume on Lumumba to the series, and the two anonymous readers of the manuscript for their excellent comments and recommendations for improving the text.

This biography of Lumumba is based on my reading and research on Congolese politics during the last fifty years, the most important product of which has been my 2002 book *The Congo from Leopold to Kabila: A People's History*. Recently, I was honored to write a long introduction to a short book of Lumumba's speeches and writings published by the Geneva-based Centre Europe-Tiers Monde (CETIM), *Patrice Lumumba: Recueil de textes introduit par Georges Nzongola-Ntalaja* (2013). I am grateful to Julie Duchatel and Florian Rochat, the CETIM editors, for having kindly associated me with this wonderful initiative for a wider dissemination of Lumumba's political thought.

It is hoped that readers of this biography will be so fascinated by Lumumba's incredible story that they will want to learn more about him and his times. Unfortunately for English-language readers, the most comprehensive narrative concerning his life, the historical context in which he came of age politically, and his journey from the lower civil service to the office of prime minister is now available only in books published in French. Of these, four sources need to be singled out. The first is the outstanding book by Jean-Marie Mutamba Makombo on the emergence of the *évolués* or African elites and their leadership of the nationalist movement in the Congo, *Du Congo belge au Congo indépendant, 1940–1960* (1998). The second and third sources are the well-researched books on Lumumba's youth, civil service career, and political activities until February 1960 by Jean Omasombo and Benoît Verhaegen entitled *Patrice Lumumba: Jeunesse et apprentissage politique, 1925–1956* (1998) and *Patrice Lumumba, acteur politique: De la prison aux portes du pouvoir, juillet 1956–février 1960* (2005). The fourth source is a look at Lumumba from the context of the history of the Sankuru region by Thomas Turner, *Ethnogenèse et nationalisme en Afrique centrale: Aux racines de Patrice Lumumba* (2000).

When we come to Lumumba's assassination, Anglophone readers have more or less full accounts of the events and the politics behind them, thanks in large part to the excellent scholarly work by Ludo De Witte, a Belgian sociologist, and Stephen R. Weissman, an American political scientist. In addition to its contribution to scholarship, De Witte's *The Assassination of Lumumba* (2001) has the rare distinction of being politically relevant because of its actual political impact in Belgium. Originally published in Flemish in 1999 and then in French translation in 2000, the book was so explosive in its revelations that it eventually led to a Belgian parliamentary inquiry on Belgium's responsibility in Lumumba's murder. Weissman, for his part, has done an outstanding job in piercing through secrecy to elucidate the U.S. role in Lumumba's political demise and assassination, first in his book *American Foreign Policy in the Congo, 1960–1964* (1974), written before the Freedom of Information Act (FOIA), and in his subsequent articles, based on documents released under the FOIA, on the involvement of the U.S. Central Intelligence Agency (CIA) in the murder. Along with the French-language publications mentioned above, the works of De Witte and Weissman have made a very useful contribution to our knowledge of the life, work, and martyrdom of Patrice Lumumba.

With particular respect to the cold war, which served as a smokescreen for the neocolonialist strategy of the West in Central and Southern Africa, invaluable information on its exploitation to justify Lumumba's assassination can be obtained from the archives of the principal players in the Lumumba drama: Belgium, the United States, the United Nations, and the Soviet Union, whose archives are now under the control of the Russian Federation. Having done research on the Congo crisis in the United Nations Archives in New York in 1986 and 1987, I was delighted to be invited to an international conference, "The Congo

Crisis, 1960–1961," organized by the Cold War International History Project (CWIHP) of the Woodrow Wilson International Center for Scholars, held in Washington, D.C., on September 23–24, 2004. The conference brought together some of the surviving actors of the Congo drama, such as Larry Devlin, the former CIA station chief in Kinshasa; Congolese politicians Cléophas Kamitatu and Thomas Kanza; and several scholars who had done research in one of the key archives: Russian, U.S., or UN. A very useful conference reader containing important documents and writings was edited by two of these scholars, Lise Namikas and Sergey Mazov. The Wilson Center has posted this collection and a transcript of the proceedings of the two-day discussions online at http://www.wilsoncenter.org/publication/the-congo-crisis-1960-1961.

Kanza, who served Lumumba as the Congo's first ambassador to the United Nations, told the conference that Lumumba was killed only three days before the inauguration of President John F. Kennedy because the latter had promised Eleanor Roosevelt that he planned to use his powers to have Lumumba released from jail and let the Congolese Parliament decide whether or not he would remain prime minister. But he did not tell us how this information was made known to the conspirators, who moved with extraordinary haste to preempt Kennedy's alleged intention.

To make the narrative easier for readers, present-day names of locations are used in the book. The colonial era and 1960–66 names of these locations are shown in the name equivalency chart. A map of the Congo and a chronology of major events in Lumumba's life are also included.

It is taken for granted that the summer "vacation" is not necessarily a holiday season for academics, most of whom devote the three months between academic years to doing research. For me, much of June, July, and August 2013 was spent on the manuscript for this biography, which meant spending long hours in my study, and thus depriving my family of my company. Having been raised in a family of professionals in which politics was a constant subject of conversation, my wife, Kulondi Jeanne Lupumba was very patient and understanding. I am grateful for her support.

During the two periods of my active involvement in Congolese politics, in 1992 and 1996, I spent nearly all of my weekends lecturing to young people all over Kinshasa on the political history of our country. Lots of questions were raised about Lumumba, and whether the country could live up to his ideals of self-determination, self-reliance, and pan-African solidarity. With the challenges of poverty, xenophobia, authoritarianism, intolerance, and other ills facing our continent today, all of the youth of Africa must reflect on these ideals. This book is dedicated to them.

Abbreviations and Acronyms

AAPC	All-African Peoples' Conference
Abako	Alliance des Bakongo
ADAPES	Association des Anciens Élèves des Pères de Scheut
AES	Association des Évolués de Stanleyville
ANC	Armée Nationale Congolaise
APCM	American Presbyterian Congo Mission
APIC	Association du Personnel Indigène de la Colonie
APIPO	Amicale des Postiers Indigènes de la Province Orientale
Balubakat	Association Générale des Baluba du Katanga
Bracongo	Brasserie du Bas-Congo
Bralima	Brasseries, Limonaderies et Malteries Africaines
Cerea	Centre de Regroupement Africain
CFS	Congo Free State
CIA	Central Intelligence Agency

CNKi	Comité National du Kivu
CNS	Conférence Nationale Souveraine
Conakat	Confédération des Associations Tribales du Katanga
CSK	Comité Spécial du Katanga
DRC	Democratic Republic of the Congo
Fédébate	Fédération des Batetela
FNLA	National Front for the Liberation of Angola
FP	Force Publique
Forminière	Société Internationale Forestière et Minière du Congo
Mistebel	Mission Technique Belge au Katanga
MNC-K	Mouvement National Congolais-Kalonji
MNC-L	Mouvement National Congolais-Lumumba
NATO	North Atlantic Treaty Organization
ONUC	Opération des Nations Unies au Congo
PNP	Parti National du Progrès
PSA	Parti Solidaire Africain
Sabena	Société Anonyme Belge de Navigation Aérienne
SGB	Société Générale de Belgique
Symétain	Syndicat Minier de l'Étain
TCL	Tanganyika Concessions Limited
UMHK	Union Minière du Haut-Katanga
UNISCO	Union des Intérêts Sociaux Congolais
YMCA	Young Men's Christian Association

Name Equivalency

Congo 2014

Ilebo
Kananga
Kinshasa
Kisangani
Likasi
Lubumbashi
Mbanza-Ngungu
Mbuji-Mayi
Ubundu

Congo 1960

Port Francqui
Luluabourg
Léopoldville
Stanleyville
Jadotville
Elisabethville
Thysville
Bakwanga
Ponthierville

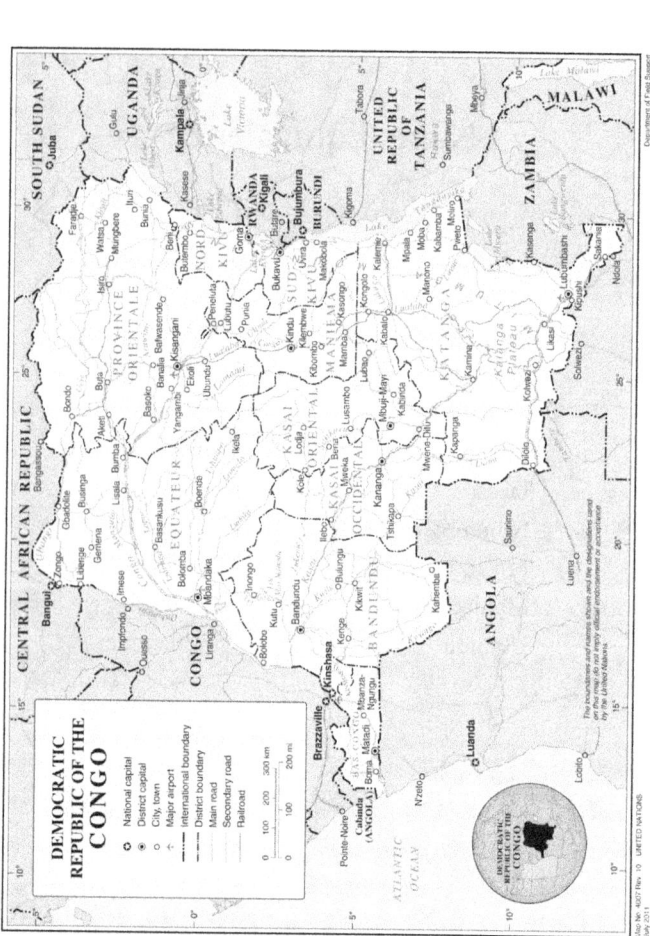

Introduction

Patrice Emery Lumumba was one of the most illustrious African nationalist leaders of the twentieth century. He was born on July 2, 1925, in the village of Onalua, which is located in the *territoire* (subdistrict) of Katako-Kombe of the district of Sankuru in the Kasai Province in the Belgian Congo. Today Sankuru is part of Eastern Kasai Province in the Democratic Republic of the Congo (DRC). Lumumba had a twelve-year career in the Belgian colonial administration (1944–56) before going briefly into business and finally devoting his life to the struggle for the independence of the Congo. He was self-taught; his major certificate of formal studies resulted from one year of technical training in a school for postal clerks in Kinshasa between July 1947 and March 1948. Despite being a school dropout, he read many books on history and contemporary affairs and took several correspondence and evening courses to enrich his knowledge of the world around him. With this education, he learned to write poetry and essays, which served as both inspiration and background to political activism. For an autodidact in a society that placed great stock in formal educational qualifications and diplomas, his social and political ascent before 1956 was remarkable.

A man of tremendous physical and intellectual energy, Lumumba read much and slept little, yet found sufficient strength to lead a very active life professionally and socially. From 1951 to 1956, while working as a postal employee in Kisangani, he held leadership positions in several voluntary organizations at the same time. These included the Association des Évolués de Stanleyville (AES), the Amicale des Postiers Indigènes de la Province Orientale (APIPO), and the Association du Personnel Indigène de la Colonie (APIC). When he moved to Kinshasa in 1957, it did not take long for Lumumba to become president of the Fédération des Associations des Batetela de Léopoldville (Fédébate/Léo). This active involvement in the life and work of civil society organizations helped him acquire skills in public debate, record keeping, and financial management, and was thus an important initiation to political life.

Consistent with his calling as an intellectual, Lumumba contributed articles to several newspapers and magazines on current issues, and particularly on questions regarding the future of the country. Before launching himself fully into politics, he acquired practical experience in business at a major brewery in Kinshasa, the Brasserie du Bas-Congo (Bracongo), where he served first in the accounts department and then as the publicity director. In the latter position, he was entrusted with the job of promoting the sales of Polar beer, a task that unleashed an intense rivalry between Bracongo and Bralima, the brewery making the rival beer Primus. It was during this "beer war" that Lumumba honed the public speaking skills that would serve him so well in political rallies and meetings.

A great political orator and strategist, Lumumba entered national politics through his election on October 10, 1958, as president of the Mouvement National Congolais (MNC), the first and at the time the only political party in the Belgian Congo that was not only multiethnic but also representative of all the strata of the Congolese population and all the regions of the country. In this capacity, he went on to participate in the First All-African Peoples' Conference (AAPC), held in Accra, Ghana, in December 1958; the first congress of Congolese political parties, held in Kananga in April 1959; and the first congress of the MNC, held in Kisangani in October 1959. He was arrested by colonial authorities because of postcongress riots and imprisoned at the notorious underground prison of Likasi, in Katanga. Lumumba was freed following the unanimous demand of Congolese delegates at the Brussels Round Table Conference (January 20–February 20, 1960), who made his participation a sine qua non for holding the negotiations on Congo's future. Lumumba returned home a real hero, and his coalition of nationalist parties won the largest number of seats in parliament to earn the right to set up the first government of independent Congo.

The democratically elected prime minister and first head of government of independent Congo, Lumumba mirrored Congolese public opinion in his reaction to the paternalistic and condescending speech by King Baudouin of the Belgians at the independence ceremony on June 30, 1960. Lumumba's militant nationalist response has become one of his political testaments in Africa. Bending to the pressure of Western governments, which perceived Lumumba's nationalism as a threat to their strategic and economic interests, President Joseph Kasavubu dismissed Prime Minister Lumumba on September 5, 1960, thus unleashing a constitutional crisis in a parliamentary regime in which the prime minister holds full power as long as he has majority support in Parliament. When Lumumba resisted this obviously illegal and illegitimate act, Colonel Joseph-Désiré Mobutu, formerly Lumumba's protégé but an informer for Belgian and American intelligence services, completed the action undertaken by Kasavubu by removing Lumumba from power by a military coup d'état on September 14, 1960.

On November 27, 1960, following a decision of the UN General Assembly to reject the credentials of his delegation in favor of the one representing President Kasavubu, Lumumba decided to flee Kinshasa, where he had been living under house arrest since the coup d'état, to join the nationalist forces in his political fiefdom of Kisangani in the east. He was arrested on December 1 at Lodi, on the left bank of the Sankuru River, brought back to Kinshasa, and held prisoner at the military base of Mbanza-Ngungu. On January 17, 1961, Lumumba and his two companions in misfortune, Maurice Mpolo (minister of youth and sports) and Joseph Okito (vice president of the Senate), were transferred to Lubumbashi, capital of the secessionist province of Katanga. At a villa not far from Lubumbashi's Luano Airport, after being tortured during the long flight, the three nationalist leaders were murdered by a firing squad made up of Belgian soldiers and policemen working for the Katanga government.

A man of principles and strong political convictions, Lumumba endured torture in prison under inhumane conditions and faced death itself with stoic demeanor and serenity. Of the memorable writings he left behind, the two that are considered as constituting his testament are his Independence Day speech, as previously mentioned, and his last letter from jail to his wife.

In addition to introducing readers to the life and work of Patrice Lumumba, this book will discuss important aspects of the history and politics of the Congo during the colonial period and the six months following independence from Belgium. Lumumba's own change from an educated African who held elitist views sympathetic to the so-called civilizing mission of colonialism to a harsh critic of the colonial system and its exploitative, repressive, and oppressive characteristics is very useful for understanding the nature of Belgian colonialism in the Congo and the reasons why the transition to independence was not as smooth as in most British and French colonies. His martyrdom in the struggle for political self-determination, economic self-reliance, and pan-African solidarity against the forces of neocolonialism and counterrevolution is the main reason why he remains such a popular figure in the Congo and in Africa.

Chapter 1 of this book reviews Lumumba's early years, from his birth at Onalua in 1925 to his departure for better opportunities elsewhere in 1944. The chapter examines his unsuccessful attempt to complete primary education in both Catholic and Protestant missions close to his village, a period in which he also spent a few months at a Methodist school for nurse's assistants. This experience introduced Lumumba to European and American Christian missionaries, who acted as willing partners of the Belgian colonial administration in subjecting Africans to the colonial state, and may have influenced Lumumba's preference for Liberals over Catholics in Belgian party politics.

Chapter 2 looks at Lumumba's career in the colonial civil service and his political apprenticeship in Kisangani between 1944 and 1956. After leaving Onalua, Lumumba worked for a few months as a sales clerk for a mining company in Maniema before moving on to Kisangani, where he started his civil service career as a clerk in local colonial administration in November 1944. But much of his career in the colonial administration was spent as a postal clerk. The chapter focuses on the more important aspect of Lumumba's life during this period, namely his political apprenticeship in several types of voluntary associations, including labor unions, elite associations, and interracial discussion clubs known as *amicales*. It was in these organizations, in which Lumumba almost invariably held one of the top leadership positions as president, vice president, or secretary, that he developed the political and organizational skills that would benefit him greatly in the struggle for independence.

It was at the height of his civil service career in 1956 that Lumumba ran into his first trouble with the colonial administration. Following his remarkable rise through self-education and organizational work to become a spokesman for the Congolese elite in Kisangani, Lumumba was invited by Belgian authorities to make a tour of Belgium. Upon his return home he was arrested on charges of embezzlement at the postal service. Chapter 3 will examine the year-long legal battle around these charges and its aftermath, which turned out to be very positive for Lumumba, for the ordeal ended with Lumumba leaving public service to work in the accounts department of a brewery in Kinshasa in September 1957, and his subsequent promotion to the post of publicity director in August 1958. The latter position not only made him widely known to beer drinkers in the middle and working classes of Kinshasa, but also helped him as a rehearsal platform for political campaigning.

Chapter 4 deals with the struggle for independence and Lumumba's central role in it between December 1958 and June 1960. It examines the major events in his rise to prominence as a political leader, together with his contribution to the independence struggle. These events include his role in the establishment and growth of the MNC; his pan-African contacts; his full-time involvement in the struggle for independence beginning on January 1, 1959; and his role in this struggle until the Brussels Round Table Conference on independence in January–February 1960.

As the first democratically elected prime minister of the Congo, Lumumba held effective power from June 30 until his dismissal from office on September 5, 1960, by President Kasavubu. Parliament rejected the president's decision as null and void, since the prime minister had majority support in both legislative houses. However, Colonel Mobutu intervened on September 14 by removing Lumumba from power and placing him under house arrest in the official residence of the prime minister. Since these two actions were illegal, Lumumba remained the legitimate but only nominal prime minister until his assassination on January 17, 1961. Chapter 5 presents a brief analysis of the political dynamics around the political elimination of Lumumba, including why Kasavubu and Mobutu took the actions they did.

Chapter 6 continues this analysis by looking more closely at the international context in which the political and physical elimination of Lumumba took place, a context that was dominated regionally by the national liberation struggle and globally by the cold war. A very important aspect of the assassination is its connection to the Katanga secession as a rallying point for counterrevolution in Central and Southern Africa during the era of decolonization. With the economic interests of the former colonial powers being threatened by radical nationalism, Brussels, London, and Paris were prepared to use their global confrontation with the communist countries to justify continued control over the former colonial territories under the pretext of not losing them to the Soviet camp. In this regard, the unanimous contempt for Lumumba in major Western capitals because of his commitment to self-determination, self-reliance, and pan-African solidarity made him a prime target for elimination from power and political assassination.

While Kasavubu, Mobutu, and other Congolese leaders were willing partners in the political elimination of Lumumba, his physical elimination was originally hatched in two separate plots by the American and Belgian governments. Chapter 7 examines these plots—the commando action of a crocodile hunter recruited to bump off Lumumba in the Belgian Operation Barracuda and the cobra venom project of a CIA scientist—and why they were abandoned in favor of concerted action with Congolese collaborators in assassinating Lumumba. In the end, Belgian security forces actually took part in the act of assassination.

Finally, chapter 8 assesses the political legacy of Patrice Lumumba for both the Congo and Africa. As a martyr and a national hero, Lumumba remains a strong political symbol for Congolese independence and national unity. Across the African continent, where his name is found in many countries in street names and other forms of commemoration, he is widely acclaimed as a symbol of pan-Africanism and African dignity. Like Gamal Abdel Nasser (Egypt), Kwame Nkrumah (Ghana), Amilcar Cabral (Guinea-Bissau and Cape Verde), Julius Nyerere (Tanzania), and Nelson Mandela (South Africa), Patrice Lumumba is highly deserving of this legacy because of his steadfast commitment to the pan-African project of political self-determination, economic self-reliance, and pan-African solidarity.

1

Early Years, Youth, and Formal Education, 1925–44

In 1925, when Patrice Lumumba was born, the Belgian colonial system had consolidated its control over African societies. Forty years of colonial rule, first under the tyranny of King Leopold's Congo Free State (CFS) between 1885 and 1908, and then under the brutal regime of the Belgian Congo, had succeeded in making two important changes. The first was ending the Swahili-Arab occupation of the Sankuru by Ngongo Letete, a military commander from the Maniema region who once worked for the Swahili-Arab slave trader Hamed bin Muhammed el-Murjebi (who is better known by his caravan name of Tippu Tip) before defecting to the CFS side. When a white officer arbitrarily executed Ngongo Letete in 1893, his lieutenants were faced with the choice of going into resistance or remaining loyal to the CFS.

The second and most important change was the subjection of African peasants to the harsh demands of forced labor, compulsory production of certain export crops, taxation without representation, and submissive obedience to colonial officials, missionaries, and African chiefs. Given the vastness of this country of 2,345,409 square kilometers, nearly eighty times the size of Belgium, colonial officials could not administer it alone. They had to depend on African chiefs, who were indispensable in helping fulfill the tasks of economic exploitation and political repression, while Christian missionaries and their African auxiliaries (catechists and teachers) were useful with respect to cultural oppression (the suppression of African values and customs), the third component of colonial rule.

Colonial economic exploitation among the Atetela, Lumumba's ethnic group, had started with the compulsory collection of wild rubber under the CFS. In the area in which Onalua is situated, the exploitation regime was supervised by Chief Wembo Nyama, who served both the CFS and the Belgian Congo between 1893 and 1940. Before that, he had served Ngongo Letete. Rather than joining the nationwide resistance by African troops against the CFS in what Belgians were to erroneously characterize as "Batetela revolts,"[1] Wembo Nyama chose to fight the rebels, and he was well rewarded for his loyalty by Belgian authorities. Ironically, the Belgians simply retained the administrative organization that the Swahili-Arabs had established, and used it for their own economic and political purposes.

Although he was Otetela,[2] Chief Wembo Nyama was not a traditional ruler, since he was not indigenous to the area under his control, nor chosen according to the customary rules and regulations regarding political office there. Imposed by the colonial administration on peoples for whom traditional political authority was organized along clan divisions, each comprising a number of villages, his rule was contested by the traditional ruler of Lumumba's clan, who eventually succeeded in obtaining a separate chiefdom from Wembo Nyama's. Lumumba's personality was obviously influenced by the political independence of Atetela clans such as his own, that of the Ewango, for which Onalua was the seat of power.

There is no doubt, however, that given his military and administrative skills, together with his longevity, Chief Wembo Nyama remained a major political figure in Lumumba's area and left his mark on it. The town he established there as the seat of his administration, Wembo-Nyama-Mibango, has remained an important religious and educational center for the Methodist Church in the Congo. In May 2013, the government of DRC President Joseph Kabila adopted a plan to transform the town of Wembo-Nyama, which is located 7 kilometers from Onalua, into a new city called Lumumbaville. It remains to be seen whether this project will actually materialize or remain a pipe dream.

Although the Catholics, with the creation of the now famous mission of Tshumbe Sainte-Marie in 1910, 38 kilometers from Onalua, were the first Christian missionaries to establish their presence in the area including Lumumba's birthplace, the Protestants did succeed in founding the first Methodist mission at Wembo-Nyama in 1914. Chief Wembo Nyama gave strong support to this initiative, at a time when Catholics were using all of their clout as members of the Belgian colonial trinity (state, church, and large enterprises) to eliminate or at least limit the Protestant presence in the Congo. On top of the historically determined animosity between these two branches of Christianity since the Reformation and the religious wars in Europe, the Belgian establishment was hostile to Protestant missionaries in the Congo because of their contribution to the international campaign against the atrocities committed under the CFS regime of King Leopold II. George Washington Williams, an African American journalist who witnessed some of these atrocities during his tour of the Congo in 1890, had declared them "crimes against humanity." To the west of Wembo-Nyama, at the confluence of the Kasai and Lulua Rivers, American missionaries William Henry Sheppard and William Morrison, at the first American Presbyterian Congo Mission (APCM) station of Luebo (established in 1891), were so active in denouncing these crimes that they were sued for libel in 1908 by the Compagnie du Kasai, a rubber-exploiting concessionary company in which the state was a major shareholder. The company lost the case in a Kinshasa court in 1909.[3]

As a youth, and later as an adult, Lumumba had no time for religious quarrels and judging people on the basis of social distinctions, religious or other. He was baptized as both a Catholic and a Protestant, and in spite of his unpleasant experience at Tshumbe Sainte-Marie—as we shall see below—he later did not hesitate to attend evening classes in Kisangani offered by the Marist Brothers, a Catholic community devoted to teaching and social work. As a lead traditional dancer who reveled in an ever-widening circle of partners, Lumumba grew up with a vision of assembling for fun or purposeful action as many people as he could under the roof. It was this vision that sustained his commitment to national unity, together with the necessity of organizing a nationwide political party to make this ideal a reality.

For children of peasants in developing countries, schooling typically starts late, often past the age of eight or nine, since boys may be needed for farming, herding, or petty trade activities, while girls have numerous household chores, including fetching firewood and water, sometimes far away from home. In Lumumba's case, he was fortunate to have a Catholic catechist in Onalua, who added to his biblical instruction duties the teaching of the equivalent of the first two years of elementary school. From 1931 to 1933, Lumumba took advantage of this less structured learning opportunity. By 1939, he had enrolled in the Methodist primary school at Wembo-Nyama, where he reached the fifth grade in 1942, only to be dismissed following accusations by a Congolese pastor of behavior unbecoming of a Christian youth, including traditional dance, which Lumumba loved and the defenders of Christian piety considered sinful.

Lumumba enrolled in the fifth grade at the Catholic school at Tshumbe Sainte-Marie in January 1943, the first month of the school year in the Belgian Congo until 1953. Unfortunately, he did not complete the school year, mostly due to the hostile learning environment created by mutual dislike between him and his teacher. The student had little respect for the teacher, whom he considered incompetent, and the teacher and the Catholic priest in charge despised Lumumba for challenging their authority.

With nearly five years of primary school under his belt, Lumumba decided to try something new. He enrolled in the Methodist school for nurse's assistants at Tunda, in Maniema, approximately 15 kilometers from the Lomami River, which separates Sankuru from Maniema. Nursing had by then become one of the prestigious occupations for Congolese contemplating entry into the middle class, along with the higher rank of medical assistant, Catholic priesthood, and white-collar employment in the state and private sectors. But Lumumba's stay at Tunda lasted only a few months. He was dismissed when the same pastor who got him expelled at Wembo-Nyama sent a note to the school calling him a "bad boy."

These three episodes demonstrate that already as a young man Lumumba was intellectually precocious, hardworking, and a person who would not suffer fools. He was invariably a leader among his peers, whether at school, at play, or in traditional songs and dance. Eager to learn and to read anything that came into his hands, he seems to have acquired more knowledge of French and some of the topics taught in classes than some of the teachers, most of whom were graduates of the same primary school in which they were teaching. One wonders what he would have become had he been raised in an environment in which he had access to better educational opportunities.

In 1943, when Lumumba left his latest formal schooling at Tunda, the Belgian Congo was at war. With Belgium quickly run over and occupied by the Nazis and its government in exile in London, the colony took up the challenge of fighting against Germany, Italy, and Japan in several theaters of war, including West Africa, Egypt, the Middle East, Ethiopia, and Southeast Asia. This required total labor mobilization through *l'effort de guerre* (the war effort), which included efforts in import substitution industrialization to make up for manufactured goods that could no longer be imported from Europe; the doubling of forced labor for peasants in 1941 from 60 to 120 days a year in order to increase the supply of food and other necessary commodities; the conscription of laborers in Kasai for mines and industries in Katanga and Kivu Provinces; and the conscription of as many young men as possible into the Force Publique (FP), the colonial army. The latter's military victories over Italian troops in Ethiopia is commemorated in Congolese cities on street signs bearing the names of Assosa, Gambela, and Saïo, localities where Congolese troops helped to free Ethiopia from Italian occupation. These victories by the FP against an

Italian contingent three times its size resulted in an Italian surrender south of the Blue Nile of over fifteen thousand troops, including at least nine generals.[4]

In these circumstances, Lumumba, who was eighteen years of age and out of school, could not stay in Onalua without being conscripted or running into trouble with the representatives of colonial authority, both Belgian and Congolese. He found himself not appreciated by either the Catholics, who were deeply involved with the colonial state, or the Methodist missionaries, most of whom were fervent believers in the ideology of white supremacy prevalent in their Dixie homeland in the United States and too timid to challenge colonial repression. Rather than being conscripted into the army or enlisted by colonial authorities to work as a mine or industrial worker, he chose to leave the rural backwater of Katako-Kombe in order to find for himself a white-collar job and better economic opportunities elsewhere. By the end of 1943 or the beginning of 1944, Lumumba and a few friends left Onalua for Maniema to seek employment at Kalima, site of an important mining industry based on cassiterite, colombo-tantalite (coltan), and wolfram. After passing a test consisting of math and French, Lumumba was hired as a sales clerk by Symétain, then the major mining company in Kalima. He stayed there for a few months before departing, first for Ubundu and then for the brighter lights of Kisangani.

2

Civil Service Career and Political Apprenticeship in Kisangani, 1944–56

Lumumba's civil service career lasted nearly twelve years, from November 20, 1944, to July 6, 1956, when he was arrested and imprisoned on charges of embezzlement of funds at the post office. This chapter examines this period of active duty as a civil servant in Kisangani, with emphasis on his activities in voluntary associations between 1948 and 1956. Politically, these were formative years, as Lumumba engaged in a wide-ranging debate on the merits and shortcomings of colonialism through newspaper articles and used the various associations to which he belonged to pressure colonial authorities to consult with the African elite, the *évolués*, on colonial policy and on issues of concern to them.

A career in the civil service reinforced the love-hate relationship that Lumumba had developed vis-à-vis the Belgian colonial system since his youth. Leopoldian propaganda through royal statements and the writings of Henry Morton Stanley and other king's men had presented the colonial enterprise in the Congo as humanitarian intervention against the Arab-Muslim slave trade and assistance in bringing the benefits of Western civilization to "darkest Africa."[1] For European colonialists, the apparently impenetrable rainforest of Central Africa was, as Joseph Conrad depicted it in his novel about the Congo Free State (CFS), the "heart of darkness." But instead of bringing freedom and light to areas formerly raided for slaves and occupied by the Swahili-Arabs, the CFS not only collaborated with Tippu Tip himself when this served its expansionist aims, but also used his former agents, such as Ngongo Letete and Wembo Nyama, to consolidate its territorial control and administer the brutal collection of wild rubber in Sankuru. Thus, colonial propaganda asking the Congolese in general and the Atetela in particular to be grateful to the Belgians for having freed them from Arab slavery was not very convincing in the face of forced labor, compulsory cultivation of cotton, conscription for military service and for labor in mines and industries far from home, and taxation without representation.

In spite of these harsh realities and his own unpleasant encounter with the representatives of the ideological institutions of the colonial system, Lumumba in Kisangani remained a fervent believer in the *mission civilisatrice* (civilizing mission) ideology of Belgian colonialism, his major opposition to the system being the color bar, inasmuch as it affected the *évolués*. In this regard, Lumumba combined tremendous enthusiasm for the quest for practical knowledge, which he saw as the major asset of the colonialists, with outright hostility toward the racism, injustice, and exclusion of the colonial system. He was therefore determined to fight discrimination in any way possible, and to overcome all the administrative restraints on fundamental freedoms and civil liberties by all peaceful means, fair and foul. For example, confronted with rigid controls on people's movements from one administrative zone to another, particularly during the war years, when colonial officials needed to keep peasants in rural areas for the war effort, Lumumba did not have valid travel papers for moving from Onalua to Kalima, and from there to Kisangani. He simply forged them.

Lumumba's history as an undocumented migrant to Kisangani who quickly rose to the top of the organizational pyramid of the *évolués* is phenomenal. It is a testimony to the historical conjuncture of postwar modernization and economic growth in the Congo, and to the characteristic traits of his personality that he developed during this period: a calm, sober demeanor in difficult times; intransigence on matters of principle; and exceptional courage in the face of danger, tireless work, and perseverance. Having only a rudimentary knowledge of French after five years of primary school and three months of clerical work for Symétain, a mining company in Kalima, Lumumba understood that his priority of priorities was to improve his education. After he succeeded in landing a clerical position in the Kisangani territorial administration, he took advantage of evening courses taught by the Marist Brothers to acquire an elementary school certificate and to learn more about the world. He even volunteered to work as an unpaid librarian at the library of the African township of Kisangani so as to read as much as he could at night and on weekends. In addition to improving his French, he read history and learned a bit about philosophy.

Since he did not have a secondary school diploma, Lumumba had to pass a competitive entrance examination to be admitted to the Postal School, a nine-month course of study on the functions and workings of the post office in Kinshasa, open to students from all over the Congo. Begun in early July 1947, the training ended on March 30, 1948, with Lumumba finishing as the third-best student in a class of thirty-four, with an average of 91.4 percent. He returned to Kisangani as a qualified postal employee, and remained committed to his vocation as a dedicated autodidact. He was able to acquire a university-level education by learning from home, through reading and correspondence courses. In this regard, Lumumba was truly five or six decades ahead of the times, as though he already had access to the Internet.

With his professional training in the theory and practice of postal service, Lumumba had achieved a position that he had always hoped for, in which he knew virtually all he needed to know about his work, and there was no one—black or white—who knew much more. But while this may have been the case at the level of craft knowledge, the reality remained that the colonial civil service was still divided by the color bar, which was also a wage bar. Whites held the best jobs and nearly all supervisory positions, and had higher wages and better working conditions than blacks, even those who were better qualified. The civil service had two categories: the *agents de l'administration d'Afrique,* which was exclusively white until token integration opened its ranks to blacks in 1957; and the *agents auxiliaires de l'administration,* for blacks. The first category had four grade levels of functions and salaries, with members of the fourth or lowest grade still earning more than Congolese medical assistants, the highest-paid state employees in the second category. Thus, a Belgian public health nurse with a secondary-level education earned more than a Congolese medical assistant with a university-level education and more responsibilities.

This discriminatory practice, which was reinforced by other aspects of the color bar, such as racial segregation in all areas of life, including housing, education, and public accommodations, was a major source of grievances for the *évolués*. Even when the two categories were finally merged into a single civil service status for Europeans and Africans (the *statut unique*) on January 13, 1959, only a handful of blacks were to be found among senior civil servants. By then, Lumumba had already taken his fight for equality from the civil service to the larger national stage. He had joined the anticolonial alliance of Congolese peasants, workers, the urban unemployed, and the middle class, most of whom realized that their economic and social rights could not effectively materialize without political rights. This was a lesson that Lumumba himself had learned from his political apprenticeship in the various voluntary associations in which he was active in Kisangani.

Lumumba's thirst for associational membership was such that in spite of his not being a former student of the Scheutist Fathers—unless one takes into account whatever instruction he received from the Onalua catechist from 1931 to 1933—he joined the Scheutist old boys' organization, the Association des Anciens Élèves des Pères de Scheut (ADAPES), of which he became vice president in 1951 and president in 1953. He also played a role in the creation in 1953 of an umbrella organization for all the important African voluntary associations of Kisangani, the Fédération des Associations de Stanleyville, of which he was elected secretary. But of all the groups to which he belonged, the most important in terms of his political apprenticeship were the Association des Évolués de Stanleyville (AES), an organization of the most prominent of Kisangani's Africans in state employment, civil society, and the private sector; the Association du Personnel Indigène de la Colonie (APIC), the nationwide trade union of Congolese civil servants; and the Amicale des Postiers Indigènes de la Province Orientale (APIPO), a fraternal organization of postal workers in Orientale Province dedicated to improving the training and welfare of its members.

The rise of the *évolués* as the petty bourgeois elite or the highest stratum of the African middle class was a function of the economic and social changes brought about by World War II, together with the rising consciousness of Congolese civil servants of their indispensable role in the smooth running of the colonial system. Emboldened by their participation in the war effort domestically through increased resource mobilization, and externally by the work of medical assistants and nurses in FP contingents in Africa, the Middle East, and Southeast Asia, Congolese *évolués* were ready to fight to obtain a special status in the Belgian Congo. On February 20, 1944, taking advantage of a popular insurrection by blue- and white-collar workers on the rail line between Kananga and Lubumbashi in solidarity with the mutiny at the FP garrison in Kananga, the *évolués* of Kananga sent a memorandum to colonial authorities demanding better treatment than "the retarded and ignorant mass." Part of the rationale for this special status was the argument that they had played a key role in limiting the impact of the insurrection by calming their less "evolved" compatriots. This project of a special status recognizing the dignity of Congolese *évolués* and ensuring their integration into the privileged world of European colonizers was the major preoccupation of this class all over the country.

In Kisangani, the AES was established on October 28, 1944, with this elitist idea of enhancing the recognition of the *évolués* as a group deserving of respect in public places (banks, post offices, hospitals, government offices, stores); reserved seats or sections in trains, ships, and buses; and residential areas away from the masses. Consistent with colonial paternalism and the moralistic character of Christian evangelization in the Congo, the association saw itself as not only preoccupied with the social, educational, and recreational needs of its members, but also serving as a watchdog over the administration of the African township, and looking after the welfare of people in need. Lumumba became its vice president in November 1953 and president in March 1954. He was removed from office in February 1956 due to hostility aroused by his meteoric rise and political ambitions.

Responding to demands by educated Africans for special recognition of their elite status, the Belgians took steps toward granting to Congolese *évolués* the status of honorary Europeans and exempting them from racist regulations applying to Africans. Following the example set by France, in 1892 the Leopoldian regime had already adopted legislation providing for assimilating a select group of Africans to European status, but this was never put into practice. In 1938, the Commission Permanente pour la Protection des Indigènes, an advisory group on colonial policy, recommended the implementation of this statute, but the Belgian government did not take action until ten years later. A *carte du mérite civique* (civil merit card) was introduced in 1948, only to be quickly superseded in importance in 1952 by a new status called *immatriculation*

(matriculation), for those Africans deemed sufficiently "evolved" culturally and otherwise to be treated like Europeans. Qualifying for matriculation required a more rigorous test of the candidate's level of Europeanization than the one for the merit card. It involved all the requirements for the merit card plus a rather humiliating home visit not once, but on two, three, or even four separate occasions by an investigative commission to look into family life, including an inspection of household goods such as furniture, silverware, linen, and bathroom furnishings, and determining whether the candidate ate at the table with his spouse and spoke with his children in French. The entire dossier had to be reviewed and approved by the court of original jurisdiction.[2]

Before 1956, most Congolese *évolués* would go to any length to drop their "native" status for assimilation to European status. Lumumba himself fought hard for matriculation, which he obtained on August 5, 1954, from the Court of Appeals in Kinshasa, after having been rejected by a lower court in Kisangani. Since the whole process was designed to promote tokenism, it yielded unimpressive figures in a large country like the Congo. By the end of 1955, only 884 persons had received the civil merit card and 116 the matriculation status. After 1956, the assimilation drive lost much of its appeal, as it became clear that while in theory matriculation gave oneself and one's spouse and children all the rights enjoyed by white people in civil and criminal law, it changed nothing in the workplace, where the color/wage bar remained a major obstacle to full integration in the world of colonial power, prestige, and privilege. Consequently, university students and many *évolués* refused to apply for assimilation, judging it to be useless.

Lumumba was elected APIPO president on November 23, 1953, and in that role he placed emphasis on professional training—to which he contributed by teaching a course on the postal service—and a better knowledge of the world and its problems. He also edited a quarterly newsletter called *L'Echo Postal.* In addition to being editor in chief and major contributor to this paper, he continued to serve as a correspondent for *L'Afrique et le Monde,* a Brussels weekly, and two major Kinshasa publications: *La Croix du Congo,* a Catholic weekly, and *La Voix du Congolais,* a monthly published by the state information service for the Congolese elite, with Antoine-Roger Bolamba as editor in chief. Between 1945 and the end of 1958, Lumumba contributed sixty-two articles to the Catholic weekly and thirteen to Bolamba's paper. Until 1956, four major themes dominated these and other articles by Lumumba: civilization and colonization, education and the emancipation of women, racial discrimination and human relations, and moral values.

Lumumba developed these themes within the hegemonic discourse of colonialism, in which obligatory tribute was paid to Belgium's "civilizing mission" in Africa, King Leopold II as a benevolent empire builder, and Henry

Morton Stanley as the Congo's savior from the scourge of the Indian Ocean slave trade. This discourse was diametrically opposed to Lumumba's Independence Day speech, in which he denounced the tyranny of the Leopoldian regime and the brutal oppression of Belgian colonialism. In his Kisangani writings, on the other hand, he remained faithful to colonial propaganda, in which the Belgian Congo was a model colony and its people the best-administered underdeveloped subjects in the world. Even when he wrote on his favorite theme of racial discrimination, Lumumba took pains to frame his arguments in nonoffensive terms as seeking to improve human relations so as to strengthen the capacity of the *évolués* to become worthwhile auxiliaries of Belgian officials. In these writings, as in his 1956 book *Le Congo, terre d'avenir, est-il menacé?* (published posthumously in 1961 and in English translation in 1962 as *Congo, My Country*), Lumumba was still operating from his prenationalism position of collaboration with the Belgian colonialists.

Little is known of Lumumba's activities in APIC, for which he served as secretary before being elected president on December 17, 1954, and reelected on April 10, 1956. As a trade union, APIC was greatly concerned with the wide difference between the remuneration of Belgian and Congolese civil servants, as indicated above, and it campaigned for "equal pay for equal work" and the abolition of the two separate categories of the civil service. Unfortunately, the trade union movement was very weak in the Belgian Congo due to colonial legal restrictions. Thus, while the Congo had the third-largest number of wage earners in Africa after South Africa and Egypt in the 1950s, with 1,146,000 African wage earners recorded at the end of 1954, it had among the lowest numbers of unionized workers in colonial Africa. By 1956, the total number of union members was 8,829, or less than 1 percent of the country's workforce. Comparable figures for French West Africa, Zambia (then Northern Rhodesia), and Nigeria were, respectively, 23, 25, and 50 percent. Unions were also kept under close watch, all of them being required to have European advisers, and colonial administrators had the right to take part in union meetings. For the Kisangani branch of APIC, Lumumba was full of praise for its European advisers.

Lumumba's own relations with whites depended on how the latter treated blacks, the *évolués* in particular. While Europeans valued his intelligence, competence, hard work, and discipline, many despised him for what they perceived as his arrogance and hostility toward them. For example, at the post office in Kisangani, some whites complained that he never greeted them and would speak with them only when it was absolutely necessary. However, by 1955, Orientale Province's fraternal organization of postal workers was opened to white members, and the two racial groups seem to have gotten along well. An advocate for integration, Lumumba joined the Liberal Circle and Study Group of Kisangani, a branch of the Belgian Liberal Party, in April 1954 and was elected vice president of the Belgo-Congolese Union, an organization devoted to interracial understanding and harmony, in March 1956. Personally, he had come to measure his relations with whites on the basis of two critical experiences: a casual encounter with a restaurant owner in 1947 in Brazzaville, and the friendship he developed with the sociologist Pierre Clément between January 1952 and April 1953.

During his year of training at the Postal School in Kinshasa, Lumumba once crossed the Congo River for a brief visit to Brazzaville, then capital of the Middle Congo and French Equatorial Africa. This beautiful city on the right bank of the mighty river represented a zone of freedom for its black neighbors on the left bank in Kinshasa, the *kinois*, who were forbidden wine and hard liquors and access to films deemed suitable for adult consumption. The *kinois* would cross the river to enjoy these forbidden fruits in the more relaxed and racially tolerant world of postwar French colonialism. Oblivious to this less racist colonial environment, Lumumba took a break from his strolling around Brazzaville on a weekend afternoon to quench his thirst at a café, with the hope of finding an African server who would bring him a glass of water. To his surprise, it was a European woman, apparently the owner of the café, who saw him, invited him to come in, gave him a seat in a place full of white customers, and brought him not the tapwater he expected but a bottle of mineral water. According to Clément, for whom Lumumba would work five years later as a research assistant, this encounter was the first revelation to Lumumba that racially speaking, "another world was possible."³ Since the civil merit card and matriculation would not succeed in ensuring to the African elite equality of access to employment, remuneration, housing, social services, and leisure opportunities in the Belgian Congo, Lumumba could now "lift up his long-bent head to dream of a country more beautiful than before," as we are urged by the Congolese national anthem.

Lumumba's friendship with Pierre Clément, a British sociologist of Belgian origin, grew out of their professional relationship. Clément was in Kisangani from January 17, 1952, to April 11, 1953, along with his colleagues N. Xyadias and V. G. Pons, as a participant in an International African Institute study mission on the social aspects of industrialization and urbanization in Africa. In the process of working for him as a research assistant in the evenings and on weekends, Lumumba became a close friend, and he accompanied Clément on a field trip to Kasai Province between December 27, 1952, and January 15, 1953, which included a visit to Wembo-Nyama and Lumumba's native village of Onalua. The friendship between the two men was so strong that Lumumba named his second child, the eldest of his four children with Pauline Opango, Patrice Pierre-Clément. For him, then, the model of good human relations between blacks and whites was this friendship based on mutual trust, respect, and reciprocity, and whites who did not meet this yardstick were useless for Congo's future.[4]

Meanwhile, Lumumba continued his quest for the social inclusion of the *évolués* in the colonial system, with equal rights for blacks and whites. Given the prominent positions he held in various elite associations, particularly the AES, he eventually became the leading spokesperson of the *évolués* vis-à-vis the colonial state in Kisangani. He established regular consultations between the AES and provincial authorities, and direct contacts with the provincial governor and with Auguste Buisseret, the Belgian minister of colonies since 1954 and a prominent member of the Liberal Party. He even surprised the Belgians and the *évolués* by holding a chat with King Baudouin during the king's first visit to the Congo in 1955. This prominence won him an invitation by colonial authorities to visit Belgium for the very first time between April 24 and May 24, 1956. In a colony characterized by some critics as "an empire of silence" because of the Belgian policy of keeping the "natives" ignorant of the outside world and "subversive ideas" like nationalism and communism, travel outside of the country was very rare indeed. Thus, for Lumumba and his companions, visiting Belgium for a whole month was a crowning achievement of their status as *évolués*.

Lumumba's meteoric rise as a leader of the Congolese elite in Kisangani, and his being listened to by Belgian officials as high as the king and the colonial affairs minister, made him unpopular among Belgian colonial officials in the Congo and aroused the jealousy of other *évolués*, especially those who considered him less qualified educationally and too much of a "stranger" to represent the local elite. These hostile sentiments were strengthened by Lumumba's apparently close ties with Buisseret and the Belgian Liberals, who were involved in a vicious quarrel with the Catholic Church in 1954–55 on the opening of public schools to the Congolese. Although he pretended to be neutral in this quarrel over secular versus religious-based education, Lumumba refused to sign Catholic petitions against a state-run educational system for blacks in competition with a state-subsidized one under Catholic and Protestant missions, and his own children were enrolled in a public school for whites. Contrary to his expressed opposition to the importation of Belgian political parties in the Congo, he was a member of the Liberal Party branch in Kisangani, of which he became vice president in September 1955. His closeness to leading power circles in Brussels and his rupture with the Catholic Church on the school issue were to have serious consequences for Lumumba. The first such consequence was his removal from the office of AES president on February 17, 1956. Major reasons for the vote against him included hostility to his prominence and the desire of fervent Catholics to punish him for his support of secular education. The second consequence was his politically motivated indictment for embezzling funds at the post office; he was arrested and imprisoned on July 6, 1956.

3

Years of Transition, 1956–58

By the end of 1955, Patrice Lumumba had risen to the pinnacle of the colonial civil service for Africans and the prestigious circles of the Congolese elite in Kisangani. In his eleven-year public career, he had attained the rank of first-class clerk as a postal employee, his annual performance reports marked as "elite." At the post office, he had been entrusted since 1951 with managing the service dealing with the money order accounts of individuals and businesses, a job that was normally reserved for a European civil servant. He had held leadership positions in nearly all the major voluntary associations in the city, including multiracial organizations like the Belgian Liberal Party, the Belgo-Congolese Union, and the fraternal organization of postal workers. Given all this, his fall from grace six months later following his arrest and imprisonment on charges of embezzlement and forgery on July 6, 1956, was brutal and demoralizing. However, with his characteristic sobriety and determination to overcome hardships with serenity, Lumumba endured prison and humiliation and came out of jail to lead a very successful venture in marketing beer before joining the struggle for Congo's independence and national unity.

The preceding chapter described the historical context in which Lumumba's violation of the law took place. Because of the color/wage bar, Lumumba, as an *évolué* with matriculation status, was still denied entry to the European category of the civil service, in which even the lowest salaries were much higher than those in the upper grade of the native category; European civil servants also enjoyed benefits such as housing and motor vehicles that were not available to Africans. Thus, in spite of the fact that his post office duties were meant for someone in the first category, he only received a first-class clerk's salary, which in January 1956 was approximately 5,000 francs a month, the equivalent of 100 U.S. dollars. With this miserable pay he had to maintain a European lifestyle that included making payments on his house mortgage, taking care of a family with three children (two of whom attended a school for whites), and paying for water, electricity, and other necessities.

Consequently, Lumumba was not alone among the *évolués* in bending rules by taking advantage of cash boxes or any money accounts to which they had access in order to make ends meet. It was an open secret that embezzlement was rationalized as "borrowing" cash for urgent needs, with the intention of reimbursing before being caught. When this involved relatively small amounts that could be covered with one's monthly paycheck, it was manageable. But once unpaid amounts became too large to escape notice, the employee responsible was in trouble. In Lumumba's case, his numerous associational activities and the demands of his assimilation status required a lot more money than his salary could bear. Dealing each day with an endless flow of money orders deposited for payment to a large department store and two major pharmacies, he found the temptation to divert some cash to his own account too strong to resist. This was made possible by the fact that he had no supervisor other than a very busy and trusting postmaster in chief, and had the necessary skills to manipulate different accounts to make sure that reasonable amounts were actually credited to each customer when expected.

In many cases, payment of the deficit and a reprimand for cheating would usually end the affair. Lumumba was not allowed this easy way out, even though he readily admitted the charges against him on the very day of his arrest, expressed his remorse about the violation of law and professional ethics, and sold his house to settle the outstanding deficit of approximately 100,000 francs (2,000 U.S. dollars) from the 126,256 francs he had embezzled since 1953 or 1954. Colonial prosecutors and the provincial administration, who resented his access to the minister of colonial affairs in Brussels and what they perceived as his arrogance and lack of respect for colonial officials in the Congo, were out to get him. Reinforced by the hostility of the Catholic Church because of Lumumba's support for secular education and his eroding support among Kisangani *évolués*, the colonialists' vendetta against him eventually turned into judicial harassment. Despite his assimilation status, they refused to release him on parole, holding him in preventive detention for fourteen months. Ironically, as Lumumba pointed out in his petitions for temporary release, the state was spending 4,000 francs a month just to feed him, while he only had a monthly salary of 4,957 francs to care for a family of five.

Following his trial on February 25, 1957, the court of original jurisdiction in Kisangani announced its verdict on March 4, 1957. It found Lumumba guilty of embezzlement of public funds, forgery, and abuse of confidence, and sentenced him to two years in prison. The office of the prosecutor found the sentence too lenient and appealed the judgment to the Court of Appeals in Kinshasa. Lumumba requested and obtained his transfer to Kinshasa so he could follow the case closely with a local lawyer. On July 4, 1957, the Court of Appeals affirmed the verdict of the lower court. Lumumba's lawyer petitioned the king for a pardon, and this was granted by royal decree on August 27, 1957. The pardon reduced the jail sentence to the fourteen months that Lumumba had already served in preventive detention, and required that his release be contingent on his finding a job. Accordingly, he was released from jail on September 7, 1957, and hired the next day by the Brasserie du Bas-Congo (Bracongo), one of the two major breweries in Kinshasa. The fact that Lumumba's trial was politically motivated and a case of judicial harassment was clearly established when Bracongo hired him to work in none other than its accounts department! But before we deal with this new chapter in his life, we need to find out what he did during his time in prison.

The first eight months of Lumumba's imprisonment, July 1956 to March 1957, were spent in a jail in Kisangani, and the last six months in Kinshasa. Given his legal status as a citizen rather than a native, he was not subjected to either hard labor or corporal punishment, both of which were the lot of Congolese prisoners. He was also distinguished from the latter in terms of lodging, clothing, and food. With ample time to himself, he read all he could find on judicial proceedings, and filed petitions to the court, the colonial administration, the colonial affairs minister, and the king; he devoted much of the last six months of 1956 to writing his book, *Congo, My Country.* Although an agreement was reached with a publisher in Brussels on December 31, 1956, the book was not published in 1957, as expected, for reasons that remain obscure. It was finally published in 1961, after Lumumba's death. As pointed out in chapter 2, this was not a revolutionary text comparable to the writings of Kwame Nkrumah, Frantz Fanon, and Amilcar Cabral, but a political essay by a Congolese *évolué* pleading for better race relations and reforms leading to greater partnership between colonial officials and the African elite in laying the foundations for Congo's future.

The manuscript echoed Lumumba's procolonialist positions on "human relations" and the Belgo-Congolese community since 1948, positions that were probably reinforced by his incarceration and need for sympathy. As Lumumba's stance began to change on the basis of his prison reflections on his career, the lessons of his month-long tour of Belgium, and the objective situation in the Congo, Africa, and the world, he seems to have lost interest in the book project. This is not surprising, for the year 1956 is an important landmark in the annals of the national liberation struggle in Africa. Coming in the wake of the Bandung (Indonesia) Conference of 1955 on Afro-Asian solidarity and nonalignment, its significance for African liberation lies in several important developments, including the failure of the Franco-British-Israeli Suez expedition and the preservation of Egyptian sovereignty; the independence of Morocco, Sudan, and Tunisia; the beginning of the decolonization process in the French colonies of West Africa, Equatorial Africa, and Madagascar; and the birth of the national liberation movement in Angola, the Belgian Congo, and Guinea-Bissau. In the Congo, a democracy movement emerged as a result of intra-elite debate on the future of the country, the opening of political space to mass participation through municipal elections, and the impact of these developments on ordinary people. Reflecting on this whole political situation nationally and internationally, Lumumba's assessment of colonialism became less laudatory and more critical.

The Congolese debate on the political future of the country arose in reaction to a publication by A. A. J. van Bilsen, a little-known professor at the Colonial University in Antwerp, entitled "Een dertigjarenplan voor de politieke ontvoogding van Belgisch Afrika" (A thirty-year plan for the political emancipation of Belgian Africa). Originally published in Flemish in November 1955, it appeared in French translation in February 1956, giving rise to a heated debate in both Belgium and the Congo among defenders of the colonial order and those advocating reforms. After months of discussion by the Congolese elite in Kinshasa, two notable reactions to the Van Bilsen plan were made public in July and August 1956, respectively. The first came from an organization of Catholic intellectuals known by the name of their occasional publication as the *Conscience Africaine* (African Consciousness) group, which endorsed the Van Bilsen plan as a good starting point for public debate on the future of the country. As the African Consciousness manifesto was being examined by the reading public, the Catholic bishops of the colony implicitly endorsed it when they published a declaration on July 2, 1956, that it was time for the Congolese to be included in the governance of their country. The African Consciousness group included Joseph Malula, a Catholic priest who would later become the second African in the twentieth century to attain the rank of cardinal in the Catholic Church; Joseph Ileo, who went on to become a prominent member of the Congolese political class until his death in 1994; and Joseph Ngalula, a distinguished journalist who played key roles in Lumumba's political life by helping to bring the latter into the world of the Kinshasa political elite in 1958, and then by joining anti-Lumumba forces in 1959 and 1960, as we shall see in chapters 4 and 5.

A more radical reaction to, and a rejection of, the Van Bilsen plan came from the Alliance des Bakongo (Abako), a cultural association of the Kongo, one of the country's major ethnic groups. Abako was originally created in 1950 by Edmond Nzeza Nlandu as the Association des Bakongo pour l'Unification, la Conservation et l'Expansion de la Langue Kikongo, and its objective was to preserve and promote the use of Kikongo, then losing ground in the national capital region of Kinshasa to Lingala, a lingua franca of commerce and popular music also used by the Belgians in the Force Publique (FP). The organization's main objective became political following the election of Joseph Kasavubu to its presidency on March 21, 1954.

In spite of the fact that he became the Congo's first president, Kasavubu's date of birth and whether or not he was part Chinese are elements of his biography that are not clearly established. He was born in a small village near Tshela in Lower Congo between 1915 and 1917. Because of his light complexion and slanting eyes, it was rumored at his birth that he might have been fathered by one of the Chinese workers on the Mayombe railroad; this notion is widely believed to be a Belgian plot to denigrate a radical nationalist leader by framing him as a product of an illegitimate birth. Oral tradition has it that his Kongo father, suspected of being a sorcerer, passed the poison ordeal to prove that he was not.

Kasavubu attended Catholic schools and completed three years of philosophy at the Kabwe Grand Seminary in December 1939. His bishop back home refused to allow him to enroll in the five-year training for the priesthood, apparently considering him unfit to be a priest. Kasavubu went on to earn his teacher's diploma in 1940, but he left mission and, after a few months, company work in 1942 for the colonial civil service, in which he became a clerk in the financial services of the central administration. Kasavubu's radicalism had already manifested itself in 1944 when, in his inaugural lecture as a member of Jean Bolikango's Union des Intérêts Sociaux Congolais (UNISCO), he shocked both colonial officials and his fellow *évolués* by advocating "the right of the first occupant," meaning that the Congo belonged to Congolese, not to Belgians, and Kinshasa belonged to his Kongo ethnic group. With a solid political base among the Kongo majority in Kinshasa, Kasavubu and Abako had the capacity to become the spearhead of the Congolese independence movement.

The Congo's independence struggle may be said to have started on August 23, 1956. This was the day on which Kasavubu held a public rally to declare Abako's rejection of the Van Bilsen plan and the African Consciousness manifesto as too timid, and to call for an orderly transition to self-government in a federal structure. The word used in the written version of the Abako counter-manifesto was *émancipation,* but Kasavubu publicly used the phrase *indépendance immédiate.* With these two words, he and Abako defined the terms of revolutionary politics in the Congo during the next four years. The organization's overwhelming victory in the municipal elections of December 12, 1957, in Kinshasa, winning 130 of the 170 communal counselors' seats contested, showed that Abako's radicalism was shared by non-Kongo Congolese. At his inauguration as mayor of the commune of Dendale (now Kasavubu commune) on April 20, 1958, Kasavubu called on Belgium and the world to recognize the Congo as a nation, and depicted his swearing-in ceremony as the initial installation of democracy in the Congo.

This is the political situation that Lumumba found upon his transfer to Kinshasa in March 1957. There were two politically active groups within the Congolese political elite: the Abako leadership around Kasavubu, which was advocating immediate independence; and the African Consciousness group of Ileo, Malula, and Ngalula, with which the old guard, comprising Bolamba, Bolikango, and others, agreed for a gradual process of decolonization amicably negotiated with the Belgians. Lumumba's Kisangani positions should have made him an ally of these political moderates, but, becoming more frustrated with the colonial system and critical of its racism, inequality, and injustice, he started moving more and more to the radical positions espoused by Kasavubu. Moreover, the latter was ahead of the moderates in having a real constituency, a mass political base that could be mobilized for political action. This appealed to Lumumba, who, like Kasavubu, understood the need to promote black consciousness not only among the colonially indoctrinated elite, but also, and more importantly, among the masses, whose mobilization was indispensable for political change.

In practice, however, Lumumba and Kasavubu could not work together. Kasavubu felt that people from other provinces of the Congo were not interested or ready to reclaim their rights the way the Kongo were, and he was ready to go it alone in the liberation of Lower Congo, and even to extend this liberation to the two other areas of the old Kongo kingdom in Portuguese Angola and French Congo, in an irredentist project of recreating that state. At the very least, he was prepared to work with other Congolese for independence, but within a federal structure in which Lower Congo would retain its autonomy. Both of these projects were anathema to Lumumba. He established relations with the leadership of the moderates as his entry point into Kinshasa's elite politics, but with the aim of radicalizing the political discourse by organizing those workers and the unemployed who were alienated by Abako's exclusionary approach to political emancipation. Thus, while sympathizing with Kasavubu on a genuine decolonization process in which the Congolese would have agency with respect to both pace and substance, he rejected the old seminarian's Kongo separatism and federalist option. These political differences were to affect their relations after independence as well. Ironically, Van Bilsen, the author of the plan rejected by Kasavubu in 1956, would become his adviser during his confrontation with Lumumba in 1960. And the independence for which he was vilified as a lunatic or subversive by the defenders of the colonial order took place twenty-six years ahead of his proposed schedule!

Following Lumumba's royal pardon in late August 1957, his Liberal Party friends were there to help him find a job in order to meet the condition of his release from jail. Even Minister Buisseret is said to have helped by recommending him to Gilbert Roland, the Bracongo general manager and a Liberal. In accordance with Bantu culture and as he had done for his friend Pierre Clément in 1952, Lumumba named a son after Roland—his third son, born in 1958—as a token of his recognition and gratitude for the support and friendship of his Bracongo boss. In August 1958, less than a year after becoming an employee of the brewery, Lumumba was appointed its publicity director, with the challenge of increasing sales through competition with the richer brewery, Bralima, established twenty years earlier than Bracongo, in 1933. With a salary of 25,000 francs a month, five times what he earned in Kisangani, plus bonuses for sales promotion, a car, and a budget for promoting the sales of Polar beer, Lumumba had all the resources he needed to do his job well. During his five months as publicity director, Lumumba succeeded in establishing this beer as a formidable rival of Primus, Bralima's beer, in what became known as the "beer war." By giving pep talks in different bars on behalf of Polar and offering bar patrons free drinks to encourage them to adopt it as their favorite beer, Lumumba not only promoted its sales significantly; he also honed his skills for future political campaigns.

In addition to political meetings and activities with his friends in the Liberal Party, Lumumba became politically active in two major groups: the Fédération des Batetela de Léopoldville (Fédébate/Léo), a grouping of the various lineage-based voluntary associations of the Atetela of Kinshasa, and a political party that came to be identified with him, the Mouvement National Congolais (MNC). While the ethnic association was primarily useful for Lumumba's knowledge of who was who in Kinshasa civil society, both inside and outside the federation, the MNC, as a national and multiethnic organization would become the center of his political life and work. Once he succeeded in wrestling it away from Ileo, Ngalula, and their moderate friends by anchoring its actions in mass-based party sections in Kinshasa and across the country, Lumumba was able to chart a new course for the national liberation movement. By then, he had made a total break with the colonial ideology of his Kisangani years.

4

The Struggle for Independence, 1958–60

Welcomed to the African Consciousness circle by Ileo and Ngalula, Lumumba outmaneuvered them by taking over their project for a national party called Mouvement National Congolais (MNC), organizing it into a genuine political party and putting his own imprint on it. In the process, he emerged as the standardbearer of the Congolese independence movement, its main mobilizer at home as well as its public face abroad. His participation in the First All-African Peoples' Conference of December 1958 in Accra, Ghana, opened his eyes even wider to the political struggles in other parts of Africa and the world, while allowing him to establish contacts that were to strengthen his political appeal in progressive circles worldwide. Instead of weakening him, intraparty squabbles and political splits increased his popularity among the people as a leader concerned with national unity and interests rather than the narrow class and ethno-regional interests of the *évolués*. Given his charisma, his national appeal, and his organizational skills, he eventually overshadowed Kasavubu as the inevitable national leader by the time independence negotiations with Belgium began in January 1960.

Lumumba's emergence as a national political leader took place between the political upheavals of 1956 and those—even more significant for the Congo—of 1959. The preceding year, 1958, was the year of the Brussels World Fair, to which colonial authorities had sent over seven hundred Congolese as a living exhibit of the success of Belgium's "civilizing mission" in Africa. It was also the year of the Working Group of Belgian parliamentarians, established in August with the mission of making recommendations on the Congo's future on the basis of consultations with representatives of the European and Congolese populations of the colony.

For those Congolese who were privileged to spend several months in Belgium as part of the world's fair, observation of the realities of Belgian life and their interactions with Belgian society helped to change their perception of whites, whom they previously considered superhuman because of white supremacy and privileged life in the Congo. Whereas European colonizers in the Congo had black domestics to do everything for them and all manual labor was done by blacks only, in Brussels the Congolese could see with their own eyes white people sweeping streets, washing dishes, and doing all kinds of lowly things that lords and masters are not supposed to do. Moreover, they found out that, contrary to the racial segregation in the colony, they were well received and served in all public accommodations, including hotels, restaurants, cinemas, and even brothels. Another world was possible, indeed, and these Congolese returned home with a yearning for independence, which they shared with family members and friends, who were anxious to hear about their adventures in the white man's world. After this experience, consultations with the Working Group were judged useless and rejected by a large segment of Congolese political opinion, including Lumumba and the MNC.

Establishing a nationwide political organization on secular and nonethnic bases had been a project of the African Consciousness group since 1956. This was all the more necessary not only to challenge the exclusionary path chosen by Abako, but also to present a common front against colonial resistance to meaningful change. *Présence Congolaise,* a weekly edited by Ngalula, became the rallying point for all those supporting the project. Twenty individuals, the majority of whom were Catholic intellectuals with deep roots in Kinshasa, signed the charter establishing the MNC on October 10, 1958. When the party's creation was announced, the surprise for most knowledgeable people was the choice of Lumumba as president of the provisional committee. After Gaston Diomi, Ileo, Ngalula, and Antoine Ngwenza each refused to assume the party's presidency, Lumumba emerged as president following a voting procedure that was actually designed to delay the choice of a president. Each member was asked to vote for himself. Since Lumumba was accompanied by a friend who was not a member of the group, but who nevertheless signed the founding charter and took part in the voting, he won two votes and the presidency.

Disappointed by their inability to deny Lumumba the presidency, the founders sought to control his actions and insisted on approving the statements he would make in public. They had underestimated Lumumba. With his intelligence, eloquence, and capacity for relentless work, he moved quickly to marginalize his more conservative colleagues by establishing mass-based party sections in the various communes of Kinshasa, and using them to radicalize the message and the work of the MNC. He also undertook efforts to expand the party all over the country, beginning with the important urban and mining centers of the Katanga region of the Copperbelt and the commercial centers of Kasai and Orientale Provinces. By the time his detractors in the party were bold enough to try to remove him from office, Lumumba had already become unstoppable, in addition to being a national and a pan-African figure.

He won the pan-African mantle at the First All-African Peoples' Conference, held in Accra from December 5 to 13, 1958. There are several narratives as to how Lumumba and his two MNC colleagues, Diomi and Ngalula, got there. The narrative presented here is the one told to me in September 1987 in London by A. R. Mohamed Babu, who attended the Accra conference as a delegate from Zanzibar and later became economic development minister in Tanzania.

According to Babu, he and the Kenyan trade union leader Tom Mboya were in transit in Kinshasa on their way to Accra from Nairobi. Concerned that a country as big and strategic as the Congo was likely to miss this great African gathering, they asked a hotel worker who spoke Kiswahili if he could put them in touch with Congolese political leaders. The worker was delighted to take them to meet Lumumba in one of the bars where he was promoting Polar beer. Babu and Mboya were so impressed by Lumumba, with whom they could converse in Kiswahili, that they sent a telegraph to the Pan-African Freedom Movement for East and Central Africa (PAFMECA) in Dar es Salaam asking for money to take a Congolese delegation to Accra.[1] The other narratives, which emphasize either the role of the Belgian pacifist Jean Van Lierde and his pro-Africa group Les Amis de Présence Africaine or that of the Ghanaian employee of the U.S. Consulate in Kinshasa Evans Lomotey as intermediaries with the organizers in Accra, are not in contradiction with what Babu told me.

Three hundred delegates representing sixty political parties and civil society organizations from twenty-eight African countries and the African diaspora took part in this conference. For the first time, Lumumba met prominent leaders of African liberation movements such as Félix-Roland Moumié of the Union of the Populations of Cameroon (UPC), Frantz Fanon of the Algerian National Liberation Front (FLN), Amílcar Cabral of the

African Party for the Independence of Guinea and Cape Verde (PAIGC), and Prince Louis Rwagasore of Burundi's Unity for National Progress (Uprona) party. He also established very useful relations with distinguished African leaders such as Kwame Nkrumah (Ghana), Gamal Abdel Nasser (Egypt), Modibo Keita (Mali), and Ahmed Sékou Touré (Guinea). Lumumba's speech to the conference on December 11, 1958, marks a total rupture with his pre-1958 positions. Colonialism is no longer seen as a harbinger of Western civilization, but a system of exploitation and injustice; colonial invaders and their successors are no longer heroes to be admired, but racists with an idiotic superiority complex; and the objective of the Congolese people's struggle is no longer racial equality in a Belgo-Congolese community, but their liberation from colonialism and the attainment of independence. Since Marxist publications were banned in the Belgian Congo, Lumumba was not familiar with the most radical of twentieth-century revolutionary ideologies. He could not conceptualize the struggle against colonialism and imperialism in a Marxist or even socialist perspective. He examined it purely from the standpoint of African nationalism, his aim being to see all the social strata and ethnic groups of the Congo unite to end colonial economic exploitation, political repression, and cultural oppression. His prestige and his confidence level were enhanced by his election to the permanent committee of the AAPC.

Following its return to Kinshasa, the MNC delegation held a large public rally on Sunday, December 28, to report on the conference and explain its resolutions, together with their implications for the independence struggle in the Congo. Lumumba was the speaker, while Diomi translated the address into Lingala. The crowd, estimated anywhere between five thousand and ten thousand people, was extremely delighted by the report of this first Congolese delegation to a major international gathering in modern history. Afterwards, Lumumba, pleased with the way things were going, decided to devote himself entirely to the struggle for independence. On January 1, 1959, he resigned from Bracongo to become a full-time political leader. The colonial administration, on the other hand, was so shocked by the success of the MNC rally that it resolved not to give the party permission to hold such public gatherings in the future. This was a self-deluding attempt to deny, as Nelson Mandela stated upon his release from prison on February 11, 1990, that it is ordinary people who make history.

Kasavubu had missed the trip to Accra (where he, too, was invited), and fearing that he would lose the independence leadership role to Lumumba and the MNC, he and Abako decided to hold their own public rally on the following Sunday, January 4, 1959, at the same YMCA site in Kalamu used by Lumumba. Organizers of public rallies and demonstrations were required to inform the appropriate authorities in advance for purposes of law and order, so that the authorities could ban the event if they wanted to. In this case, the letter sent to the Belgian mayor of Kinshasa on Tuesday, December 30, 1958, did not reach City Hall until Friday, January 2, 1959. The mayor responded the next day that if the proposed meeting did not have the "private character" its planners seemingly intended, they would be held responsible for any consequences. As law-abiding *évolués* familiar with the political nuances of administrative correspondence, the Abako leaders interpreted the mayor's letter as a ban. They decided to reschedule the meeting for January 18, so as to obtain the necessary authorization and react to the anxiously awaited government policy statement on Congo's future, which Brussels had promised to release on January 13.

Meanwhile, by January 4, the originally scheduled date of the meeting, thousands of Abako supporters had gathered at the YMCA, and on being told by Kasavubu and the Abako leadership that the meeting had been banned and they should go home, the crowd refused to disperse peacefully. Reinforced by many of the twenty thousand football (soccer) fans coming out of a nearby stadium, the demonstrators, throwing rocks, attacked the police, passing white motorists returning home from weekend or Sunday afternoon outings in the countryside, European-owned shops, and other symbols of white privilege and authority. In a relatively short time, virtually all the African townships of Kinshasa joined the rebellion, which lasted for four days. Although official figures obtained from hospitals and burial services indicated only 49 people dead, all Congolese, and 116 injured, including 15 Europeans, more credible estimates of people killed were as high as 300. Many Africans were buried by relatives and friends without any formalities, and not all the people injured sought hospital care.

As a tribute to the mass action on that day in 1959, which sounded the death knell of Belgian colonialism in the Congo, January 4 is a national holiday, Independence Martyrs' Day, in the DRC. *Indépendance immédiate*, the slogan of the Kinshasa protesters, soon became a non-negotiable demand of the mass democratic movement all over the country. This revolt marked a new and truly revolutionary phase of the independence movement, the phase of the radicalization of the struggle. In this phase the initiative passed from the *évolués* to ordinary people. The Kinshasa revolt was entirely spontaneous, with workers and the urban unemployed taking matters in their own hands to make the slogan a reality. The entire course of Congolese history was changed by their action.

Both the Belgians and the *évolués* were shocked by the violence of the masses. For the Belgians, it was a clear demonstration that contrary to their colonial myth of "natives with happy faces," the Congolese rejected as utter nonsense the notion that they were the best-administered subjects, living in a "model colony." Faced with a demand for total and immediate independence, the lack of political will in Belgium for an Algerian-type colonial war, and an international context in which decolonization was the order of the day, Belgian authorities had to accept the idea of a negotiated independence. This was the gist of two separate policy statements released on January 13, 1959, by both the Belgian king and government, with the royal declaration going much further in explicitly endorsing the idea of independence. For the *évolués,* initial fears of mass violence were generally pushed aside by the realization that the threat of violence was a useful means of obtaining concessions from the colonialists. Unfortunately, all political parties used violence where it was of maximum profit to them: against their Congolese rivals in electoral competition.

The masses not only initiated the decolonization process; they also influenced its pace. A major reason for the Belgian decision to grant independence in 1960 was the fact that several areas of the country had become totally ungovernable, most dramatically the rural areas of Lower Congo and Bandundu, where peasants in particular had ceased to recognize the authority of the colonial state and were willing to take orders only from Abako and the Parti Solidaire Africain (PSA), respectively. They refused to pay taxes and to respect administrative regulations, and some went so far as to reject any contact with the social services provided by the colonial state, which in their minds had become illegitimate and an enemy. The radicalization of the independence struggle intensified during the period from September 1959 to January 1960. In addition to the well-organized civil disobedience and the widespread boycott of the December 1959 local elections in Lower Congo and Bandundu, major incidents included the violent disturbances of October 30–November 1 in Kisangani, and colonially instigated ethnic violence in Kasai and in the trust territory of Rwanda.[2]

In spite of its ethnic basis, it can be said that Kasavubu's Abako was the first real political party in the Congo, and one whose actions had positive consequences for the independence struggle. Lumumba's MNC, on the other hand, was the first truly national party, and played a crucial role in the political agitation for independence beginning with the rally of December 28, 1958, without which the events of January 4, 1959, would not have taken place. The political reforms of 1957 and the Working Group mission led to the emergence of numerous political parties in 1958. In addition to Abako, MNC, and PSA, parties that were to play a major role in independence politics included Balubakat, the political association of the Luba-Katanga, led by Jason Sendwe; the Centre de Regroupement Africain (Cerea) of Anicet Kashamura, which was based in Kivu; and the Confédération des Associations Tribales du Katanga (Conakat) of Moïse Tshombe, who would later be responsible for the Katanga secession.

In July 1959, the MNC split in two over personality conflicts and policy differences between the moderate leaders—led by former African Consciousness group members Ileo and Ngalula along with trade union chief Cyrille Adoula—and Lumumba. Under the influence of Belgian Catholic and Liberal circles as well as that of the Congolese priest Joseph Malula, the moderates accused Lumumba of communistic and dictatorial tendencies. These unfounded charges were essentially a reflection of the accusers' uneasiness with the manner in which Lumumba was transforming a reformist movement into a radical political party and with his trips outside the country, whose funding by the groups that invited him was external to the MNC. His destinations included Nigeria, where he delivered an address on African unity and national independence at the closing session of the International Seminar of the Congress for Freedom and Culture at the University of Ibadan on March 22; Conakry, Guinea, where he attended a meeting of the permanent committee of the AAPC from April 15 to 17; and Brussels, for numerous meetings, speeches, and lectures from April 22 to 25. Earlier in April, the Kinshasa elite had tried to limit Lumumba's role in the first congress of Congolese political parties favorable to a unitarist structure of the state, held in Kananga April 9–12. Ironically, Albert Kalonji, the MNC provincial leader for Kasai and the man chosen by Kinshasa to host the meeting, was a federalist.

On July 16, 1959, the old guard dissolved the provisional MNC committee and created a new one in which the presidency was to be held collegially by the chairs of three commissions: political (Martin Ngwete), economic and social (Adoula), and propaganda (Ngalula). The next day, Lumumba reacted by convening an extraordinary assembly of the sectional committees of the party in Kinshasa, which confirmed him in the position of president of the new provisional committee pending the party congress. By the end of October 1959, the two wings of the MNC had become two separate parties, the Mouvement National Congolais-Lumumba (MNC-L) and the Mouvement National Congolais-Kalonji (MNC-K), after the moderates had chosen Kalonji as their new president. In spite of having prominent non-Luba leaders such as Adoula and Ileo among its founders, the MNC-K eventually became a predominantly Luba-Kasai party. The MNC-L, on the other hand, established itself as the only truly national and multiethnic political party during the struggle for independence. The only other party with national and multiethnic credentials was the Parti National du Progrès (PNP), an organization of middle-level black civil servants and traditional chiefs set up by the colonialists as a conservative alternative to the nationalist movement and its call for immediate independence. The contempt for the PNP in Congolese public opinion was expressed in its being derisively called, in a play on its acronym, the "Parti des Nègres Payés" (party of paid niggers).

Lumumba's political star rose higher again with the holding of the first MNC-L congress October 23–28 and an extraordinary congress of nationalist parties in Kisangani October 29–30, 1959. The first congress, in which

Albert Kalonji took part with the hope of reconciling the two rival wings of the party before his own congress was to start in Lubumbashi on October 31, was a great success. Reflecting the bitter debate between the colonial administration and Congolese political parties on the local elections planned for December 1959, Lumumba ended the MNC-L congress with a militant speech in which he called on his followers to boycott the elections and resort to civil disobedience if the Belgians persisted in undermining democratization as an indispensable component of the decolonization process. The governor of Orientale Province seized on these pronouncements as a violation of law, and an arrest warrant was issued against the MNC-L leader. The Kisangani incidents began on the afternoon of Friday, October 30, as a response of the African population to the violence used by the security forces against innocent people when they came to arrest Lumumba in the Mangobo commune, where he was presiding over the second congress. The area was calm until three trucks and six jeeps full of helmeted soldiers with fixed bayonets on their guns entered, throwing smoke grenades. Residents responded with whatever weapons they could put their hands on, with white persons and property as their targets. Predictably, other African communes of Kisangani joined the rebellion, which lasted until Sunday, November 1. The human toll, according to official sources, was at least twenty deaths and a hundred or so people wounded on the Congolese side, and three wounded on the European side, including a security officer who was hit with a spear.

Like the Kinshasa uprising of January 1959, the Kisangani incidents were a proindependence protest against Belgian colonialism and the administration's arrogance in trying to push down Congolese throats a reformist agenda in place of total and immediate independence. The martyrs of Kisangani paid dearly for following Lumumba in daring to say "no" to the Belgians. His trial took place January 18–21, 1960; he was found guilty of inciting violence and condemned to six months at hard labor. On January 22, he was transferred to the notorious underground prison at Likasi. His detention made him a very popular figure and a rallying point for the independence struggle.

When the Round Table Conference of independence negotiations between Belgian and Congolese leaders opened on January 20, 1960, in Brussels, the Congolese formed a common front and insisted that Lumumba's release from jail so he could participate in the conference was a nonnegotiable condition for pursuing the talks. Lumumba was released on January 24, and arrived in Brussels the next day. January 27, his first day at the conference, coincided with the decision at the conference to fix the date of Congo's independence at June 30, 1960. That evening, the Congolese delegates celebrated their victory to the rhumba rhythms of Joseph Kabasele (known as Grand Kalé), leader of the African Jazz Band in Kinshasa. He apparently composed "Indepéndance Cha Cha" the same day he played it, a song that ranks high among the classics of Congolese popular music. Lumumba took an active part in the conference proceedings, and played a key role in the decision on the structure of the future state, which would be unitarist, but with large decentralization.

Why did the Belgians accede to nearly all of the political demands of the Congolese, including the recognition of the conference not as a consultative forum, but as a body whose decisions would be binding on both parties; the release of Lumumba from jail only three days after his conviction; and the setting of the date of independence, after their intransigence with respect to the December 1959 elections? The Belgians made all of these concessions because they were confident that their continued presence in the Congo would protect and advance their interests. As they saw it, they would remain associated with state power through the army, in which Belgian officers were to retain command and train future Congolese officers; and through the government, the judiciary, the civil service and state enterprises, in which Belgian experts and senior civil servants would provide advice and guidance to Congolese officials. As for the other two pillars of colonial rule, the economy and culture, Belgian companies would continue to exploit Congolese resources and to sell goods and services in the former colony, while Catholic missionaries would remain engaged in their religious, educational, and health ministries. Even radical nationalists like Lumumba understood that in an underdeveloped country with a shortage of technical cadres like the Congo, independence could not be total, at least initially.

After dancing to "Indépendance Cha Cha" in Brussels and returning home to adoring crowds that treated them like heroes, Lumumba and his Round Table colleagues had no clear understanding of the economic aspects of the transfer of power, which had a lot to do with the limits of national sovereignty and the expectations of ordinary people for material prosperity. Their ignorance of political economy and their inexperience in managing a modern economy led them to neglect crucial issues of assets ownership, the public debt, and economic policy. Although all major leaders attended the Political Round Table Conference in January–February, Conakat leader Tshombe was the only prominent politician who bothered to attend in its entirety the Economic Round Table Conference, which met in Brussels from April 26 to May 16, 1960. Lumumba, for his part, sent Mario Cardoso, a teaching assistant in psychology and education at Lovanium University in Kinshasa, as head of the MNC-L delegation to this important conference. Other major parties also relied on university students and recent graduates, who were asked to negotiate with prominent Belgian experts, some of whom were their economics professors. Negotiating with such young, inexperienced, and politically insignificant delegates who needed Belgian expertise to make sense of the complex issues at stake, the Belgians laid the groundwork for the third rape of the Congo, economically speaking, the first and second having taken place under King Leopold II and the colonial state, respectively. Although the Congolese delegates had clearly indicated that the Congo could not make any commitment before it became master of its destiny, Belgian authorities cynically used the resolutions of the conference to privatize the enormous state portfolios in major colonial trusts such as the Comité Spécial du Katanga (CSK) and the Comité National du Kivu (CNKi) and transferring these assets to Belgium. They also allowed many private companies operating in the Congo to transfer their headquarters to Belgium, thus denying the new state a large amount of tax income, while leaving to it virtually all of the public debt.

Thus, while the political conference was apparently a great victory for the Congo, it was at this economic conference that the Belgians sealed the fate of the country. The Congolese leaders were evidently true believers in the Nkrumahist gospel that once you obtain the political kingdom, everything else will follow more or less automatically afterwards. In the transition to independence in the Congo and in the rest of Africa, the political kingdom has done wonders for African ruling classes—who have gone from middle-class life to join the rich and superrich of the globalized world—but yielded little or no economic benefits for the popular masses. Lumumba had hoped to do better, but the objective conditions he inherited and the hostility he faced from his internal and external enemies would limit his chances to even try to fulfill the people's expectations of independence.

5

The Short Political Life of Congo's First Prime Minister, 1960–61

Two factors are essential for understanding the political crisis that Lumumba faced shortly after taking power on June 30, 1960. The first had to do with the hostility against him by the Belgians along with their Western and Congolese allies, who were determined to do whatever was necessary to make him fail and lose power. The second was the people's disappointment in their expectations of independence; the major manifestation of this disappointment was the mutiny of the FP, which unleashed the first major crisis of independent Congo, known universally as the "Congo crisis." This was in fact a crisis of decolonization, due to the manner in which the Belgians managed the transfer of power with a view to retaining as much control over the Congolese state and economy as they could, and the unpreparedness of Lumumba and the radical nationalist leaders to grasp fully the reins of power. Add to this equation the secessions of the mineral-rich province of Katanga and the diamond-rich region of South Kasai,[1] plus the intervention of the international community through the United Nations, and the result is a very complex political situation whose immediate consequences were the illegal removal of Lumumba from office in September 1960 and his assassination in January 1961. This chapter looks at Lumumba's tenure primarily from the standpoint of domestic politics, but a full picture of why he lost power and his life so fast requires an examination of the international context, which was dominated regionally by the national liberation struggle and globally by the cold war. This is the subject of the next chapter. The assassination itself is analyzed in detail in chapter 7.

Internally and externally, hostility to Lumumba arose from the ideological split in the nationalist movement between radicals and moderates, as already shown with respect to the split of the MNC in chapter 4. The radicals were progressive nationalists who sought to create mass-based political parties and saw independence as an opportunity for changes likely to benefit ordinary people economically and socially. In African and international politics, they espoused the Bandung principle of "positive neutralism," or nonalignment between the Western and the Soviet camps.[2] For them, a strong central government in a unitary state was the most appropriate agency for fulfilling these aims. Their popularity within the industrial working class, the most politically conscious sector among ordinary people, is best exemplified by the fact that the important Luba-Kasai population of the urban and mining centers of Katanga remained loyal to Lumumba and his MNC-L, even after the split between him and Luba-Kasai leader Albert Kalonji.

In addition to Lumumba, the most prominent radicals were Antoine Gizenga and Pierre Mulele of the progressive wing of the PSA, and Anicet Kashamura, president of Cerea. A regionally based party like the PSA, the Cerea sought to mobilize the people of the Kivu province behind the goals of unitarism, pan-Africanism, and nonalignment. The fourth member of the radical coalition was the Katanga cartel of unitarist parties, led by Balubakat. Although an ethnically based political party of the Luba-Katanga, Balubakat earned its radical nationalist credentials for its fight against separatism and the secessionist movement in Katanga. It was led by Jason Sendwe, a medical assistant and a devout Methodist, whose lieutenants were Prosper Mwamba Ilunga, Ildephonse Masengwo, and the youth leader Laurent Kabila.

The moderates, on the other hand, were nationalists who were more conservative in their political outlook generally, whether they were unitarists or federalists. Given their apparent readiness to accept Western tutelage, they enjoyed support from Belgium and other Western governments and corporate circles. The most prominent leader in this group was Joseph Kasavubu, who started his political career as a radical nationalist and federalist, but whose radicalism mellowed as he sought to position himself for postcolonial leadership vis-à-vis Lumumba in the eyes of both his former adversaries in Kinshasa (Adoula, Ileo, Ngalula, etc.) and the West. In addition to Kasavubu, Tshombe, Kalonji, Ileo, and Adoula, the principal moderate leaders included Cléophas Kamitatu, leader of the conservative wing of the PSA; Victor Nendaka, who created a third and short-lived breakaway group of the MNC known as MNC-Nendaka; Justin-Marie Bomboko, the first Congolese to study at the Free University of Brussels; and Joseph-Désiré Mobutu, the former FP sergeant and MNC-L representative in Brussels.

Following the May 1960 independence elections, Lumumba's party won a plurality of seats in the House of Representatives, the lower house of Parliament. They captured 33 of the 137 seats, and with the support of the national alliance cartel of radical parties, Lumumba could easily count on 71 votes, 2 more than the 69 votes needed for a majority. In spite of this reality, Walter J. Ganshof van der Meersch, the Belgian minister in charge of managing the transition, sought to bar Lumumba from the premiership by making Kasavubu the prime minister–designate on June 17, with the task of forming the first government of independent Congo, despite the fact that Abako had won only 12 seats in the House. Kasavubu failed miserably, and Ganshof was forced to entrust this task to Lumumba on June 21. Although Lumumba did succeed in forming a government and throwing the weight of his coalition behind Kasavubu's bid for the mostly ceremonial post of head of state, this attempt to block his accession to the office of prime minister boded ill for the radical alliance. A bad precedent had been set in the manifold compromises that resulted in the formation of the first national government, with each of the opposing camps occupying a seat in the dual executive. From then on, the moderates won the power struggle in all its decisive stages: Mobutu's return to active military duty as a result of the mutiny; Kasavubu's coup of September 5, 1960; Mobutu's first coup d'état of September 14, 1960; Lumumba's fall and assassination; the elimination of the Lumumbists from the political scene; and the crushing of the Lumumbist-led "second independence" movement. Hostility to Lumumba and his followers had become the cornerstone of the politics of the moderates and their backers in the West.

The second factor of the crisis was that the Congolese people saw very early on and clearly that their expectation that independence would usher in a new era of fundamental freedoms and material prosperity was unlikely to be met. Members of the new ruling elite had neglected to protect the country's assets from Belgian looting, seemingly more concerned with enjoying the material benefits that colonialism had denied them than with a radical transformation of the inherited state and economy to meet the people's expectations of independence. At the conclusion of the May elections, hundreds of newly elected Congolese leaders went to Kinshasa and to provincial capitals as the representatives of the people.

Their first official act, after they had fought each other for the important leadership positions, was to accept not only the privileges that had been enjoyed by the Belgians before them, but also some new privileges of their own creation. In the national capital, for example, parliamentarians voted to increase their remuneration from 100,000 to 500,000 francs a year (2,000 to 10,000 U.S. dollars), in a country where the annual per capita monetary income for Africans was below 50 U.S. dollars.

The other social classes, well aware of this greed, asked for their fair share of the fruits of independence. The working class began staging strikes in Kinshasa, Mbandaka, and elsewhere. Teachers threatened not to return to their classrooms if salaries and working conditions were not improved. And for peasants and the unemployed, the politicians were simply liars, and it became fashionable to equate "telling lies" with "talking politics." Having forgotten the wonderful promises they had made during the electoral campaign for jobs, better wages, free health care, free primary and secondary education, and in some cases the abolition of both forced labor and taxes, the new *évolué* leaders felt confident that they could count on the FP to maintain law and order. They were mistaken. They had failed to understand the implications of independence for the other social classes, and it was precisely because of this failure that the FP mutiny caught them by surprise.

To the soldiers demanding change and immediate Africanization of all officer ranks, Lumumba and other leaders preached patience, and showed their elitism by promising to provide additional training for soldiers before they were given higher promotions. This was good logic but bad politics. It was the soldiers' turn to ask the politicians, "If higher studies are required for promotions, what higher studies have *you* had to become what you are now?"[3] The soldiers rebelled. Their question was based on the fact that at independence, the FP remained unchanged from the way it was during the colonial period, with all officer positions occupied by Belgians. Until 1959, when the rank of warrant officer was opened to Congolese noncommissioned officers, the highest rank for a Congolese was that of sergeant-major. While it was true that most of the African countries in which independence was achieved through peaceful negotiations maintained European officers at the higher ranks of general, colonel, and major, the former Belgian Congo presented an extreme case in that not even a single second lieutenant was Congolese.

The depth of discontent in the armed forces was well known to General Emile Janssens, the FP commander, who had an excellent intelligence service. Moreover, he had personally witnessed acts of indiscipline at Camp Leopold II in Kinshasa on July 4, and heard news of saber rattling from the elite mechanized brigade at Camp Hardy to the south, in Mbanza Ngungu. In this context, the general meeting of the troops that he convened in Kinshasa on the morning of July 5 can only be interpreted as a conscious effort at instigating revolt within the FP. On a big blackboard in front of the excited troops, Janssens wrote in capital letters the following words: "Before independence = After independence." For the men in uniform, he told them, there would be no changes as a result of independence; discipline would be maintained as usual, and white officers would remain in command. Unless he was simply a fool, Janssens was deliberately provoking rebellion among the troops, not involuntarily doing so, as Auguste Maurel, an otherwise keen observer of Belgian policy in the Congo, suggests.[4] Given the climate of discontent within the FP, his arrogant and patronizing speech was part of Belgian attempts to destabilize the Lumumba government in order to cause its fall. These destabilization efforts included instigating the mutiny of the FP and pushing the Katanga province to secede.

Janssens's arrogant and patronizing speech simply added fuel to the fire. Convinced without doubt that they were being denied the fruits of independence available to civilians, the soldiers rose up to demand salary increases, promotions, and the dismissal of all Belgian officers. Using the excellent communications network of the armed forces, they informed their comrades all over the country, who immediately expressed their solidarity and moved on to disarm all of their Belgian superiors. In many garrisons, the men actually took it upon themselves to elect their own officers.

To calm the situation, Lumumba began the process of Africanizing the officer corps by appointing Victor

Lundula—a former FP staff sergeant who served as a medical assistant during World War II in Asia and since January 1960 as the burgomaster of the Kikula commune in Likasi—a major general and commander in chief of the army, which he renamed the Armée Nationale Congolaise (ANC). He also appointed Joseph-Désiré Mobutu, a former FP quartermaster sergeant and a junior minister in the prime minister's office, as a colonel and chief of staff of the ANC. Both appointments were ill advised. Lundula did not have the necessary qualifications to manage a modern army. As for Mobutu, Lumumba made a serious blunder based on his political naivety and his overconfidence with regard to commanding the loyalty of the people in his entourage. He refused to listen to apparently well-founded rumors about Mobutu's ties to the Belgian and American intelligence services. In appointing Mobutu to this sensitive position, he had unwittingly chosen his own Judas.

If Janssens's intention in instigating the mutiny was to discredit Lumumba's leadership and push him out of power, the immediate results were the panic and flight of European civil servants and settlers, which deprived the economy and the state of most of their professional and technical cadres. Unfortunately, acts of violence were committed against Belgian officers resisting arrest and whites refusing to surrender their firearms or vehicles commandeered by the mutineers, as well as a few acts of rape against white women by soldiers intoxicated by alcohol and rage. Horrible as these cases were, including the gang rape of two women in the Madimba subdistrict of Lower Congo, exaggerations of their magnitude in the European rumor mill set off and intensified white flight, even in the absence of a single reported death among Europeans, and provided a pretext to the Belgian government for military aggression against an independent and sovereign state.

Belgium had no logistical challenges in invading its former colony. Following World War II, Belgium had established two military bases for metropolitan troops not detached to the FP, at Kamina in Katanga Province and at Kitona in Lower Congo. Within the context of the cold war, these bases were part of the Western defense architecture under the North Atlantic Treaty Organization (NATO). Belgium had already begun sending troop reinforcements to these bases in May 1960, presumably to reassure the Belgian population of approximately a hundred thousand people that Brussels was doing everything necessary to protect them. Using this rationale, on July 10 Belgium invaded the Congo with these troops and new reinforcements flown in from Belgium. On the following day, Katanga Province declared its secession from the Congo, using the nationwide instability and Lumumba's alleged communist ties as reasons for establishing an independent state of Katanga in friendship with Belgium. This was not a pure coincidence. A clear indication of their true intentions was that the Belgians disarmed all non-Katangese soldiers of the Congolese army and expelled them from the province. They retained those who were native to the province ethnically to enroll them in the Katanga Gendarmerie. By so doing, Belgium took part in the criminal enterprise of ethnic cleansing that was so dear to Godefroid Munongo, Katanga's powerful interior minister and a descendant of the Nyamwezi king Msiri, who had migrated to Katanga from Tanzania around 1850. This involvement showed how desperate Brussels and its corporate allies were in trying to make the secession an African affair. In reality, Munongo and Tshombe, the provincial president, served as the African front for the more powerful interests of mining companies and white settlers.

The unilateral military intervention by Belgium and the Katanga secession added new challenges for Lumumba to the already difficult tasks he had undertaken to reestablish discipline in the ANC and restore law and order throughout the country. He and President Kasavubu made several trips in the interior to cool tempers and reassure Europeans, and were united in considering several options with regard to foreign assistance to establish peace and security. These included U.S. military assistance, which was in fact requested without Lumumba's knowledge by Gizenga, his supposedly "communist" deputy prime minister, and Bomboko, the foreign minister. U.S. ambassador Clare Timberlake made it known to Gizenga and the Lumumba government that they could not count on U.S. support. For him, the best solution would be UN intervention. It is clear that for Timberlake and the U.S. government, the presence of UN troops was the best way of protecting Western interests in the Congo, and the ambassador also hoped that the unilateral Belgian intervention could be legalized by placing it under a UN umbrella. This idea of a UN cover for Western and specifically American interests became an integral part of U.S. policy in the Congo.

On July 12, Lumumba and Kasavubu made the fateful appeal for UN intervention. Dag Hammarskjöld, the UN secretary-general, was already waiting for the request, having been alerted to it by his deputy, Ralph Bunche, who was already in Kinshasa. With the United States convinced that the UN was the best instrument for protecting Western interests in the Congo, and the Soviet Union attentive to the strong Afro-Asian solidarity with Lumumba, the Security Council moved rapidly to approve the deployment of a UN peacekeeping force to the Congo two days later, on July 14, at 3 a.m. On the evening of July 15, in less than forty-eight hours, the first contingents of the United Nations Operation in the Congo (ONUC) had arrived in the Congo, a record in the annals of UN peacekeeping.

In view of Hammarskjöld's refusal to confront the Belgian troops and white mercenaries in Katanga militarily, Lumumba decided to take matters in his own hands by equipping the ANC to do what was needed. As the central government was making preparations for sending its troops to Katanga, the diamond region of South

Kasai rebelled from central authority on August 8, 1960. Since Albert Kalonji, the Luba-Kasai leader, announced the South Kasai secession from the Katanga capital of Lubumbashi, it was evident that the two secessions were intertwined. In fact they were both supported by Belgian corporate interests. It was thus logical for the Lumumba government to issue an order to the ANC to put an end to the rebellion in little South Kasai before crossing the provincial border into Katanga. The ANC entered the so-called Autonomous State of South Kasai without much resistance during the night of August 26–27, 1960. Unfortunately, ANC soldiers considered all the residents of South Kasai the enemy, and committed atrocious massacres, the most important of which involved thousands of innocent civilians who had taken refuge in the Catholic cathedral of Mbuji-Mayi, capital of the secessionist enclave. Erroneously characterized by Hammarskjöld as acts of genocide, these massacres gave Kasavubu the excuse he needed to dismiss Lumumba from his job as prime minister.[5] He did so on September 5, 1960.

If it makes sense for the prime minister as both defense minister and head of government to be held ultimately responsible for acts committed by his troops, what about the other responsible officials in the chain of command: (1) the commanders in the field, who either gave the orders to kill unarmed civilians or could not control their unruly soldiers; (2) Colonel Mobutu, the ANC chief of staff; and (3) Kasavubu himself, in his capacity as the supreme commander of the armed forces? In this regard, whoever gave the ANC the order to crush the rebellion in South Kasai before moving on to Katanga—be it Lumumba or Mobutu—the entire chain of command, including Mobutu, Lumumba, and Kasavubu, must be held politically responsible for the heinous crimes against humanity committed by the ANC. Criminal responsibility, on the other hand, would require evidence that the minister of defense and/or the chief of staff had actually given authorization to the troops to commit these crimes. Morally, Kasavubu had no justification for blaming Lumumba alone while holding Mobutu and himself above blame. Legally and politically, he had no authority to dismiss a prime minister enjoying majority support in Parliament, as both legislative houses indicated by their votes declaring the president's action null and void. Since Lumumba's removal from office could not be accomplished legally, Colonel Mobutu revealed his true political colors by staging a coup d'état against Lumumba on September 14, 1960. He did so with technical advice and support from General Ben Hammou Kettani, head of the Moroccan ONUC contingent and deputy UN force commander.

Having failed to bring Lumumba down through the FP mutiny, his internal and external enemies used the secessions of Katanga and South Kasai as traps by which he could be ensnared. He was charged with the sin of communism in the first instance, and accused of the crime of genocide in the second. These two secessions not only made it possible for the Congolese moderates to eliminate their formidable foe from the political scene; they also reinforced their anticommunist axis with two rendition centers to which they could send Lumumba and his followers for torture and assassination. The political mafia chieftains in Kinshasa collaborated with the very secessionist forces they were supposed to fight, even allowing South Kasai to remain in rebellion by recalling the ANC troops that had conquered it. By so doing, they gave themselves an opportunity to resort to deniability regarding any crimes committed on their instigation in Lubumbashi and Mbuji-Mayi. If the participation of Katanga's leaders in "one of the most important assassinations of the twentieth century"[6] is well known, the role of South Kasai's Kalonji is less known, and yet he was so accommodating to his Kinshasa allies that he turned Mbuji-Mayi into the preferred location for slaughtering Lumumba's followers. The best known of these victims is Pierre Finant, the first elected governor of Orientale Province and father of the famous Congolese singer Abeti Masikini (Betty Finant). For its eager participation in the renditions orchestrated by Kinshasa, the South Kasai capital came to be known as the *boucherie* (slaughterhouse). Both Tshombe and Kalonji did not understand that Kinshasa's alliance with them was tactical rather than strategic, their common opposition to Lumumba and his partisans being the only factor uniting them temporarily in a common effort. Once Lumumba was assassinated and his followers weakened politically, the moderates in Kinshasa had no use for them, and succeeded in ending the secession of South Kasai by supporting a mutiny in Kalonji's own army in September 1962, and that of Katanga through UN military action in January 1963.

By then, the unitarists among the moderates had already taken control of the central state machinery through a powerful clique known as the Binza Group. This control was exercised through the medium of key organs of state power closely linked to external sources of assistance and pressure. The most important of these organs were the army, the security police, the foreign ministry, the central bank, and the internal affairs apparatus (incorporating the police and the administration of provinces), which remained under the control of Mobutu, Nendaka, Bomboko, Albert Ndele, and Damien Kandolo, respectively. These five men formed the nucleus of the Binza Group, so called because its members usually met in the elite Kinshasa suburb of Binza, where they maintained private residences. They worked closely with American, Belgian, and UN officials in furthering their own interests and those of their Western allies. Just as they had used Kalonji and Tshombe to get rid of Lumumba, they, too, were secondary actors and pawns in the Western-supported counterrevolution against the national liberation struggle in Central and Southern Africa. Patrice Lumumba was the first major casualty of this counterrevolution.

6

Lumumba and the Counterrevolution in Central and Southern Africa

The international context of Lumumba's demise was dominated regionally by the national liberation struggle and globally by the cold war. This chapter intends to show that if the cold war provided the ideological pretext or justification for his political and physical elimination by a coalition of Western interests, the major reason for his assassination lies in the Western-backed counterrevolution against the national liberation struggle in Central and Southern Africa. What was this counterrevolution, why was it backed by the West, and how did Lumumba become its first major victim in the region? These are the questions that need to be answered before we look at the details concerning his assassination.

After his return to power in France in June 1958, General Charles de Gaulle made a memorable speech in Brazzaville on August 28 in which he told Africans that whoever wanted independence could seize it. But when Ahmed Sékou Touré and his followers did so on October

2, 1958, the French cut off all ties with Guinea; departing French civil servants destroyed office equipment and furniture, shredded or burned documents, cut off phone lines, and took away such essential papers as building and bridge plans. The message could not be any clearer: independence was acceptable to Paris so long as the leadership of the new African country was pliable in its dealings with the French establishment, the best examples being puppets like Ahmadou Ahidjo in Cameroon, Léon Mba in Gabon, and the priest-president Fulbert Youlou in Congo-Brazzaville. This was the message that the Belgians, too, were sending to Lumumba and other Congolese leaders. They were prepared to work with moderate leaders like Adoula, Ileo, Kalonji, Kasavubu, and Tshombe, but not radicals like Lumumba.

In the Congo case, what was at stake concerned more than the interests of the former colonial power. The counterrevolution of which Lumumba became a victim involved the whole African subcontinent from Katanga to the Cape of Good Hope. Mining companies and white settlers in that area were reluctant to concede their political control and economic privileges to the forces of African nationalism, and for as long as they could, they retained power by convincing Western powers that they were better protectors of Western economic and strategic interests than African independence and liberation movements. Geographically and economically, the Katanga region of the Copperbelt has been an integral part of the Southern African economic complex. This is a relatively interdependent region of world capitalism with a highly developed industrial structure in South Africa and an abundance of mineral resources throughout the whole area. Through corporations like the British South African Company (BSAC), Tanganyika Concessions Ltd. (Tanks or TCL), Anglo-American, Consolidated Gold Fields, and De Beers, South African capital had been invested in nearly all the countries of the region, particularly in the mining industry. Most of these countries were also providing the apartheid economy with cheap migrant labor and with markets for South African goods and services, including transportation and marketing.

As a country with enormous wealth in natural resources and transportation linkages to Atlantic and Indian Ocean ports, the Congo was progressively integrated in the Southern African economic complex via the mining industry and the transportation network. When the Union Minière du Haut-Katanga (UMHK), the giant mining company and the single most important corporation in colonial Congo, was established in 1906, TCL was the second major private shareholder after the Société Générale de Belgique (SGB), the largest Belgian transnational. It was also the founder and majority owner of the Benguela Railway, which connects the Katanga to the Atlantic Ocean ports of Benguela and Lobito in Angola. Throughout the colonial period, mining equipment, coal, foodstuffs, and even wage earners found their way north to Katanga from South Africa, Zimbabwe, Malawi, Zambia, and Angola. White miners from the south brought with them values and behavioral patterns that greatly reinforced the racism of the Belgian colonial system. With white South Africans and Rhodesians as their reference groups, Belgian settlers sought to create a colonial-settler system and to subordinate the political economy of the province to their interests, but they were repulsed in their quest for state power by the Belgian corporate elite, which did not wish to concede a higher portion of the economic surplus to the settlers.

Later on, however, the prospects of independence under a radical nationalist government led by Lumumba brought a rapprochement between the corporate leaders, represented by the top management of UMHK and other SGB companies in Katanga, and the settlers. While these two white groups were instrumental in preparing the secession, in an international environment marked by overwhelming support for self-determination, national independence, and majority rule, they needed black allies to give it credibility. And they found them in Tshombe's Conakat, which became the auxiliary arm of settler politics and the voice of the UMHK and other companies speaking through African mouths. With the backing of the Belgian government, Katanga's independence was proclaimed on July 11, 1960, by Tshombe, while its white architects and strategists remained in the background. Thus was an "internal settlement" scheme imposed on

Katanga Province long before the Rhodesian rebel government of Ian Smith coined the term to designate the agreement signed with Bishop Abel Muzorewa, the Reverend Ndabaningi Sithole, and Chief Jeremiah Chirau on March 3, 1978, for a limited measure of power sharing with the white settlers in Zimbabwe.

At the very time that African countries were achieving their independence from European colonial rule, this counterrevolution against national liberation was rearing its ugly head from the Congo basin all the way to the Cape of Good Hope, with mining companies, white settlers, and their backers in the Western establishment waging a vigorous campaign to preserve European interests and white supremacy in Central and Southern Africa. Against the national and social aspirations of the black masses for freedom and material prosperity, the counterrevolution was aimed at coopting traditional rulers and reactionary or moderate intellectuals in the preservation of the status quo in the name of bogus formulas such as "partnership," "internal settlement," "homeland independence," or independent statehood emptied of its emancipatory thrust. In this perspective, the idea was to join an independent Katanga to the Federation of Rhodesia and Nyasaland (Malawi, Zambia, and Zimbabwe today), the Portuguese colonies of Angola and Mozambique, and the apartheid state of South Africa (including Namibia) against the forces of radical nationalism represented by the liberation movements of Southern Africa and the MNC-L and its allies in the Congo. Consequently, winning the battle for Katanga was likely to give a tremendous boost to the war against the national liberation struggle in the whole region.

As a country that claims to support anticolonial revolutions like its own war of independence, the United States played a key role in the counterrevolution by participating in the assassination of Lumumba; supporting the Portuguese colonial wars through NATO; and condoning apartheid in Namibia and South Africa through the policies of "linkage" and "constructive engagement," which were detrimental to African freedom fighters.[1] Only public pressure mobilized by the African American lobby TransAfrica and the disinvestment campaign by universities and churches succeeded in having Congress override President Ronald Reagan's veto of the Comprehensive Anti-Apartheid Act in 1986. All of the prosettler U.S. positions can be understood with reference to the cold war, or the confrontation between the Western camp, led by the United States, and the communist bloc led by Soviet Union. Instead of fighting each other directly in a theater of war, these two blocs used economic, political, and cultural resources in their competition for the souls and minds of the developing countries of Africa, Asia, and Latin America, but they also engaged in proxy wars between their respective clients, and in the destabilization of those regimes perceived as threatening their interests. In Central and Southern Africa, the United States maintained military and intelligence collaboration with Portugal and South Africa, with the latter's mercenaries being critical as Belgium's allies in backstopping the Katanga secession, while the Soviet Union and other socialist countries provided assistance to African liberation movements, including Lumumba's government in the Congo.

Before the Congo crisis, Western hostility to political regimes committed to using the natural resources of their countries to improve the living standards of their people had already manifested itself in the destabilization of governments perceived as threatening to Western interests. The best-known African case in this regard was the Anglo-French-Israeli aggression against Egypt in the wake of the nationalization of the Suez Canal by President Gamal Abdel Nasser in 1956. Although this attempt to regain Western control of the canal failed thanks to Soviet threats and U.S. reluctance to enter the fray, it followed the classic pattern of destabilization, which involved humiliating the targeted leader, weakening him politically, and thus making it easier to remove him from power. This strategy was perfected under the administration of U.S. President Dwight D. Eisenhower by Secretary of State John Foster Dulles and his younger brother Allen Dulles, head of the Central Intelligence Agency, with CIA-engineered coups d'état against Prime Minister Mohammed Mossadegh of Iran in 1953 and President Jacobo Arbenz of Guatemala in 1954. Britain participated in the destabilization in Iran, as London was equally opposed to Mossadegh for having nationalized a British oil company. In the case of

Guatemala, the Dulles brothers served on the board of the United Fruit Company (and Allen had actually worked for it), the major U.S. corporation whose interests were at stake. Six years later, Allen Dulles would supervise the CIA destabilization campaign against Lumumba.

The U.S. role in modern Congolese history goes well beyond economic motives and interests, even though the latter are not insignificant. The best-known U.S. economic interests in the Belgian Congo were the shares of the Thomas Ryan and Daniel Guggenheim group in the Société Internationale Forestière et Minière (Forminière), with interests in diamond mining in Kasai, plantation agriculture in Mayombe, and gold and cattle in the east; and those of the Rockefeller group in UMHK through TCL. However, these interests paled in importance next to the strategic interest of the U.S. in Congolese uranium, which the UMHK made available to Washington for purposes of making the first atomic weapons, the bombs that President Harry Truman dropped at Hiroshima and Nagasaki. A major consequence of this Congolese contribution to the war effort was that the United States found for itself a vital national interest in the strategic minerals of the Congo, including uranium, copper, cobalt, and industrial diamonds. This strategic interest expanded in the postwar period to imply a Western stake in preventing the Soviet Union and its allies from gaining influence in Central Africa. For Washington and its Cassandras, nonalignment was a dirty word and leaders like Lumumba who espoused it were either "communist sympathizers" or naïve about the communist threat. Using this cold war discourse as a rationalization of their hostility to independent-minded leaders, U.S. policy makers thus agreed with Belgium that Lumumba had to be removed from power. The question was "how to do it," and the answer was "by all means necessary," including hired killers, corrupt politicians, and the United Nations. Like Britain, the United States had a strong Katanga lobby, whose prominent members included Senators Barry Goldwater (Arizona), Thomas Dodd (Connecticut), and Strom Thurmond (South Carolina).

It was through the cold war perspective common to U.S. policy makers in Washington and to senior American civil servants in the UN Secretariat in New York that the Congo crisis was perceived. Several weeks before the outbreak of the crisis, UN secretary-general Hammarskjöld had already mapped out a scenario in which the rapid transfer of power in the Congo was likely to result in an international crisis for which UN intervention would be required. The brilliant Swedish diplomat also thought that given the lack of adequate preparation on the part of the Congolese to manage a modern state, such a crisis would create a great opportunity to put in practice his ideas on world governance, with the UN acting as an agent of nation building. Accordingly, he sent UN undersecretary-general Ralph Bunche to Kinshasa in late June 1960 to represent the UN at the independence ceremonies and to stay for a few weeks to advise the new government and explore the requirements for UN assistance. Instead of a few weeks, Bunche stayed on for over two months, becoming in the process the first special representative of the secretary-general (SRSG) in the Congo and the interim force commander of ONUC. With ONUC, Hammarskjöld departed from previous practice, by which the Security Council (SC) itself kept direct control over peacekeeping operations, by centralizing management and supervision within the Secretariat, with the secretary-general, the SRSG, and the force commander as key decision makers. In the Congo, a position of chief of civilian operations was also created, in view of the importance of the large nation-building mandate of ONUC.

A major dispute arose between Lumumba, who had requested UN intervention, and Hammarskjöld, who took part in framing SC resolutions in view of global political realities, on the interpretation of these resolutions. On the surface, the ONUC mandate as described in the SC resolutions of July 14, July 22, and August 9 is broadly supportive of the Congolese government's demand for (1) the withdrawal of Belgian troops from the entire national territory, including Katanga; (2) military assistance to restore law and order; and (3) technical assistance to ensure the smooth running of essential services. In reality, and given the British and French support for the Katanga secession and their sympathies with Belgium, Hammarskjöld did not have Western support "to take all necessary action" to speed up Belgian withdrawal as called for in the

July 22 resolution. More importantly, he did not believe in confronting the Belgians militarily, as he was convinced that they would leave on their own once UN troops had restored law and order and brought the situation under control. While this worked out for the rest of the country, it could not apply to Katanga, where Belgian soldiers and white mercenaries were the backbone of the secession, without which it would collapse.

Because of UN refusal to assist his government in expelling the Belgian troops and the white mercenaries from Southern Africa and Europe who were supporting it, Lumumba felt compelled to seek military assistance elsewhere. He obtained some help from the Soviet Union for the airlift of troops and supplies to Katanga and South Kasai, including two hundred technicians, trucks, and thirteen troop transport planes. Both UN and U.S. officials raised such a fuss about this assistance that it was largely forgotten that the first shipment of military equipment and supplies to independent Congo was part of the Soviet contribution to the UN operation, which included the ferrying of Ghanaian troops from Accra to Kinshasa. Moreover, as Moscow argued in a note to the UN secretary-general, "the sending by the Soviet Union of help to the government of the Republic of the Congo—in the form of civil aircraft and motor vehicles—was not contrary to the terms of the resolutions of 14 and 22 July 1960, since the said resolutions set no limit on the right of the [Congo] government to ask for or be given direct bilateral aid."[2]

Hammarskjöld's indulgent attitude to the Belgian support for secession in Katanga, and his open hostility to Soviet bilateral support to Lumumba, showed his cold war bias. The secretary-general and his chief collaborators in the Congo crisis shared a common cold war outlook with Western policy makers, and saw their mission in the Congo as preserving the then existing balance of forces in the world. Two diplomats who had great admiration for Hammarskjöld have testified as to his pro-West bias. Thomas Kanza, Lumumba's representative at the UN and a young man who looked up to the secretary-general as a mentor, has written that Hammarskjöld "believed that the West had a sacred mission towards Africa in general, and especially the Congo."[3] Rajeshwar Dayal, who served as SRSG in the Congo between September 1960 and June 1961, reports that his boss "had little respect for the Soviet Under-Secretary, G. P. Arkadiev, and though Arkadiev's functions were political, he was rather pointedly excluded from participation in the Congo discussions."[4] Dayal does not tell us why a senior UN political affairs official was so excluded by a man he claims was committed to nonalignment.

The secretary-general apparently believed that a UN official from the Soviet Union would remain loyal to the foreign policy of his country, while those from the West would act as neutral international civil servants. This is why the "Congo discussions" were dominated by Hammarskjöld's senior American aides: Ralph Bunche, his deputy; Andrew Cordier, his executive assistant; and

Heinrich Wieschhoff, his éminence grise. As Arkadiev's subordinate, Wieschhoff was entrusted with the custody of the Congo files, but he could not show them to his immediate boss. While Bunche and Wieschhoff were more diplomatic in following the secretary-general's caution on being extremely careful not to create the impression that they were "out to get Lumumba,"[5] Cordier the cold warrior had no such scruples. During his brief tenure as acting head of ONUC between Bunche's departure on August 28 and Dayal's arrival on September 8, 1960, there was no doubt as to the fact that the United Nations had become a simple instrument of U.S. policy in the Congo. He and U.S. ambassador Timberlake worked hand in hand to advance U.S. policy objectives, which by then had as a priority the political and physical elimination of Lumumba. Cordier helped engineer and execute the illegal removal of Lumumba from power by Kasavubu on September 5, 1960. He closed the airports, to prevent Lumumba from bringing troop reinforcements from Kisangani, and the national radio station so that he could not use it to appeal to the people, knowing full well that Kasavubu could cross the river and use Brazzaville Radio, which was under the control of his ethnic kin, President Youlou of Congo-Brazzaville.

Bunche, the winner of the Nobel Peace Prize in 1950 for his mediation of the armistice between Israel and the Arab states following the 1948 Israeli-Arab war, was very hostile to the radical and anti-imperialist type of

African nationalism espoused by Lumumba, Nasser, and Nkrumah, which was dismissed in Hammarskjöld's entourage as "emotional pan-Africanism."[6] During Bunche's tenure as SRSG in the Congo, his cable traffic with the UN Secretariat went through the U.S. Embassy in Kinshasa. Others who played key policy-making roles on the Congo included General Carl von Horn, Hammarskjöld's compatriot, who served as the first force commander in the Congo, and the secretary-general's British assistant, Brian Urquhart. Given their worldview and the prevailing climate of the times, all of these international civil servants from the West had a negative perception of Lumumba. Wittingly or unwittingly, they provided to those seeking his demise the justification and the opportunities they needed to remove a democratically elected leader from office by illegal means.

On August 31, 1960, when told of U.S. concerns over Soviet assistance in ferrying ANC troops to Kisangani for the campaign against the secession, Hammarskjöld reassured Washington "that he had given strict orders not to permit any 'unauthorized landings' by Soviet planes transporting Lumumba's troops to Katanga."[7] In so doing, Hammarskjöld was violating paragraph 4 of the SC resolution of August 9, according to which "the United Nations Force in the Congo will not be a party to or in any way intervene in or be used to influence the outcome of any internal conflict, constitutional or otherwise." Hammarskjöld himself wanted this clause in the resolution to avoid any UN military action in Katanga against the Belgians, but he was not ashamed to violate it to interfere with the lawful action of a democratically elected government to uphold the constitution and crush an externally supported secession. In this particular case of Soviet assistance to Lumumba, UN actions were also part of a wider propaganda campaign designed to convince world public opinion that Lumumba was facilitating Soviet expansion in the heart of Africa. As Kanza points out, the campaign was "part of the necessary psychological preparation for a major coup in the Congo, a coup inspired and supported by Western powers."[8] For this coup to succeed, the support of the UN Secretariat, particularly through Andrew Cordier, and ONUC, through General Kettani, was indispensable.

The United States and its Western allies had every reason to congratulate themselves for having won the cold war in the Congo by taking effective measures to preempt or frustrate Soviet attempts to support Lumumba in his rightful defense of Congolese national interests. The Soviet Union could not match the military, political, diplomatic, and economic assets that the West could deploy in promoting its interests. More importantly, the Soviet Union saw its involvement in the Congo as a small price to pay for the propaganda dividends that Lumumba's demise at the hands of the imperialists would bring to Moscow. It was not prepared to fight the Western-backed counterrevolution in Central Africa.

In the end, both Lumumba and Hammarskjöld would die while trying to end the Katanga secession. Hammarskjöld, who died in a plane crash on the night of September 17–18, 1961 (exactly eight months after Lumumba), during a mission to negotiate with Tshombe in Ndola, Zambia (then Northern Rhodesia), was a victim of the settler and right-wing elements of the counterrevolution. Ironically, his anti-Lumumba positions had strengthened these elements, which provided financial and military support to the Katanga secession. With Lumumba already out of the picture, the secession had lost its value for major Western powers, whose interests were better served in a unitary Congo under the control of moderates. Lumumba, on the other hand, died for attempting to uphold constitutional order, national unity, and territorial integrity. He was a victim of the coalition of all counterrevolutionary forces, operating within the logic of the cold war against the national liberation movement as a struggle for self-determination, self-reliance, and pan-African solidarity.

7

Lumumba's Assassination

The Congo's first democratically elected head of government was assassinated on January 17, 1961. Lumumba, the victim, was only thirty-five years old; he had been in power for a little over two months; and he was murdered only six and a half months following Congo's independence. This heinous crime was a culmination of two interrelated assassination plots by the U.S. and Belgian governments, which used Congolese accomplices to carry out the deed. Ludo De Witte, the Belgian author of *The Assassination of Lumumba*, the most definitive scholarly work on the subject, has called it "one of the twentieth century's most important political assassinations."[1] The assassination's historical importance lies in a multitude of factors, the most pertinent being the global context in which it took place, its long-term impact on Congolese politics, and Lumumba's overall legacy as a nationalist and pan-Africanist leader.

As pointed out in the preceding chapter, this assassination cannot be fully understood without reference to the world context, then dominated by the national liberation struggle in Africa and the cold war internationally. In this context, it was inevitable that the U.S. and its Western allies would not be prepared to let Africans have effective control over strategic raw materials, on the pretext that these might fall in the hands of their enemies in the Soviet camp. It is in this regard that Lumumba's determination to achieve genuine independence and to have full control over Congo's resources in order to utilize them to improve the living conditions of its people was perceived as a threat to Western interests. To fight him, the United States and Belgium used all the tools and resources at their disposal, including the UN Secretariat under Hammarskjöld and Bunche, Lumumba's Congolese political rivals, and hired killers.

One of the tools that appealed to both the Americans and the Belgians was assassination. In the wake of the Cuban Revolution and Fidel Castro's turn to the left, President Eisenhower and CIA chief Allen Dulles adopted assassination as a major foreign policy tool against nationalist leaders considered anti-Western or hostile to the interests of the capitalist West. On August 18, 1960, Dulles had as usual given President Eisenhower his daily briefing on world affairs, including the Congo, prior to a meeting of the National Security Council (NSC) on the same day. This was the day when Lawrence Devlin, his station chief in Kinshasa, had sent him a cable stating that "a classic communist takeover" was under way in the Congo, and that "there may be little time left [to] avoid another Cuba."² It was in these circumstances that the NSC discussion on the Congo crisis ended with the president's cryptic question about "getting rid of this guy," which the CIA boss understood perfectly as a presidential directive to assassinate Lumumba, for U.S. presidents were then held by conventions of deniability never to say such nasty things openly.

Thus, while people like C. Douglas Dillon, the then undersecretary of state, did not understand what was going on—he told the U.S. Senate Select Committee on attempted assassinations of foreign leaders in 1975 that he did not think that the president meant to assassinate Lumumba—the evidence is that Dulles, who already considered Lumumba "a Castro or worse," got the right presidential message. Back at CIA headquarters at Langley, Virginia, he gave instructions to Sidney Gottlieb, the agency's top scientist, to move expeditiously on implementing the presidential order. Accordingly, the Special Group of the NSC, a high-level interagency group charged with overseeing covert operations, discussed the issue of "getting rid of Lumumba" a week later, in its meeting of August 25.³ On August 27, Dulles sent a cable to Devlin stating that the removal of Lumumba "must be an urgent and prime objective and that under existing conditions this should be a high priority of our covert action."⁴

Dr. Gottlieb, the CIA scientist, would later land in Kinshasa on September 26 as "Joe from Paris," equipped with a deadly substance made of cobra venom, to be applied to Lumumba's food or toothpaste. To Devlin, the spy chief in Kinshasa and the man who had recruited Mobutu for Uncle Sam between 1958 and 1960 in Brussels, this type of adventure *à la* James Bond appeared ludicrous. Who was going to penetrate Lumumba's security in order to poison him? he asked. For Devlin, the best course of action was to work with Lumumba's Congolese rivals to eliminate him politically and, maybe later, physically. This is actually what happened, in accordance with another plan conceived by the NSC Special Group to bribe Kasavubu and other Congolese moderates to collaborate in the elimination of Lumumba, known as Project Wizard. The first public disclosure of this project came out in an article by Steve Weissman in the *Washington Post* of July 21, 2002. Its success would depend on collaboration with both Belgium and the Congolese moderates.

By September 1, ANC troops had successfully invaded South Kasai and were advancing toward Katanga from the north and the west. Frightened by reports of the boldness of these troops, Tshombe and Kalonji, the secessionist leaders, appealed to Kasavubu, their moderate and federalist ally, to stop Lumumba's antisecessionist drive. Two critical factors gave Kasavubu the impetus he needed to make the move against Lumumba. The first was that the ANC military action in South Kasai had resulted in massacres of innocent civilians in several locations, notably at Mbuji-Mayi and Kasengulu, near Tshilenge. With Hammarskjöld cynically exploiting these unfortunate killings by describing them as "genocide" against the Luba-Kasai—in fact they did not fit the definition of genocide in international law as an act with the intent to eliminate in whole or in part a group defined along the lines of race, ethnicity, religion, or other criterion—Kasavubu found it convenient to charge the prime minister with this crime. The second factor was the presence in Kinshasa of Hammarskjöld's executive assistant, Andrew Cordier, the American cold warrior who threw the weight and prestige of the UN behind U.S. and Belgian demands that Kasavubu dismiss Lumumba.

On the evening of September 5, 1960, the Congolese were startled to hear the little, squeaky voice of President Kasavubu on the airwaves announcing his dismissal of Lumumba. This action was based on a controversial and little-understood article of the interim constitution handed down by the Belgians, but it was clearly a civilian coup in a parliamentary democracy in which the government enjoyed majority support in both legislative houses, and therefore illegal. Both houses declared Kasavubu's decision null and void, and gave a vote of confidence to the prime minister. Lumumba reacted by dismissing Kasavubu, whom he had supported for the ceremonial presidency against Jean Bolikango for purposes of appeasing the strong Abako constituency in Kinshasa. But Parliament refused to remove Kasavubu from office, in spite of his illegal action, which created a constitutional crisis for the young republic.

There were only two ways of resolving this crisis: by reconciling Lumumba and Kasavubu, or by forcibly removing one of them from power. Diplomats from a number of African countries and the new UN envoy, Rajeshwar Dayal, chose the first option, but failed. The path of reconciliation had already been made into an obstacle course by the good works of Cordier, the U.S. Embassy in Kinshasa, Kasavubu's Belgian advisers, and Mobutu's CIA and ONUC friends. On September 13, a joint meeting of the two houses of Parliament gave Lumumba full powers. The next day, Kasavubu suspended Parliament, and Mobutu staged his first military coup d'état.

Officially, Mobutu declared his intention as temporarily *neutralizing* both Lumumba and Kasavubu politically. He promised that until the situation improved or returned to normal, the country would be run by a college of general commissioners made up of university graduates and upperclassmen under the presidency of Bomboko, the foreign minister. Rather than a calming measure, this was actually a coup against Lumumba, who was denied access to his office, while the equally "neutralized" Kasavubu continued to discharge his official functions, including swearing in the college of general commissioners into office and receiving foreign envoys. Mobutu also closed the Soviet and Czech embassies in Kinshasa, clearly showing on which side of the cold war he stood. And Bomboko, the first commissioner general, was actually one of the four cabinet ministers who had countersigned Kasavubu's executive order dismissing Lumumba. Like Kasavubu and Mobutu, he was one of the moderate leaders receiving CIA money under Project Wizard.

Having succeeded in removing Lumumba from office, the anti-Lumumba alliance of UN officials, Belgian authorities, U.S. diplomats, and Congolese moderates was now preoccupied with how to prevent him from regaining state power. Timberlake, the U.S. ambassador, was totally obsessed with this question, and sought UN approval for Lumumba's arrest. More elegant and diplomatic than the Yankee envoy, Hammarskjöld played for time, so as not to create the impression that he was "out to get" Lumumba. But, like his American and Belgian allies, that was just what he was, as made clear by his derogatory statements about Lumumba in communications to his entourage and his conversations with Western officials, his appeasement of the Belgians in Katanga, his refusal to be tough with Tshombe, and his slavish obedience to directives from Washington on the Congo question.

The Belgians had no scruples about their intentions. The Belgian ruling class, including King Baudouin, the prime minister, the ministers of foreign and African affairs, and Belgian officials in Brazzaville, Kinshasa, and Lubumbashi, was actively working for Lumumba's assassination. A Belgian assassination plan came into existence in mid-August 1960, when the cabinet authorized a "secret fund" of 20 million Belgian francs (or 400,000 U.S. dollars) for this purpose on August 26. Operationalizing the plot, known as the Barracuda Plan, was the joint responsibility of Major Jules Loos, military adviser to Count Harold d'Aspremont Lynden, the Belgian minister of African affairs, and Colonel Louis Marlière, Colonel Mobutu's Belgian military adviser, whose operational base was Brazzaville. In an interview with De Witte, Loos was apparently proud of having offered to Marlière "a crocodile hunter to bump off Lumumba."[5] Since Marlière was working for Mobutu and yet had to spend a lot of time with other Belgian conspirators across the river, the ANC chief of staff was therefore working with both the Belgians and the Americans against his former mentor.

The Barracuda Plan, like the CIA cobra venom plan, was eventually abandoned once Lumumba was placed under house arrest on October 10, with a ring of Ghanaian blue helmets around his residence flanked by an outer ring of ANC troops. But both the Americans and the Belgians did not abandon their determination to see Lumumba dead. Already, on October 6, Count d'Aspremont Lynden had sent a note to his subordinates stating that the solution to the crisis was "the final elimination of Lumumba." Washington and its allies put sufficient pressure on the UN General Assembly to recognize the Kasavubu delegation over the rival delegation representing Lumumba and his democratically elected government. With this UN credentials vote on November 22, the process of eliminating Lumumba from the political scene had won international endorsement, even as he remained extremely popular among the peoples of the Third World.

Consequently, Lumumba realized that the only way to regain power was through popular support and armed struggle led by the legitimist forces then gathering in Kisangani under the leadership of Antoine Gizenga, the deputy prime minister. He had to escape imprisonment in his own residence. On November 27, Lumumba fled Kinshasa in an attempt to reach his stronghold of Kisangani. U.S. and Belgian intelligence services were quick to offer their assistance to Mobutu and security police chief Victor Nendaka in tracking Lumumba's movements. The Belgian airline Sabena provided a helicopter to Gilbert Pongo, Nendaka's deputy, for this purpose. And Raymond Linard, pilot and co-owner of Air Brousse, an airline providing services to small airstrips in the Congo, also joined the chase.

Lumumba was captured on December 1 at Lodi, on the left bank of the Sankuru River, and denied UN protection by the Ghanaian contingent at Mweka the next morning when he had succeeded to run away from his captors. He was handed over to Pongo at Ilebo, and flown with the latter to Kinshasa on an Air Congo DC-3 airliner. After enduring more humiliation and brutal beatings at the Binza parachutist camp in Mobutu's presence and spending a miserable night in Nendaka's garage, Lumumba was transferred to the elite armored brigade camp at Mbanza-Ngungu in the Lower Congo. Even in jail, he continued to pose a threat to the moderate leadership in Kinshasa and to its Western backers. In response to Lumumba's arrest, the Lumumbist government under Antoine Gizenga in Kisangani began expanding its control and authority in the eastern part of the republic, capturing Bukavu, the capital of Kivu Province, by Christmas 1960. Its victories against Mobutu's army and its threatening drive against the secessionist forces in Katanga thus encouraged Lumumba's followers all over the country to continue the struggle for genuine independence, national unity, and territorial integrity.

U.S. and Belgian officials were greatly alarmed by these developments, with the U.S. embassy in Kinshasa preoccupied with rumors of a pro-Lumumba coup. Given a series of mutinies among troops in both Kinshasa and Mbanza-Ngungu between January 7 and 14, there was also fear among the moderate Congolese authorities that the soldiers guarding Lumumba at Mbanza-Ngungu might free him. For Washington and Brussels, the time to get rid of Lumumba physically had arrived, but there was a need to get his Congolese enemies involved in the conspiracy to kill him. The Congolese conspirators were the moderate leaders in Kinshasa, including some members of the college of general commissioners, and the secessionist leaders of Katanga and South Kasai. Since Washington had limited ability to operate on the ground, direct responsibility for Lumumba's assassination was assumed by the Belgians, who carried out this odious act through a chain of command running from the ruling class in Brussels to Belgian noncommissioned officers in the Katanga Gendarmerie.

De Witte has given an excellent account of how the whole process unfolded.[6] There were three separate levels of responsibility. At the very top, there was a Congo committee, chaired by Prime Minister Gaston Eyskens and including African Affairs Minister Harold d'Aspremont Lynden and Foreign Minister Pierre Wigny. It was the last two who orchestrated the entire assassination plan. D'Aspremont Lynden, the former head of the Belgian technical assistance mission (Mistebel) to secessionist Katanga and nephew of Gobert d'Aspremont Lynden, the king's chief of staff, was the minister who gave the final order for Lumumba's transfer to Lubumbashi, where any sane person would have known that he would be killed. The transfer took place on January 17, 1961, in a Sabena DC-4 under the command of Captain Piet van der Meersch.

The second level comprised the major Belgian representatives in the Congo, both military and civilian. The military officers included Colonel Frédéric Vandewalle, former head of the security police in the Belgian Congo and coordinator of Belgian military affairs in Katanga; Colonel Louis Marlière, Mobutu's military adviser; Major Guy Weber, Tshombe's military adviser; Major Armand Verdickt, a Belgian intelligence officer serving in Katanga; and Captain-Major René Smal, another member of the Katanga advisory team under Professor René Clemens of the University of Liege. In addition to this éminence grise of the Katanga secession, the civilian advisors included Victor Tignée, Godefroid Munongo's chief of staff, Jacques Bartelous, and Jacques Brassinne.

All of these senior officials were in one way or another involved in the assassination plot, at least in the assignments they gave to subordinates in the third group or those who had to execute the actual deed of murder. These included police superintendents Frans Verscheure, Georges Segers, and Gérard Soete; Captain Julien Gat, the chief executioner; plus Lieutenants Gabriel Michels and Claude Grandelet and Lance-Sergeant François Son.

Stories that had long circulated as rumor in the Congo, but that were also told to the UN commission of inquiry, have now been confirmed as historical facts. Lumumba and his two companions, Youth and Sports Minister Maurice Mpolo and Senate Vice President Joseph Okito, were severely beaten on the long plane ride to Katanga, in the presence of two Luba-Kasai members of the college of general commissioners, Ferdinand Kazadi, the general commissioner for defense, and Jonas Mukamba, the general commissioner for internal affairs. Not too far from the Luano airport in Lubumbashi, the three dignitaries were once more tortured at the Brouwez villa, located 8 kilometers from downtown; personally assaulted by the Katanga interior minister Godefroid Munongo, other Katanga leaders, and Belgian officers; and shot somewhere in the bush by an execution squad under the command of Captain Gat. The next day, police officer Soete and his brother removed the bodies from the burial site, cut them into small pieces, and dissolved them in sulfuric acid.

It should be noted that UN troops stood by as Lumumba was tortured by his captors at Ilebo and in Kinshasa, on December 2, 1960, and at the Lubumbashi airport on January 17, 1961. When this is added to decisions taken by the secretary-general and his executive assistant mentioned above, it is evident that for the plot against Lumumba to succeed, the support, or at the very least the apparent neutrality, of the UN Secretariat was indispensable. At every critical juncture in Lumumba's drama, UN officials and troops were involved, by acts of commission or omission. Thus, even if the United Nations was not as directly involved in Lumumba's assassination as Belgium and the United States were, it was nevertheless an accessory before the fact. This was a result of the very broad mandate that the Security Council had given to the UN mission in the Congo, and Hammarskjöld's interpretation of that mandate in accordance with U.S. and Western interests in their confrontation with the communist bloc in the cold war.

Of the three external actors in this drama, only Belgium has recognized its responsibility in Lumumba's death. The Belgian parliamentary inquiry established in response to De Witte's book concluded on November 16, 2001, that Belgian authorities both on the ground and all the way up to the king had a moral responsibility in Lumumba's assassination, for failing to prevent it when they knew that sending him to Katanga would result in his death. The Belgian House of Representatives accepted the commission's conclusions on February 5, 2002, and the government endorsed them as well, except for the criticism against the king. While this is far from satisfactory, it is much better than the silence from the United Nations and the hypocrisy of U.S. authorities. None of the secretary-generals who have succeeded Hammarskjöld have seen it appropriate to create a commission of inquiry on the involvement of UN officials in the conspiracy leading to Lumumba's assassination. In the United States, the Senate Select Committee on Alleged Assassination Plots Involving Foreign Leaders conducted hearings in 1975 that included an inquiry into Lumumba's assassination.[7] After detailing all that the CIA did in planning the assassination and helping Lumumba's Congolese rivals to kill him, the committee absolved the agency, since it did not actually pull the trigger or carry out the act of assassination. This was a complete whitewash and an intellectually dishonest exercise. What we know today about Project Wizard and the CIA station's complicity in the rendition of Lumumba to Katanga makes it clear that the United States bears a major responsibility for Lumumba's assassination and its negative consequences for the Congo.

Of the Congolese conspirators in Lumumba's assassination, Kasavubu and Tshombe died in 1969, less than four years following their overthrow as president and prime minister of the Congo by General Mobutu in November 1965. Kasavubu apparently died due to Mobutu having refused to allow him to leave Boma for medical treatment abroad. Tshombe, who was living in exile in Spain, was kidnapped and taken prisoner to Algeria on June 30, 1967, when the small plane in which he was traveling in the Mediterranean region was hijacked by a mercenary working for Mobutu. He died exactly two years later, on June 30, 1969, allegedly, according to Algerian authorities, of a heart attack. Other major actors to die before the assassination became an issue of public debate in the Congo in 1991 included Gilbert Pongo, who was captured in Bukavu on January 1, 1961, by troops loyal to the Gizenga-led government and executed in Kisangani in retaliation for Lumumba's assassination; Cyrille Adoula, who had taken part in Kinshasa discussions on the fate of Lumumba; and Ferdinand Kazadi, the former general commissioner for defense.

Godefroid Munongo, Tshombe's right-hand man as Katanga's interior minister, died of a heart attack on May 22, 1992, during a session of the Sovereign National Conference (CNS) at the People's Palace in Kinshasa. He had reportedly traveled to Mobutu's hometown of Gbado-Lite the day before to inform him that he wanted to tell the whole truth about Lumumba's assassination to the national conference. The CNS was a democratic forum of all relevant social forces designed to take stock of what had gone wrong in the past and to chart a new course for the nation. One of its twenty-three commissions was devoted to gathering all the information available on the major assassinations that had taken place in the country since 1960, and Munongo was apparently ready to reveal what he knew about Lumumba's case. While no autopsy was conducted, most people in the Congo then believed that the heart attack resulted from poisoning. Since the report of the assassination commission was never made public by decision of the CNS president, Monsignor (and now Cardinal) Laurent Monsengwo, it is hard to ascertain whether Justin Bomboko, Joseph Ileo, Albert Kalonji, Jonas Mukamba, Albert Ndele, and others who have been named as having something to do with the assassination were ever asked to testify before the commission and what testimony, if any, they gave on their individual recollections of what happened in December 1960 and January 1961.

Both at home and abroad, impunity has been the general rule for all those who were involved either directly or indirectly in Lumumba's assassination. At home, the main reason for this was that from September 1960 to May 1997 the country remained under the control of the very people who played a key role in Lumumba's assassination, beginning with Mobutu and his Binza group partners. Externally, the lack of justice for the Congo and Congolese victims of crimes against humanity is a function of the weakness of African states in the current international system. The only way to improve our standing in this system is to realize the dream of Patrice Lumumba for greater pan-African solidarity and unity.

8

The Political Legacy of Patrice Lumumba

During his U.S. exile in the 1980s, Holden Roberto, leader of the National Front for the Liberation of Angola (FNLA), visited my office at Howard University with one of his aides. In order to contradict the accusations (actually well founded) against him as a client of the CIA, my two visitors stood up and recited in its entirety Lumumba's Independence Day speech of June 30, 1960. This gesture, which greatly touched me, bore testimony to the attachment of the African continent as a whole, even among its stray sheep, to this martyr of African nationalism and the struggle for liberation of oppressed peoples around the world. Rare are African countries in which one does not find streets or even large avenues bearing the name of Lumumba. Many African children born after his assassination were given his name.

For a self-educated person, it is remarkable how Lumumba's name is evoked in the company of such great thinkers of African liberation as Amilcar Cabral, Frantz Fanon, and Kwame Nkrumah. Due to the Belgian ban on the importation of "subversive literature" in the Congo, Lumumba was not as well acquainted with revolutionary ideas and movements as these three men, who were even politically active in Europe. And yet, for someone who until 1956 was singing the praises of Belgian colonialism, his political discourse and action since December 1958 make a perfect fit with the theory and practice of progressive political movements in the twentieth century. As an intellectual who produced beautiful poetry and excellent essays, he epitomizes the leader who embodies the trials and tribulations of his people, as well as their hopes for a better future. Of the writings put together by his Belgian friend Jean Van Lierde in a book published in 1963 as *La pensée politique de Patrice Lumumba*,[1] four stand out as symptomatic of the remarkable depth of his political thought and analysis: a 1959 poem entitled "Pleure O Noir Frère bien-aimé" (translated into English as "Weep, O Beloved Black Brother"); his combative Independence Day speech; his last recorded message to the Congolese people from prison; and, also from prison, his last letter to his wife, Pauline.

Lumumba's poetry bears a great affinity to the reaffirmation of African humanity and dignity by the *Négritude* movement and years later by the Black Consciousness Movement, whose leaders included Steve Biko. There is no satisfactory record of Lumumba's poems, but it is known that he enjoyed reading a poem at the beginning of some important gatherings, as he did at the meeting of

October 10, 1958, in which he was chosen interim president of the MNC. "Weep, O Beloved Black Brother," his best-known poem, was published in September 1959 in the MNC-L newspaper *Indépendance*. It is a masterpiece in both its rhetorical brilliance and its compelling narrative, which consists of a summary of African history since the slave trade, including a look at the African diaspora in North America, together with its contribution to black awakening and the fight for dignity, and the perspectives of freedom and prosperity that the coming independence was heralding in Africa. In marking the break with colonialism, the poem asks Africans to tell their European master "in a loud voice" that "this country is no longer his, as in older days," and that their lands and their riches henceforth belong to them. To the Congolese, this means that "the shores of the great river, full of promises" henceforth belong to them, but they have a duty to "make the Congo a free and happy nation, in the heart of this gigantic Africa."[2] This challenge has yet to be met by his compatriots, whose land can provide food, water, and electricity to the whole continent of Africa, but is today incapable of doing so for approximately 70 million souls in the DRC itself.

Lumumba returns to this theme of self-determination and its responsibilities in many of his texts, particularly in his Ibadan University address of March 22, 1959. Like other African liberation leaders, he insists that as a struggle aimed at rooting out colonialism and imperialism from Africa, liberation is a fight against a system of domination, and not against Europeans, or even their culture. For him, Africans should be able to take from Western culture "what is good and beautiful and reject what is not suitable for us," and thus "give Africa a civilization of a new type, an authentic civilization corresponding to African realities."³ A "passionate and idealistic fight," as Lumumba describes it in his now famous Independence Day speech, the national liberation struggle was waged in the name of self-determination, economic well-being, and African unity. Accordingly, he makes a commitment to economic and social justice for all, with everyone entitled to just remuneration for his or her labor.

This legacy of support for radical change in order to meet the deepest aspirations of the Congolese people for democracy and social progress was best exemplified in the "second independence" movement, the mass insurrections of 1963–68 against the neocolonial state and the Binza Group, the clique in control of state power in Kinshasa. Within the Lumumbist leadership of the revolutionary movement, the most positive aspect of the legacy was manifest in the selfless devotion of Pierre Mulele not only to the uncompromising defense of the interests of the popular masses, but also to an unshakeable resistance against any foreign or oligarchic stranglehold over the natural resources of the African continent. In this regard, it is useful to distinguish between Lumumbism in words and in deeds, or between façade Lumumbists simply using the name of our national hero for their own narrow class interests and real Lumumbists like Mulele who fought for the welfare of ordinary people.

In addition to self-determination and economic and social justice, Lumumba was a fervent believer in pan-Africanism. For him, the independence of the Congo represented "a decisive step toward the liberation of the entire African continent." He was so committed to promoting pan-African solidarity that in spite of the political crisis in which he was embroiled, he organized and hosted a ministerial-level pan-African conference in Kinshasa between August 25 and 31, 1960. The conference was attended by delegates from Egypt (then known officially as the United Arab Republic), Ethiopia, Ghana, Guinea, Liberia, Mali, Morocco, Togo, Tunisia, and the provisional government of Algeria, plus representatives of several liberation movements. In his opening address to the conference, Lumumba outlined his pan-African vision in eight points, including support for the total liberation of Africa; nonalignment as a basis for genuine independence; removal of all colonially inherited linguistic barriers to African integration; and inter-African cooperation in the commercial, military, information, and scientific fields. He was a visionary and the only Congolese leader to have such a clear-cut commitment to pan-African unity. His legacy for the progressive wing of pan-Africanism was thus established, as the majority of participating states at the Kinshasa conference would later attend the Casablanca Conference of January 4–7, 1961, where they declared their support for Lumumba, then a prisoner in the Congo. As shown above, in spite of this support, both Ghana and Morocco, through the actions of Generals H. T. Alexander and Kettani, the respective commanders of their UN contingents in the Congo, who were allies of Lumumba's enemies, failed to save Lumumba from his torturers and executioners.

The greatest legacy that Lumumba has left for the Congo is the ideal of national unity, which has been internalized by an overwhelming majority of the Congolese people. In his address to the Congolese youth in August 1960, the Congo's prime minister saluted the brave young people who died for independence in the major anticolonial rebellions of January 4, 1959, in Kinshasa and October 30, 1959, in Kisangani, and exhorted the youth, both male and female, to remain steadfast in their defense of national unity. He not only fought against the Katanga secession; he laid down his life to end it in defense of national unity. Consequently, the people of the Congo are likely to remain steadfast in their defense of their national unity and territorial integrity, come hell or high water.

The last two documents through which Lumumba's political thought is expressed were products of his life in prison: a message to the Congolese people and a letter to his wife, Pauline. The message, recorded by an Italian radio station in December 1960 or January 1961, is perhaps one of the most comprehensive statements of Lumumba's political legacy, including his commitment to fight and, if necessary, to die for freedom and national sovereignty. For freedom, he maintains, "is the ideal for which, in all times and through centuries, men have fought and died." He also welcomes struggling for independence. For him, "History has shown that independence is never handed down on a silver platter. It is snatched away."[4]

Finally, in his last letter to his wife, Lumumba remains confident about the ultimate triumph of the "sacred cause" to which he has dedicated his life, and concludes by affirming his faith in the future of the Congo and Africa as follows:

> Neither brutality, nor physical cruelty, nor torture has ever led me to beg for mercy, because I prefer dying with my head held high, with unshakeable faith and deep confidence in the destiny of my country, rather than living in submission and contempt for sacred principles. History will one day have its say, but it will not be the history taught in Brussels, Washington, Paris, or at the United Nations, but the one taught in the countries emancipated from colonialism and its puppets. Africa will write its own history, and it will be from north to south of the Sahara a history of glory and dignity.[5]

This biography is a modest contribution to that history.

Chronology

1925   July 2: Patrice Lumumba (PL) is born in the village of Onalua in the Sankuru district of Kasai Province.

1944   PL holds his first job as a sales clerk for Symétain in Kalima (Maniema) for a few months, before departing for Kisangani via Ubundu.

November 20: PL begins his civil service career as a clerk in the territorial administration of the urban region of Kisangani.

1947   July 1: PL begins his training at the Postal School in Kinshasa.

1948   March 30: PL successfully completes his postal service training, finishing as the third-best student in a class of thirty-four, with an average of 91.4 percent.

April: PL returns to Kisangani as a qualified postal employee and begins his meteoric rise in the civil service and the *évolué* circles of Kisangani.

1954   March 5: PL is elected president of the Association des Évolués de Stanleyville (AES), the most important organization of the Congolese elite in Kisangani.

April: Following the nomination of Auguste Buisseret of the Liberal Party as Belgium's minister of colonies, PL joins the Liberal Circle and Study Group of Kisangani, a branch of the Belgian Liberal Party.

May 19: PL leads an AES delegation to first meeting with the new governor of Orientale province, André Schöller, during which the principle of consultation on important issues is established.

August 5: PL obtains *immatriculation* (matriculation status), thus joining the elite stratum of the *évolués*, or Congolese with theoretically identical civil rights with Europeans.

October 31–November 1: PL meets with Colonial Affairs Minister Buisseret during the latter's visit to Kisangani, and establishes a very good relationship with him.

1955   June: During King Baudouin's first visit to the Congo, PL astonishes the Belgians and the Congolese dignitaries present at the provincial governor's reception by holding a chat of approximately ten minutes with the king.

1956   February 17: PL loses his position as president of AES, due in part to jealousy of his newly found prominence and his support of Buisseret's policy of secular education for the Congolese, which was opposed by the Roman Catholic Church.

April 24–May 24: First visit by PL to Belgium as part of a group of sixteen Congolese dignitaries invited by the governor-general to tour the metropolis.

July 6: PL is arrested and indicted for embezzlement of funds at the post office in Kisangani and placed in preventive detention.

1957 February 25: PL trial in the court of original jurisdiction in Kisangani.

March 4: The court verdict is announced, and PL is condemned to two years of prison. The state prosecutor considers the punishment too lenient and appeals the ruling to the appeals court in Kinshasa. PL requests transfer to Kinshasa, and this is granted.

June 13: The appeals court hears PL's case.

July 4: The appeals court rejects the state's arguments and affirms the decision of the lower court.

August 27: A royal pardon is issued in PL's favor, but his liberation from jail is contingent on his finding a job.

September 7: PL is freed from jail.

September 8: PL is hired by the Brasserie du Bas-Congo (Bracongo), a major Kinshasa brewery, to work in its accounts department.

November 24: PL is elected vice president of the Liberal Circle of Kinshasa.

1958 August: PL is promoted to publicity director at Bracongo.

October 10: PL is elected president of the provisional committee of the Mouvement National Congolais (MNC).

October 26: PL is elected president of the Fédération des Batetela (Fédébate).

December 5–13: PL, Gaston Diomi, and Joseph Ngalula represent the MNC at the First All-African People's Conference (AAPC) in Accra, Ghana.

December 28: PL and MNC hold a public rally in Kinshasa to report on the Accra Conference.

1959 January 1: PL resigns from Bracongo to devote all his time to political work.

January 4–7: Proindependence public uprising in Kinshasa.

January 13: Belgian king and government issue declarations favoring independence.

March 22: PL gives a major address on African unity and national independence at a seminar of the Congress for Cultural Freedom at the University of Ibadan in Nigeria.

April 9–12: PL takes part in the first congress of Congolese political parties in Kananga.

April 15–17: PL participates in an extraordinary meeting of the AAPC in Conakry, Guinea.

April 22–28: PL gives several lectures and news conferences in Brussels.

July 16: Attempt to remove PL from the MNC presidency, and the beginning of the split of the party into two wings: MNC-L and MNC-K.

August 7–September 12: PL in Kasai, first for the liberation of Albert Kalonji and then to build the MNC.

October 3–19: PL in Accra for George Padmore's funeral, a meeting of the Executive Committee of the AAPC on the ninth, and other business.

October 23–28: PL at the first MNC-L Congress in Kisangani.

October 29–30: PL hosts the congress of nationalist parties in Kisangani

October 30–November 1: Kisangani incidents; PL is arrested

1960 January 20: Round Table Conference on Congolese independence begins in Brussels; Congolese delegates form a common front and request Lumumba's release from jail and his participation in the conference.

January 21: Following a four-day trial, PL is convicted of inciting violence in Kisangani and condemned to six months in prison.

January 22: PL is transferred to the underground prison at Likasi.

January 24: PL is released from jail and arrives in Brussels the next day to take part in the Round Table Conference.

January 27: Round Table Conference fixes Congo's independence day as June 30, 1960.

February 20: Round Table Conference ends; PL and other delegates return home to manage the transition and campaign for the May general elections.

June 21: Following Kasavubu's failure to form a government, the Belgian minister in charge of the transition reluctantly names PL as prime minister–designate.

June 30: PL's Independence Day speech upsets Belgian king and the West.

July 5: FP mutiny.

July 7–8: PL begins process of Africanizing the FP, which he renames the Armée Nationale Congolaise (ANC).

July 10: Belgian military intervention.

July 11: Katanga Province secedes.

July 12: PL and Kasavubu request UN intervention.

July 24–August 8: PL goes on mission to New York and Washington to seek assistance in resolving the crisis.

August 8: South Kasai secedes.

August 18: U.S. President Eisenhower orders the assassination of PL.

August 25–31: PL hosts Pan-African Conference in Kinshasa.

August 26: The Belgian government authorizes a secret fund for the assassination of PL.

August 26–27: ANC troops enter South Kasai.

September 5: Kasavubu dismisses PL.

September 13: Parliament gives full powers to PL.

September 14: Mobutu stages coup d'état against PL.

November 22: PL delegation loses the credentials battle at the UN General Assembly in New York.

November 27: PL flees his residence in Kinshasa to go to Kisangani.

December 1: PL is arrested in Kasai, sent back to Kinshasa the next day, and eventually jailed at the elite ANC armored brigade camp at Mbanza-Ngungu.

1961 January 17: PL and his two companions, Maurice Mpolo and Joseph Okito, are transferred to Lubumbashi and murdered in the evening by a Belgian execution squad.

Notes

Chapter 1: Early Years, Youth, and Formal Education, 1925–44

1. As Guy De Boeck has shown in his book *Baoni: Les révoltes de la Force publique sous Léopold II, Congo, 1895–1908* (Antwerp: EPO, 1987), these revolts against King Leopold's rule involved people from all over the Congo.

2. Singular of *Atetela*.

3. The most readable account of these crimes can be found in Adam Hochschild, *King Leopold's Ghost: A Story of Greed, Terror, and Heroism in Colonial Africa* (Boston: Houghton Mifflin, 1998).

4. Unfortunately, this kind of information on the African role in both world wars is not generally known. On February 29, 2012, I received an e-mail from Lensa Idossa, an Ethiopian student at Columbia University, commenting on an article I had written on the assassination of Patrice Lumumba, and asking me to explain why there is a place called "The Congo Cemetery" at Dembi Dollo, a city in western Ethiopia. The FP's triumphs in World War II were preceded by similar feats in World War I, such as the crushing defeat of the German army at Tabora (Tanzania). The resulting Belgian control of the western part of German East Africa led to the League of Nations awarding Rwanda and Burundi to Belgium as mandated territories.

Chapter 2: Civil Service Career and Political Apprenticeship in Kisangani, 1944–56

1. Having become famous for "finding" David Livingstone at Ujiji in 1871, Stanley made an epic 999-day journey across the African continent from Zanzibar in 1874 to Boma in the Congo in 1877. Since Britain showed no interest in acquiring the vast territories of the Congo basin through which he passed, Stanley was hired by King Leopold II to help the latter lay claims to these territories. He became the king's number one agent in the acquisition of the Congo.

2. The U.S. equivalent is the federal district court.

3. Pierre Clément, "Patrice Lumumba (Stanleyville, 1952–1953)," *Présence Africaine*, no. 40 (1st trimester 1962): 57–78.

4. For Clément's own account of this relationship, see Clément, "Patrice Lumumba (Stanleyville, 1952–1953)."

Chapter 4: The Struggle for Independence, 1958–60

1. Founded in 1958, PAFMECA added "Southern" to its name to become the Pan African Freedom Movement of East, Central, and Southern Africa (PAFMECSA) at its February 1962 meeting in Addis Ababa, Ethiopia, in order to allow the nationalist organizations of South Africa, Southwest Africa (Namibia), and the British High Commission Territories (Botswana, Lesotho, and Swaziland) to join. Responding to a militant speech by African National Congress (ANC) leader Nelson Mandela describing the inadequacy of nonviolent methods in fighting settler colonialism, the organization amended its constitution by removing references to nonviolence.

2. Between 1925 and 1960, Rwanda and Burundi were annexed to the Congo in a single administrative unit known as Belgian Congo and Ruanda-Urundi, with a single governor-general in Kinshasa, a single civil service, and a single army, the FP.

Chapter 5: The Short Political Life of Congo's First Prime Minister, 1960–61

1. The secessionist state of South Kasai was carved out of a predominantly Luba-Kasai area comprising the current cities of Mbuji-Mayi and Mwene-Ditu as well as the districts of Tshilenge and Kabinda (minus the *territoires* or subdistricts of Kabinda and Lubao). Recognized by the central government as a province in 1962, it was enlarged by including both the Kabinda and Sankuru districts to become the province of Eastern Kasai in 1966.

2. Bandung is an Indonesian city in which the first Afro-Asian summit met in 1955 to express strong support for decolonization and opposition to both nuclear war and alignment with one or the other of the two blocs in international politics.

3. A paraphrase of a sentence from a letter by a group of Congolese soldiers published in *Emancipation,* a Kinshasa newspaper, on March 19, 1960, and cited in Francis Monheim, *Mobutu, l'homme seul* (Brussels: Éditions Actuelles, 1962), 72.

4. Auguste Maurel, *Le Congo de la colonisation belge à l'indépendance* (Paris: L'Harmattan, 1992), 301.

5. In international law, genocide consists of crimes committed with the intent to destroy in whole or in part a group of people defined on the basis of race, ethnicity, language, religion, or other category. However heinous the crimes committed and however many people were killed in South Kasai, these killings did not fit the definition of genocide.

6. Ludo De Witte, *The Assassination of Lumumba,* trans. Ann Wright and Renée Fenby (London: Verso, 2001), xviii.

Chapter 6: Lumumba and the Counterrevolution in Central and Southern Africa

1. The policy of linkage made Namibian independence hostage to the withdrawal of Cuban troops from Angola, who

were there to help defend the country against South African aggression. Constructive engagement, on the other hand, was a failed policy of fighting apartheid without sanctions.

2. Cited in Thomas Kanza, *Conflict in the Congo: The Rise and Fall of Patrice Lumumba* (Baltimore: Penguin, 1972), 282.

3. Ibid., 220.

4. Rajeshwar Dayal, *Mission for Hammarskjöld: The Congo Crisis* (Princeton: Princeton University Press, 1976), 308.

5. Madeleine G. Kalb, *The Congo Cables: The Cold War in Africa—From Eisenhower to Kennedy* (New York: Macmillan, 1982), 137.

6. See Hammarskjöld's cable to Cordier on August 15, 1960, from author's research in UN Archives, B472.

7. Kalb, *The Congo Cables*, 69.

8. Kanza, *Conflict in the Congo*, 284.

Chapter 7: Lumumba's Assassination

1. De Witte, *The Assassination of Lumumba*, xviii.

2. Kalb, *The Congo Cables*, 53.

3. U.S. Department of State, *Foreign Relations of the United States, 1964–1968*, vol. 23, *Congo, 1960–1968* (Washington, DC: U.S. Government Printing Office, 2013), 20–21. The NSC Special Group was a high-level interagency working group on covert operations coordinated by Gordon Gray, President Eisenhower's national security advisor, and including the CIA director and the deputy secretaries of state and defense.

4. Ibid., 22.

5. De Witte, *The Assassination of Lumumba*, xviii.

6. Ibid., chaps. 4 and 5.

7. See U.S. Congress, Senate, Select Committee to Study Government Operations with Respect to Intelligence Activi-

ties, *Alleged Assassination Plots Involving Foreign Leaders: An Interim Report of the Select Committee to Study Governmental Operations with Respect to Intelligence Activities, United States Senate* (New York: W. W. Norton, 1976); and *Final Report: Foreign and Military Intelligence,* bk. 1, by the Select Committee to Study Government Operations with Respect to Intelligence Activities, 94th Cong., 2nd Sess., April 26, 1976.

Chapter 8: The Political Legacy of Patrice Lumumba

1. Patrice Lumumba, *La pensée politique de Patrice Lumumba*, ed. Jean Van Lierde (Paris: Présence Africaine, 1963); trans. Helen R. Lane as *Lumumba Speaks: The Speeches and Writings of Patrice Lumumba, 1958–1961* (Boston: Little, Brown, 1972).

2. Ibid., 69–70. My own translation from the French original in *La pensée politique de Patrice Lumumba*.

3. Ibid., 24–30. My own translation.

4. Ibid., 394–98. My own translation.

5. Ibid., 389–91. My own translation.

Bibliography

Clément, Pierre. "Patrice Lumumba (Stanleyville, 1952–1953)." *Présence Africaine*, no. 40 (1st trimester 1962): 57–78.

Dayal, Rajeshwar. *Mission for Hammarskjöld: The Congo Crisis*. Princeton: Princeton University Press, 1976.

De Boeck, Guy. *Baoni: Les révoltes de la Force publique sous Léopold II, Congo, 1895–1908*. Antwerp: EPO, 1987.

Devlin, Larry. *Chief of Station: A Memoir of 1960–67*. New York: Public Affairs, 2007.

De Witte, Ludo. *The Assassination of Lumumba*. Translated by Ann Wright and Renée Fenby. London: Verso, 2001.

Gibbs, David. *The Political Economy of Third World Intervention: Mines, Money, and U.S. Policy in the Congo Crisis*. Chicago: University of Chicago Press, 1991.

———. "The United Nations, International Peacekeeping and the Question of 'Impartiality': Revisiting the Congo Operation of 1960." *Journal of Modern African Studies* 38, no. 3 (2000): 359–82.

Hochschild, Adam. *King Leopold's Ghost: A Story of Greed, Terror, and Heroism in Colonial Africa*. Boston: Houghton Mifflin, 1998.

Kalb, Madeleine G. *The Congo Cables: The Cold War in Africa—From Eisenhower to Kennedy*. New York: Macmillan, 1982.

Kanza, Thomas. *Conflict in the Congo: The Rise and Fall of Patrice Lumumba*. Baltimore: Penguin, 1972.

Lumumba, Patrice. *Lumumba Speaks: The Speeches and Writings of Patrice Lumumba, 1958–1961*. Edited by Jean Van Lierde, translated by Helen R. Lane. Boston: Little, Brown, 1972. Original French edition: *La pensée politique de Patrice Lumumba*. Edited by Jean Van Lierde. Paris: Présence Africaine, 1963.

———. *Patrice Lumumba: Recueil de textes introduit par Georges Nzongola-Ntalaja*. Geneva: CETIM, 2013.

Maurel, Auguste. *Le Congo de la colonisation belge à l'indépendance*. Paris: L'Harmattan, 1992.

Mazov, Sergei. *A Distant Front in the Cold War: The USSR in West Africa and the Congo, 1956–1964*. Washington, DC: Woodrow Wilson Center Press, 2010.

Monheim, Francis. *Mobutu, l'homme seul*. Brussels: Éditions Actuelles, 1962.

Mutamba Makombo, Jean-Marie. *Du Congo belge au Congo indépendant, 1940–1960: Émergence des "évolués" et genèse du nationalisme*. Kinshasa: Institut de Formation et d'Études Politiques, 1998.

Namikas, Lise. *Battleground Africa: Cold War in the Congo, 1960–1965*. Washington, DC: Woodrow Wilson Center Press, 2013.

Nzongola-Ntalaja, Georges. *The Congo from Leopold to Kabila: A People's History*. London: Zed Books, 2002.

Omasombo, Jean, and Benoît Verhaegen. *Patrice Lumumba, Acteur politique: De la prison aux portes du pouvoir, juillet 1956–février 1960*. Tervuren: Africa Institute; Paris: L'Harmattan, 2005.

———. *Patrice Lumumba: Jeunesse et apprentissage politique, 1925–1956*. Tervuren: Africa Institute; Paris: L'Harmattan, 1998.

Schmidt, Elizabeth. *Foreign Intervention in Africa: From the Cold War to the War on Terror.* Cambridge: Cambridge University Press, 2013.

Turner, Thomas. *Ethnogenèse et nationalisme en Afrique centrale: Aux racines de Patrice Lumumba.* Paris: L'Harmattan, 2000.

U.S. Congress, Senate, Select Committee to Study Government Operations with Respect to Intelligence Activities. *Alleged Assassination Plots Involving Foreign Leaders: An Interim Report of the Select Committee to Study Governmental Operations with Respect to Intelligence Activities, United States Senate.* New York: W. W. Norton, 1976.

U.S. Department of State. *Foreign Relations of the United States, 1964–1968.* Vol. 23, *Congo, 1960–1968.* Washington, DC: United States Government Printing Office, 2013.

Van Bilsen, A. A. J. "Een dertigjarenplan voor de politieke ontvoogding van Belgisch Afrika." *De gids op maatschappelijk gebied: Maatschappelijke werken, sociale wetgevingen, rechtsvragen, volkshuishoudkunde* 46, no. 12 (1955): 999–1028.

Weissman, Stephen R. *American Foreign Policy in the Congo, 1960–1964.* Ithaca, NY: Cornell University Press, 1974.

———. "An Extraordinary Rendition." *Intelligence and National Security* 25, no. 2 (2010): 198–222.

———. "Opening the Secret Files on Lumumba's Murder." *Washington Post,* July 21, 2002.

Index

Alexander, H. T., 139
American Presbyterian Congo Mission (APCM), 32
Arkadiev, 112–13
Armée Nationale Congolaise (ANC), 98, 114, 124, 147; birth of ANC, 93, 95, 96, 146; South Kasai campaign, 97–99, 120, 146

Babu, A. R. Mohamed, 69–70
Balubakat (Association Générale des Baluba du Katanga), 76, 87
Bandung Conference and legacy, 58, 86, 151
Barracuda Plan, 124
Bartelous, Jacques, 128
Baudouin, King: first visit to the Congo and chat with Lumumba, 51, 142; Independence Day speech and Lumumba's response, 22; pardon for Lumumba, 56, 143; role in Lumumba's assassination, 123, 127, 129–30
Belgian Congo, 19, 29, 30, 34, 35, 71, 91, 108, 127; decolonization, 7, 21, 58; emergence of the *évolués*, 43–50; and Ruanda-Urundi, 150; World War II and its impact, 35–36
Belgium: Brussels Economic Round Table Conference, 82–83; Brussels Political Round Table Conference, 80–82; Brussels World Fair, 67–68; military intervention and support for Katanga's secession, 94–100; role in the counter-revolution, 107, 109–11; Parliamentary inquiry into Lumumba's assassination, 11, 129–30; role in Lumumba's assassination, 122–29; Royal and government declarations on Congo's future (Jan. 13, 1959), 75
Binza Group, 100, 132, 137
Bolamba, Antoine-Roger, 46, 62
Bolikango, Jean, 61, 62, 121
Bomboko, Justin-Marie, 88, 95, 100, 122, 132
Brassinne, Jacques, 128

Bunche, Ralph, 96, 109, 110, 112–14, 118

Cabral, Amilcar, 28, 57, 70, 134
Catholic Church, 32, 52, 55, 59, 142
Central Intelligence Agency (CIA). *See under* United States of America
Clemens, René, 127
Clément, Pierre, 49–50, 64, 150
cold war, 8, 11–12, 27, 86, 94, 101, 106, 109, 112–13, 115–16, 118, 122, 129
colonial trinity, 32
Comité Spécial du Katanga (CSK), 83
Congo-Brazzaville, 49, 101–2, 113
Congo Free State (CFS), 29–30, 32, 38
Conscience Africaine group, 59
Cordier, Andrew, 112, 115, 121

d'Aspremont Lynden, Gobert, 127
d'Aspremont Lynden, Harold, 124, 127
Dayal, Rajeshwar, 112, 122
decolonization, 7, 27, 58, 62–63, 75, 79, 85, 151; De Gaulle and, 101–2
de Gaulle, Charles: and decolonization, 101–2
Devlin, Lawrence (Larry), 12, 118–19, 120
De Witte, Ludo, 10–11, 117, 124, 127, 129, 151
Diomi, Gaston, 68, 69, 72, 144
Dodd, Thomas, 109

Dulles, Allen, 107–8, 118

Egypt, 28, 35, 48, 58, 71, 107, 138
Eisenhower, Dwight D., 107, 118–19, 142
Ethiopia, 35, 138, 149
évolués, 20, 37–39, 41–48, 51–52, 54, 56, 61, 66, 73–75, 141–42
Eyskens, Gaston, 127

Fanon, Frantz, 57, 70, 134
Finant, Pierre, 99
forced labor, 29, 35, 38, 90
Force Publique (FP), 35, 43, 60, 85, 88, 90–94, 98, 146, 149, 150
France, 44, 49–50, 101–2

Ganshof van der Meersch, Walter J., 88
Gat, Julien, 128
German East Africa, 149
Ghana, 21, 28, 66; All-African People's Conference (1958), 21, 66, 69–72, 144; Ghanaian UN troops in the Congo, 111, 124–25, 138–39. *See also* Alexander, H. T.; Nkrumah, Kwame
Gizenga, Antoine, 87, 95, 125–26, 131
Goldwater, Barry, 109
Gottlieb, Sidney, 119–20
Grandelet, Claude, 128
Guinea, 71, 77, 102, 138, 144. *See also* Sékou Touré

Hammarskjöld, Dag, 96–97, 109–10, 112, 114, 116, 118, 120–21, 123, 129–30
Hochschild, Adam, 149
Horn, Carl von, 114

Ileo, Joseph, 59, 62, 65, 66, 68, 77, 78, 88, 102, 132
indépendance immédiate, 62, 74
Independence Martyrs Day, 74

Janssens, Emile, 91–93

Kabila, Laurent, 87
Kalonji, Albert, 77–79, 87–88, 97, 99–100, 102, 120, 132, 145. *See also* South Kasai secession
Kamitatu, Cléophas, 12, 88
Kandolo, Damien, 100
Kanza, Thomas, 12, 112, 115
Kasavubu, Joseph, 22, 26–27, 60–64, 66, 72–73, 76, 87–89, 95–98, 102, 113, 120–24, 130–31, 146
Kashamura, Anicet, 76, 87
Katanga, 21, 23, 27, 35, 69, 76, 83, 85, 87, 92; and the counterrevolution, 102–16; role in Lumumba's assassination, 126–33; secession, 94–100. *See also* Munongo, Godefroid; Tshombe, Moïse
Kazadi, Ferdinand, 128, 131
Keita, Modibo, 71
Kennedy, John F., 12
Kettani, Ben Hammou, 98, 115, 139
Kinshasa anticolonial rebellion (January 4–7, 1959), 72–76
Kisangani anticolonial rebellion (October 30–November 1, 1959), 76–80

Leopold II, King, 8, 32, 46, 83, 91, 149
Leopoldian system, 37, 44, 47
Livingstone, David, 150
Loos, Jules, 124
Lovanium University, 82
Lumumba, Patrice Emery
  birth and early years, 29–36
  postal studies, 19, 40–41
  civil service career in Kisangani, 37–52
  arrest and imprisonment on work-related offenses, 53–58
  meteoric rise in nationalist politics in Kinshasa, 59–77
  as a political prisoner, 78–80
  as a participant at the Brussels Roundtable Conference, 80–84
  electoral victory, 88–89
  Independence Day speech, 47, 134, 135, 137, 146
  as prime minister, 85–100
  dismissal and arrest, 97–100
  and the counterrevolution in Central and Southern Africa, 101–6
  assassination, 117–33
  political legacy and inspiration, 134–40

Lumumba, Patrice Emery (*cont.*)
  national hero, 28, 138
Lundula, Victor, 93

Malula, Joseph, 59, 62, 77
Mandela, Nelson, 28, 72, 150
Marlière, Louis, 124, 127
matriculation system (*immatriculation*), 44–45, 50, 54, 142
Maurel, Auguste, 92
Mboya, Tom, 70
Mbuji-Mayi: as a human "slaughterhouse" for Lumumbist political prisoners, 99; massacre at the Catholic cathedral, 97, 99, 120
Michels, Gabriel, 128
mining companies, 8, 95, 102, 105
Mobutu Sese Seko (Joseph-Désiré), 88, 89, 93, 97, 98, 100, 131, 132; coup d'état against Lumumba, 22, 26, 89, 122, 147; role in Belgian and U.S. assassination plots against Lumumba, 27, 120, 122–27
Morocco, 58, 138, 139
Morrison, William, 32
Moumié, Félix-Roland, 70
Mouvement National Congolais (MNC), 21, 26, 65–66, 68–69, 72, 76–77, 86, 144; Mouvement National Congolais-Kalonji (MNC-K), 78, 144;
Mouvement National Congolais-Lumumba (MNC-L), 78–79, 82, 87–88, 105, 136, 144–45
Mpolo, Maurice, 23, 128, 147
Msiri, King, 95
Mukamba, Jonas, 128, 132
Mulele, Pierre, 87, 137–38
Munongo, Godefroid, 95, 128, 131–32
Mutamba Makombo, Jean-Marie, 10

Nasser, Gamal Abdel, 28, 71, 107
Ndele, Albert, 100, 132
Nendaka, Victor, 88, 100, 125
Ngalula, Joseph, 60, 62, 65, 66, 68–69, 77–78, 88, 144
Ngongo Letete, 29–30, 38
Nigeria, 48, 77, 144
Nkrumah, Kwame, 28, 57, 71, 83, 114. *See also* Ghana
nonalignment, 58, 86, 87, 108, 112, 138
Nyerere, Julius, 28
Nzeza Nlandu, Edmond, 60

Okito, Joseph, 23, 128, 147
Omasombo, Jean, 10
Opango, Pauline (Lumumba's wife), 50, 135, 139

Pan-Africanism, 28, 87, 114, 138
Parti Solidaire Africain (PSA), 75–76, 87–88. *See also* Gizenga, Antoine; Kamitatu, Cléophas; Mulele, Pierre
Pongo, Gilbert, 125, 131

Roland, Gilbert, 64
Rwagasore, Louis, 71

Segers, Georges, 128
Sékou Touré, Ahmed, 71, 101–2. *See also* Guinea
Sendwe, Jason, 76, 87
Sheppard, William Henry, 32
Smal, René, 127
Société Générale de Belgique (SGB), 103, 104
Société Internationale Forrestière et Minière du Congo (Forminière), 108
Soete, Gérard, 128, 129
Son, François, 128
South Kasai secession, 85, 97–100, 111, 120, 126, 146, 151
Stanley, Henry Morton, 37, 47, 150
statut unique, 41

Tanganyika Concessions Limited (TCL or Tanks), 103, 108
Tanzania, 28, 70, 95, 149
Thurmond, Strom, 109
Tignée, Victor, 128
Timberlake, Clare, 95, 113, 123
Tippu Tip (Hamed bin Muhammed el-Murjebi), 29, 38
Tshombe, Moïse, 76, 82, 88, 95, 99, 100, 102, 104, 116, 120, 123, 127, 130–31. *See also* Katanga
Tshumbe Sainte-Marie, 31, 33, 34
Turner, Thomas, 10

Union Minière du Haut-Katanga (UMHK), 103, 104, 108
United Kingdom (Britain), 107, 109, 150
United Nations: Cordier and Kasavubu's dismissal of Lumumba, 113, 115, 121–22; Gen. Kettani and Mobutu's coup d'état, 98, 115, 139; Hammarskjöld's anticipation of the Congo crisis, 96, 109–10; pitfalls of UN intervention, 129–30; pro-West/anti-Lumumba bias in the UN Secretariat, 112–15; UN Operation in the Congo (ONUC), 96, 98, 110, 113, 115, 122
United States: CIA role in Lumumba's assassination, 11, 118–23; and the counterrevolution, 106–9; President Eisenhower's assassination order, 118–19, 146; Senate's whitewash of U.S. responsibility in the assassination, 130, 152; strategy of using the UN as a cover for Western interests, 95–96
uranium, 108
Urquhart, Brian, 114

Van Bilsen, A.A.J. (Jef), 59–61, 64
van der Meersch, Piet, 127

Vandewalle, Frédéric, 127
Verdickt, Armand, 127
Verhaegen, Benoît, 10

Weber, Guy, 127
Weissman, Steve, 10
Wembo Nyama (Chief), 30–32, 38
Wembo Nyama (Methodist mission, town), 31–32, 33, 34, 50
white settlers, 8, 95, 102, 105

Wieschhoff, Heinrich, 113
Wigny, Pierre, 127
Williams, George Washington, 32
Wilson Center's Cold War International History Project, 11–12

Youlou, Fulbert, 102, 113

Zanzibar, 69, 150. *See also* Tippu Tip

OHIO SHORT HISTORIES OF AFRICA
THOMAS SANKARA
AN AFRICAN REVOLUTIONARY
ERNEST HARSCH

THOMAS SANKARA, often called the African Che Guevara, was president of the West African country of Burkina Faso until his assassination during the military coup that brought down his government. An avowed Marxist, he outspokenly asserted his country's independence from France and other Western powers and at the same time sought to build genuine pan-African unity.

Ernest Harsch traces Sankara's life from his student days to his political awakening and increasing dismay at his country's poverty and political corruption. As Sankara rose to leadership positions, he used those offices to mobilize people for change and to counter the influence of the old, corrupt elites. He and his colleagues initiated economic and social policies that shifted the country away from dependence on foreign aid and toward a greater use of its own resources. Although Sankara's sweeping vision and practical reforms won him admirers both in Burkina Faso and across Africa, a combination of domestic opposition groups and factions within his own government and army finally led to his assassination in 1987.

This is the first English-language book to tell the story of Sankara's life, drawing on extensive first hand research in Burkina Faso, including interviews with the late leader. Decades after his death, Sankara remains an inspiration to youth throughout Africa for his integrity, idealism, and dedication to independence and self-determination.

Ernest Harsch is a research scholar at the Institute of African Studies at Columbia University. He worked on African issues at the United Nations for more than twenty years and is the author of *South Africa: White Rule, Black Revolt*.

Thomas Sankara

An African Revolutionary

Ernest Harsch

OHIO UNIVERSITY PRESS

ATHENS

Ohio University Press, Athens, Ohio 45701
ohioswallow.com
© 2014 by Ohio University Press
All rights reserved

To obtain permission to quote, reprint, or otherwise reproduce or distribute material from Ohio University Press publications, please contact our rights and permissions department at (740) 593-1154 or (740) 593-4536 (fax).

Printed in the United States of America
Ohio University Press books are printed on acid-free paper ⊚ ™

24 23 22 21 20 19 18 17 16 15 14   5 4 3 2 1

Library of Congress Cataloging-in-Publication Data
Harsch, Ernest, author.
 Thomas Sankara : an African revolutionary / Ernest Harsch.
   pages cm. — (Ohio short histories of Africa)
 Includes bibliographical references and index.
 ISBN 978-0-8214-2126-0 (pb : alk. paper) —
 ISBN 978-0-8214-4507-5 (pdf)
1. Sankara, Thomas. 2. Presidents—Burkina Faso—Biography. 3. Burkina Faso—Politics and government—1960–1987. I. Title. II. Series: Ohio short histories of Africa.
 DT555.83.S36H37 2014
 966.25052—dc23
                    2014029649

Cover design by Joey Hi-Fi

Contents

List of Illustrations	7
Preface	9
1. "Another Way of Governing"	13
2. The Forging of a Rebel	20
3. Onto the Political Stage	37
4. The State Reimagined	52
5. Mobilizing the Nation	71
6. Development for the People	88
7. A Foreign Policy of One's Own	108
8. The Last Battles	127
9. "Is It Possible to Forget You?"	146
Selected Bibliography	155
Index	159

Illustrations

Thomas Sankara	16
Sankara during his officer training	25
Sankara serving as a soccer referee	57
Active elders in community mobilizations	75
Members of the Women's Union of Burkina	83
Water reservoir	89
Sankara and a colleague planting a tree seedling	100
Sankara at a conference in Ouagadougou	120
Sankara with President Jerry Rawlings of Ghana	123
Captain Compaoré, Commander Lingani, and Captain Zongo	129
Pibaoré villagers rallying in support of the Sankara government	145

Preface

Writing this short account of the life of Thomas Sankara required making a number of choices and judgment calls. Given space limitations, which aspects to explore in some detail, which to touch only lightly? Although Sankara was a complex, multisided individual, he was above all a political actor. So the focus here is on his political views and undertakings, especially during his four years as president.

I knew Sankara. I spoke with him directly on half a dozen occasions, a couple times at length. I was also able to observe him giving public addresses and in other interactions while I was covering developments in Burkina Faso as a journalist. This limited familiarity has led me to highlight certain aspects of his personality and style. It may as well introduce some subjective bias. I do not apologize for my sympathies, but simply wish to alert the reader that my interpretations may differ from those of scholars who were less favorable to Sankara's revolutionary outlook. At the same time, I take note of certain shortcomings of his time in office that some of those who idolize him might prefer to pass over.

Sankara clearly played a leading, even preponderant role in his country's revolutionary process, but it was nevertheless a collective enterprise. It had many other actors, both in the leadership and on the ground. Their contributions cannot be given their due attention in a biography such as this, which necessarily focuses on an individual. Nor is it possible to assess Sankara's precise role and influence with full certainty. Some initiatives obviously were his own. Yet his convictions led him to work through collective leadership bodies, making it hard to pinpoint precisely how his views and actions shaped developments. Accounts by some of his contemporaries have helped shed patches of light on these questions. I hope that future scholarship will illuminate yet more.

In my research on this period in the history of Burkina Faso, I am indebted to a number of individuals. Some of those I interviewed are cited in the bibliography. In particular, I would like to thank Paul Sankara for his personal observations about his brother, and Madnodje Mounoubai for sharing several anecdotes about his time working with Sankara. Others living within Burkina Faso or outside the country also provided insights, but I will refrain from thanking them by name.

Among scholars, Bruno Jaffré has conducted the most detailed research into Sankara's life, and his *Biographie de Thomas Sankara* was invaluable in the writing of chapters 2 and 3 in particular. I thank him for reviewing this book's manuscript and making several useful observations. I also appreciate Eloise Linger's sharp editorial eye, as well as the comments and suggestions of the publisher's two anonymous reviewers.

To date, the most comprehensive source for Sankara's own words is the collection published by Pathfinder Press, *Thomas Sankara Speaks: The Burkina Faso Revolution, 1983–87,* available in both English and French editions. The reader interested in more than the short passages from Sankara used in this biography is directed to that collection. I am grateful to the publisher for permission to use its English translations of the quotations drawn from it. For the many quotations taken from other sources, the translations from the original French are my own.

1

"Another Way of Governing"

The women had traveled from across Burkina Faso, packing the tiered seats and spilling into the aisles of the central auditorium of the House of the People in Ouagadougou. There were more than three thousand of them, young and old, a few with babies on their laps, most dressed in multicolored traditional fabrics, often in the red, white, and dark blue pattern of the Women's Union of Burkina. They had come to the capital to celebrate their day—March 8, International Women's Day—with speeches, slogans, stories, songs, and dance. They cheered and chanted with leaders of the women's union, who spoke sometimes in French and sometimes in Mooré, Jula, or Fulfuldé, three of the country's indigenous languages.

That day in 1987 they also came to hear their energetic young president, Thomas Sankara, who had already initiated numerous measures to improve women's standing and opportunities. Sankara's speech did not disappoint. He had made some of the main points before: that women had to organize, that traditional customs had to shed their oppressive features, that social inequality had to be combated, and that the revolution would triumph only if women became full participants. But this time he also anchored his arguments to an exhaustive review of women's oppression through eight millennia of social evolution and gave numerous examples of its signs in contemporary Burkinabè society, sometimes in poetic flights of oratory. He scathingly criticized Burkinabè men—including some among his fellow revolutionaries—who hampered advancement for the women in their own families. Transformation would be incomplete, he said, if "the new kind of woman must live with the old kind of man," drawing much applause and laughter.

Sankara's interaction with the women that day was not unusual. Since becoming president in August 1983 at the head of a revolutionary alliance of young radical military officers and civilian political activists, he had repeatedly traveled across the country to outline his government's ambitious initiatives and projects. On his tours he met with villagers, youth leaders, elders, artisans, farmers, and other citizens. He addressed enthusiastic audiences. Many listeners knew that his words were not just the promises of another politician or government official. They had already seen tangible improvements in their own towns and villages: new schools, health clinics, sports fields, water reservoirs, and irrigation dams. People were impressed by the uncharacteristic vigor of this leader, who was not only impatient to battle poverty but also quick to jail bureaucrats caught stealing from the meager public treasury. Some certainly were alarmed by the revolutionaries' rhetoric about class struggle and calls to crush those who opposed the government. Yet Sankara himself demonstrated a particular ability to convey his sweeping vision of societal transformation in concrete terms and actions that could be readily appreciated by ordinary people and by reformers across ideological boundaries. Until he was cut down in a military coup in October 1987, Sankara was widely seen as having done more to stimulate economic, social, and political progress than any previous leader.

Sankara left a mark beyond his own country. During visits elsewhere in Africa or at international summit meetings, his speeches struck listeners with their forcefulness and clarity. His frank criticisms of the policies of some of the world's most powerful nations were all the more notable coming from a representative of a small, poor, landlocked state that few had previously heard of.

The French authorities had heard of it, at least by the name Haute-Volta (Upper Volta), as they called the territory they had colonized and ruled from 1896 to 1960. When President François Mitterrand visited Ouagadougou in November 1986, he encountered a changed country, with a different kind of leader. President Sankara greeted his guest not with the usual diplomatic niceties and ceremonial toasts. He offered a "duel" of ideas and oratory. Sankara began with a plea for the rights of the Palestinian people; defended Nicaragua, then under attack by

Thomas Sankara (1949–1987). *Credit: Ernest Harsch*

US-backed "contras"; and scolded Paris for its policies in Africa and toward African immigrants in France. Recalling the spirit of the French revolution of 1789, he said his government would be willing to sign a military pact with France if that would bring to Burkina Faso shipments of arms that he could then send onward to liberation forces fighting the apartheid regime in South Africa. If Sankara's verbal jousts took Mitterrand off guard, the French president recovered quickly. He set aside his prepared remarks and took on Sankara point by point. He also praised the Burkinabè president's directness and the seriousness of his questions. With Sankara, Mitterrand said, "it is not easy to sleep peacefully" or to maintain a calm conscience. Half jokingly, he added, "This is a somewhat troublesome man, President Sankara!"

It was not only the Sankara government's daring foreign policy positions that resonated across Africa. People noticed the way he set about governing his own country—with dramatic shake-ups of lethargic state institutions and procedures, prompt trials and prison sentences for wayward officials, and a major shift in public services away from the privileged elites and toward the poorest and most marginalized. Such steps struck many as examples of the kind of deep reforms needed in so many African countries after decades of repressive and corrupt misrule. The rhetoric of Sankara's revolution was not about Western-style representative democracy—for most of Africa, that wave of change was still a few years off, in the 1990s. But it was about reorienting the state back toward the initial promise of the independence era: to overcome the inequalities bequeathed by colonialism, to see to the welfare of the common citizen, and to build a sovereign Africa, free of foreign tutelage.

Radicals and restive youths across the continent were easily drawn to Sankara's example. So were some reform-minded professionals, including Colonel Ahmadou Toumani Touré in neighboring Mali. He later told me that already in the 1980s he was deeply disturbed by the corruption and autocratic methods of Mali's longtime ruler, Moussa Traoré. At the time, he looked to Burkina Faso as a model of "another way of governing, a departure from the form in which a president replaces the colonizer but lives exactly like the colonizer, completely cut off from the living society." (Several years after Sankara's death, Touré led a coup against the Traoré dictatorship and initiated a constitutional process that brought multiparty elections and the restoration of civilian rule. A decade later, Touré, then a retired general, was elected president, although his tenure was not as innovative as many had hoped. As Mali plunged into rebellion and chaos, he too was ousted in a coup in March 2012.)

Improving the ways of governing in Africa has never been easy. As Sankara was to tragically discover in his own country, efforts to restructure state institutions, carry out controversial reforms, and chip away at elite privileges can foster resistance and opposition, both from within and from powerful external forces. Mistakes, brash initiatives, and heavy-handedness can shake the confidence of potential supporters. And seemingly minor differences with close comrades can deepen under pressure. Sankara was killed by some of those comrades on October 15, 1987. That act cut short the life of one of contemporary Africa's more innovative leaders.

However brief Sankara's passage, his life is worth examining. This short account looks at the influences that helped shaped him, the ideas and visions of a self-professed dreamer, and the concrete achievements, ambitious projects, and unfinished work of his presidency. In the process it may help provide some small understanding of why so many youths across the continent continue to see Sankara, decades after his death, as an embodiment of their hopes and dreams.

2

The Forging of a Rebel

Thomas Sankara was born on December 21, 1949, in the small town of Yako in central Upper Volta, as the territory was then called. He too initially bore a different name: Thomas Noël Isidore Ouédraogo. Ouédraogo is one of the most common family names among the Mossi, the largest ethnic group and the mainstay of the old precolonial Mossi empire. Yet Thomas was not Mossi. He was Silmi-Mossi, a socially marginal category descended historically from both Mossi and Peulh. His father, Joseph Sankara, was Silmi-Mossi, but had assumed the name Ouédraogo when he joined the French army in World War II at the request of the Mossi chief of Téma, to whom his family was allied. In the army Joseph also converted to Catholicism from the Islam practiced by most Sankaras. Thomas's mother, Marguerite Kinda, was Mossi by birth and herself had sometimes used the name Ouédraogo. Only later, when Thomas was in his teens, did Joseph change the family name back to Sankara.

Thomas grew up in a large family. Two sisters were born previously, but he was the first son. Eight more brothers and sisters came afterward (and another sister died in infancy). As the oldest boy, Thomas saw it as his duty to help care for and protect his siblings.

His early years were spent in Gaoua, a town in the humid southwest to which his father was transferred as an auxiliary gendarme. As the son of one of the few African functionaries then employed by the colonial state, Thomas enjoyed a relatively privileged position. The family lived in a brick house with the families of other gendarmes at the top of a picturesque hill overlooking the rest of Gaoua. But Thomas played with other children and sat alongside local classmates once he started primary school, so he soon became aware of their conditions and of the wider world around him.

In the 1950s, Upper Volta was still a colony of France. The territory had initially been conquered by French army contingents in 1895–96, when they drove the Mossi emperor (*mogho naba*) from Ouagadougou. It took several more years for them to conquer the Bobo, Samo, Lobi, Gourounsi, Gourmantché, Peulh, Tuareg, and other peoples. Even then, not all communities were "pacified" until the suppression of a major revolt among the peoples of the west and of the northern Sahel in 1915–16. At the time, the territory was part of a larger French West African colony. Only in 1919 was it formally established as a separate colony called Upper Volta. Viewed from Paris, Upper Volta was a minor colonial possession, of little material value except to grow cotton or to provide conscripted young men to work on roads, railways, and plantations in other French colonies. Its marginal status was confirmed when in 1932 the official colony of Upper Volta was dissolved and most of its territory merged into the neighboring Côte d'Ivoire (Ivory Coast), only to be reconstituted yet again in 1947.

Compared with the practice in France's richer colonial territories, Paris sent relatively few French administrators or colonists to Upper Volta. There were enough in Gaoua, however, for the young Thomas to notice how differently they lived from the African population and how much more privileged were the European children of his age. Occasionally he got into scraps with European children in school or around the town. Although his father often took his side in such disputes, he also disciplined him at home for getting into conflicts. When Thomas was eleven years old, just a few days before Upper Volta attained its formal independence from France, he and some friends organized their own mock ceremony to lower the French flag and raise the colors of the new nation. That led to a brawl between European and African boys. Although Thomas himself was not involved, the school director demanded that his father punish him with a beating. His father refused.

Most of the time Thomas applied himself seriously to his schoolwork, excelling in math and French. He went to church often, participated in a church scout troop, and devoted time to religious studies. Impressed with his energy and eagerness to learn, some of the priests encouraged Thomas to go on to seminary school once he had finished his primary courses. He initially agreed. But he also took the exam required for entry to the sixth grade in the secular educational system, and passed. When his father told the priests that Thomas would not be joining a seminary after all, they responded that he had not prayed hard enough for his son.

Thomas's decision to continue his education at a *lycée* (state secondary school) proved to be a turning point. That step got him out of his father's household, since the nearest lycée was in Bobo-Dioulasso, the country's commercial center. He spent hours exploring the large city on a bicycle. At the lycée (named after Ouezzin Coulibaly, a preindependence nationalist), Sankara made some close friends, including Fidèle Toé, years later to be named a minister in his government. Soumane Touré, soon to become another longtime friend, was in a more advanced class, where he participated in a student strike against the school's rather rigid disciplinary rules. Sankara continued to concentrate on his regular studies. He still did well in math and French, took part in theater productions, went to the movies, and started a regimen of physical exercise.

Meanwhile, the country was experiencing political turmoil. Upper Volta's first president, Maurice Yaméogo, was never a particularly inspiring figure, having acceded to independence rather reluctantly. He maintained a strong connection to France, with numerous French "advisers" working in both the army and the civil administration. Over time Yaméogo became more autocratic and jailed many critics. He appointed relatives to key positions and engaged in extravagant personal spending, while simultaneously imposing austerity on state employees and cracking down on the trade unions. He appeared oblivious as his unpopularity grew. On January 3, 1966, workers launched a general strike, and large crowds of students, unemployed youths, workers, petty traders, and others poured into the streets of Ouagadougou in a veritable popular insurrection. After army officers refused to follow the president's orders to disperse the demonstrators by force, it was clear that Yaméogo was finished. He agreed to resign and hand power over to the army commander, Lieutenant Colonel Sangoulé Lamizana.

Those events in the capital stirred few immediate ripples in Bobo-Dioulasso. Sankara was focused on his final secondary school exams. He did hear over the radio, however, that Lamizana had established a new military academy in Ouagadougou, the first in the country, and that as part of its first class of prospective junior officers it would take in three students who had just obtained their secondary school certificates. The military was popular at the time, having just ousted a despised president. It was also seen by some young intellectuals as a potentially national institution that might help discipline the inefficient and corrupt bureaucracy, counterbalance the inordinate influence of traditional chiefs, and generally

Sankara during his officer training in the late 1960s.
Credit: Courtesy Paul Sankara

help modernize the country. Besides, acceptance into the military academy would come with a scholarship; Sankara could not easily afford the costs of further education otherwise. So he took the entrance exam and passed. He joined the academy's first intake of 1966, at the age of seventeen, stepping onto the same career path that his father had once pursued.

As with his earlier studies, Sankara took the challenges of the military academy seriously. Although the physical training was rigorous, especially for someone of modest build, he persisted and strengthened himself. He also discovered that he had an aptitude for leadership—the basic goal of the academy, after all, was to train officers for a new army that had relatively few.

The academy also taught its trainee officers a variety of academic subjects, including in the social sciences. For those topics it employed civilian professors. One was the academic director, Adama Touré, who taught history and geography. Although known for some progressive ideas, Touré did not openly air all his views; that would have been risky in such a politically and socially conservative country. Only years later was it revealed that he belonged to the clandestine African Independence Party (PAI), a regional Marxist group centered in Senegal and with branches in several other former French colonies. Touré invited a few of his brightest and more politically inclined students—Sankara among them—to join informal discussions outside the classroom. Touré talked about imperialism and neocolonialism, socialism and communism, the Soviet and Chinese revolutions, the liberation movements in Africa, and similar topics. Although Sankara had already started to become politically aware, this was the first time he was exposed, in a systematic way, to a revolutionary perspective on Upper Volta and the world.

Besides his official studies at the academy and extracurricular political activities, Sankara also made the time to explore Ouagadougou and widen his network of friends. He pursued his passion for music and played the guitar more often.

Three years later, Sankara completed his studies at the military academy. He was one of just two graduates then selected for more advanced officer training in Antsirabé, in Madagascar, an island nation off the continent's southeastern coast and another former French colony. When Sankara arrived in October 1969 he encountered a country very different from the poor, arid nation he knew. Madagascar was lush with vegetation; its main cities were filled with many historic buildings, monuments, and gardens; and the level of economic development was notably higher.

At the Antsirabé academy, the range of instruction went beyond standard military subjects. Sankara was particularly drawn to courses on agriculture, including how to raise crop yields and better the lives of farmers—themes he would later take up in his own country. Madagascar's army was innovative in another respect: it had not only combat personnel but also members of public service units—the "green berets"—who focused primarily on development activities. Sankara was so impressed that he asked for a year's extension in Madagascar to work with the units.

Beyond widening his knowledge and range of skills, Sankara used his time in Madagascar to improve his mastery of French. He was especially fond of coining words and phrases and engaging in humorous wordplay, which made him a more interesting and effective public speaker. He honed his writing skills, even becoming the editor of the academy newsletter. And he lost no opportunity to supplement his official instruction with further political education. Among the works used in his classes were some by Marxist authors or the well-known French development thinker René Dumont. Several professors were left-wing French academics, and Sankara sometimes had dinner with them.

Sankara advanced his political education through more than books and discussions. He was able to personally witness revolutionary change. His last year in Madagascar coincided with an unprecedented period of political upheaval marked by peasant revolts, general strikes, huge public demonstrations against a conservative pro-French regime, and finally a military takeover that steadily brought ever more radical officers into high positions of power. Sankara and a friend from Mali traveled to the capital in the hopes of meeting Captain Didier Ratsiraka, the most radical of the officers and then foreign minister (later to become president). They did meet, but Ratsiraka was busy and rushed off after a few minutes.

When Sankara finally returned to Upper Volta in October 1973, he was a trained officer ready to command. But his head was also bursting with new notions of how an institution such as the army could be used to promote development—and of the need for wider political and social changes. Now twenty-four and a second lieutenant, Sankara received his first command, to train new recruits in Bobo-Dioulasso.

Sankara moved to that city with his much younger brother and sister, Paul (ten) and Pauline (twelve). Sankara felt that the two had not had enough parental discipline, since his mother was indulgent by nature and his father became less strict with age. "He always used to say we were spoiled," Paul recalled. He and Pauline lived with Thomas in the officers' quarters. They both received considerable attention, in contrast to family life in Ouagadougou, where they were just two of many children. Thomas, Paul remembered, "would always check on our homework, pretty much every day." Although there was a domestic servant to help with chores, "We had to take care of our own clothing, washing, putting things in order. That was it, military discipline." The rigorous upbringing included physical exercise. Paul went running with the soldiers, and liked it. The habits he learned from Thomas stayed with him the rest of his life.

Sankara's approach to the new army recruits under his charge was not too different. He found the established military training programs rather archaic, largely copied from those of the French army in the era of Napoléon Bonaparte. So he adapted them and coupled the military training with civic education, as he had learned in Madagascar. In addition to sports and athletic activities on Sundays, he organized civics classes on Saturday mornings, covering topics such as the rights and duties of citizens and the powers of the legislature, military, and courts. At first the recruits were resentful that some of their free time was taken up by the courses, but eventually they became more interested. According to Bruno Jaffré, one of his biographers, Sankara regarded the recruits' awakened interest in civic affairs as "confirmation of his optimism in human nature and encouragement to engage in other similar actions."

Sankara's experiments in Bobo-Dioulasso had begun to draw attention from others in the military but were cut short, to his regret, when he was transferred to Ouagadougou in March 1974. There he was assigned to the army's engineering corps, where he tapped into the technical skills he had acquired during his last year in Madagascar. Sankara spent much of his time traveling around the country, overseeing the building of roads, houses, and other structures. In the process he discovered that certain army officers and government officials were diverting funds, materials, or food or giving their own relatives lucrative jobs. He openly criticized the dealings of several, including the army quartermaster and the minister of transport—even though the latter was a son of the traditional chief of Téma, to whom Sankara's father owed some allegiance. None of the errant officials were punished, but senior officers did start to wonder about this young upstart.

In December 1974, a brief war broke out between Upper Volta and Mali, growing out of a dispute over a contested region stretching nearly 100 miles along their common border. Sankara was among the many sent to the border. He commanded a small group that staged an ambush and captured some Malian soldiers. The exploit was mentioned in the press, contributing to an image of Sankara as a "war hero." Although that label was sometimes cited when he later became politically prominent, it was not one that Sankara used himself. In fact, he thought the war was senseless, having erupted over some badly drawn lines on a colonial map and pitting against each other two poor African countries with shared cultural and ethnic affinities. The experience of the war also appears to have further alienated Sankara from the military's higher command. It confirmed in his eyes that the officers were more attentive to lining their own pockets than to the conditions of their troops or the need for an efficient, professional army capable of defending the country. It was not hard to see that the army was outmatched by the Malian armed forces, and was saved from defeat only by the intervention of regional mediators who helped arrange a truce in early 1975.

Although Sankara shared his views selectively with some other young officers and with his left-wing civilian friends, he did not express them openly at the time. Yet some of his observations about the weaknesses of the country's army did gain a hearing among his superiors. President Lamizana in particular appreciated Sankara's evident energy and talents. Already at that time, Lamizana recalled years later, he regarded Sankara as an "officer of the future" who was destined to lead. Lamizana was less concerned than some of his colleagues about the unconventional political views circulating within the junior officer corps. Sankara, for his part, treated Lamizana with respect and paid courtesy calls to the general's house on holidays.

In 1976 Lamizana appointed Sankara, now a full lieutenant, to take charge of a new national commando training center. Based in Pô, a relatively small town not far from the southern border with Ghana, the center was designed to train the elite fighting units that the army lacked. For the more than four years he commanded the center, the position provided Sankara with an opportunity to develop more fully the kinds of innovative training programs he had first started in Bobo-Dioulasso—and without having to report daily to any superiors, since he was the highest-ranking officer in Pô. The center's regimen was rigorous, with an emphasis on imparting advanced military skills to the soldiers, who came to Pô from units around the country. Sankara also saw to their well-being.

When he discovered that the military camp lacked a secure source of water, he bought a motorized pump without going through the army's normally slow requisition channels, and then presented the bill directly to Lamizana (who covered it from a presidential account). Noticing that the younger soldiers often spent all their pay early in the month, he ensured that they set up savings accounts at a local bank and learned how to manage their money.

Sankara worked as well to raise the soldiers' civic awareness and intellectual acumen. Yet organizing educational activities was not a simple task. Books were few in Pô, so every time Sankara or his colleagues went to Ouagadougou, they came back with books, some of a political nature. Since the goal was to produce citizen-soldiers who viewed themselves as serving the wider society, Sankara also initiated development projects in which his troops worked directly with local communities. In one instance, the center joined with a nongovernmental organization to dig wells and improve residents' access to water. On another occasion, he secured a contribution of musical instruments, which were given to soldiers with some aptitude to form a band. Sankara, with his guitar, participated in the rehearsals and even some of the performances. As the soldiers got better, they joined with civilian musicians to launch the Missiles Band of Pô, often playing at weekend dances and other events.

In 1978, while Sankara was away for a short training course, there was a physical altercation between some soldiers and local youths. A superior officer in Ouagadougou sided with the soldiers, worsening the tensions. Sankara then rushed back to Pô, disciplined the soldiers involved, and arranged a reconciliation meeting between the army and the residents.

Since Pô was less than a hundred miles from the capital, Sankara was able to travel there regularly, both to meet with his army superiors and to see his friends. During this period, he met a young woman, Mariam Serme. They began seeing each other regularly, and the romance deepened. They married in Ouagadougou in 1979, in a simple ceremony in a small Catholic church. Since the couple's combined income was relatively modest, they originally planned to invite only a hundred guests to the reception. But friends contributed generously, and attendance ultimately swelled to three hundred. A little more than two years later, in August 1981, Sankara became a father with the birth of his and Mariam's first child, Philippe.

Though focused on his responsibilities at the training center and on his new family life, Sankara remained painfully aware of the desperate conditions facing his country's people. In one of the poorest nations in the world, Upper Volta's 7 million inhabitants had an annual average per capita income of just $210 in 1980. Less than one in ten lived in a city, and the adult literacy rate scarcely reached 11 percent. Only 18 percent of school-age children were in primary school, and a bare 3 percent made it to secondary school. Recurrent droughts, soil erosion, and stagnant crop yields meant that hunger was common. Poor nutrition and disease cut lives very short: average life expectancy was an abysmal forty-four years.

Fueled by anger at such a reality, Sankara's conviction deepened that fundamental change must come. During his visits to Ouagadougou, and on yet more military training missions to France and Morocco, he systematically pursued contacts with those who thought likewise. Some were in the military, including Blaise Compaoré, whom Sankara first met during the war with Mali and then again at a training course in Morocco. In 1978 he made Compaoré his deputy commander at the Pô training center. Other contacts were with civilians, members of a number of small, leftist groups. A few groups had followings in the trade unions, but the newer ones were most often based among academics and students. Ideologically, they tended to identify as Marxist, with the supporters of the African Independence Party (PAI) generally politically sympathetic to the Soviet Union and the rest looking to either China or Albania for inspiration. Some groups spent a lot of time debating arcane theoretical points and did not always seem fully aware of the daily problems facing ordinary people.

Although Sankara valued and learned from these activists' debates and discussions, he avoided joining any of the civilian groups. He remained closest to his small circle of friends among the junior officers, and he encouraged interactions between them and the civilian activists, some of whom regularly visited the commando center in Pô.

To Sankara and his colleagues, a scent of change seemed to be in the wind. The politicians of the old conservative political parties were in disarray. Strikes were becoming more common across the country. Public anger was mounting over the recurrent exposure of corruption scandals involving both military officers and civilian bureaucrats. Yet Sankara's study of revolutions had taught him that it could be foolhardy to act precipitously. So he bided his time—at least for a little while longer.

3

Onto the Political Stage

As the 1980s opened, the government of Sangoulé Lamizana had already been in office for nearly a decade and a half. Compared to the experience of some of Upper Volta's more volatile and highly repressive West African neighbors, Lamizana's rule was relatively stable and not especially strict. Yet his government's relative laxity came with a corollary: there was very little effort to tackle the country's severe social and economic problems. Development initiatives were minimal at best, while those in high office—with the apparent exception of the president himself—freely used their positions to advance their own personal interests and aggrandizement. As Lamizana complained in a 1980 New Year's address, the elites cared little for the good of the country and instead worshipped "the religion of power and money."

For many other military officers of Lamizana's generation, this was not particularly troubling. What did concern them was the government's inability to end the incessant bickering of leading civilian politicians or rein in the restive student and labor movements, which were becoming more active.

On November 25, 1980, a group of senior officers led by Colonel Saye Zerbo mounted a coup. Adopting the rather unwieldy name of the Military Committee for the Enhancement of National Progress (CMRPN), they deposed the government, detained Lamizana and other officials, scrapped the constitution, dissolved the National Assembly, and suspended all political parties and activities. Zerbo, a veteran of French military campaigns in Indochina, cited an "erosion of state authority" under Lamizana among the reasons for his coup. He vowed to instill discipline within the state and fight corruption, and to that end set up commissions to study civil service reform and investigate malpractices by officials of the previous regime. The coup was initially popular. The new government set up by the CMRPN included some progressive nationalist civilian ministers and enjoyed the support of some trade unions.

Sankara took no part in that coup. Even though some young officers rallied to the CMRPN and Sankara and his closest friends were sympathetic to the new regime's promises to root out corruption, they remained suspicious of the political conservatism of the colonels now in power. Their position was a delicate one. On the one hand, as members of a military hierarchy, they were obliged to follow their superiors. On the other, they hesitated to accept public positions in the new government out of concern that to do so might compromise their strategic goal of fundamental political change. The reality was that the radical wing of junior officers represented by Sankara was not yet strong enough to decisively influence events.

Nevertheless, the radicals' support was growing among the ranks of the military, just as their ties were deepening with the student and labor movements and with the civilian revolutionary groups. For the officers of the CMRPN—whose early popularity soon began to wane—this support was a political asset that could shore up their hold on power. They embarked on a game of seduction to draw in the young radicals.

As an acknowledgment of Sankara's military command abilities as well as his political following, he was promoted to captain in January 1981 and named head of the army's operational division. He soon was asked to take on a ministerial position in the government. Sankara refused. In a carefully worded letter to Zerbo, he cited "a personal, free, and conscious decision to not accept any political post." Some of his civilian revolutionary friends agreed with that decision. Others urged Sankara to take up the offer, arguing that outright rejection could expose him and his comrades to retaliation. Finally, after some negotiation, Sankara reluctantly agreed to become minister of information. He insisted, however, on two conditions: that his deputy at the commando training center in Pô, Blaise Compaoré, take over as its commander; and that Sankara serve as minister for only two months until a replacement could be found (although his tenure ultimately stretched to seven months).

On September 13, 1981, Sankara assumed his first official political position. Even though he viewed his new duties as temporary, he set about fulfilling them with the same seriousness and attention to detail as he devoted to other tasks. He brought in a trusted friend from his secondary school days, Fidèle Toé, to act as his chief of staff and recruited several promising young journalists to help him oversee the work of the state-owned media.

From the outset, Sankara functioned like no other government minister up to that time. With a flair for the dramatic gesture, he pedaled to work each day on a bicycle rather than drive a state-issued car. The sight of a cabinet minister bouncing along Ouagadougou's dusty streets just like other citizens sent a clear message of the kind of public servant he intended to be.

To journalists, Sankara's approach to the work of the Ministry of Information was very different from that of his predecessors. He did not urge them to mince their words or paint official life in glowing colors, but instead quietly encouraged them to report what they saw. Years of state intimidation were not easy to shake off—and some reporters may well have been suspicious of this new minister in uniform. But gradually the general tenor of the official media became more probing. Exposés of high-level scandals now appeared not only in *L'Observateur*, a private newspaper, but also in the state-owned weekly *Carrefour africain*. Articles revealed massive embezzlement at a publicly owned investment bank by its former head and raised questions about an official in the Ministry of Trade who was suspected of taking bribes in exchange for authorizing illegal wheat imports.

The revelations stirred public outrage, but the only trials at the time were of several corrupt post office personnel. Predictably, conservative state officials were not happy with the exposés. Security police called in the director of the national news agency for questioning, accusing him of publicly leaking details of the investment bank scandal. Sankara reacted immediately by protesting directly to the minister of the interior. In a follow-up letter he argued that such acts could divert the press from its basic mission: to provide citizens with "the most accurate information possible."

Meanwhile, political and social tensions in the country were again sharpening. While the CMRPN's promises to clamp down on corruption and profiteering proved to be of limited substance, its reaction to political dissenters took on a much harder edge. Outspoken student activists were detained. As labor unions continued to demand better living and working conditions, the authorities responded by suspending the right to strike; dissolving the most militant of the union federations; and ordering the arrest of its central leaders, including Soumane Touré, one of Sankara's secondary school friends. Touré was reported to have evaded arrest by fleeing to Pô in the automobile of Ernest Nongma Ouédraogo, Sankara's cousin. The CMRPN's ever more repressive and antilabor turn prompted Sankara and other radical junior officers to step up their own political activities, through "circles of reflection" within the military and in discussions of strategy with their colleagues in the student and union movements.

Sankara also decided that the time had come to end his participation in the government. Since the CMRPN had ignored his earlier requests to be relieved of his functions, Sankara finally took the initiative himself. He made his exit in a particularly theatrical and politically charged fashion. On April 12, 1982, just three days before the officers of the CMRPN were to hold the first major review of their time in office, Sankara sent a formal letter of resignation to the president. In it he criticized the CMRPN for its "class" character and for serving the "interests of a minority." He also announced his resignation publicly—and live over the radio—during a speech at the closing session of a conference of African ministers responsible for cinema. With President Zerbo present at the event, he issued a strong plea for freedom of expression, concluding with the words: "Woe to those who would gag their people."

The senior officers reacted promptly by arresting Sankara. They also demoted him in rank and deported him to a military camp in the western town of Dédougou.

Sankara's open defiance reflected a broader split between the conservatives and the radical junior officers. It widened further during the review assembly three days after Sankara's exit, leading to the resignations from the CMRPN of Compaoré and Henri Zongo, another captain close to Sankara. They too were exiled to remote military bases.

Although communication among the core leaders of the radical officers' wing was now more difficult, they were able to remain in sporadic contact, while others took a more direct role in keeping the network active. They were emboldened by the CMRPN's increasing political isolation. Some of Zerbo's rivals within the factionalized army raised the idea of another coup, and quietly approached the radicals to join the anti-Zerbo plotters. In discussions with his colleagues, Sankara rejected that option, arguing that a strictly military takeover would not be able to initiate fundamental political and social change. Instead, he maintained, it was necessary to first elaborate a political platform in conjunction with the civilian movements and revolutionary groups.

Though Sankara's supporters held back, other officers moved ahead to military action, led principally by Commander Gabriel Somé Yorian, the army chief of staff. On November 7, 1982, they overthrew Zerbo's CMRPN and proclaimed a new military-led government, which they called the Council for the Welfare of the People (CSP). The new body was a coalition of individuals and factions united only by opposition to the Zerbo regime. It initially had no agreed political platform and no established leadership, enabling the radicals to push it in a somewhat progressive direction. Their influence was evident in the CSP's first declarations, which condemned the Zerbo regime for waste, corruption, illicit enrichment, and repression of students and workers. They also won agreement to restructure the CSP as a wide consultative body of 120 representatives from all military units in the country.

Sankara himself happened to be in Ouagadougou at the time of the coup, having received permission to visit his family after the birth of his second son, Auguste, just a few weeks earlier. His presence in the capital fueled inaccurate rumors that he had been a key force behind the coup. Given the leadership vacuum in the CSP, some of his supporters did in fact put forward his name for the presidency, which he declined. Others nominated Somé Yorian, but the radicals blocked that choice since the commander was known as a political conservative who was close to Maurice Yaméogo, the country's first president. Ultimately, Jean-Baptiste Ouédraogo, the little-known head of the army's medical service, was the compromise choice as president.

Although the revolutionary-minded junior officers were just one component of the broad coalition in the new CSP, they exerted greater influence than ever before. Two close Sankara allies, Commander Jean-Baptiste Lingani and Second Lieutenant Hien Kilimité, became secretary-general and deputy secretary-general, respectively, of the CSP. One of the body's first acts was to restore Sankara, Compaoré, and Zongo to their previous ranks as captain.

As he did when he was minister of information, Sankara used this new opening as a public platform to agitate for more change. Although he was not yet a member of the government, the CSP sent him to speak on its behalf in late December to a congress of the secondary and university teachers' union, one of the most militant in the country. Telling the teachers that the army was facing "the same contradictions as the Voltaic people," Sankara affirmed that "struggles for liberty" were gaining within the military barracks and vowed that the new government would support union rights. A commentary in the independent newspaper *L'Observateur* noted that while fiery pronouncements were routine for trade union leaders, this was "the first time an officer of the Voltaic armed forces had made such engaged statements in public."

The following month, on January 10, 1983, an extraordinary assembly of the CSP acknowledged Sankara's growing political standing by naming him prime minister. This time he readily accepted. He thus became the official number two to President Ouédraogo and, more importantly, was in charge of coordinating the day-to-day work of the various ministries.

When Sankara took his formal oath of office on February 1, he vowed that he and other government members were there to serve the people, "not to serve themselves." And by "the people," he specifically meant peasants, workers, artisans, artists, students, and democratic organizations that defended the interests of the "popular masses." The people wanted freedom, he said, but "this freedom should not be confused with the freedom of a few to exploit the rest through illicit profits, speculation, embezzlement, or theft." He urged state personnel to get out of their air-conditioned offices, experience the concrete living and working conditions of ordinary citizens, and set a practical example of "probity, honesty, and love of work well-done."

As prime minister, Sankara had his first opportunity to represent his country on the world stage. In late February, much to the unease of France, other Western powers, and some neighbors such as Côte d'Ivoire, Sankara paid an official state visit to Libya. He was greeted there with considerable fanfare and promises from Muammar al-Qaddafi to send substantial aid. That visit (along with a brief stopover in Upper Volta by Qaddafi that April) provided some grist for claims from sections of the media and from Sankara's political opponents that he was a lackey of the mercurial Libyan leader. Qaddafi did indeed press Sankara to adopt his idiosyncratic political theories, but Sankara was reported to have replied: "We are not exactly political virgins. Your experience interests us, but we want to live our own."

Sankara also represented Upper Volta at a summit meeting of the developing countries' Non-Aligned Movement in New Delhi the second week of March. There he actively sought out various revolutionary leaders, including Fidel Castro of Cuba, Samora Machel of Mozambique, and Maurice Bishop of Grenada. In his speech to the summit, Sankara openly sided with the more radical wing of the Non-Aligned Movement, including by supporting anti-imperialist rebels in El Salvador and the revolutionary Sandinista government in Nicaragua.

Within Upper Volta, Sankara also became more overt in expressing his revolutionary views. On March 26, 1983, the CSP organized a mass rally in Ouagadougou featuring its top officials. Commander Lingani, as secretary-general of the CSP, gave a short introduction, vowing opposition to "exploiters" and "imperialist subversion attempts." Sankara, as prime minister, took the podium next. He strenuously defended his foreign policy initiatives, including his overtures to various revolutionary leaders around the world. But most pointedly, he also took sharp swings at virtually all sectors of Upper Volta's social and political elites: bureaucrats, businessmen, party politicians, religious and traditional leaders, corrupt officers. He spiced up his characterizations of these "enemies of the people" with a lively litany of colorful animal imagery, such as "fence-sitting chameleons" and "hungry jackals." Throughout the speech, he employed a call-and-response method to elicit the crowd's vocal participation:

> Are you in favor of keeping corrupt civil servants in our administration?
>
> [*Shouts of "No!"*]
>
> So we must get rid of them. We will get rid of them.
>
> Are you in favor of keeping corrupt soldiers in our army?
>
> [*Shouts of "No!"*]
>
> So we must get rid of them. We will get rid of them.

When Sankara finished, President Ouédraogo stepped to the podium to read his own speech. But he had been clearly upstaged by his prime minister. His own address was delivered in a markedly lower key and had a more moderate message.

Some weeks later, on May 14, another rally was organized in Bobo-Dioulasso. A similar scenario played out. Sankara elicited a very enthusiastic response from the members of the youth organizations invited to the rally. When President Ouédraogo stood up next to address them, he was greeted at first with silence. Then as he spoke the crowd began to disperse, amid chants of "Sankara! Sankara!"

Sankara's various pronouncements, at home and abroad, cemented his alliance with the country's main revolutionary political groups. But they also alarmed the more conservative officers in the CSP—and apparently the French authorities as well. Two days after the Bobo-Dioulasso meeting, Guy Penne, the African affairs adviser to President François Mitterrand, arrived in the country for an official visit. Early the next morning, May 17, armored units surrounded Sankara's home and took him into custody. Others took up strategic positions around the capital and arrested Lingani. Although surrounded, Captain Zongo rallied a number of troops and vowed to resist, but relented after speaking by phone with Sankara, who urged him to avert a bloodbath. His friend and political activist Valère Somé managed to evade arrest and traveled to Pô, where he alerted the commandos about the coup. In the absence of Captain Compaoré (who was traveling), the commandos mobilized and took control of the town. When Compaoré joined them, they decided to openly refuse to recognize the legitimacy of the authorities in Ouagadougou.

The new government—widely known as the CSP-II—still had Jean-Baptiste Ouédraogo as its titular president, but Somé Yorian was now the real power behind the regime. With Sankara out of the way, Ouédraogo met later that day with Penne, who promised generous financial aid from France.

If Sankara's ouster was supposed to restore political stability, it soon became obvious that the move was backfiring. Protests erupted almost immediately. Over May 20–21, large and sometimes violent demonstrations rocked Ouagadougou, involving high school students, youths from poor neighborhoods, and some trade unionists. Protesters cried, "Free Sankara!" and chanted anti-imperialist slogans, particularly against France, widely regarded as the promoter of the coup.

The demonstrations, together with the defiance of the commando base in Pô, prompted the authorities to relent somewhat. Sankara and Lingani were freed for a while in an effort to start negotiations. Sankara was even permitted to travel to Pô, where he was greeted as a hero. Sankara, Lingani, and Zongo were soon rearrested, however.

As a political stalemate seemed to set in for the next two months, the "Sankarist" camp gradually consolidated its position. Sensing that a new regime change was imminent, political discussions between the young officers and civilian groups advanced to the point of sketching out a general political platform and deciding who would be named to key ministerial posts. Meanwhile, clandestine committees of civilian supporters were formed, drawn from the leftist groups, student movement, and trade unions. Messengers shuttled back and forth between the oppositionists in Ouagadougou and the commandos in Pô, where some students and other youths underwent military training. Meanwhile, Sankara continued to negotiate with President Ouédraogo in the hopes of arranging a peaceful political transition and avoiding bloodshed. At a meeting with Sankara on August 4, Ouédraogo reportedly indicated his willingness to resign as president.

According to some accounts, Captain Compaoré's forces in Pô obtained information that Somé Yorian was preparing a decisive initiative of his own: to assassinate Sankara, Lingani, and Zongo; push President Ouédraogo aside; and assume power in his own name. That prompted the rebels to strike first. On the afternoon of August 4, 1983, commandos from Pô headed for the capital, leaving the Pô garrison under the guard of armed civilians. The commandos traveled quickly in trucks commandeered from a Canadian construction firm, slipped into the capital, and took up positions around key locations: the presidency, radio station, security and gendarme headquarters, and the armored group at Camp

Guillaume. The clandestine civilian groups played a central supporting role, as guides and by cutting the city's power. At 9:30 p.m., in a closely coordinated operation, the commandos seized all their main targets, as junior officers led takeovers at the air base and the artillery camp. They confronted only minimal resistance, and as a result very little blood was shed. (However, Somé Yorian and another conservative officer, Fidèle Guébré, were captured several days later and shot, supposedly during an "escape attempt.")

By 10:00 p.m. on August 4 Sankara was on the radio to announce the overthrow of the government and the start of a new revolutionary process. In a declaration broadcast several times during the night in French, Mooré, and Gourounsi, he proclaimed the creation of the National Council of the Revolution and called on citizens throughout the country to form popular committees to safeguard it. The new government's main goal, he said, was to defend the people's interests and to help them achieve their "profound aspirations for liberty, true independence, and economic and social progress."

4

The State Reimagined

When Sankara and his colleagues took power on August 4, 1983, they called their leading body the National Council of the Revolution (CNR). The name signaled to anyone who might have been in doubt that their goal was sweeping political and social change. The next day, Ouagadougou witnessed a huge welcoming demonstration, the first of many support marches and rallies over the following weeks and months in towns and villages across the country. The response in the streets indicated that major sectors of the public—especially young people—had high expectations that finally something would be done to fundamentally refashion their country.

Sankara, then just thirty-three, did not waste time. He soon outlined the broad sweep of his revolutionary vision: an overhauled state to serve the interests of all citizens; the elimination of ignorance, illness, and exploitation; and the development of a more productive economy to reduce hunger and improve living conditions.

While the CNR would be in the lead in spurring such changes, Sankara insisted that ordinary people also had to organize and take initiative. In response to his first radio broadcast as president appealing to everyone, "man or woman, young or old," to form popular organizations, new Committees for the Defense of the Revolution (CDRs) began to emerge within a few days. The first arose in a rather disorganized manner in Ouagadougou's poorer neighborhoods and then spread more systematically over the next few months to other towns and most of the approximately seven thousand rural villages.

Throughout his presidency, Sankara spoke and acted in the name of two institutions, the government and the CNR. The government, which implemented policy, comprised both military and civilian ministers, the latter chosen because they represented the main left-wing parties or because of their particular technical or managerial skills. The CNR, also a body of soldiers and civilians, deliberated periodically on broad policy matters and guided the work of the government. The CNR's precise membership was kept secret for security reasons, although it was widely known that Sankara, Compaoré, Zongo, Lingani, and Valère Somé were among those belonging to it. Decision making in the CNR was collective—and on some occasions proposals favored by Sankara were overruled. But Sankara clearly was the CNR's most influential member, and his energy, acumen, and oratorical skills ensured that he would be its most visible public face.

Revolutionary Vision

Sankara delivered the CNR's main programmatic declaration, known as the "political orientation speech," in October, two months after the takeover. It included a broad critique of the established order as well as an ambitious agenda for transformation. There was little difference between colonial rule and "neocolonial society," Sankara said, except that some nationals had taken over as the agents of foreign domination. While the twenty-three years of Upper Volta's independence was "a paradise for the wealthy minority, for the majority—the people—it is a barely tolerable hell." Echoing the themes of his "enemies of the people" speeches in May, Sankara identified the main domestic opponents of revolutionary change as the "parasitic classes" and the traditional "reactionary forces" in the countryside. In contrast, the main proponents were the "people," principally workers, the petty bourgeoisie, and peasants.

The character of the revolution, he said, was "democratic and popular." Its long-term goal was "to eliminate imperialist domination and exploitation and to purge the countryside of all the social, economic, and cultural obstacles that keep it in a backward state." In place of the old state machinery, a new one would be built that would be "capable of guaranteeing the democratic exercise of power by the people and for the people," with the CDRs as the main agents of that process.

Sankara's use of the term "democratic," it should be noted, drew from notions of participatory democracy, not Western-style electoral models. In fact, one of the CNR's first measures was to outlaw the country's established political parties, which were seen as tools of the old elites. No elections to representative parliamentary bodies were envisaged. The absence of elections—except within the framework of the obviously partisan CDRs—was later seen as one of the Sankara government's major shortcomings, even by most of those who continued to follow his ideas. Despite the rhetoric of people's participation, there were insufficient channels through which popular ideas and grievances could be transmitted upward.

Throughout Sankara's October 1983 address and in other speeches, the influence of Marxist ideas was evident. Sankara readily acknowledged his appreciation of the Russian, Chinese, and Cuban revolutions. During visits to his office it was easy to spot volumes by Marx and Engels on his bookshelves and a bust of Lenin on his desk. Sankara read widely, including the Bible and Koran and writings by many non-Marxist revolutionaries and other progressive thinkers. Whatever his personal views, Sankara was careful to not tag the labels of "socialism" or "communism" onto the revolutionary process he was helping to lead. Upper Volta, he pointed out, was an extremely underdeveloped country, with little industry and just a tiny wage-earning working class. Under the circumstances, the process there was "an anti-imperialist revolution" that was unfolding "within the limits of a bourgeois economic and social order." The most important tasks facing revolutionaries were therefore to fight against external domination, construct a unified nation, build up the economy's productive capacities, and address the population's most pressing social problems, such as widespread illiteracy, hunger, and disease.

To symbolize that rebirth, the CNR changed the country's name in August 1984, during the first anniversary of its assumption of power. The territory once labeled Upper Volta would henceforth be called "Burkina Faso," translated roughly (from two different indigenous languages) as "land of the upright people." Besides emphasizing integrity and probity as essential characteristics of the new state, the name also signaled its indigenous identity, with its citizens—now known as Burkinabè—projected to be proud Africans.

Leadership Style

Whatever people thought of Sankara's grand ideas for the country, they soon became aware that his day-to-day conduct was markedly different from that of any previous president. At times with theatrical symbolism, he openly disdained the customary pomp and ceremony that generally come with high office. Official portraits of the president—so common in public buildings across Africa—were prohibited. Young activists were discouraged from chanting his name. He was normally driven to meetings and public events not in limousines, but in modest cars. Once a week he played soccer with his advisers and staff, and passersby could see him dressed in shorts and jersey. Sometimes he appeared unannounced at public events, participants only gradually becoming aware of his presence when they glanced to the side or

Sankara serving as a soccer referee. His presidential style was very informal. *Credit: Courtesy Paul Sankara*

rear and saw him quietly standing there, perhaps wearing a tracksuit.

Such informality was designed to send a message: that leaders should be modest, and that especially in such a poor country, they should not live the high life. In 1987, Sankara's last year, he publicly declared all the sources of income and assets of himself and his wife, Mariam. They were quite modest: he clearly had not used his position to amass wealth. His two sons remained enrolled in public school. Mariam continued to report daily for her job at the government's shipping agency, where she was a transportation specialist. His parents lived in the same house they occupied before in Ouagadougou's Paspanga neighborhood, his father now retired but his mother still selling spices and condiments to bring in some extra income.

Paul, his younger brother, said that Sankara told all family members that they should not anticipate any benefits because of his political position, in contrast to the common practice in much of Africa. "He explained to everybody how we shouldn't expect anything from him." He also warned them to "be careful of people coming with gifts," since they would likely seek some favor in return. Sankara noted in an interview with a Burkinabè journalist: "I've taught those close to me that they should in no way try to profit from the fact that one of their relatives now happens to be president. Whatever they may earn, let them earn it because they've worked for it, not because they're members of the president's family, neither my wife, nor my brothers and sisters, nor my other relatives or my children when they grow up a bit more."

Sankara did name a few personal friends to high positions, as well as a cousin, Ernest Nongma Ouédraogo, as interior minister. All had been politically active for years. Sankara trusted their loyalty, as well as their willingness to tell him what they thought, rather than what they thought he wanted to hear. "Friendship was important to him," recalled Paul. His brother believed that "real friends tell me exactly what they want to tell me, even if I don't like it."

Alfred Sawadogo, who worked with Sankara as an adviser on nongovernmental organizations from 1984 until the coup, has described a complex, multisided individual: "He was always surprising: Sometimes exuberant, quarrelsome, teasing, funny, friendly, and warm. Sometimes hard, withdrawn, quick-tempered, stony faced. Sometimes lyrical and poetic, his words powerful, deep, and real. But always true to himself: a nationalist to his core, an idealist, demanding, rigorous, an organizer."

Sankara could be stubborn in his views, even when they were unpopular. Yet he could also reverse himself when persuaded that he was wrong. In a draft of a speech that he was to have given to a group of military comrades on the day of his death, Sankara noted that "we have benefited each time that someone considered it necessary to raise an opinion different from mine, to defend a position different than mine. . . . These I have adopted and implemented, along with advice, suggestions, and recommendations."

Sankara was always eager to learn new things, including new technologies. At a time when personal computers were still rare in Africa, he and his cabinet ministers took courses in how to use them. He also began to learn English.

Sankara's methods of work were unconventional. Although trained at military academies in rigorous planning and strategic thinking, he sometimes took initiatives in an ad hoc fashion, with little evident forethought about how they could be implemented. "Sankara was the antithesis of a bureaucrat," Sawadogo commented. Sankara hated formalism and cumbersome, slow procedures. Functioning alongside the president, Sawadogo learned to "work fast, think fast, act fast, make decisions and be fully responsible for them." Sankara did not like it when anyone told him that a particular initiative had never been tried before or was impossible to carry out. He frequently declared, "That which man can imagine, he can achieve." Over time, Sawadogo recalled, those who worked with the president learned that by aiming for the seemingly unattainable, they were able to accomplish much more than they had ever dreamed—they could push the boundaries of what was possible.

Ordinary Burkinabè seemed to readily embrace Sankara's approach, as they mobilized in their local communities to quickly build new schools, health clinics, and other facilities that had once seemed but a remote fantasy. But many of the country's civil servants were less eager to step up the pace. Sankara discovered that he had to combine persuasion with a good bit of coercion to get them to move more quickly and effectively in responding to people's needs.

Disciplining the Bureaucracy

An early priority was to convince state employees—and the population at large—that the CNR was serious when it said that public property was sacred and that civil servants were there to serve the public, not themselves. Up until then, the record had been otherwise. During the first two decades of the country's independence, only about thirty cases of economic crime were brought before the courts, and very few of those involved high-level perpetrators.

That changed dramatically with the creation of the People's Revolutionary Tribunals (TPRs). Their purpose was both repressive and educational, to punish crimes of corruption and embezzlement, and to instill a greater sense of morality in public life. Ernest Nongma Ouédraogo, interior minister under Sankara, later explained to me that the aim of the TPRs was "to awaken people, to put them on guard against corruption, and to prevent those who might be tempted by corruption to pull back." Sankara made a similar point in his speech at the opening of the first TPR trial, declaring, "To the immoral 'morality' of the exploiting, corrupt minority, we counterpose the revolutionary morality of an entire people acting in the interests of social justice."

Ordinary citizens, moreover, were to help implement that justice. Departing from the practice of the old courts, in which a single magistrate ruled over a case, the new tribunals were established as panels of professionals and lay judges, including one magistrate, perhaps a military or police officer, and five or six civilians chosen by local CDRs. The trials were public, often drawing large audiences and with the proceedings broadcast live over the radio. Cassette tapes recorded from the trial broadcasts sold briskly in marketplaces.

The first trial, in January 1984, was of General Lamizana, who was charged with diverting money from a special presidential fund. After hearing extensive testimony that Lamizana had used the fund mainly to help a variety of individuals, not for his own personal enrichment, the panel decided by majority vote to acquit him. Not everyone was so fortunate. A dozen more TPR trials over the next six months included among their defendants forty-four former government officials of cabinet rank or above. A dozen were acquitted, but the rest were ordered to pay stiff fines and reimburse money they had embezzled. A number also received jail sentences, with Colonel Saye Zerbo drawing an eight-year term for embezzlement, illicit enrichment, and tax fraud. Overall, about forty tribunal sessions were held under the CNR, most of them taking up multiple cases, with nearly one thousand individuals tried.

For other government functionaries who might be tempted to improperly benefit from their positions, the message was clear: henceforth, state office was to be regarded as a public trust, with public goods and affairs managed on behalf of the population, not in the officeholder's own interests.

Not all disciplinary measures led to trials. To help shake up a bureaucracy that moved at a lethargic pace, a number of civil servants were simply fired for incompetence, spending working hours in bars, or being politically disloyal.

In a country where civil service salaries were far above the incomes of most other Burkinabè and the public sector took up a big share of the state budget (leaving little for public services or investment), Sankara's CNR also tightened up considerably on the incomes and perks that state employees had come to expect. Numerous bonuses were simply eliminated. Various "solidarity" funds were set up to aid drought victims or contribute to public investment campaigns, with the contributions deducted directly from government employees' pay packets. These measures caused considerable disgruntlement throughout the civil service, even though the higher echelons generally had to give up a bigger share.

Government ministers and other senior officials lost their expense accounts. Two-thirds of the government's auto fleet was sold off, and only small cars were kept, even for ministers. Officials who were assigned individual cars were strictly prohibited from keeping them outside working hours without permission (to prevent them from using the vehicles for informal business activities).

In August 1985, with no prior warning, the CNR dissolved the government. It relieved all cabinet ministers of their titles and reassigned them to collective farming projects in the countryside. Most were subsequently reappointed. A similar government dissolution/reconstitution occurred each of the following two Augusts. Sankara explained that this was a "revolutionary pedagogic formula," designed to destroy the "myth" that ministerial appointment was an irrevocable sinecure for the individual holding the office. "Everyone must know that a minister is only a servant, and that each militant must be prepared to take on governmental duty."

An Army of the People?

Like other state institutions, the military itself was marked for change. Sometimes the political rhetoric became overheated, as leaders of the CNR stressed the need to "decolonize" the army and transform it from an instrument of the bourgeoisie into a servant of the oppressed. Sankara, in line with his earlier work in the army, often emphasized the importance of raising the political and civic consciousness of the ranks, stating that "a soldier without training is just a criminal in power."

Yet the process of reforming Burkina Faso's armed forces was rather more orderly and measured than the verbiage might have suggested. The military chain of command continued to operate normally—except that its very pinnacle was essentially lopped off, both by the death or imprisonment of those senior officers who had opposed Sankara's radical wing and by the compulsory retirement of all the army's remaining generals. Since no other officers were promoted to that rank, the Burkinabè army remained devoid of generals until many years later.

Like other parts of the state administration, the military too had suffered from corruption and profiteering under the old regimes. To clean house, the CNR hauled a number of senior officers before the TPRs, and some were found guilty and imprisoned. New "revolutionary discipline" councils were set up within the armed forces to hear cases of embezzlement, theft, unauthorized absence from duty, and other infractions. New "garrison committees" were also established, along the lines of the civilian CDRs, with representatives elected by general assemblies of officers and ranks. The instructional program at the commando training base in Pô was expanded for the first time to include basic officer training, so that trainee officers no longer had to be sent abroad for their initial studies.

Most significantly, Sankara's earlier experiment in linking military training with public service and development work was made systematic. Military bases around the country started farms to grow food and raise livestock, engaged in tree planting to combat deforestation, cleaned up trash from towns and villages, dug wells, and built schools, health clinics, roads, and other facilities. Aside from its practical impact, this kind of activity had an educational function: to help prevent soldiers from developing superior attitudes and to convince civilians that the army, alongside its usual functions, could also contribute to the country's economic advancement.

By farming, Sankara told me in 1984, soldiers would be further reminded of how ordinary Burkinabè labor and suffer, so that they would continue seeing themselves as part of the people, not members of a privileged group. "This is the way we are going to produce a new mentality in the army." At the same time, he added, military training was being extended to civilian supporters through the CDRs and establishment of a reserve militia, in effect serving to "demystify the military arts." Henceforth the defense system would be composed not only of the army. "It is composed of all the people. This is possible because the people trust us. In how many African countries do you see them giving arms to civilians?"

Yet the reality was not quite so rosy. Arming young and inexperienced CDR activists led to abuses. And some of the underlying weaknesses of the regular army were highlighted during another brief border war with Mali in late December 1985. The Malian government attacked, using the presence of Burkinabè census takers in a disputed region as a justification. The Burkinabè armed forces, with only a small air force and very few tanks or armored cars, were no match for the larger and better-equipped Malian military. The Burkinabè side suffered serious setbacks. Fortunately, mediators negotiated a ceasefire five days later, and both countries agreed to submit their border dispute to arbitration by the International Court of Justice.

Some armed CDR and militia units had joined the army in trying to defend the country during the war, but the sobering reality was that popular mobilization could not compensate for the military's fundamental shortcomings. Sankara acknowledged that the CNR had neglected equipping the army, believing that it would have been "criminal to spend money on arms." Throughout his presidency, total regular troop strength remained steady at nine thousand men. Military expenditures, as a share of total spending, hovered around 19 percent, only slightly higher than when the CNR first took over.

Decentralization

The new state envisaged by the CNR was not only one intended to be less corrupt and more effective, but also one that extended—practically for the first time—outside the main cities and towns. Previous regimes had tried to govern the countryside only indirectly, largely through traditional chiefs and other local notables. They saw little need for building up an administrative apparatus outside Ouagadougou and a few other centers. But if the Sankara government was to extend public services to the rural population and initiate reforms to break the hold of the chiefs, then it needed to extend the state's limited geographical reach considerably.

The CDRs played a major role in this. Although their main functions were to help mobilize local communities for development projects and to support the CNR politically, they also had a quasi-state role. Sankara referred to them as "representatives of revolutionary power in the villages, the urban neighborhoods, and the workplaces."

The CDRs' fundamental decision-making body was the general assembly, a regular meeting of all members to discuss pressing questions and make decisions by majority vote. The assemblies elected nine-member CDR bureaus to direct activities and liaise with higher-level CDR bodies. The local CDR units were genuinely popular and not just for the educated few, filled with people from humble social origins, many of them illiterate and unable to speak languages other than their own.

The CDRs had to undertake a wide range of local responsibilities, from ensuring the provision of basic social services and day-to-day security to helping out with the national census and publicizing government directives. In much of the countryside, CDRs were the main centers of political power, especially given the "insufficiency of official services," as one CDR report put it. For all practical purposes, the CDRs were the basic building blocks for a restructured state apparatus.

The CDRs played their roles in direct competition with the traditional chiefs. This was the first time in the country's postcolonial history that institutions other than the chieftaincy or councils of elders existed in the villages, representing at least the beginnings of a shift in authority to commoners. The central government itself stepped in to weaken the position of the chiefs. Although the chiefs' prerogatives had been challenged before, Sankara went further. In December 1983 he decreed the abolition of all laws on the designation of chiefs and their territorial jurisdictions and stripped them of any remaining state benefits or rights to collect taxes, tributes, or labor services.

A month earlier, the CNR started a process of creating new territorial divisions and local government structures. Thirty provinces were created, significantly smaller in size than the old regions to ensure better administrative coverage of their populations. Below the provinces were three hundred new departments, an average of ten per province. And below them were the villages and urban communes. Each department was managed by a council selected by the village and town CDRs within that department, but headed by a prefect directly appointed by the central government. The thirty urban communes that served as provincial capitals were run by government-appointed "special delegations," with mayors chosen by the CDRs (except in Ouagadougou, where the mayor was a government appointee).

In trying to extend its authority down to the local level, the government faced numerous challenges, not least of which was its limited personnel. Since it did not have money to simply recruit additional civil servants to staff the new provincial structures, it opted to partially decentralize some of the functions and personnel of the central ministries, setting a quota for each relevant ministry to shift an additional 10 percent of its employees to the provinces.

In the past, most ordinary Burkinabè had scarcely any contact with state representatives. Now, for better or worse, the state was starting to become a much more active presence in their daily lives.

5

Mobilizing the Nation

On an especially hot day in March 1987, during a visit I made to Doundouni, about 40 miles west of Ouagadougou, some 50 residents crowded into the village's only primary school classroom. They were especially proud of the new facilities they had built themselves: a health post, an entertainment hall, a nearby cereal bank, and a headquarters for the local Committee for the Defense of the Revolution (CDR). "This is a great day to do things, to involve the whole population," commented one villager. Observed another: "Before, people didn't know how to work together. But now they've learned to work together equally. That's why things are changing in this country."

Scenes like the one in Doundouni were common across the country. In big urban neighborhoods and small villages alike, people mobilized collectively to build new infrastructure, clean up their locales, and tackle many other day-to-day problems. Burkinabè had long been known for their spirit of self-help, hard work, and collective engagement, but to many residents and foreign observers the intensity and pace of community mobilizations clearly had picked up.

"The popular masses are going faster than the government in this matter," Sankara said a day before my Doundouni visit. "When we ask a province to build four schools, they end up building twelve. This causes problems, since we have to provide the seats, tables, chalk, schoolmaster, and so on. Perhaps it's better like this—that the people are zealous, that they're committed and enthusiastic—than if they pull back." While the popular clamor for more education may present the government with some "painfully joyful" difficulties, he added, it was preferable to the situation in some neighboring countries, where the authorities were "sorrowfully lucky" to not have people placing so many demands on them.

Within just a few weeks of the takeover by the National Council of the Revolution (CNR) in August 1983, the collective labor mobilizations began. The initial calls came from the central authorities in Ouagadougou, and at the local level were often initiated by the defense committees. Although social and political compulsion sometimes played a role, the initiatives generally drew a ready and sometimes exceptionally enthusiastic response. Most of the specific goals were of obvious and immediate benefit to the communities: cleaning school and hospital courtyards; graveling roads; building mini-dams to capture or channel scarce water for farm irrigation; and, when building materials could be secured, even starting construction on schools, community centers, theaters, and other facilities. There was also some consultation in the selection, with proposals often raised or discussed during public CDR assemblies.

Bigger projects required more elaborate organization. In the town of Kaya, neighborhood and workplace CDRs spent a week simply gathering the necessary materials to begin construction on a new residential zone. Some days were devoted to locating and transporting large stones or sand. Civil servants and members of the CDR women's units gathered gravel. And different neighborhoods were organized into daily shifts to produce bricks.

In the villages the mobilizations were scheduled to not conflict with normal farming or market activities. In the cities, where the rhythm of life was set more by the standard workweek of salaried employees, neighborhood general assemblies and work mobilizations usually took place on weekends. The pace initially seemed quite hectic. Over the weekend of November 12–13, 1983, alone, seventy-seven separate CDR activities were reported in major towns, nearly half of them being either collective labor mobilizations or other forms of development work.

These community mobilizations were put on a more systematic basis in the People's Development Program (PPD), launched in October 1984. Through the program the government and CDRs tried to coordinate local efforts more systematically on a national scale, extend them into provinces where they had previously been weak, and integrate them better into the government's more general economic, social, and political undertakings. Over the fifteen months of the PPD, 351 schools, 314 maternal health centers and dispensaries, and 88 pharmacies were built, as were 274 water reservoirs and 2,294 wells and boreholes. Across the thirty provinces, people's actual contributions of money and labor (expressed as a rough monetary equivalent) were estimated to have averaged 27 percent of the total costs of the provincial programs, with the remainder funded by the provincial and national governments and by external donor agencies. According to Planning Minister Youssouf Ouédraogo, the PPD was regarded by the government as "a popular school for the masses" to bring them new technical and organizational skills, "so that they themselves can solve the problems that come up in the provinces."

Young people were the most eager participants in the mobilizations, as they were in CDR activities more generally. Sometimes urban youths went to rural areas, as when the CDR in Somgandé, on Ouagadougou's northern periphery, mobilized to help farmers in nearby villages. Noted the weekly magazine *Carrefour africain,* the initiative helped the urban youths appreciate the hard work of village life, while at the same time making villagers more open to "the innovative ideas of the youths."

In the traditional social structures of Burkina Faso, as elsewhere in Africa, elders usually held the greatest social status and often monopolized decision making. But with the arrival of the CNR—many of whose members were themselves relatively young—urban and rural youths finally saw new avenues to break from old social

Youth were most active in community mobilizations, but efforts were also made to draw in elders. *Credit: Ernest Harsch*

constraints. By actively supporting their communities, they not only acquired new organizational skills but also enhanced their own sense of social worth.

Social mobilizations were not a monopoly of the CDRs alone. Across the country, new self-help organizations proliferated, many without any direct connection to the government. Between 1983 and 1987 more than 160 new civil associations were formed, while the membership of an established group such as the "naam" peasants' movement in Yatenga province increased nearly thirtyfold.

Commando Campaigns

Beyond the local level, the CNR launched a variety of "commando" mobilization campaigns to tackle problems of national importance. Participants generally included volunteers, CDR activists, and civil servants reassigned from their normal duties for a few days or weeks at a time. One campaign focused on digging irrigation canals in the Sourou River valley to support agricultural cooperative projects. Another organized people to plant millions of trees to help combat deforestation and the spread of desert areas.

The Battle of the Rail, launched in February 1985, had an especially high profile. Its goal was to extend deeper into the isolated northeast the sole railway line, which then ran from the Côte d'Ivoire border only as far as Ouagadougou. Although the northeast had unexploited manganese deposits, the World Bank and other donor agencies considered extension of the railway to be uneconomical, and therefore declined to fund it. The Sankara government hoped to change their minds by building an additional 100 kilometers of track from Ouagadougou to Kaya through its own financing and labor mobilizations. Within seven months, about a third of the distance was covered, with some four hundred laborers mobilized each day, usually on a rotating basis from different CDRs, government offices, civil associations, and volunteers (including some foreign visitors). By October 1987, when the government was overthrown, track had been laid to within just a few kilometers of Kaya.

Not all commando mobilizations were so productive. In 1985 Sankara proclaimed a "white city" campaign to mobilize townspeople to paint their houses white, as part of a broader effort to improve urban appearances. Many residents strongly resented the effort, however. They objected to the cost of the paint, but mostly they thought the choice of color was ridiculous: with winds blowing around the fine ocher sand of the Sahel, not much stayed white for very long. The campaign was soon abandoned.

The Alpha Commando literacy campaign was better received. Launched in February 1986 and lasting two and a half months, it mobilized mainly volunteer instructors—students, CDR activists, civil servants, and some teachers. They taught basic literacy and numeracy to some thirty thousand rural people, mostly members of peasant associations. With follow-up, about half eventually managed to acquire a measure of functional literacy.

By most estimates, the greatest triumph was the Vaccination Commando, a child immunization campaign. Previous vaccination campaigns were carried out strictly through the government's regular and very limited health services—and thus reached only a tiny fraction of children, even in Ouagadougou. Reflecting Sankara's typical impatience with slow, bureaucratic procedures, the cabinet decided in September 1984 to launch a commando-style campaign to vaccinate most Burkinabè children against the key childhood killers (measles, meningitis, and yellow fever)—and to do so over a period of only two weeks, just two months later. Foreign donor agencies advised against such a fast and extensive campaign and suggested a more cautious, measured approach. The UN Children's Fund

(UNICEF) and a few other donors agreed to support the effort, although with serious misgivings about its feasibility.

According to Paul Harrison, in his 1987 book *The Greening of Africa*, what the international agencies failed to take into account was the government's commitment and ability to mobilize very large numbers of people: "There were radio programmes and posters in local languages; there were travelling theatre groups. But in a country with poor roads, where only a minority have radios, person-to-person communication was central." The CDRs, he noted, were crucial in creating awareness and mobilizing people. "The response was overwhelming. Mothers almost took the vaccination points by assault. They walked long distances, and formed queues often more than a kilometre long, waiting whole days and nights for their turn."

By the end of the two weeks, some 2 million children had received a vaccination, about three times the number in previous campaigns. Rural coverage was almost as high as in the cities. According to a joint evaluation by UNICEF and the Ministry of Health, sensitization of the population to health issues was "the most spectacular aspect of the operation." In addition, health worker morale increased significantly, as did greater overall public demand for better health services. Most immediately, the Vaccination Commando meant that in 1985 the usual epidemics of measles and meningitis—which often claimed the lives of between 18,000 and 50,000 children—did not occur.

Women's Advancement

Even more than male youths, Burkinabè women previously had very few opportunities to mobilize in defense of their social and economic interests, organize politically, or engage directly with state institutions. The weight of traditional, patriarchal relations bore down on them especially heavily. Most women were effectively relegated to the status of minors, whatever their age. From birth to death, many basic life decisions remained in the hands of their fathers, husbands, uncles, and other male relatives. As Sankara observed, "Our society—still too primitively agrarian, patriarchal, and polygamous—turns the woman into an object of exploitation for her labor power and of consumption for her biological reproductive capacity."

From the start, the new Burkinabè leadership emphasized that the emancipation of women was one of its central goals. In Sankara's 1983 political orientation speech, it featured second in a list of national priorities, after reform of the national army but before a section devoted to economic reconstruction. Repeatedly, speeches by Sankara and other leaders chastised "corrupt" and "feudal" husbands for treating their wives and daughters as "beasts of burden" and pledged to act against the many customary practices judged to be oppressive to women.

Specific measures for women were built into many social and economic programs, from literacy classes specially targeted toward women, to the establishment of primary health units in each village, to support for women's cooperatives and market associations. A new family code was drafted. Among other things, it sought to set a minimum age for marriage, establish divorce by mutual consent, recognize a widow's right to inherit, and suppress the bride-price and the practice whereby a widow had to marry one of her late husband's brothers. Vigorous public campaigns were launched against female genital mutilation, forced marriage, and polygamy.

Such practices were deeply rooted in Burkinabè society, however. They could not be eliminated by simple government decree or moral arguments. That did not stop Sankara and his colleagues from trying, but many of their efforts met with widespread rejection and incomprehension—including from some women themselves.

In the political realm, however, the government did have the power to take unilateral initiatives. At a time when hardly any women had reached high political or administrative positions in Africa, Sankara named several to cabinet posts, including as ministers of family affairs, culture, health, and the budget. In each of the last two cabinets under Sankara, in 1986 and 1987, the number of women reached five, or about a fifth of the total; previous governments had, at best, one or two women ministers. Other women were appointed as judges, department prefects, provincial high commissioners, and directors of state enterprises (the national airline, television network, and foreign trade agency).

Women appointees, though highly capable, were not always welcomed. In the province of Passoré, where Aïcha Traoré was named high commissioner, merchants strenuously resisted her efforts to rebuild the central marketplace in Yako. Supporters of the old conservative parties tried to use the presence of a woman in such a high office to rally men against the government.

Yet many women appreciated finally seeing someone of their own sex in at least a few positions of authority. Though more of a gesture than a genuine shift in power between the genders, such appointments sent a strong signal of encouragement to women at all levels.

Some women also received military training—a particularly radical notion in such a society. In some cases, as at the Pô commando base, the training began with the wives of soldiers, partly to enable them to play stronger leadership roles in the defense committees and other organizations. But more formal training programs were also established for women around the country, most of them members of the CDRs. Some women were recruited directly into the armed forces, with a few rising to become tank drivers and air force pilots.

The annual celebrations of International Women's Day, held in both Ouagadougou and the provinces, became high-profile events and provided women with occasions to speak out on issues of immediate concern. Provincial women's assemblies were also held, as in Bam, where women raised problems like female circumcision, forced marriage, inequitable divorce practices, poor sex education, and the banishment of young women who became pregnant outside of marriage.

The most numerous openings for women to organize came through the CDRs. Initially, women took part in the defense committees to only a limited extent, even though they often participated in greater numbers than men in the local community clean-up and development mobilizations. During the very first defense committee elections, almost no women were elected to the local CDR bureaus, in part because few were bold enough to step forward as candidates. In an effort to overcome this gap, the official statutes of the CDRs, issued in May 1984, mandated that at least two positions in each nine-member bureau had to be filled by women, that of deputy chairperson and the executive member responsible for women's mobilization. In some rare cases, more than two women actually were elected.

To help coordinate the work of female CDR activists nationally, a special body was created within the CDR national secretariat, the Directorate for Women's Mobilization and Organization. It sought to direct the women's cells within the CDRs and to encourage women's participation in general assemblies, community development projects, and militia training, although with uneven success. By the second national conference of the CDRs in 1986, one-third of the elected delegates were women.

Members of the Women's Union of Burkina. Sankara stressed the importance of women's political advancement. *Credit: Ernest Harsch*

In September 1985 the Women's Union of Burkina (UFB) was set up by directive of the CDRs' national secretariat. Local UFB bureaus were elected by general assemblies of women, but the chairperson, initially, was the CDR bureau member responsible for women's mobilization. Although it was not independent and UFB members sometimes found themselves relegated to stereotypical female roles such as preparing meals for conferences, the women's union gradually acquired a more distinct profile. During the 1986 literacy drive, for example, a UFB representative sat on each five-member regional management committee. The UFB complained that only limited places had been allotted to women; of the nearly 1,000 literacy centers, just 69 were exclusively for women and 396 for both sexes. These complaints prompted Sankara to promise that future literacy drives would be organized so that more women could take part.

A Nation for All

Like many other African countries, the territory known as Upper Volta/Burkina Faso was something of an artificial creation. The French conquest brought into one entity peoples who spoke some sixty different languages; observed Islam, Christianity, or indigenous African religions; and followed widely varied practices and customs. True, because of the reach of the old Mossi empire, the country's geographical boundaries were perhaps less arbitrary than those of some of its neighbors. And the relatively easygoing relations among the various ethnic groups meant that tensions among them were historically not that severe, despite some resentment over the tendency of the Mossi to dominate. At the same time, the French decision to divide Upper Volta among Côte d'Ivoire, Mali, and Niger between 1932 and 1947; the absence of a strong nationalist movement for independent statehood; and the pervasive influence of French administrators for years after independence tended to impede the development of a robust national identity. Moreover, the sheer weakness of the state and its extremely minimal contact with people in the countryside meant that there was not much of an institutional framework within which a sense of common citizenship could arise.

When Sankara's CNR came to power, it consciously pursued a policy of inclusion, to open up social and political life to more of the country's different ethnic groups. The CNR itself had numerous Mossi in it, but also Bobo, Gourounsi, Peulh, and others. Sankara, who was Silmi-Mossi (of mixed Mossi and Peulh ancestry), personified that mixed composition.

In rejecting the territory's former name, Upper Volta, in favor of Burkina Faso, the government sought to project a new national identity: First, an identity that would be local and African, against the French designation of "Haute-Volta." Second, a pan-territorial identity that encompassed the country's multiple cultures. Roughly translated as "Land of the Upright People," the name Burkina Faso is itself a multilingual composite: *burkina* from Mooré, the language of the Mossi, meaning "worthy people" or "men of dignity"; and *faso* from Jula, signifying, among other definitions, "house" or "republic." The "bè" suffix in Burkinabè came from Fulfuldé, the language of the Peulh.

Even during the year before the name change in August 1984, the state media started to actively promote Burkina Faso's multiplicity of indigenous cultures and languages. Television news was no longer delivered only in French, but also in Mooré and occasionally other languages. Because very few Burkinabè had access to television, radio remained the main means of communication, and it employed eleven of Burkina's indigenous languages. At the anticorruption trials held before the People's Revolutionary Tribunals (TPRs), a radio translator would often sit in a corner with a microphone, to provide a running summary of the proceedings in Jula or one of the other national languages for broadcast.

During the colonial era, all school instruction had been in French, and only later were Mooré, Jula, and Fulfuldé introduced in some primary schools on an experimental basis. Because of the neglect, by the 1980s, only thirty-six of the approximately sixty languages had been studied in any depth, and of those, just fourteen had been given a written form. The Sankara government drafted a new educational reform proposal that projected a greater use, over time, of the national languages in the schools. Although that reform was not implemented, the literacy campaign of 1986 was conducted in nine indigenous languages, despite the scarcity of written materials in them.

The government also supported numerous cultural festivals, at which participants from around the country could share their varied forms of artistic expression. At a weeklong national cultural festival in Gaoua in December 1984, for example, dance troupes, musicians, weavers, sculptors, writers, and painters from different ethnic groups displayed their talents and competed for jury prizes. Among the novelists, poets, playwrights, and short-story writers, there were winners for works in French, Mooré, Jula, and Fulfuldé. Such displays were not confined to occasional festivals. Major political rallies, professional conferences, and other events also were frequently preceded or followed by dance and musical performances by troupes from different ethnic groups.

The Sankara era saw an unprecedented blossoming of African cultural and ethnic representations. Many Burkinabè acquired a strong sense of pride in their specifically African identity and in the cultural richness of their country. Years after the CNR's demise, significant sectors of the population, including leading figures who once were politically hostile to the Sankara government, seem to readily accept their identification as citizens of Burkina Faso, as Burkinabè.

6

Development for the People

Sankara's vision of Burkina Faso's economic transformation was a basic one: improve the lives of its people. When the US magazine *Newsweek* asked him how a poor country like his could develop, he did not lay out a sweeping agenda of industrialization or land redistribution, as the interviewer might have expected from someone who spoke of revolution. Sankara talked instead about building irrigation dams to help grow more food, constructing schools and health clinics, and setting up networks of small stores throughout the countryside so that villagers could secure their daily necessities. "Our economic ambition," Sankara explained, "is to use the strength of the people of Burkina Faso to provide, for all, two meals a day and drinking water."

Most people in richer countries might take for granted access to safe drinking water and more than one meal a day. But in Burkina Faso that was indeed a revolutionary notion.

When I visited the northeastern region of Yatenga, on the edge of the Sahara Desert, it was obvious just how painstaking and incremental economic and social development would be. Even on the outskirts of Ouahigouya, the regional capital, the ground was hard and sunbaked, covered here and there by patches of sandy soil that could support little more than a few shriveled stubs of grain. Only an infrequent jagged tree or parched brown bush dotted the landscape. Yet Traoré, a local farmer, had been able to harvest a modest crop of millet and sorghum a few months earlier. He showed off the rows of rocks that he and his two brothers had piled up along the contours of the land to slow soil erosion and retain crop debris, a new technique he had just learned to marginally

A water reservoir built through community mobilizations. For such a poor, arid country, expanding access to water was a revolutionary measure. *Credit: Ernest Harsch*

improve fertility. Not far from Traoré's farm there were some new wells, a few hand pumps, and numerous small dams and channels to capture and direct water on the rare occasions when it did rain. A few miles farther away the scenery turned unexpectedly green. Farmers tended gardens of carrots, okra, cabbage, and other vegetables. A nearby water reservoir built a couple years before provided the irrigation.

The government's emphasis on such small, tangible improvements did not mean it lacked a grand vision. In Sankara's 1983 political orientation speech, he declared that the aim was nothing less than the construction of a national economy that was "independent, self-sufficient, and planned at the service of a democratic and popular society." That goal was echoed in the first five-year economic development plan, launched in 1986. The slogan of "self-sufficiency," as generally used by Sankara and other leaders, did not mean cutting Burkina Faso's national economy off from the rest of the world. But it did imply reorienting it more toward domestic markets and interests.

Easy to proclaim, excruciatingly difficult to accomplish. Since much of the economy was dominated by family agriculture, with little industry of any kind, there were few sources of domestic revenue to finance expansion of productive capacities or social services.

Yet the National Council of the Revolution (CNR) did set out on a path of gradual transformation. Throughout its various programs, projects, and initiatives, several recurrent themes stood out. First, economic projects had to use local materials, labor, and financing as much as possible in order to reduce reliance on foreign aid and imports. Second, with equity as a watchword, those at the top had to lose some of their perks so that those at the bottom could benefit. Third, whatever limited financial resources the government had at its disposal were allocated as a priority to rural areas, not the urban centers. And fourth, in a country of scant rainfall and a harsh climate, environmental concerns had to be integrated into all development efforts. Previous governments had espoused some of these aims, but none had ever put much effort into trying to implement them.

"We Have to Depend on Ourselves"

At a time when many African leaders behaved like supplicants eager to do anything to attract Western financing, the Burkinabè government insisted that national priorities came first. As the five-year plan put it, Burkina Faso's development strategy had to "base itself on national resources, both human and material, to build the new society."

If Western donor agencies were willing to help finance those national programs, fine. However, Foreign Minister Basile Guissou told me, "we don't wait for anything from anyone. No one will come to develop Burkina Faso in place of its own people." Planning Minister Youssouf Ouédraogo put it in similar terms: "Foreign aid, technical aid, will only be as a support, no longer the determining factor in the construction of the national economy."

They were both echoing Sankara. "We could use and we need aid from developed nations," the president told *Newsweek*, "but such aid is not so generous or forthcoming in these times." Aid from the United States, he noted, was "ridiculously small, especially when you see the wealth and prosperity of that country." Despite the CNR's revolutionary rhetoric, most of Burkina Faso's donors maintained their aid programs. However, much of that aid was tied to specific projects, over which the donors continued to exercise considerable decision-making authority, in contrast to funds allocated directly to the central budget, which the government controlled. France, the largest donor, halted all general budgetary support after 1983. The World Bank did the same after January 1985.

One reason for the Burkinabè authorities' reticence about foreign aid was their concern that it often came with strings attached. Justin Damo Barro, who was finance minister during Sankara's first year, later revealed that he had tried on four occasions to persuade the president to ask for assistance from the International Monetary Fund, but Sankara declined on the grounds that IMF "conditionality" would spell the end of the revolution, by shifting decisions over basic economic policy away from Burkinabè and toward an external entity. During a discussion with me in March 1987, Sankara said that he had earlier asked the US government to stop financing contingents of Peace

Corps volunteers and instead provide an equivalent sum as direct budget support. The United States refused, so the Burkinabè government suspended the Peace Corps program. Even when foreign volunteers carried out useful projects, Sankara said, they might end up fostering "a psychology of dependence on outside aid." As he put it in the *Newsweek* interview, "In the final analysis, we know we have to depend on ourselves."

Austerity of a Different Kind

Since the government's own treasury was not very large, the budget ministry consistently sought to reduce unnecessary and ostentatious spending. This was reflected in the early measures to cut the perks of ministers and other high civil servants. "We have tightened the belt from the top," Sankara remarked. On several occasions, the authorities even organized public discussions of the annual budget, to promote greater understanding of the budgetary process and to solicit more ideas about where to cut. Sankara closed one such conference by inviting citizens to find further ways to economize. He criticized civil servants and state enterprise personnel who still engaged in absenteeism, self-enrichment, laziness, and wasteful working methods. The CNR also strengthened the other side of the ledger sheet by enhancing the collection of taxes (levied mainly on property owners) and other sources of revenue. Meanwhile, it abolished the regressive colonial-era "head tax," a modest amount that every citizen had to pay annually, but which was onerous for poor villagers who had little cash income.

The combination of budgetary rigor and enhanced tax collection—along with foreign aid when it was available on acceptable terms—enabled the government to significantly increase investments, especially in basic infrastructure (roads, wells, market facilities) and essential social services. Between 1983 and 1987 the annual budget increased notably. Expressed as a percentage of gross domestic product, government expenditures rose from 13.4 percent to 17.4 percent and revenue from 13.5 percent to 16.3 percent. On the expenditure side, social services were strongly favored. From 1983 to 1987 public spending on education increased by 26.5 percent per person and on health by 42.3 percent.

Across Africa at the time, "austerity" was a very unpopular word. It generally was introduced at the insistence of the IMF and World Bank, as part of their "structural adjustment programs." The cuts often came in government jobs, education, and health, while the elites were usually able to continue pursuing their profligate ways. In Sankara's Burkina Faso, by contrast, it was the poor who saw the tangible benefits of austerity and those at the top who had to make do with less.

Into the Fields

Burkina Faso is an overwhelmingly agrarian country. In the 1980s more than 90 percent of its population still lived and labored on the land. Farmers had little to work with. In the entire country, less than 6 percent of the land that could be irrigated actually was. The remainder depended almost entirely on rainfall, which was often inadequate and unreliable. Only 10 percent of all farmers used animals for plowing. Most had nothing more advanced than the *daba,* a short-handled hoe. Few livestock herders had access to fodder, and usually roamed the countryside in search of grazing land and watering spots.

In some areas of central and western Burkina Faso, commercial farmers grew cotton, a crop first introduced by force in the colonial era. Since cotton exports still secured nearly half the country's foreign earnings, most official agricultural extension services, fertilizers, and other assistance went to those cotton zones, not to food farmers. As a result, cereal production stagnated. In 1984 the same amount of millet and sorghum—the main staple grains of rural Burkinabè—was grown as in 1960, although the country's population was 50 percent larger. So hunger remained prevalent across much of the countryside, even in "normal" times. In years of drought, many villagers were seriously threatened by famine.

For Sankara, the choice was obvious. Agriculture would be "the nerve and principal lever of our economic and social development," he said in a speech to tens of thousands during a celebration of the government's first anniversary. Most investments would be devoted to agriculture, "especially in favor of food crops." To modernize the country, he said, it would be essential to raise farm yields, put under cultivation all land that could be developed, and reorganize existing agricultural production channels.

In the regular annual budgets, a greater share of spending was shifted directly to agriculture. In the five-year plan, some 71 percent of projected investments for the productive sectors were allocated to agriculture, livestock, fishing, wildlife, and forests. An even larger amount in recurrent spending was planned for irrigation, sanitation, and other water projects, with major portions of health, education, and transport investments destined for rural areas.

Total cereal production rose by a spectacular 75 percent between 1983 and 1986. Much of that increase was due to more favorable rains, and output declined somewhat in 1987 because of poor weather. Yet the improvement in yields was also due to 25 percent more land being placed under irrigation between 1984 and 1987. In the Sourou Valley a dam was built within a few months almost entirely by volunteer labor, with about 8,000 hectares of irrigated land devoted to cereals, rice, and market gardening and another 8,000 to growing sugarcane for a new sugar refinery. Across the country, use of fertilizer increased by 56 percent between 1984 and 1987. Because of the high costs of imported chemical fertilizer, much of this increase involved greater use of organic fertilizers. In 1987, some 180 tractors were imported for a number of large-scale cooperative projects.

To help farmers better store and market their crops, hundreds of village cereal banks were built through collective labor mobilizations organized by the Committees for the Defense of the Revolution (CDRs) and other rural organizations. In the past, villagers, with no way to store any surplus grains, often had no option but to sell them to local merchants (since the state grain marketing agency had the capacity to buy up only about a tenth of the country's crop). The merchants sometimes hoarded cereals to drive up prices, then later resold the grains back to the same villagers at perhaps twice the original cost. But the cereal banks, now managed by farmers groups, allowed villagers to buy back grain when they needed it at only a little more than the initial price (as long as not too much cereal had spoiled in the rudimentary local granaries).

In August 1984 the government enacted a new agrarian reform law, which, among other things, nationalized all land. Previously, most rural land had been owned communally, with the chiefs generally deciding who could farm it. In some areas, however, private land ownership had begun to develop, as urban land speculators sometimes acquired titles, either illegally from village chiefs or from commercial farmers who failed and had to sell their land. For most villagers, the agrarian reform's shift from communal to state ownership would not bring any real change in their relationship to the land; their rights to farm the land remained the same. Yet by ending the risk that farmers could lose land to creditors or speculators, the law aimed to bring farmers greater security of tenure. Sankara emphasized that point at a large rally in the agricultural town of Diébougou the year after the law was adopted. "Improve your land and farm it in peace," he told the residents. "The time is over when people, sitting in their parlors, can buy and resell land on speculation."

The agrarian law also was designed to change how decisions about land were made. In theory, traditional chiefs' powers of land allocation were to be handed over to new commissions run by the village CDRs. That shift could not be put into practice, however. There were very few land-use maps and it was the chiefs who had detailed knowledge about established tenure patterns and rights. Despite the advent of the CDRs, many chiefs still enjoyed considerable authority among ordinary villagers. So when plans for new land management commissions were finally drafted in 1987, they provided for involving local chiefs. However, with the overthrow of the Sankara government later that year, implementation of the new land law ground to a halt.

"Struggle for a Green Burkina"

One other aspect of the agrarian reform, Sankara noted in an October 1985 speech on food security, was to encourage Burkinabè to become more responsible for managing land in a rational way and for preserving the environment more generally. "One cannot imagine the development of agriculture and an increase in its productivity without a program for the regeneration and conservation of nature," he said.

In Africa at the time, the close interrelationship between environmental sustainability and economic development was not yet widely understood by decision makers. Some African leaders were even suspicious of calls for environmental protection, seeing it as a diversion from efforts to industrialize and diversify their economies. The idea that environmental conservation and economic development were complementary gained wider acceptability among African leaders only after they took part in the United Nations' groundbreaking "Earth Summit" in 1992 in Rio de Janeiro, Brazil. In appreciating the importance of the natural environment—"the struggle for a green Burkina," as he put it—Sankara was well ahead of most of his African counterparts.

To many of Sankara's fellow citizens, however, the point was more than obvious. The daily reality of their harsh environment constantly drove the issue home: scarce and fickle rainfall, water holes and rivers that often ran dry, vegetation that became increasingly sparse in the savannah regions, and a sandy, windswept desert that each year seemed to edge farther and farther south from Burkina Faso's northern provinces. Even residents of the capital, Ouagadougou, became acutely aware of the problem one day in March 1985 when the fine red sands of the Sahara Desert blew in on the harmattan winds, blocking the sun, filling the air, and covering everything with a thin coating of grit. "Every one of us understood that the desert is advancing," Sankara remarked a few weeks later, "that the desert is already at our doors."

As early as the 1970s, when Sankara traveled around the country to implement community development and civil engineering projects for the army, he recognized how vital water sources and trees were to ordinary Burkinabè. After becoming president, one of his first acts was to create a Ministry of Water, the first time the country had a ministry devoted exclusively to that essential resource. His government's People's Development Program of

Sankara and a colleague planting a tree seedling. His government was an early proponent of environmental conservation.
Credit: Courtesy Paul Sankara

1984–85 featured many community projects to dig wells and water reservoirs, and included mobilizations to plant more than 10 million trees.

To help raise public awareness and combat the alarming loss of vegetation, Sankara launched a campaign in early 1985 known as the "three struggles." One "struggle" sought to end the unregulated and abusive cutting of trees for firewood, a problem worsened by unlicensed wood merchants who oversaw the wholesale razing of woodlands. Henceforth, Sankara decreed, merchants would have to be licensed to cut only from designated areas and could transport wood only in specially marked vehicles, with violators subject to criminal charges. Another struggle penalized the practice of setting brush fires to clear farmland, an activity that easily escaped control in the dry season. Finally, livestock herders were discouraged from allowing their cattle to wander unsupervised into farming areas where they could trample crops. Sankara warned bluntly that "any grazing animal that destroys a planted tree or cultivated grain will be shot, pure and simple."

The first two aspects of the campaign had only mixed results. While the trade in firewood did undergo some greater regulation, poor villagers continued to cut trees for firewood in the absence of alternative energy sources. And for farmers without heavy tools or equipment, setting brush fires was still often the quickest way to clear land. In face of such prevalent practices, the government and the CDRs simply lacked the capacity to effectively enforce the new prohibitions. Worse, the struggle to halt animals' destruction of trees and crops turned into an unmitigated disaster. Some CDR activists took to extremes Sankara's call to shoot roaming animals. Many were shot, whether they were trampling vegetation or not, and ended up on spits for CDR feasts. A few herders who resisted the practice were also killed, and many fled with their herds, some into neighboring countries. Since farmers and herders often hail from different ethnic groups (many herders are seminomadic Peulh), ethnic tensions also flared. Recognizing that the effort to control wandering livestock was an utter failure, the first national conference of the CDRs in early 1986 decided to abandon it.

According to Alfred Sawadogo, who worked with Sankara to draft the "three struggles" campaign, this experience convinced the president to search for more peaceful, systematic ways to preserve Burkina Faso's environment. The accent shifted from criminalizing harmful practices to involving the population more actively in positive conservation efforts. Speaking at an international conference on trees and forests in Paris in 1986, Sankara emphasized that "our struggle for the trees and the forests is first and foremost a democratic and popular struggle," waged by the people.

Tree-planting initiatives became more pervasive. People were encouraged to plant trees on virtually every family or cultural occasion, from weddings and christenings to the presentation of awards or visits by dignitaries.

Farming families that acquired new tracts of land developed near dams and water reservoirs were each obliged to plant a hundred or more tree seedlings. The traditional village practice of maintaining sacred forests devoted to the ancestors—which fell into disuse with the spread of Christianity and Islam—was partially resurrected under the slogan of "one village, one tree grove." Each community was expected to create a tree nursery to begin reviving protected forest areas in their locale.

State and Market

Reform of the Burkinabè administration was essential not only for enhancing the functioning of the state and its various institutions. Because of the weakness of the country's private sector, the effectiveness of the state was also central for the country's economic development. When Sankara's CNR came to power, it inherited about thirty state-owned enterprises, which included utilities and service agencies as well as firms engaged directly in production, such as gold mining.

These state enterprises, however, were a "poisoned legacy," as the government's *Sidwaya* newspaper put it. They often had very different structures, styles of management, and methods of internal and external control, making it hard for the central authorities to gain a clear picture of their financial position, let alone supervise their functioning. Managers had often given relatives, friends, and political clients jobs in the enterprises, and pilferage and embezzlement became widespread in some of them.

The CNR soon handed over the most grievous cases of outright theft and embezzlement to the People's Revolutionary Tribunals. Many directors and other senior personnel were dismissed for incompetence and negligence, and replaced by others considered more qualified or trustworthy. In 1984 the government decreed a more uniform set of structures, operations, and control mechanisms for all state enterprises. Each was now run on a day-to-day basis by a government-appointed director. Each also had a new administrative council—composed equally of government appointees and representatives of the trade unions and CDRs—that met annually to supervise performance, budgets, investment plans, personnel policies, salary scales, and other matters.

For the first time, the operations of the state enterprises were opened to public scrutiny. In July 1986 and March 1987, public hearings were organized in Ouagadougou's House of the People, at which state enterprise directors, administrative councils, and financial experts had to give an accounting of their performance, financial records, and policies over the previous three years. They did so before large public audiences, as well as some twenty cabinet ministers, sometimes headed by Sankara himself. When state property and interests were at stake, Sankara told the managers, "there can be no sentimentalism." He ordered all directors and senior officers to make full disclosures of their assets. "All personnel must be sensitized to the risks of corruption," he said. "Those who are corrupt and those who corrupt them must be denounced. From now on, failure to expose them will be considered a sign of complicity."

While allowed to operate, private businesses also came under greater scrutiny. They soon found that the era of anything-goes was over. Sankara assured them that they could continue to make money, especially those sectors of "national capital" engaged in direct production. "Private property is a normal thing at this stage of our society. It is normal that it should be protected," he said shortly after taking power. But what could not be accepted, he added, "is private property dishonestly acquired."

Merchants, especially those engaged in hoarding, price-fixing, and various extortionate practices, discovered that the CNR was more energetic than previous regimes in trying to regulate their activities and intervene more directly in market operations. Large businesses had to contend with tax officials demanding that they pay their due share.

However, indigenous producers and entrepreneurs—as against those linked more directly to external capital—gained new opportunities with the CNR's emphasis on building a national economy. Despite the complaints of importers, higher customs duties were imposed to better protect domestic goods from stiff foreign competition.

Under the slogan "Let's produce and consume Burkinabè," the Sankara government also encouraged manufacturers to produce more from local materials and consumers to buy more goods made locally. Bakers were urged to include a small portion of local corn (maize) flour in their bread, rather than just wheat, which was mainly imported. Beverage companies were asked to introduce some sorghum malt in their beer production, and to diversify into bottling mango and other fruit juices. Although modest, such efforts strengthened domestic demand in ways that also gave incentives to farmers to grow more surpluses for commercial sale.

One initiative in particular had multiple economic, social, and political implications—the promotion of dresses, shirts, pants, and other clothing known as Faso dan Fani. In the past, women in traditional villages and in Catholic-run mission stations wove fabrics from local cotton. The practice virtually died out, however, as residents bought more clothes made from imported fabrics and almost all cotton was exported. The CNR acted energetically to revive the manufacture of local clothes. Networks of women weavers were organized in cooperatives to produce Faso dan Fani outfits for both men and women, often in basic blue and white, but also in more elaborate colors and designs. To create a ready market for the clothes, the government obliged all civil servants to wear Faso dan Fani outfits to official ceremonies and events. Some state employees also regularly wore them to work, whether they genuinely liked the outfits or to curry favor with their supervisors, since wearing Faso dan Fani was often portrayed as a patriotic act. Sankara himself frequently wore Faso dan Fani, and he stirred wider interest when he addressed an Organization of African Unity summit in Ethiopia in 1987 in a Faso dan Fani outfit.

For the women who produced the clothes, Faso dan Fani carried more than a political message. It became a major source of revenue, estimated in 1987 at about CFA600 million, or more than US$1 million. That not only gave them additional income but also often enhanced their social status within their families and communities.

7

A Foreign Policy of One's Own

When South African Foreign Minister Pik Botha, one of the most hard-line figures in the apartheid regime, visited Paris in February 1985, Sankara fired off a sharp telegram to his French counterpart. Receiving Botha, he admonished President François Mitterrand, "means strengthening apartheid," adding to the misery of millions of South Africans and delaying the release of Nelson Mandela, the liberation leader imprisoned since 1962. "Receiving Pik Botha is an official way of supporting and legitimizing the most odious crime in the world."

Before the arrival of Sankara's government, such an official protest to the country's former colonial power would have been unthinkable. Upper Volta, like most of France's former colonies in Africa, generally hewed closely to the foreign policy outlook of the authorities in Paris. The French embassy in Ouagadougou was conveniently located right next to the old presidential palace.

Sankara's determination to break from an external policy dictated largely from Paris already had been prefigured in early 1983, during his foreign trips as prime minister in the previous regime, prompting the involvement of French officials in his ouster. After he then became president a few months later, he continued to make bold pronouncements on a wide variety of contentious international topics and more trips to forge new alliances.

True to his frugal ways back home, Sankara ensured that the costs of official travels were kept to a minimum. With no presidential or personal jet at his disposal, he often hitched rides to international meetings with other African heads of state. Now Burkinabè officials traveling abroad were required to fly economy class and stay at the most modest accommodations, including official consular or embassy residences. A staff member of Burkina Faso's UN mission in New York recalled Sankara's 1984 visit there. Mattresses were put on the mission floors for government ministers accompanying him. "There's nothing wrong with that," Sankara told the ministers. "This should bring back to some of you memories from the time you were students." The money saved on hotel bills, he reminded them, would be better used for new wells and schools back home. Such lack of ostentation in Burkinabè officials' travels did not diminish the power of their messages. For some observers, it even enhanced their impact.

From Sankara's numerous declarations on international issues, several themes stand out. First, he sought to establish, in the clearest terms, that Burkina Faso no longer followed direction from Paris—or from

Washington or other Western capitals. Second, as a sovereign nation, Burkina Faso would establish relations with any state it wanted to. Third, in keeping with its revolutionary ideals, the National Council of the Revolution (CNR) would stand in solidarity with oppressed peoples and liberation movements. And finally, it would press for genuine pan-African unity, which Sankara believed could be achieved only through *action* by African governments and peoples, not through an occasional common declaration issued at the close of a summit meeting.

This radically internationalist approach won Burkina Faso new friends in far-flung places and raised its global stature well beyond the country's small size and economic power. It also generated alarm in Western capitals—and among the conservative governments in some of its African neighbors.

Breaking with Tradition

Sankara's face-to-face verbal duel with François Mitterrand in November 1986 (highlighted in chapter 1) was only the most dramatic expression of his government's determination to move away from France's political "sphere of influence." In his October 1984 speech to the United Nations General Assembly, Sankara was implicitly critical of the French military intervention in Chad. He called overtly for the Indian Ocean island of Mayotte, under French control, to be returned to the Comoros, an independent African state. On other occasions, Sankara expressed support for the proindependence Kanak movement that sought an end to French rule over the Pacific territory of New Caledonia.

In November 1984 the Burkinabè minister of trade warned French businesses in the country that the government would no longer maintain "privileged relations" with them, and the finance ministry ordered state banks to briefly suspend financial transfers between those businesses and France. Although Sankara had taken part a year earlier in one of the Franco-African summits that the French government organized periodically with the leaders of its former African colonies, in December 1984 he decided to boycott the next one—and never went to another. A CNR statement explained that the Burkinabè government would participate in international conferences only on the basis of its own economic and political interests. "Our aim is to have the political courage to openly break with an old tradition."

Burkina Faso did attend a February 1986 summit of La Francophonie, a loose cultural grouping of nations that utilize the French language. In a message to the summit read on his behalf by Captain Henri Zongo, Sankara noted that Burkina Faso's use of French was a legacy of its colonial past. Even though only about a tenth of all Burkinabè actually spoke it, the language remained useful for international communication. In his message Sankara observed with some irony that it was through French that he and other Burkinabè revolutionaries learned about the struggle of the Vietnamese people, defended the rights of immigrant workers, read the works of "the great educators of the proletariat," and sung the "Internationale," the song of the world communist movement. If the grouping of Francophone countries was to have any continued relevance, however, it had to acknowledge that there were "two French languages," that spoken within France and "the French language spoken in the five continents." It was a not-so-subtle dig at the efforts of the official Académie Française, supported by the French government, to get French speakers everywhere to conform to the grammar and usage of France itself. Instead, Sankara insisted, the French language—if it was to better serve the democratic ideals of the French revolution of 1789—had to be open to the idioms and concepts of other peoples.

Sankara had traveled to Paris himself a few days before the summit, met François Mitterrand, and signed a series of new cooperation agreements between France and Burkina Faso. On the surface at least, relations between the two countries had eased somewhat, and Sankara's visit to Paris paved the way for Mitterrand to visit Ouagadougou later that year. After Mitterrand's Burkina Faso visit, a journalist asked the French president what new aid France had agreed to provide. He responded, "But President Sankara didn't ask me for anything!"

Earlier, Sankara summarized his government's attitude toward contacts with France: "What is essential is to develop a relationship of equals, mutually beneficial, without paternalism on one side or an inferiority complex on the other."

Sankara's "White House" in Harlem

For the US government, Upper Volta had been a little-known backwater, of no apparent strategic importance to Washington. Although there was a US embassy in Ouagadougou, it mostly oversaw US aid programs and contingents of Peace Corps volunteers. On most political issues, the US authorities seemed content to leave direct involvement to their French counterparts.

According to some accounts, while Sankara was preparing to travel to the United States in 1984 to address the UN General Assembly, the White House asked to see a draft of his planned remarks. The ostensible reason was to consider any possible responses, but it probably was also to determine whether Sankara would be welcome for a White House visit with President Ronald Reagan. Judging the tone of Sankara's draft to be too critical of the major powers, the United States reportedly requested a few alterations. Sankara ignored the request, and no White House invitation was issued. Sankara also was not authorized to stop off in Atlanta, where he had been invited by Mayor Andrew Young, a prominent African American leader.

With his visit limited to New York, Sankara reached out to a different audience. He first spoke publicly before a crowd of more than five hundred African Americans who packed the auditorium of the Harriet Tubman school in Harlem the evening of October 3. It was a relatively short speech that began and ended with a charged litany of call-and-response slogans: "Imperialism," to which the crowd called out, "Down with it!" "Racism," and they shouted, "Down with it!" Sankara's slogan, "Dignity," brought a roar of "To the people!," followed by "Power," and "To the people!" Praising Harlem as a center of Black culture and pride, Sankara asserted that for African revolutionaries, "our White House is in Black Harlem." His words resonated strongly with the audience, especially when he affirmed the connections between the struggles of Africans in Africa and their descendants in the diaspora. Together, he said, they could more strongly fight their common oppressors. When he affirmed that he was "ready for imperialism" and hoisted up his holstered pistol, the audience erupted in laughter and applause. He told them that the next day he would address the United Nations, to speak about injustice, racism, and hypocrisy. "I will tell them that we and you, all of us, are waging our struggles and that they would do well to pay attention."

True to his word, Sankara's speech the following day to the UN General Assembly was hard-hitting and touched on a wide range of global injustices. They spanned the paternalism of Western aid policies and the major powers' armed interventions in poor nations, to the struggle against the apartheid regime in South Africa. Although he was speaking in the United States, he did not mince words when discussing US policies. He said that Burkina Faso stood side by side with the Palestinian struggle "against the armed bands of Israel," a country that for twenty years had defied the international community "with the complicity of its powerful protector, the United States." He condemned the "foreign aggression" against the Caribbean island of Grenada, where the United States had intervened militarily the year before. And he affirmed solidarity with the Sandinista revolutionaries in Nicaragua, "whose harbors are mined, whose villages are bombed," a reference to the "contra" war against Nicaragua supported directly by the Reagan administration.

A Diversity of Relations

As part of its effort to assert greater autonomy from France, Burkina Faso assiduously sought new political, economic, and cultural relations with other countries. Among the traditional donor powers, it signed new aid agreements with the Netherlands, Japan, and Canada. A month after his UN speech, Sankara visited China, which helped build a major sports stadium in Ouagadougou and provided an interest-free loan of $20 million for agricultural development, among other forms of assistance. In 1986 Sankara led a large delegation on a weeklong visit to the Soviet Union, which previously had provided some agricultural equipment, along with other economic assistance. Such Soviet aid did not keep Sankara from publicly criticizing the Soviet military intervention in

Afghanistan, which he did in his UN speech and on other occasions. Nor did Sankara's earlier relations with Libya prevent the Burkinabè government from publicly criticizing the mediocre quality of Libyan assistance.

Sankara exhibited a strong personal affinity for Cuba. After his speech as prime minister at the Non-Aligned summit in New Delhi in March 1983, Cuban president Fidel Castro invited him to his suite one evening to get to know him better, and the two became friendly. Just a few months after the CNR was established, in December 1983, Burkina Faso signed a scientific, economic, and technical cooperation agreement with Cuba. Under it, Cuba sent some two dozen medical personnel to Burkina Faso and provided aid in agriculture, economic planning, stockbreeding, transportation, education, and dam construction. On his way to New York for the UN General Assembly, Sankara first stopped off in Cuba, where he was awarded the Order of José Martí, Cuba's highest honor. In accepting it, Sankara remarked, "Cuba and Burkina Faso are so far and yet so near, so different and yet so similar, that only revolutionaries can understand the sincere love that pushes us irresistibly toward one another." In November 1986 Sankara traveled once again to Cuba, where he met with Castro twice.

From Cuba, Sankara made a short side trip to Nicaragua, returning a visit that Nicaraguan president Daniel Ortega had made to Burkina Faso three months earlier. In Nicaragua, Sankara spoke to a crowd of two hundred thousand on behalf of all foreign delegations attending a celebration of the twenty-fifth anniversary of the ruling Sandinista National Liberation Front, which had overthrown a US-backed dictatorship seven years earlier. As he did in his UN speech, Sankara expressed solidarity with Nicaragua in face of the US-supported "contra" war.

The CNR's decision to establish new ties with a range of governments that were generally at odds with Paris and Washington stirred some critical reactions from those powers. "People accuse us of being the pawn of Libya, Cuba, the USSR, and Algeria," Sankara noted. He denied that accusation, and dismissed the notion that the CNR was copying those political models. "The Burkinabè revolution is not an imported revolution."

Challenging African Leaders

Sankara was a strong champion of pan-African unity and the principles of the then Organization of African Unity (OAU, now the African Union). Yet he held no illusions about the willingness or ability of most African leaders to take concerted action in defense of the continent's common interests. At annual summit meetings of the OAU and in his frequent trips in Africa, he often prodded and cajoled his peers to match their conference speeches with concrete deeds.

The struggle for freedom in South Africa and Namibia was the issue on which he was most persistent. The seeming intractability of the apartheid regime—despite international sanctions and near-universal condemnation within Africa—was an affront to all Africans, Sankara believed. As long as the basic rights of the majority of South Africans and Namibians were denied, Africa as a whole could not achieve true unity or advance economically and politically.

One of the earliest acts of Sankara's CNR was to rename a central thoroughfare in the capital Nelson Mandela Avenue. The government symbolically issued Mandela a Burkinabè passport, in effect claiming him as a citizen. Of more practical effect, South African goods were barred from sale in Burkina Faso. Local activists mounted a campaign against Shell Oil, one of the country's main oil suppliers, as part of an international boycott of the company for its dealings in South Africa, and the Sankara government responded by exploring arrangements with alternative suppliers. Encouraged by frequent Burkinabè media accounts of the horrors of apartheid and the struggles of the African National Congress (ANC) in South Africa and the South West Africa People's Organization (SWAPO) in Namibia, a number of local antiapartheid committees emerged, based largely at the university and secondary schools.

In many of his speeches on international issues, Sankara cited the importance of the Southern African freedom struggles and the need to make sanctions against the apartheid regime more effective. At an OAU summit in 1986 he publicly offered ten rifles to ANC and SWAPO fighters. As some African leaders started to chuckle, Sankara continued, "Ten rifles represent something really big to a poor country like Burkina Faso." He then challenged the other OAU leaders: "If every one of the fifty OAU states did the same, it would mean that 500 African National Congress or South West Africa People's Organization soldiers would be armed."

Though couched in military terms, Sankara's real point was political. If African countries actually took some action—rather than limit themselves to flowery speeches and impassioned denunciations—then the movement in solidarity with the Southern African freedom struggles might make more headway. That was the main theme of a pan-African antiapartheid conference held in Ouagadougou October 8–11, 1987 (just a few days before the coup). The Bambata Forum—named after an early South African rebel—had the government's blessing, but was mainly organized and financed by local activist groups. Most of the deliberations focused on how people in various African countries could mobilize support for the ANC and SWAPO without necessarily relying on their governments to take action.

Another struggle within Africa that Sankara championed was that of the independence movement in Western Sahara. It was originally a colony of Spain, which relinquished control in 1975 to Morocco and Mauritania; a few years later Mauritania withdrew, and Morocco occupied the remaining territory as well. That occupation, however,

Sankara at a pan-African antiapartheid conference in Ouagadougou just a few days before his death. Supporting the liberation movements in Southern Africa was a keystone of his foreign policy. *Credit: Ernest Harsch*

encountered the resistance of a movement known as the Polisario Front, which proclaimed its own state, the Sahrawi Arab Democratic Republic (SADR). The Burkinabè government officially recognized the SADR, and at the end of March 1984 Sankara became the first head of state to visit areas of Western Sahara under the control of the Polisario Front. He then pushed strongly within the OAU for wider recognition of the SADR. Before the year was out, the OAU did officially admit the Sahrawi republic, prompting Morocco's withdrawal from the organization and irritating France, which generally supported Morocco's claim to the territory.

At the time, one of the most burning economic issues confronting Africa was the continent's enormous foreign debt, some $200 billion in 1986. The annual payments on those debts, generally owed to Western donor agencies, banks, and financial institutions, consumed about 40 percent of African countries' export earnings, on average. That left little for essential imports and basic services, let alone development. Individual African countries, and since 1984 the OAU itself, pleaded with creditors for some relief. But only small portions of Africa's debts were forgiven, with creditors usually agreeing only to postpone payments somewhat. In exchange for even that, they insisted on strict domestic austerity measures, which in some countries led to serious rioting and political instability.

Believing that African leaders' entreaties to Western creditors were too timid, Sankara made a bold proposal at a July 1987 summit of the OAU: that Africa, collectively, simply refuse to pay. He cited two arguments. First, African countries just did not have the money to keep up repayments without plunging their economies and peoples into even deeper crises. "We cannot repay the debt because we have nothing to pay it with." Second, many African countries originally took the loans, at steep interest rates, on the advice of Western financial experts, who ultimately bore responsibility for the mushrooming of the debt. "Those who led us into debt were gambling, as if they were in a casino. As long as they were winning, there was no problem. Now that they're losing their bets, they demand repayment." Individually, African countries would be too weak to refuse to pay, Sankara pointed out. So he proposed that African leaders stand together and create a "united front" against the debt. The OAU never followed Sankara's advice, although at the end of that year it did adopt a common position on the debt proposing a "constructive dialogue" to reduce Africa's debt payments to "reasonable and bearable" levels.

Ripples in the Neighborhood

Of all countries in its immediate region, the Sankara government enjoyed the closest relations with Ghana. Those dated back to when Sankara was prime minister in early 1983. The year before, radical junior military officers, led by Flight Lieutenant Jerry John Rawlings, allied with civilian leftist groups and seized power in Ghana, proclaiming

Sankara with President Jerry Rawlings of Ghana. Among West African leaders, the two were especially close political allies. *Credit: Service de la presse présidentielle/Bara*

their own revolutionary and anti-imperialist intentions. Prime Minister Sankara commented at a mass rally in Ouagadougou in March 1983: "When Rawlings says, 'No way for kalabule!'—that is, stop the corruption—he says this in the interests of the Ghanaian people. But in fact it is in the interests of all peoples, because the Voltaic people too are against corruption." After Sankara was ousted as prime minister and his supporters established a base of resistance in Pô, they made clandestine contacts with the Rawlings government in Ghana, whose border was only 20 kilometers south of Pô.

Just a little more than a month after the radicals took power in Ouagadougou, Rawlings himself traveled to Pô to meet with Sankara. In February 1984 he returned for a large welcoming rally in Ouagadougou. On that occasion, Sankara publicly revealed that Rawlings had "dared to support us with all his military, political, and diplomatic strength" during the period leading up to the CNR's triumph. By that point, Burkinabè and Ghanaian military forces had already organized a series of joint military maneuvers, codenamed Bold Union, to dramatically signal their mutual solidarity. They organized a second, longer set of joint maneuvers in 1985. According to Sankara, the affinity was based on a common "spirit of liberty and dignity, of counting on one's own resources, of independence, and of consistent anti-imperialist struggle."

Of Burkina Faso's other immediate neighbors, relations with Benin, which was headed by a left-leaning government that had its own conflicts with France, were moderately warm, while those with Niger were usually relatively cordial. However, political contacts with the three other countries with which Burkina Faso shared a common border—Togo, Mali, and Côte d'Ivoire—were generally tense. All were politically close to France, gave sanctuary to Burkinabè opponents of the Sankara government, and were worried about the potential for revolutionary contagion. When they experienced domestic opposition, they often pointed a finger of blame at Ouagadougou, as the Togolese government did after a failed coup attempt in 1986.

Some analysts saw the Malian government's decision to provoke the brief December 1985 border war with

Burkina Faso as motivated, at least in part, by a fear that Sankara's popularity among some sectors within Mali could lead to overt challenges. Sankara may have stoked that concern to some extent. In a September 1985 speech to a mass rally in Ouagadougou in which he took up various threats against the CNR from the region's more conservative governments, Sankara pointedly stated, "The revolution of the Burkinabè people is at the disposal of the people of Mali, who need it. . . . Only revolution will allow them to free themselves."

The government of neighboring Côte d'Ivoire was similarly nervous about developments next door—an anxiety heightened by the fact that up to 2 million Burkinabè lived and worked there. President Félix Houphouët-Boigny, who had governed that country since independence in 1960, was one of France's closet allies in Africa. In November 1984 Côte d'Ivoire hosted its largest-ever joint military exercises with France, involving two thousand French and three thousand Ivorian troops and assorted jet fighters and helicopter gun ships. It was not necessary to make any overt threats against the CNR. The message of the exercises was clear: they were held by the Comoé River, along the border between Côte d'Ivoire and Burkina Faso.

Given Côte d'Ivoire's economic and political weight in the region and the presence of large numbers of Burkinabè citizens in that country, the Sankara government was careful in its dealings with President Houphouët-Boigny. It was not easy. A first planned visit by Sankara to Côte d'Ivoire in May 1984 was cancelled when the Ivorian government refused to let Sankara visit Abidjan, the largest city, apparently out of concern over the welcome he might receive from its inhabitants. A visit was finally organized the following February, not in Abidjan, but in the political capital, Yamoussoukro, a much smaller town. Some eighteen hours before Sankara's arrival, a bomb exploded in the hotel suite where he was supposed to stay. But the visit went ahead anyway, and Sankara met with Houphouët-Boigny. Though it was not Abidjan, thousands of Ivorians and Burkinabè nevertheless turned out to greet Sankara.

On the surface at least, relations between the two governments remained proper. In 1986, Houphouët-Boigny visited Ouagadougou and was given a cordial welcome. As he had done in several other countries in West Africa, the Ivorian president also put out feelers to potential political allies within Burkina Faso. He scored a notable advance in this when in June 1985 Chantal Terrasson de Fougères, who was raised in Houphouët-Boigny's household as an adopted daughter, married the Burkinabè minister of defense—Captain Blaise Compaoré.

8

The Last Battles

The day of the coup that ended Sankara's life, October 15, 1987, I was in the small village of Pibaoré, a hundred or so kilometers northeast of Ouagadougou. Like others in rural Burkina Faso, the residents of Pibaoré could point to tangible changes: a recently formed peasants' union, a brick schoolhouse, a cereal bank for surplus grain, literacy classes, several thousand newly planted trees, a water reservoir, and improved harvests of millet and sorghum. They had rallied in Pibaoré's central square to celebrate those achievements. A few younger participants wore T-shirts bearing Sankara's image. As elsewhere, the inhabitants of Pibaoré identified the revolution with their president. "He doesn't just make promises, like the old politicians," one commented. "He gets things done." A moment's thought, and then he added, "He's shown us that we can get things done."

After the rally ended, some youths listening to Radio Ouagadougou started to hear military music rather than the normal programming. They were puzzled. Then sometime between 5 and 6 p.m. came a stunning announcement: "patriotic forces" in Ouagadougou had brought an end to "the autocratic power of Thomas Sankara." The day's celebratory mood first turned to disbelief, then to grief and sadness.

The next morning, back in Ouagadougou, I learned what everyone there already knew: Sankara had been not only overthrown, but also killed. The radio broadcast very little hard information—not even an official announcement of Sankara's death. It reported only that the National Council of the Revolution (CNR), government, and a few other institutions had been dissolved and replaced by a mysterious "Popular Front," headed by a new president, Captain Blaise Compaoré. The airwaves were also filled with invective. Sankara was vilified as a "traitor" to the revolution, a "petty-bourgeois" who "consorted with bourgeois potentates" and was guided by "mystic forces," a "messianic" who ran a "one-man show," a "fascist," even a "paranoiac misogynist."

Few people I spoke with in Ouagadougou believed the accusations. Many found them quite distasteful. They were also disgusted when they learned that Sankara and twelve comrades slain with him had been buried unceremoniously, with no grave markers, in Dagnoën cemetery, on the edge of one of the capital's poorer neighborhoods. As news of the location spread by word of mouth, first small groups and then hundreds trekked by foot to the cemetery to lay flowers on the grave mounds and to weep.

Captain Blaise Compaoré (*left*), who seized the presidency after Sankara's assassination, with Commander Jean-Baptiste Lingani and Captain Henri Zongo a year after the coup. Lingani and Zongo were summarily executed in 1989.
Credit: Ernest Harsch

How did this stunning turn of events happen? How could one of Sankara's closest comrades—and personal friends—carry out such a bloody coup? For some months, there had been rumors of divergences within the revolutionary leadership but few clear explanations of what the differences entailed. I last spoke with Sankara four days before his death, and he gave no hint of serious problems. One of his aides—Frédéric Kiemdé, who was to die in the same fusillade—did confide that there were disagreements over issues of political organization and the use of repression against government critics. Yet no one seemed to expect such a dramatic outcome. Only in retrospect was it possible to piece together a plausible explanation of some of the factors that contributed to the assassination and coup.

From Outside and Within

Sankara's revolutionary project obviously had external enemies, and a number of analysts pointed to the likelihood of foreign involvement in the 1987 coup. France stood at the top of the list of suspects, a natural assumption given its previous part in the ouster of Sankara as prime minister in early 1983. So far, no solid evidence has emerged indicating a direct French role in the 1987 coup, although Jacques Foccart, a key French intelligence figure with extensive networks of influence throughout Africa, was known to be hostile to Sankara and may well have encouraged regional allies to make a move. The governments of Togo and Mali were closely allied with France and openly supported Burkinabè opponents of Sankara's CNR. But it was the regime in Côte d'Ivoire that was best positioned to foment a coup from within, especially with President Houphouët-Boigny's growing ties with Compaoré. Some also suspected that Libya's Qaddafi may have been implicated, since his relations with Sankara had become somewhat strained and his post-coup ties with Compaoré were markedly warm. Two Liberian warlords (Prince Johnson and John Tarnue) later stated publicly that they had been asked to help Compaoré oust Sankara, although details of their accounts were contradictory.

Whatever the nature or extent of foreign involvement in the coup, the most compelling—and troubling—evidence pointed to domestic forces. Not only were the immediate perpetrators Burkinabè, but they came from among Sankara's collaborators in the CNR, government, and military command.

Historically, revolutions and revolutionary efforts worldwide have often been beset by internal differences and conflicts. Frequently even minor divergences have widened under the pressures of domestic opposition and a hostile external environment. As an avid student of revolutions, Sankara was quite conscious of such dangers. He was also well aware that over time revolutionary leaderships may abandon their original ideals; lose touch with their people; become more hardened, inward-looking, and repressive; and succumb to corruption and self-interest. In a number of public statements, especially during the last two years of his life, Sankara seemed particularly concerned that such a fate could be in store for Burkina Faso. He urged diligence and corrective measures "to prevent the revolution from turning in on itself, to prevent the revolution from ossifying, to prevent the revolution from shriveling up like a dried fig."

Between Coercion and Persuasion

In trying to advance the revolutionary process, Sankara had not hesitated to use repressive means when that seemed necessary. He favored firm action against those who directly opposed the government or who engaged in activities considered threatening to political stability. The dangers were not imagined. In 1984 Colonel Didier Tiendrébéogo, several other officers, and some civilian collaborators were caught plotting a coup; a military court acquitted more than a dozen, but ordered the execution of the leaders. In 1985 saboteurs blew up army ammunition depots in Ouagadougou and Bobo-Dioulasso, taking several lives. An army captain suspected of those attacks fled the country and was later detected by Burkinabè intelligence among the Malian forces that attacked Burkina Faso that December.

As the CNR gradually consolidated its position and overt security challenges were contained, Sankara shifted focus. He increasingly found himself trying to discipline those within the military, police, state bureaucracy, and Committees for the Defense of the Revolution (CDRs) who used their repressive powers arbitrarily, against potential allies or even ordinary citizens. Sankara drew a distinction: "While the revolution means repression of the exploiters, of our enemies, it must mean only persuasion for the masses—persuasion to take on a conscious and determined commitment."

Initially, some of the greatest problems came from a layer of activists in the CDRs. Some went to extremes against perceived enemies, ordering beatings and arbitrary arrests. In 1984 the offices of the only private newspaper, *L'Observateur*, were burned down, many suspected by zealous militants. Abusing their positions as representatives of the CNR, some CDR members wielded authority not in defense of the revolution but to lord it over others, get back at personal enemies, and engage in extortion. Some embezzled funds or broke into people's homes. Among the armed members of the CDRs' vigilance brigades, a few used their weapons for shakedowns and armed robberies. Such activities alienated people from the CDRs and stained the image of the government and CNR. Years later, many Burkinabè remembered the misdeeds of the CDRs even more than the successes of their popular mobilizations.

As early as a month after coming to power, Sankara recognized the potential danger of the CDRs' repressive powers, acknowledging "a risk of seeing them degenerate." By late 1985, a few of the most extreme cases of "gangster CDRs" were brought to trial before the People's Revolutionary Tribunals. Then early the next year many frank self-criticisms were aired at the first national conference of CDRs. Sankara, in the closing address, was especially scathing. Some CDR leaders, he said, had "set themselves up as veritable despots in the local districts, in the villages, and in the provinces. . . . [r]eigning and holding sway like warlords." Sankara admonished them: "The CDR office must not be a locale of torturers but the complete opposite: an office where you find people who lead, who organize, who mobilize, who educate, and who struggle as revolutionaries."

Subsequently, many CDRs were reorganized and undisciplined leaders purged. The security functions of the CDRs were downgraded, with fewer armed patrols and other operations by their vigilance brigades. However, the absence of alternative mechanisms of expression outside the CDRs made it hard to keep them in check.

The CDRs were not the only institutions that leaned toward coercion when faced with dissidence. The government and CNR also reacted with a heavy hand, at least initially with Sankara's apparent approval. The repression started with the detention of leaders of the old elite political parties but eventually extended to some of those originally seen as revolutionary allies.

Relations with the trade unions, especially those in the public sector, soured over the dismissal of state employees. Some were let go because of incompetence but others because they were suspected of political disloyalty, sometimes for little more than past party affiliations. Most dramatically, a serious conflict developed between the CNR and the main primary school teachers union, led by supporters of Joseph Ki-Zerbo, an internationally known historian, then living in exile in Senegal, who had been close to the previous military regime of Colonel Saye Zerbo. In March 1984 the authorities ordered the arrest of several of the teachers' leaders. That prompted a three-day protest strike, to which the Ministry of Education responded by dismissing some 1,300 teachers. Many Burkinabè were shocked by the severity of the reaction.

That same year, political differences within the CNR and government led to the ejection of supporters of the African Independence Party (PAI). One of the group's best-known leaders, Soumane Touré, also led a major labor federation, so the rift further strained relations with the unions. Over the next three years, Touré and other unionists were repeatedly detained. Matters came to a head in May 1987 when members of a CDR in Ouagadougou again arrested Touré, along with several others. Accusing them of planning antigovernment protests, the CDR publicly called for their execution, an especially provocative act since Sankara and Touré were known to be personal friends. Kiemdé, Sankara's aide, told me that Sankara opposed the detentions as damaging to the revolution. He quietly pressed for their release, and several of the lesser-known detainees were freed. Within the CNR Sankara also fought to block the executions—which were favored by all but one of the political groups in the council. The loudest calls for execution came from the Union of Burkinabè Communists, which was close to Blaise Compaoré. According to Valère Somé, who sided with the president, Sankara's intervention in the CNR "was decisive in saving Soumane Touré's life." Sankara later told a group of journalists that because of his stance, "There's now a campaign against me. I'm accused of being a sentimentalist."

Sankara's position on Touré's case was motivated not just by friendship. It reflected a broader shift during 1986 and 1987 to try to ease up on coercion and reduce social tensions. A number of the imprisoned officials of previous governments were let go, and several hundred of the dismissed teachers were rehired. Two months before the coup, Sankara urged the reintegration of more teachers and instructed all cabinet ministers to find ways to reinstate civil servants who had been fired for political reasons. Sankara also announced a "pause" in efforts to carry out various projects, an apparent acknowledgment of the signs of fatigue exhibited by sectors of the population over the frenetic pace of the CNR's social mobilizations.

Repeatedly, Sankara tried to persuade his comrades that the revolution could advance only if people were won over to its goals, of their own free will, not through compulsion. The revolution, he said, "needs a convinced people, not a conquered people—a convinced people, not a submissive people passively enduring their fate." The aim should be to win over everyone. "We are eight million Burkinabè; our goal is to create eight million revolutionaries." Failing to rely on persuasion, he said just before the coup, would inevitably lead to yet more repression: "A conquered people means an endless series of prisons.... For revolutionaries, victory lies in the disappearance of prisons. For reactionaries, victory lies in the construction of a maximum number of prisons. That's the difference between them and us."

"Rich with a Thousand Nuances"

Sankara's views on coercion related closely to his thinking on the kind of political organization that could best move the revolutionary process forward. Many of his colleagues focused on how to best unify the disparate leftist groups that supported the CNR—and usually maneuvered to try to position their own organization in the lead. Sankara, however, regarded the existing groups as too narrow and self-absorbed. He repeatedly emphasized opening up to broader sectors of the population, starting with the many activists not affiliated with the established political groups.

When the CNR came to power in August 1983, there were two civilian organizations allied with Sankara's radical military current: the PAI, which operated publicly as the League for Patriotic Development (Lipad); and the Union of Communist Struggle-Reconstructed (ULCR), led by Valère Somé. The ULCR's support did not extend much beyond students, professors, and other professionals. The PAI/Lipad had a notable base in the unions. Sankara and most of the other officers in the CNR constituted themselves as the Revolutionary Military Organization (OMR). Following the expulsion of the PAI/Lipad from the CNR and government in 1984, three other groups emerged and joined the CNR: the Union of Communist Struggle (ULC), the Burkinabè Communist Group (GCB), and the Union of Burkinabè Communist (UCB). All were very small, with roots mainly in the student movement and among academics and media personnel. The UCB also had support from sectors of the officer corps, leading some of its rivals to label it "militarist." Most of these groups' leaders were ideological disciples of Stalin,

Mao, or Enver Hoxha (of Albania), reflecting their dogmatic, intolerant views.

In 1986, all the political formations in the CNR signed an agreement to dissolve themselves as separate groups and merge into a united political party. But the negotiations were bogged down by ideological differences, personal rivalries, sectarianism, and divisive factional maneuvers, including by Compaoré and other officers. Sankara was in favor of exploring renewed ties with the PAI/Lipad, but any overtures were cut short by the May 1987 arrest of Soumane Touré, seemingly at the UCB's instigation. The ULCR, which often sided with Sankara, also found itself under attack by the UCB and the other groups, with some of its activists at the University of Ouagadougou even detained by soldiers.

Sankara tried to mediate among the factions, largely in vain. He also tried to get them to look beyond their own organizational identities, to keep in mind the real issue that concerned most Burkinabè: bettering their daily lives. He made it clear that he favored unification of the various revolutionary currents, but not through a narrow, mechanical merger of the established groups. "Our democratic and popular revolution sets itself aside from all sects and sectarian groupings," he said. To think that "only a certain nucleus, only a certain group, is worth anything" would end up isolating the leadership. Sankara warned that creating a political vanguard through a simple amalgamation of existing organizations could lead to a "nomenklatura of untouchable dignitaries," using the Russian word for a Soviet-style list of state positions reserved solely for party appointees.

Above all, Sankara insisted, a revolutionary organization should be open to many viewpoints. It was necessary to "guard against making unity into a dry, paralyzing, sterilizing, monochromatic thing. On the contrary, we would rather see a manifold, varied, and enriching expression of many different ideas and diverse activities, ideas and activities that are rich with a thousand nuances."

Fighting the "Gangrene of Corruption"

Besides pressing on issues of coercion and organization, Sankara also sought to reinvigorate the battle against corruption. In his government's early years that struggle concentrated mainly on politicians and functionaries from the previous administrations, through the trials before the People's Revolutionary Tribunals (TPRs). Now the emphasis was to be on *current* officeholders. Sankara was concerned about corruption not just among ordinary civil servants or CDR activists, but most especially among members of his own leadership team. Just a few days before the coup, Sankara told a group of journalists that "today there are people in power who live better lives than the population, who engage in small-scale trade with Syrian-Lebanese merchants, who find positions for their families, their younger cousins, all the while speaking in very revolutionary language."

According to Fidèle Toé, who was minister of labor at the time, one of Sankara's last acts was to propose a "revolutionary code of conduct." He first introduced the idea at a council of ministers meeting chaired by Compaoré on October 7, 1987, and then led a discussion of the topic at an October 14 council meeting (chaired by Sankara and in Compaoré's absence). The broad outlines of such a code, Toé later recounted, were to ensure that all leadership cadres had the endurance and intellectual capacity to fulfill their responsibilities and conducted themselves with honesty, integrity, and "revolutionary morality."

The most important measure to try to ensure such morality had come earlier that year. In February Sankara established the People's Commission for the Prevention of Corruption (CPPC). Its main purpose was to collect and investigate information on the incomes and assets of all high officials to see whether they were living beyond their means. Any anomalies were to be passed on to the police for further investigation, and if there was evidence of a possible crime, the perpetrator would be charged before a TPR. The CPPC's function, said a CNR declaration, was to help "preserve our society and our revolution from the gangrene of corruption, a weapon used by imperialism and the bourgeoisie to lead astray revolutions from within."

Sankara was the first to appear before the CPPC. According to his declaration of assets, he owned one house, on which he was still paying a mortgage, two undeveloped plots of land, an automobile, several bicycles, a refrigerator, kitchen appliances, and several guitars. His monthly salary was CFA136,736 (equivalent to US$462 at the time), while his wife's was CFA192,690. Their combined bank accounts totaled just CFA532,127. He also reported that foreign leaders had given him gifts while traveling abroad, including four cars and more than CFA850 million in cash, all of which as a matter of policy he had handed over to the state treasury.

After his declaration, Sankara noted in an interview with a Burkinabè newspaper that while the earlier efforts to punish corruption through the TPRs were extremely important, those accomplishments remained "very fragile." He continued: "Every day we are tempted by corruption. People come and offer us opportunities. They often come in the guise of caring. They promise you this or that. They even try to convince you that it's in the interests of the country that they come to praise you and offer you a gift. We are tempted to take it." He hoped that mechanisms such as the CPPC would help his comrades avoid being corrupted, knowing that some day they might have to give an accounting.

Publicly, Sankara denied that he had any specific comrades in mind. But some of his colleagues later recalled that he sometimes expressed concern about the influence of Chantal Terrasson de Fougères, Compaoré's wife, who made little secret of her taste for luxuries. Compaoré himself was "not very enthusiastic about the struggle against corruption," Ernest Nongma Ouédraogo, who was then interior minister, later explained to me. After declaring his own assets, according to Ouédraogo, Compaoré was subsequently "reproached for having hidden certain properties of his wife, such as a massive gold clock given to her by President Houphouët-Boigny" of Côte d'Ivoire.

It would be unfair to pin too much blame on Compaoré's wife. He was known to be politically ambitious. As early as August 1983, just before the advent of the CNR, Compaoré reportedly told one of Sankara's security aides that he, Compaoré, would be president and Sankara prime minister. Once Sankara and the other leaders learned of that position, they collectively "clarified" who among them would be the best face of the new government. Frustrated at the outset, Compaoré may have viewed his marriage to someone from Houphouët-Boigny's family as a step toward a beneficial future alliance.

Revenge of the Elites

Whatever the weight of individual ambition or corruption in the developments that led to Sankara's death, it is likely that the coup plotters also counted on support (tacit or otherwise) from wider segments of disgruntled social layers. All those who lost some of their powers and privileges as a result of Sankara's revolutionary venture—the social elites, land speculators, big merchants, traditional chiefs—had good reason to see him go. In the months leading to the coup, anonymous leaflets circulated in Ouagadougou and other cities calling on Mossi to unite against the government of the "stranger," an implicit rallying cry in favor of Compaoré, a Mossi, and against a non-Mossi president who had sought to curtail the authority of the predominantly Mossi traditional chiefs.

Within the state bureaucracy itself, there were many senior civil servants, public functionaries, and military officers who did not see why they should have to make sacrifices to free up funds for rural development. They resented the trimming of their bonuses and resisted efforts to reassign them to provincial towns, far from the capital's relative comforts. The CNR's stern anticorruption measures stymied their aspirations for self-enrichment.

Sankara recognized the risks of challenging this layer. In a 1985 interview, he told me: "The revolution in Africa faces a big danger, since it is initiated every time by the petty bourgeoisie. The petty bourgeoisie is generally made up of intellectuals. At the beginning of the revolution the big bourgeoisie is attacked. That's easy. . . . But after one, two, or three years, it's necessary to take on the petty bourgeoisie. And when we take on the petty bourgeoisie, we take on the very leadership of the revolution. . . . To take on the petty bourgeoisie means keeping the revolution radical, and there you will face many difficulties. Or you can go easy on the petty bourgeoisie. You won't have any difficulties. But then it won't be a revolution either—it will be a pseudorevolution."

"It's Me They Want"

On the morning of Thursday, October 15, 1987, Sankara met for several hours with Valère Somé at the presidential residence to discuss various matters. The most pressing among them, according to Somé, concerned the ongoing strains between Sankara and Compaoré and among the various political currents within the leadership. Also that morning, Sankara drafted a speech to a meeting of the Revolutionary Military Organization to be held that evening. In it he proposed a "purification" of the CNR and implementation of the code of conduct, among other measures, so as to dispel the "distrust and suspicion" that were infecting the revolution's supporters and lessen the "factionalism" among its leaders. But it was a speech he would never get to deliver.

That afternoon, Sankara had a scheduled meeting with his small team of advisers. They gathered about 4:15 p.m. at the old Conseil de l'Entente headquarters, which for some time had served as an office of the CNR. The meeting was under way for only a brief time when shooting erupted in the small courtyard outside, around 4:30 p.m. or shortly after. Sankara's driver and two of his bodyguards were the first to be killed. Upon hearing the gunfire, everyone in the meeting room quickly took cover. Sankara then got up and told his aides to stay inside for their own safety. "It's me they want." He left the room, hands raised, to face the assailants. He was shot several times, and died without saying anything more. If his exit from the room was intended to save his comrades inside, it failed. The gunmen, all in military uniform, entered the meeting room and sprayed it with automatic weapons fire. Everyone inside was killed, except for Alouna Traoré,

Villagers rallying in Pibaoré in support of the Sankara government, shortly before Sankara's assassination later that day. *Credit: Ernest Harsch*

who survived his wounds and later gave the only eyewitness account of the attack.

Compaoré denied that he had issued orders for Sankara's assassination, and claimed to have been at home in bed ill at the time of the killing. Many found it hard to believe that his men would have acted on their own. And they *were* Compaoré's men. The killers included Sergeant Hyacinthe Kafando, Compaoré's aide de camp. He and the other known assailants all served directly under Captain Gilbert Diendéré, then the commander of the Pô commando base and soon to become head of Compaoré's military security force.

Because of their actions, Compaoré was no longer just the number two. By that evening, he was the new president.

9

"Is It Possible to Forget You?"

Some months before the October 1987 coup, a colleague of mine presented to Sankara my proposal for a book of speeches, interviews, and other documents from the revolutionary process in Burkina Faso. Sankara liked the overall idea. But he objected that the proposal focused too much on him. "The story of our revolution needs to be told, so that the world can know what we are trying to achieve," he told my colleague. "But I am not this revolution, and cannot be the only one to carry this revolution. If this is the case, then we don't have a revolution."

Reflecting on those comments in the aftermath of Sankara's death—and the evident collapse of much of the popular initiative that had given momentum to the changes he tried to carry out—it seemed that Sankara had been too optimistic. He was correct in one sense: it was not just about him. Many tens of thousands of Burkinabè found inspiration in the revolutionary venture, and gained some confidence that the leadership was serious about bringing fundamental improvements. Yet ultimately, that leadership proved to be quite thin.

Among the top leaders, few other than Sankara demonstrated a clear ability to inspire popular support. Only Valère Somé and several others belonging to the ULCR and OMR openly stood with him in the contentious debates that divided the CNR. If the issues in dispute had been pursued solely through political discussion—and taken before the public—it is possible Sankara might yet have prevailed. But his most determined opponents worked in the shadows, through conspiratorial means, not in the arena of contending political ideas. Within the military itself, the plotters managed to take those officers and men who were loyal to Sankara off guard, and arrested many. A garrison in Koudougou led by Captain Boukary Kaboré refused to recognize Compaoré's new Popular Front government, but its defiance was suppressed by force, with the loss of many lives and Kaboré's flight to neighboring Ghana.

This is not the book to recount what happened in the wake of the coup or to analyze the nature of the new regime and its policies. It is enough to note that Compaoré's initial claim that he was trying to "rectify" the revolution and set it back on track soon proved hollow. From the outset the new authorities enjoyed very little popular support. Beyond the tiny political groups that participated in the coup, they relied mainly on backing from the social elites, bureaucrats, merchants, traditional chiefs, and leaders of the old parties of the 1960s and 1970s. Within a few years, even the paper-thin veneer of revolutionary rhetoric was peeled away. Politics increasingly revolved around material favors, corruption, and outright repression. Various human rights groups catalogued the detention or killing of scores of political dissidents, student activists, journalists, and ordinary citizens over the years. Norbert Zongo, the country's leading investigative journalist, was assassinated with three colleagues in 1998, apparently by members of the elite presidential guard. The majority of Burkinabè remained mired in poverty. In 2012, according to the United Nations, the level of "human development" in Burkina Faso was the fifth lowest in the world.

Meanwhile, in the wake of the coup, relations with Burkina Faso's more conservative neighbors, especially the governments of Côte d'Ivoire and Togo, grew close. Ties with France improved markedly. The French authorities not only regularly welcomed Compaoré to Paris but even awarded their National Order of the Legion of Honor to Colonel (later General) Gilbert Diendéré, the officer who commanded Sankara's executioners.

So what was left of Sankara's revolution? The most obvious answer is: the memory of the man, and the ideas he so passionately defended.

Thousands of Burkinabè expressed their deep emotional attachment to Sankara in the days immediately after his death. They walked to the Dagnoën cemetery to pay their respects at his graveside. Some laid flowers and wept. Others left handwritten messages: "Long live the president of the poor." "The jealous, power-hungry, and traitors murdered you." "Mama Sankara, your son will be avenged. We are all Sankara." "Is it possible to forget you?" "A hero never dies."

In the first few years after the coup, it was very risky for any Burkinabè to publicly proclaim their admiration for the late president. Many who had worked closely with Sankara or refused to support the new regime were detained, beaten, or driven into exile. Commander Jean-Baptiste Lingani and Captain Henri Zongo, the two other surviving "historic" military leaders of the CNR's seizure of power, were summarily executed in 1989. Although they had not backed Sankara two years earlier, neither were they active in Compaoré's coup; they thus were suspect.

By the start of the 1990s, domestic opposition built up and spilled into the streets with calls for greater freedom. That opposition, combined with pressure from donors, obliged the government to grudgingly allow multiparty elections. Compaoré's party—with direct access to state resources, financing from business, and some fraud—easily dominated the elections. But the slightly greater openness of the political system also made it possible for new parties to arise. A dozen or more groups identifying themselves as "Sankarist" eventually organized and won legal recognition. Some fielded candidates in elections, often citing Sankara's example and his ideas to attract votes. The various Sankarist parties consistently won a notable minority of the electorate, rising from more than

100,000 votes in 2002 to nearly twice that in 2012. Despite their disunity, these Sankarists managed to elect a handful of deputies to parliament and to stand out as a distinct voice among a plethora of opposition forces.

Attitudes in favor of Sankara extended far beyond the electoral arena—kept alive by widespread dissatisfaction with political and social conditions in the country. Young people, artists, musicians, and activists often recalled his ideas, and during times of crisis in particular protesters often held up his portrait or shouted slogans from Sankara's revolutionary era.

As early as 1991, the strength of this pro-Sankara sentiment obliged the government to officially acknowledge him as a "national hero." Yet it continued to refuse calls for a judicial inquiry into his death. Then in the wake of a prolonged series of antigovernment protests and strikes in 1998–99, after Norbert Zongo's assassination, the authorities tried to appease critics by agreeing to a series of political reforms and promising to build a monument to Sankara and the three other official national heroes (Ouezzin Coulibaly, Philippe Zinda Kaboré, and Nazi Boni). That Monument to the National Heroes was finally inaugurated in Ouagadougou in December 2010, during celebrations to mark the country's fiftieth anniversary of independence.

Sankara's grave also continued to serve as an informal monument, now encased in a concrete enclosure, whitewashed and adorned with the Burkinabè national colors.

Supporters and admirers of Sankara have held commemorative gatherings there each year. The one on October 15, 2007—the twentieth anniversary of his death—was especially large. Many thousands turned out, with unruly crowds growing so big that the organizers had difficulty controlling them. An emotional highpoint was the appearance of Mariam Sankara, the late president's widow, who had gone into exile with her two sons shortly after the coup. Returning to Burkina Faso for the first time since then, she laid flowers at her husband's gravesite. While some of the organizers had known Sankara personally, many in the crowd were too young to have had any direct memories of their own. "The ideal of Thomas Sankara is still here, through all these youth who are mobilized, all these people," his widow told a reporter.

Sankara's ideas were clearly starting to reach a new generation. Even the state-owned daily *Sidwaya* felt compelled to acknowledge that Sankara was viewed as a pan-African hero, within Burkina Faso and across the continent, in league with figures such as Marcus Garvey, Kwame Nkrumah, Malcolm X, Patrice Lumumba, Sékou Touré, and Cheick Anta Diop. "Twenty years after his death," the newspaper commented, "his pan-Africanist ideas remain intact in the memory of Africa's peoples, in particular its youth."

A demonstration of Sankara's external appeal came during the twentieth anniversary commemoration as well. Weeks before, an international "Thomas Sankara

Caravan" departed from Chiapas, Mexico. It was initiated by Odile Sankara, one of the late president's sisters, and a Chadian musician teaching in Mexico. The group of Africans and Mexicans then flew to France, and by land passed through Switzerland and Italy, addressing rallies of hundreds of people along the way and picking up more international participants. They then flew to Senegal and traveled by land through Mali, addressing yet more rallies, before finally arriving in Ouagadougou on the eve of the anniversary to a large welcoming crowd.

Whether at anniversary commemorations or on other occasions, it has not been uncommon to see young people across West Africa wearing Sankara T-shirts. Activists can readily find his words, whether from printed collections of his speeches and interviews (published in French as well as English editions) or on the website http://thomassankara.net. Hip-hop and reggae musicians from Mali, Senegal, and Burkina Faso have released popular songs and videos sampling passages from Sankara's speeches. In Senegal, the rapper-activists of "Y'en a marre," an opposition group with a fervent following among youths in poor neighborhoods, have gone to rallies sporting T-shirts with Sankara's portrait and the message, "I'm still here."

"Above all, Sankara's ongoing popularity is due to the ideas and values he embodied," Demba Moussa Dembèlè, director of the African Forum on Alternatives in Dakar, has written. "If Sankara arouses as much fervor today as he did more than two decades ago, it is because he embodied and defended causes that resonate today among the world's oppressed."

Selected Bibliography

Andriamirado, Sennen. *Il s'appelait Sankara*. Paris: Jeune Afrique livres, 1989.

———. *Sankara le rebelle*. Paris: Jeune Afrique livres, 1987.

Bazié, Jean Hubert. *Chronique du Burkina*. Ouagadougou: Imprimerie de la direction générale de la presse écrite, 1985.

Englebert, Pierre. *Burkina Faso: Unsteady Statehood in West Africa*. Boulder, CO: Westview, 1996.

Harrison, Paul. *The Greening of Africa*. Harmondsworth: Penguin, 1987.

Harsch, Ernest. "Burkina Faso: A Revolution Derailed." *Africa Report* 33, no. 1 (January–February 1988): 33–39.

———. "The Legacies of Thomas Sankara: A Revolutionary Experience in Retrospect." *Review of African Political Economy* 40, no. 137 (September 2013): 358–74.

———. "Thomas Sankara (1949–1987)." In *Dictionary of African Biography*, vol. 5, edited by Emmanuel K. Akyeampong and Henry Louis Gates, Jr., 268–70. Oxford: Oxford University Press, 2012.

Jaffré, Bruno. *Biographie de Thomas Sankara: La patrie ou la mort . . . .* 2nd ed. Paris: L'Harmattan, 2007.

———. *Burkina Faso: Les Années Sankara, de la révolution à la rectification*. Paris: L'Harmattan, 1989.

Otayek, René, Filiga Michel Sawadogo, and Jean-Pierre Guingané, eds. *Le Burkina entre révolution et démocratie (1983–1993)*. Paris: Karthala, 1996.

Prairie, Michel, ed. *Thomas Sankara Speaks: The Burkina Faso Revolution, 1983–87*. 2nd ed. New York: Pathfinder Press, 2007.

Sankara, Thomas, and François Mitterrand. "La joute verbale Sankara Mitterrand (texte intégral), 17 novembre 1986," http://thomassankara.net/spip.php?article32 (accessed October 23, 2012).

Sawadogo, Alfred Yambangba. *Le président Thomas Sankara. Chef de la révolution Burkinabè: 1983–1987. Portrait*. Paris: L'Harmattan, 2001.

Skinner, Elliot P. "Sankara and the Burkinabè Revolution: Charisma and Power, Local and External Dimensions." *Journal of Modern African Studies* 26, no. 3 (September 1988): 437–55.

Somé, Valère D. *Thomas Sankara: L'espoir assassiné*. Paris: L'Harmattan, 1990.

Ziegler, Jean, and Jean-Philippe Rapp. *Sankara: Un nouveau pouvoir africain*. Paris: Editions Pierre-Marcel Favre, 1986.

Interviews by Ernest Harsch

Basile Guissou. Ouagadougou, March 12, 1985.

Ernest Nongma Ouédraogo. Ouagadougou, March 4, 1999.

Youssouf Ouédraogo. Ouagadougou, March 15, 1985.

Paul Sankara. Washington, DC, May 30, 2013.

Thomas Sankara. New York, October 2, 1984, and Ouagadougou, March 17, 1985.

Ahmadu Toumani Touré. New York, September 26, 1996.

Website

http://thomassankara.net

Videos

Association Baraka. *Sur les traces de Thomas Sankara . . . Héritage en partages.* Baraka Studios, 2008, 180 minutes.

Balufu, Bakupa-Kanyinda. *Thomas Sankara.* Paris: Myriapodus Films, 1991, 26 minutes.

Ho, Thuy Tien. *Burkina Faso, un révolution rectifiée.* Paris: Solferino Images, 2011, 52 minutes.

Shuffield, Robin. *Thomas Sankara: The Upright Man.* Amazon/CreateSpace, 2009, 53 minutes.

Index

Afghanistan, 116
African Independence Party. *See* PAI
African Union. *See* OAU
agrarian reform, 97–98
agriculture, 89–90, 94–97
Algeria, 117
Alpha Commando, 77, 83
ANC (African National Congress), 118–19
anticorruption, 61–63, 139–42; asset disclosures, 104–5, 140–42
armed forces reforms, 64–67, 81

Bambata Forum, 119–20
Barro, Justin Damo, 92
Battle of the Rail, 76
Benin, 124
Bishop, Maurice, 46
Bobo, 21, 85
Boni, Nazi, 150
Botha, Pik, 108
Burkina Faso, 84; ethnic groups, 84–85; languages, 84–86; name change, 56, 85; poverty, 34–35, 148; religions, 84; territorial divisions, 69–70. *See also* Upper Volta

Burkinabè Communist Group. *See* GBC

Canada, 115
Carrefour africain, 40, 74
Castro, Fidel, 46, 116
CDRs (Committees for the Defense of the Revolution), 53, 66–69, 78, 81–83, 97–98, 104; abuses by, 102, 132–35
Chad, 110
chiefs, traditional, 68–69, 98, 143
China, 115
CMRPN (Military Committee for the Enhancement of National Progress), 38–43
CNR (National Council of the Revolution), 51–54, 72, 90, 110–11; differences within, 128–31, 137–39, 144, 147
Committees for the Defense of the Revolution. *See* CDRs
Comoros, 110
Compaoré, Blaise, 35, 39, 44, 49–50, 53, 126, 128–29, 135, 140–42; coup (1987), 127–30, 143–47, 149; post-coup practices, 147–48
Côte d'Ivoire, 22, 84, 124–26, 130, 148

Coulibaly, Ouezzin, 23, 150
Council for the Welfare of the People. *See* CSP
CPPC (People's Commission for the Prevention of Corruption), 140–42
CSP (Council for the Welfare of the People), 43–51
Cuba, 46, 116–
culture, 86–87

daba (hoe), 95
Dagnoën cemetery, 128, 148
decentralization, 67–70
Dembélé, Demba Moussa, 152
democracy, 17, 55
Diendéré, Gilbert, 145, 148
Diop, Cheick Anta, 151
Directorate for Women's Mobilization and Organization, 82
Dumont, René, 28

economic policy, 88, 90–93; aid, 91–93; austerity, 63, 93–94; foreign debt, 121–22; private sector, 105–6; state enterprises, 103–5; taxation, 93–94, 105
education, 72, 77, 83–84, 94
elders, 74–75
El Salvador, 46
environment, 98–103; "three struggles," 101–2; tree planting, 100, 102–3

Faso dan Fani, 106–7
Foccart, Jacques, 130
France, 21–23, 48–49, 92, 108–2, 121, 125, 130, 148; as colonial authority, 15, 21–22, 84

Francophonie, La, 111–112
French language, 13, 51, 85–86, 111–12
Fulfuldé, 13, 85–87

Garvey, Marcus, 151
GBC (Burkinabè Communist Group), 137
Ghana, 122–24
Gourmantché, 21
Gourounsi, 21, 51, 85
government, 53, 64, 80
Grenada, 46, 115
Guébré, Fidèle, 51
Guissou, Basile, 91

Harlem, 113–14
Harrison, Paul, 78
Haute-Volta. *See* Upper Volta
health, 77–78, 94
Houphouët-Boigny, Félix, 125–26, 130, 142

IMF (International Monetary Fund), 92, 94
Israel, 115

Jaffré, Bruno, 30
Japan, 115
Johnson, Prince, 130
Jula, 13, 85–87

Kaboré, Boukary, 147
Kaboré, Philippe Zinda, 150
Kafando, Hyacinthe, 145
Kiemdé, Frédéric, 129, 135
Kilimité, Hien, 44
Ki-Zerbo, Joseph, 134

labor mobilizations, 71–76
Lamizana, Sangoulé, 24, 32–33, 37–38, 62

League for Patriotic Development. *See* Lipad
Liberia, 130
Libya, 46, 116–17
Lingani, Jean-Baptiste, 44, 47–50, 53, 129, 149
Lipad (League for Patriotic Development), 137–38
literacy campaign, 77, 83–84, 86
Lobi, 21
Lumumba, Patrice, 151

Machel, Samora, 46
Madagascar, 27–29
Malcolm X, 151
Mali, 18, 84, 124–25, 130, 152; wars with Burkina Faso, 31–32, 66–67, 124–25, 132
Mandela, Nelson, 108, 118
Mauritania, 119
Military Committee for the Enhancement of National Progress. *See* CMRPN
Mitterrand, François, 15, 17, 48, 108, 110, 112
mogho naba (Mossi emperor), 21
Mooré, 13, 51, 85–87
Morocco, 119, 121
Mossi, 20–21, 84–87, 142–
Mozambique, 46

"naam" peasants' movement, 75
Namibia, 117–120
National Council of the Revolution. *See* CNR
Netherlands, 115
New Caledonia, 111
Newsweek, 88, 92–93
Nicaragua, 15, 46, 115–17
Niger, 84, 124
Nkrumah, Kwame, 151

Non-Aligned Movement, 46, 116

OAU (Organization of African Unity), 107, 117–19, 121–22
Observateur, L', 40, 45, 132
OMR (Revolutionary Military Organization), 137, 144, 147
Ortega, Daniel, 116
Ouédraogo, Ernest Nongma, 41, 59, 61, 141–
Ouédraogo, Jean-Baptiste, 44–45, 48–50
Ouédraogo, Youssouf, 74, 91–92

PAI (African Independence Party), 26, 35, 135, 137–38
Palestine, 15, 115
pan-Africanism, 110, 117, 119, 151
Penne, Guy, 48–49
People's Commission for the Prevention of Corruption. *See* CPPC
People's Development Program. *See* PPD
People's Revolutionary Tribunals. *See* TPRs
Peulh, 20–21, 85
Pô, 32–35, 39, 48–50, 123
Polisario Front, 121
Popular Front, 128, 147
PPD (People's Development Program), 73–74, 100–101

al-Qaddafi, Muammar, 46

Rawlings, Jerry John, 122–24
Ratsiraka, Didier, 28–29
Reagan, Ronald, 113
repression, 41–42, 131–36, 148–49

Revolutionary Military Organization. *See* OMR

SADR (Sahrawi Arab Democratic Republic), 121
Samo, 21
Sankara, Auguste, 44
Sankara, Joseph, 20–21
Sankara, Marguerite (née Kinda), 20
Sankara, Mariam (née Serme), 34, 58, 151
Sankara, Odile, 152
Sankara, Paul, 29, 58–59
Sankara, Pauline, 29
Sankara, Philippe, 34
Sankara, Thomas
  childhood, 20–24
  family, 20–23, 29, 34, 58–59
  military training, 24–29
  army commands, 29–34, 39
  in Mali war (1974), 31–32
  as minister of information, 39–42
  as prime minister, 45–48
  arrest (1983), 48–49
  August 4, 1983, takeover, 50–53
  and CNR, 53–54
  ideology, 15, 47, 52–55
  leadership style, 14, 40, 56–61
  assets, 140–41
  death, 19, 127–28, 144–45
  legacy, 149–53
Sankarists, 149–50
Sawadogo, Alfred, 59–60, 102
Senegal, 26, 152
Sidwaya, 103, 151
Silmi-Mossi, 20, 85
Somé, Valère, 48, 53, 135, 137, 143–44, 147

Somé Yorian, Gabriel, 43–44, 49–51
South Africa, 17, 108, 114, 117–20
Soviet Union, 115–17, 139
SWAPO (South West Africa People's Organization), 118–19

Tarnue, John, 130
Terrasson de Fougères, Chantal (Compaoré), 126, 141–42
Tiendrébéogo, Didier, 132
Toé, Fidèle, 23, 40, 140
Togo, 124, 130, 148
Touré, Adama, 26–27
Touré, Ahmadou Toumani, 18
Touré, Sékou, 151
Touré, Soumane, 23, 41, 135, 138
TPRs (People's Revolutionary Tribunals), 61–63, 65, 86, 104, 133, 139–40
Traoré, Aïcha, 81
Traoré, Alouna, 144–45
Traoré, Moussa, 18
Tuareg, 21

UCB (Union of Burkinabè Communists), 135, 137–38
UFB (Women's Union of Burkina), 13, 83–84
ULC (Union of Communist Struggle), 137
ULCR (Union of Communist Struggle-Reconstructed), 137–38, 147
UNICEF, 77–78
Union of Burkinabè Communists. *See* UCB
Union of Communist Struggle. *See* ULC

Union of Communist Struggle-Reconstructed. *See* ULCR
unions, 41, 45, 134–36
United Nations address, 110, 114–15
United States, 17, 92–93, 113–15
Upper Volta, 15, 21–22, 31, 84. *See also* Burkina Faso

Vaccination Commando, 77–78
Vietnam, 112

water, 89, 96, 100–101
Western Sahara, 119, 121

women, 13–14, 79–84, 106–7
Women's Union of Burkina. *See* UFB
World Bank, 76, 92, 94

Yaméogo, Maurice, 23–24, 44
"Y'en a marre," 152
Young, Andrew, 113
youth, 74–75

Zerbo, Saye, 38–39, 42–43, 62, 134
Zongo, Henri, 42, 44, 48–50, 53, 111, 129, 149
Zongo, Norbert, 148, 150

www.ingramcontent.com/pod-product-compliance
Lightning Source LLC
Chambersburg PA
CBHW060906300426
44112CB00011B/1359